William Ross Hartpence

History of the Fifty-first Indiana Veteran Volunteer Infantry

A Narrative of its Organization, Marches, Battles and Other Experiences in Camp

and Prison - From 1861 to 1865

William Ross Hartpence

History of the Fifty-first Indiana Veteran Volunteer Infantry
*A Narrative of its Organization, Marches, Battles and Other Experiences in Camp and Prison -
From 1861 to 1865*

ISBN/EAN: 9783744755894

Printed in Europe, USA, Canada, Australia, Japan

Cover: Foto ©ninafisch / pixelio.de

More available books at **www.hansebooks.com**

HISTORY

OF THE

Fifty-First Indiana

Veteran Volunteer Infantry.

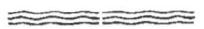

A NARRATIVE OF ITS ORGANIZATION, MARCHES, BATTLES
AND OTHER EXPERIENCES IN CAMP AND PRISON;

FROM 1861 to 1866.

WITH REVISED ROSTER.

By WM. R. HARTPENCE,

SERGEANT MAJOR.

HARRISON, OHIO.:
PUBLISHED BY THE AUTHOR.

CINCINNATI, O.:
THE ROBERT CLARKE COMPANY, PRINTERS AND BINDERS.

1894.

COLONEL A. D. STREIGHT.

CONTENTS.

ILLUSTRATIONS.

WM. R. HARTPENCE.

W H Y ?

TO preserve the memory of the experiences through which we passed during the great War of the Rebellion, from 1861 to 1866, and to furnish our posterity with the record of our faithfulness to the old flag, that represents the superior civilization, intelligence, purity and nobility of American institutions, the unity and integrity of our Nation, and the unqualified freedom which abides in every part of our broad domain; to provide a ready and comprehensive summary in chronological order, of the organization of the Fifty-First Regiment of Indiana Volunteers, its marches, battles, skirmishes, hardships and most thrilling incidents, which occurred during its long service; is the object of this book.

The Fifty-First was *one of eighty-eight regiments* among the thousands of distinctive organizations in all the magnificent armies of the United States, that bore the distinguished title of "VETERAN," which a celebrated writer of war history has pronounced "the grandest name the war originated."

This book also demonstrates and defends the title of our old commander to the leadership in the wonderful and celebrated delivery of Union prisoners from the infamous Libby Prison through a tunnel; and it forever quiets the lying tongues of envious traducers.

It lays no claim to literary merit. The story is told in

vii

an easy conversational style ; and is almost purely a collation of facts obtained from old letters, personal interviews with comrades, and the Official War Records ; and is the fruitage of years of labor. If the accuracy of any statement is questioned ; the burden rests upon the authority whence it originated ; which has always been the very best that could be obtained. If its jokes and funny things seem to require a "diagram ;"—they were understood and appreciated by the comrades with whose experiences they are associated. *They are true!* If any comrade fails to find proper mention of his own individual exploits, let him turn the muzzle of his mud-gun toward himself ; for he has been besought in many ways, and space would have been gladly given, for scores of incidents no one but themselves knew.

COMRADES : Our marches and encampments are over ; our "swords have been beaten into plowshares," and our "spears into pruning-hooks ;" and we are endeavoring to perpetuate our work of saving the Nation, by strengthening the union of our great Republic along the pleasant lines of peace. Let us ever preserve the honorable record we made during those eventful years ; and add to its luster the even more glorious emblazonry of the Cross ; that when we are mustered out here, we may be transferred to that comradeship that is eternal and of unfading glory.

W. R. H.

Fifty-First Indiana Regiment.

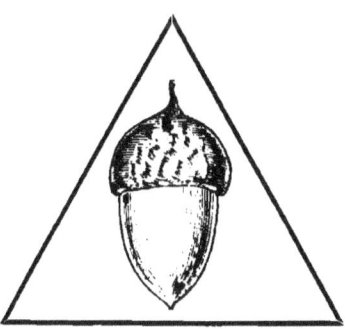

THE History of any single regiment engaged in the War of the Rebellion, may seem unimportant, and easy of accomplishment. But, the vast results of that awful struggle between loyalty and treason depended on the faithfulness of each individual; and if a record were made of each incident on which the outcome of movements of both armies in some way, direct or remote, was contingent, "the world itself could not contain the books that should be written."

A battle of any considerable magnitude, is so extensive, that no one man's description of it can convey an adequate idea of what it is like. A battle in which from 25,000 to 45,000 men on each side are engaged, covers an immense area of ground, embracing usually hills, plains, woods and hollows; so that the movements on one part of

the field may be unseen and unknown to those who fight
on another part; the sudden changes in the conflict resembling the shifting scenes of a panorama; in short, no one
ever saw, nor ever will see, the whole of a battle. For this
reason, the exact truth about any conflict of our war, or
any considerable operation, whether on the march or in
camp, is hard to get, and can only be obtained by taking
the statements of a large number of reliable persons who
were actually present; and even then great care and discretion must be observed in harmonizing the various statements, keeping in mind the fact that each witness made
his observation from a different standpoint, and that dif-
ferences as to details may refer to different situations on
the same field. The account of any soldier is of value,
according to his reliability for accuracy and veracity.

No State in the Union was more prompt in furnishing
men and money than was Indiana, nor no troops more
faithful, zealous and true. Many of the most noted generals of the War went from Indiana. There were Wallace,
Hovey, Davis, Meredith, Reynolds, Kimball, Crittenden,
Foster, Cruft, Harrow, Colgrove, Miller, Cameron, Veach,
Coburn, Hascall, Wilder, Grose and many others. There
were besides, ten thousand in the ranks, equally capable,
splendid fighters, and only lacking the opportunity.

The success that attended the Union forces during the
first few months, in which some Indiana regiments figured
somewhat favorably, caused a general impression that the
war was about over, and the Union was saved. The Bull
Run disaster, however, convinced every intelligent citizen
of the great need of more soldiers, and of the fact that the
Rebellion was not going to be "put down in ninety days."
As the bloviating confidence of the South increased, the
faith of the North weakened. Treasonable organizations
sprang up among our own homes, and discouraging letters
from relatives and neighbors flooded the mails. In all this
disheartenment, Governor O. P. Morton never lost his self-

possession, nor his confidence in the ultimate subjugation of the traitors. This he sought continually to impart to his soldiers, whom he never distrusted, and who loved and honored him with a devotion never accorded by them to any other man.

The three months' regiments were reorganized for the three years' service; and the winter of 1861-62 found most of them in the field.

It is quite impossible, at this distance from the War, when a large majority of those who lived till the close, and were discharged with the regiment, have "passed over the river," and are now mustered with the "silent majority," and the records in the Adjutant General's office at Indianapolis have been so thoroughly destroyed or scattered, to obtain even a brief biographical sketch of anything like a considerable number of the comrades, if there were room in our limited space to insert them in these pages. Whatever is omitted must be supplied as well as may be from the Adjutant General's Report.

At the request of Governor Morton, Abel D. Streight, a book publisher in Indianapolis, recruited the Fifty-First Regiment of Indiana Volunteers. He was commissioned Colonel of this regiment, September 4, 1861, and the regiment was organized in Indianapolis, October 11, though it was not mustered in until December 14. Colonel Streight was joined on September 27, by J. G. Doughty, a printer of Indianapolis, who was commissioned Quartermaster; and October 9, by Wm. H. Colescott, of Shelbyville, commissioned Major. October 11, nearly all of the original line officers were commissioned, their date of muster being December 14, with a few exceptions. Benj. J. Spooner, of Lawrenceburg, was the first Lieut.-Colonel of the Fifty-First, the date of his commission being December 4, 1861. He resigned June 16, 1862, to accept a commission as Colonel of the 83d Indiana. He was a brave and efficient officer, and led his command gallantly through many hot conflicts; losing an arm in the bloody charge on Kenesaw Mountain, Georgia, on the morning of June 27, 1864.

Company A was made up chiefly from North Salem and Brownsburg, in Hendricks county, with a few from each of the towns of Pittsboro, Danville and Lebanon.

Company B was made up mostly in Newton county, Kent Station furnishing the largest number, and Morocco, Freedom, Pilot Grove and Indianapolis furnished each a small number.

Company C found most of its members in Hendricks county; New Winchester, Brownsburg, Lizton and Pittsboro furnishing the bulk of them.

Company D resulted from general work in Hancock and Johnson counties; Greenfield, Fairfield and Franklin supplying the greater number.

Company E secured its complement chiefly in Knox and Brown counties; Vincennes, Wheatland, Nashville, Bruceville, Oaktown and Busseron contributing in proportion with the order of their mention.

Company F went out from Shelby county; Shelbyville sending at least one-half; while Morristown, Marion, Fairland and Marietta were all well represented; with a small contingent from Indianapolis.

Company G was made up in Peru, Miami county; and in addition to the regimental band, fully one-half of that company went from that city. There was also a fair representation from Mexico, in the same county, and from the city of Logansport.

Company H found one-half of its members in Bruceville, Knox county; the balance being about equally made up from Vincennes, Wheatland and Edwardsport, in the same county.

Company I drew chiefly for its make-up on the southern part of Hancock county, and the northern part of Shelby county; London and Fairland contributing the major part, with a fair donation from Indianapolis.

Company K was a sort of "ground-hog necessity" to the completion of the regiment, and brought together some of the best soldiers from every part of the State: Putnam, Hancock and Knox counties making the best showing in numbers; especially Oak Station, in Knox; with six or eight from each of the towns of Greenfield, Carpentersville, Curryville, Wheatland and Linton. Many of these served in the 7th Indiana Regiment, in the three months' service.

Each company had more or less from every part of the State; Company H being the nearest to an exception, and Company I being badly scattered. It is possible that this fact created a necessity for each to stand by the other, that ripened into a fraternity that was not excelled, and rarely equalled, by any other regiment in the field.

When the President called for 300,000 more men, the heart of every loyal Hoosier leaped, and his patriotic zeal was inflamed to an almost passionate eagerness to enlist. Hundreds of fathers and mothers, in selfish affection, had exacted a promise from dutiful sons, before leaving home, that they would not enlist without their parents' consent. But the sounds of the fife and drum, and the glare of brass buttons shut out all other sounds and sights, drowned the voice of filial duty, and swept the boys clear off of their feet. The blue uniform, with its warlike belongings, were simply resistible. When the word went home that the boy had enlisted, a season of grief swept over the family, and their hearts were torn as though death had suddenly entered the fold. But with a philosophy born of patriotism, the father took up the son's burden on the farm or in the shop; while mother and sister, who could not go to war, found many ways to help at home. They too buckled on the armor, and were faithful through all the terrible ordeal. Among sweethearts there was a sudden crystallization of love that years of "billing and cooing" could not have accomplished.

The cause of the war, and its progress up to the date

of the enlistment of the Fifty-First Indiana, is passed over, as well as the individual experience of each comrade in leaving home and joining the regiment, as such details would be quite voluminous, and would possess little interest to the average reader. Very few of the old boys are left to read this, and it must be comprehensive enough to interest others.

We were all burning with eagerness to encounter the rebels; and the Union army was only awaiting our arrival to settle the matter at once and for all. Everything and everybody were at high pressure; and the best blood of the State was concentrated in the northeast part of Indianapolis, on the commons adjoining Prof. R. T. Brown's home, the camp line bounded on the west and south by Central and Christian Avenues.

When the writer arrived at Indianapolis, in the fall of 1861, he applied to W. R. Holloway, who was at that time Governor Morton's private secretary. The two young men had been printer apprentices in the same town, and the fresh aspirant for military honors and experiences relied greatly on the private secretary's judgment in directing him to the exact spot where glory awaited him, and where his valuable services were most needed, and would be best appreciated. The recruit was introduced as the new drum major; but as there was no special use for such a luxurious adornment, and the regulations didn't call for it, he soon found his name on the roll among the H's, in the regular way, and was paired off with Rev. Wm. Hancock, a sort of back number, who had figured among the Center township worshipers as a local exhorter, and who soon found a place in a hospital, and finally in the Corps d'Afrique.

It is quite impossible to describe the transformation from the condition of an ordinary citizen to that of a full-fledged soldier; how we stood before the brilliant young West Pointer, Major T. J. Wood, and worked our arms, wriggled our fingers, champed our teeth and marched back and forth a few paces, to demonstrate our physical perfection. It is a pity the Pension Department could not have been there. It would have saved a great deal of trouble in hunting up evidence they might have gathered there in a few minutes. Then we held up our hands and were solemnly sworn to defend "the Constitution and the flag." The climax of our fondest dreams was reached when we donned the blue uniform, and stood in the full panoply of war.

CAMP "STREIGHT."

One of our first experiences was a visit from our home folks, who were accompanied by huge baskets loaded with bread, roast beef, chicken, cake, butter, pies, doughnuts and jellies. They were always welcomed with yells of delight, and were saluted with yells on their departure. All the boys were well provided with lungs, and it seemed as natural for them to yell at everything that excited them, as it was to breathe or eat.

Our camp was a model of regularity. Each day the quarters were carefully policed, and our bunks, resembling mortar-beds filled with straw, were well aired and "made down." Our parlor, kitchen and bedroom furniture partook of the same elegance and convenience, being selected more for use than ornamentation.

We had a continual and burning desire to perfect ourselves in the manual of arms, and a terrible concern about the exact position of our feet, in our military maneuvers. There was also a consuming dread lest the war would be over before we had an opportunity to exhibit our prowess. We got over all this in time.

OUR FIRST REVIEW.

On Thursday, November 21, the Fifty-First took part in a grand review in Military Park, a few squares northwest of the State House. There were eight regiments of infantry, one thousand cavalry and two batteries of light

artillery. The Fifty-First received praise for its splendid
appearance and for the best drill. We were very proud of
this; but our souls were far from happy. We yearned for
scenes of carnage, and would not be comforted. But it
came at last.

LEAVING INDIANAPOLIS.

At 4:35 p. m., Monday, December 16, 1861, we left
Indianapolis for "the front." One train carried the baggage, horses and wagons, and two other trains carried the
soldiers. The *Indianapolis Journal* of next morning had
the following:

"The people of Indianapolis have never seen a more complete military pageantry than that exhibited in our streets yesterday. Early in
the day the 51st regiment, Col. Streight, struck tents in the northern
part of the city, and marched in true army style to trains on the Madison and Indianapolis Railroad, which were in waiting to convey them
to the Ohio River, over which, by steamboat, they expect to be conveyed
to Louisville or some other prominent point in Kentucky. The regiment marched in complete order, and elicited the admiration of everybody. It has always been justly credited for sobriety, and its movements
were marked by that decorum which is ever characteristic of good and
true men. The regiment marched in solid columns through our streets
to the depot, followed by its baggage wagons and the guard detailed to
pick up stragglers. It got aboard the cars in good order, and departed
without any unnecessary fuss or parade.

The departure of Col. Streight's infantry   was more warlike,
systematic and business like in appearance than any demonstration
heretofore witnessed in this city. We accept this display as an evidence
that the art of war is being rapidly learned by our people, and that those
who have had an opportunity of practising it, even on the peaceful and
unstained fields of Indiana, have so far progressed as to be able to do
effective and substantial service as soon as opportunity offers."

At Franklin, we were delayed an hour, during which
we were surrounded on the platform by scores of beautiful
girls, to whom the boys immediately made love, and then
left the darlings in sadness and tears. Our trip was free
from mishaps, and was attended with much pleasure. We
reached North Madison about 11 o'clock that night, and
disembarked from the cars. The moon shone brightly,
and the night was lovely. Mr. Branham, superintendent

of the railroad, conducted us from the top of the incline
to the wharf, where we arrived about 2 o'clock next morning. In the meantime the baggage train was run down the
incline.

EN ROUTE FOR "DIXIE."

At Madison we embarked on the steamers "City of
Madison" and "Lancaster," the right wing occupying the
former, and the left wing the latter. The equipage, consisting of 65 horses and 35 wagon loads of quartermaster's
stores, was stowed among the decks of the vessels. At 3
P. M. we were ready, and sailed for Louisville. We had
gone but a short distance, before the fog became so dense,
that we were obliged to lay to until nearly 9 o'clock in the
morning of the 18th, when it cleared away, and we arrived
at Louisville at 12 : 30.

In three hours we were prepared for the march. By
that time several thousands of citizens had gathered, to
welcome us to their city, and many were the invitations to
supper. There were also many solicitations from prominent citizens, to march through certain parts of the city ;
but it was decided to take the shortest route to the camp.
This took us through the center of the city for nearly two
miles, during which there was one continued ovation, flags
and handkerchiefs waving, and cheers ringing from every
side. We halted just below town ; naming our first camp
on the enemy's soil, after Adjutant Ramsey.

On the way, a comrade of Co. F, contemplating our
hospitable reception, exclaimed, "By gracious ! we are on
the enemy's soil ! I'd like to see a live rebel." Instantly
a full-muscled dame of near two hundred weight strode to
the front, and cracking her fist, replied, "Well, sir, here's
one ; what do you want?" His curiosity was satisfied.

Next morning we were assigned to Gen. E. Dumont's
brigade, Department of the Ohio. Everybody was drilling
vigorously ; and it was confidently expected that in less
than forty hours we would be in the very heat of battle.

Our camp presented a very military appearance that first morning in "Dixie." The monster Sibley tents were spread out in all their conical symmetry, while the various designs drawn on them with charcoal, gave undoubted indication of the bloodthirsty warriors congregated beneath their shelter. There were such inscriptions as "Bengal Tigers," "Bull Pups," "Wild Cats," and a score of other names, equally terrifying.

The first evening, the regimental band went to town and serenaded George D. Prentice, editor of the *Journal*, for which they received distinguished mention next day.

SWEARING THEM IN.

The bravery of some of the boys was equaled only by their impudence. The next morning, as soon as it was known where we were going, and while the stars were still twinkling in the sky, Logan Russell, O. F. Brown and J. P. Smith, the Tennessee mountaineer, started on, with a view to foraging, (for that spirit manifested itself in some at the very start,) and for whatever experience they might encounter. They soon met a lot of milk-and-water rebels, whom they asked if they were "Union" or "secesh."

"Neutral," was the reply.

"Here," said Russell, "we are the advance guard of twenty thousand Union soldiers; we want you to holler for Lincoln."

"O, no; we cain't do thet."

Three guns came down promptly, and their muzzles were directed straight at the "neutrals." With firm tone, Logan then said:

"Holler for Lincoln! Hats off!"

In very feeble voices came "Hurraw fer Lincoln!"

"Louder!" shouted the Union leader.

"*Hurraw fer Lincoln!*" yelled the Kentuckians; after which they were permitted to pass.

When the command came up that night, our heroes

received a reprimand that kept them in ranks ever after.

That day we marched out ten miles on the Bardstown pike, camping in a lovely grove. As we went to supper, a good Union lady, who had been considerably enthused by the music, as we filed off of the road into camp, sent over a jug of milk for the band. There were among the band two violins, a flute and clarinet. With the addition of a cornet and tenor horn, this sextette made a very creditable orchestra ; and an hour or two after supper, they went to the house and serenaded the family. They were invited in, and enjoyed a rare treat of cakes, pies and raspberry cordial. After leaving the residence, they were followed out to the "big road" by a number of darkies, who were nearly wild for some music ; and when the orchestra began to play, they began to dance, keeping it up for some time, and describing some of the most fantastic figures.

On Saturday, March 21, we marched 21 miles, going through Mt. Washington and Bardstown, proceeding to Camp "Spooner," (or Camp "Mud," as some called it.) three miles east of the latter town.

As we marched down the main street of Bardstown, a soldier seeing a little darkey, with his head stuck over the gate, inquired if he could get some milk ; at the same time presenting his canteen and a dime.

"Deedy yo kin," replied the boy : and grasping both canteen and money, he disappeared like a flash ; returning in a very short time with the milk, which the soldier took with that confidence that was universally reposed in the loyalty of the negro. This soldier had been raised in the city, and had not acquired a fondness for buttermilk. So, when he discovered the contents of his canteen, he made a remark that would not do to put in here. His captain, who had served in Mexico, advised him to cork his vial of wrath, and his canteen also, till both were needed. Along toward night, when he got very thirsty, that buttermilk tasted delicious ; and from that time on he has been very fond of that refreshing beverage. This does not apply to everything we learned to eat or drink in the army.

A heavy rain fell on Sunday, making it exceedingly difficult to get about. Here we experienced our first real hardship; but we did not stay long, moving on Tuesday, to the farm of Mr. Grigsby, where we fared much better, receiving every attention that gentleman and his wife and handsome young daughter, Ella, could bestow.

Next day, Wednesday, was Christmas. How little we thought that we should pass the fifth anniversary of that holiday on the stormy beach at the southern extremity of far away Texas. Shortly after going into camp, one of the boys captured a 'possum, which we skinned and roasted for breakfast next morning. "Possum fat am good."

THE ARMY OVEN.

At this point our quartermaster furnished us with an army oven, a sort of sheet-iron box on wheels; that doubtless netted the inventor a good round sum, but ought to have sent him to a penitentiary. It was a most withering failure and a fraud. It never was on hand when needed; and when it did appear, it was so rusty and dirty, that it would have turned the stomach of a william-goat. Our headquarters cook, Charley, roasted the 'possum for us, and made one or two batches of biscuits in our oven; and we never saw it afterwards.

Although flour was rarely issued, we got some occasionally. Then we would have biscuits and pies, baked in the skillet-oven, or flapjacks, made in the frying-pan. In this latter exercise, we acquired great skill in turning the broad disks of leathery batter in the air, seldom miscalculating the distance one of them would gravitate while it described a half-revolution.

NO TWO WATCHES AGREE.

While we were camped at this place, the writer was sent to town on an errand, his pass being good till 4 P. M.

As no two watches came anywhere near agreeing, and the corporal of the patrol that overtook him on his way out of town, having his watch fifteen minutes too fast, the writer was marched down to the jail, where he might have stayed all night, but for the kindness of his keeper, who took him across the street to General Wood, commanding the post, who released the prisoner, and rebuked the patrol.

On New Year's day, we left our friendly camp, on the Grigsby farm, marching through Bardstown, to "Camp Morton," about four miles south. Our command was now known as "20th Brigade, Department of the Ohio," Col. J. W. Forsythe, 64th Ohio, commanding, and consisted of the 64th and 65th Ohio, 51st Indiana and 3d Kentucky. As we passed through town, Mrs. Grigsby was standing on one of the principal corners, waving us farewell, while her eyes were flooded with tears.

The first soldier buried by our regiment in the honors of war, was probably Sebron S. Jones, a musician in Co. D, whose remains were conveyed in solemn procession to a spot near Bardstown, some time during the first week in January. No data can be found for positive identification.

The following order was received:

"HDQRS. DEPT. OF THE OHIO,
Louisville, Ky., Jan. 16, 1862.

Brig. Gen. T. J. Wood, Commanding at Bardstown:

SIR—The general commanding desires to have the road from Danville to Somerset put in good order, and for this purpose he assigns you to the duty, and to the command of the troops to be engaged in it. Proceed to Lebanon, move with the 20th Brigade, Col. Forsythe commanding, and begin from Danville. 1000 axes, 1000 picks, 500 shovels, 500 spades are ordered sent to Col. Forsythe from here to-day, and will reach him to-morrow. The 21st Brigade, Col. Carr commanding, will be under your command. He is impressed with the importance of the work, as the supply of troops depends on the early completion of the road. The road must be corduroyed, with logs to make a species of puncheon floor, not less than 16 feet wide. Gen. Thomas has orders to work in like manner on the Somerset end. It is hoped it will not occupy more than ten days. Draw supplies from Lebanon. JAMES B. FRY, Chief of Staff."

A letter from Buell to Thomas, Jan. 17, says, "Wood, with three regiments is building the road from Danville." Again, on the same day, Buell to Wood. "Ray's regiment (49th Indiana.) is put under Wood's command, to work on the road." We broke camp on the following Monday, passing through Bardstown to a pretty little knoll about six miles from that town, covered with lovely cedars. The next day, about 9 o'clock, we started from there, marching slowly all day, making fourteen miles, and camping just below Springfield, on a finely wooded farm, with plenty of water, above and below, a drenching rain pouring down as we put up our tents. Next day we proceeded to Lebanon, in a continuous drizzle of rain, going into camp a mile from town, feeling more like drowned rats, than proud and gallant soldiers. Next morning was cold and clear, the bright sunshine affording an opportunity to dry ourselves out. Many of us went to town, and had a "picnic." On Tuesday, the 21st, we marched fifteen miles, and as many more the next day; camping in sight of the residence of Colonel Fry, the hero of Somerset, with whose family the writer spent the evening in a delightful manner. Eleven miles more brought us to Stanford, next day, and the day following we halted three miles below. Next day, which was Friday, we marched four miles, to where our next date is made.

HALL'S GAP.

January 26, 1862, we were on the mountain, at Hall's Gap, seven miles south of Stanford, Ky., building corduroy road, in almost unfathomable mud, in order for the advance of our troops, to take part in the battle at Somerset, in which the rebel Zollicoffer was killed. Col. Streight was in command of four regiments, and superintended the work. We cut down the huge chestnut trees, that were abundant there, quartered them, and laid them in 16-foot lengths across the road. Our boys amused themselves in the meantime making pipes and trinkets of the laurel root, which also abounded. Many of our boys had the measles, and many were troubled with diarrhœa, of which latter disease some died. Flour was issued to us, which we took to the citizens' houses, and had baked into biscuits, which was payed for with coffee.

At this place a man named Rains, of the 19th Kentucky, died and was buried near his home at the foot of the mountain.

From February 1, to April 30, we were known as the 6th Division. From here dates indiscriminate "foraging" also. Here Mrs. Bridgewater's servant, a snaggly quadroon, brought pies, turkeys, etc., of which Jim Douglas, of the band, bought an immense stack, paying for them with a $5 note on the N. W. Railroad Bank of New York, as pretty money as you ever saw, and giving Jesse Zern ("sutler,") as surety for its redemption.

Returning to Lebanon, February 12, the entire regiment was vaccinated; there being smallpox in the town. We left Charles Holden, of Co. I, with congestion of the lungs, at Stanford, where he died.

Buell to Mitchell—Feb. 13, 1862: "Wood will have his division at Munfordsville to-morrow."

Wood to Fry—Feb. 14, 1862: "Some regiments have been waiting at the depot [Munfordsville] nearly 24 hours; one train was detained two hours at the Junction; 4 regiments have gone, and 5 are now embarking; impossible to send the remaining two before to-morrow."

Buell to McClellan—Feb. 15, 1862: "Wood's, a raw division, reaches Green River to-day."

Buell to McCook—Feb. 15, 1862: "The three batteries of Nelson's division leave with Wood's division at Munfordsville."

We arrived at Munfordsville, a mean looking village of 300 inhabitants, February 14, by railroad, through most picturesque country. Here we experienced our first great distress, from snow and rain. Dumped from the box cars unceremoniously at night, into the snow, without fuel or shelter, exposed to the inclement weather, it was one of the most distressful experiences of our army service. The train stood on the track there all night; and it is inexpli-

cable why our inexperienced boys were not permitted to
occupy them.   Many of the boys next day visited the ruin
of the bridge, and the battle-ground where Willich's 32d
Indiana fought the Texas rangers under Buckner.   Kettle
says of this fight :

"On December 17, four companies of the 32d Indiana, thrown out in
advance of Munfordsville, on the Louisville & Nashville Road, 42 miles
north of Bowling Green, encountered a party of Texan Rangers, who
charged them, and were received with a sharp fire.   The infantry were
then ordered to rally on an adjoining wood.   In the act they were
charged by the Texan horsemen, and a desperate hand-to-hand encounter ensued, the Indianians making use of their sword bayonets.   They
soon gained the woods, when the Texans fled, leaving many dead,
including their colonel, upon the field.   The Federal loss was 13 killed,
and as many wounded."

There is probably a mistake here, as Col. Willich took
two other companies of his own regiment and went to the
relief of the two already engaged.   Besides this, they did
not get to the wood, but formed a hollow square in open
field, and finally repulsed the enemy.   The Fifty-First got
there just in time to be too late, and occupied the deserted
camp of the 32d, on the east side of the railroad, taking
possession of several barrels of sour krout, that had been
issued to Willich's dutch regiment, and deserted by them
when they went into the fight with the Texans.   On the
opposite side of the railroad lay a battery, principally composed of Germans, who, observing our desolate condition,
divided several camp-kettles of delicious soup with us ; for
which we have ever since been grateful.   Possibly the generous fellows, by sharing with us, had to go without their
next meal, or at least to reduce their allowance materially.

The railroad was torn up to Bowling Green, and on
the evening of February 23 our regiment was sent forward
with the wagons, to get them up the mountain side, four
or five miles below.   That night, during a temporary halt
of several hours, a company of us visited Osceola Cave,
a branch of the Mammoth.   We were in fine spirits once
more, as we had news of the capture of Fort Donelson,

and we *knew* then that the war was certainly about over.

At least 99 per cent. of Union soldiers knew nothing of card-playing before entering the service. It came to all as a positive necessity, and was as generous and edifying to the moral and mental manhood, as coffee was to the physical. This habit did not take precedence of everything else, but with many was alternated with reading the testament. It was simply a diversion to vary the weary monotony of camp life, and by nearly all was discontinued soon after their return home. It was quite common to see a little testament in the blouse pocket, but rarely a pack of cards; and just before a battle those who had cards, would throw them away.

As we did not often hear church-bells, and we could not well carry calenders, it frequently occurred that we did not know what day of the week it was. At the close of a march one day, two members of a "mess" whose duty was to get wood and water, hastened to perform their task, and then sat down to rest on a log; and to make it more restful, one of them produced a deck of cards, and soon they were deep in the mystery of euchre. Just then one of the unregenerate passed, and observing the game, said to one of the players:

"Why, I thought you was a Christian."

"Well, that's all right; what o' that?"

"Do you know what day this is?"

"No; do you?"

"Yes, it's Sunday; 'n' I didn't think your church 'lowed that."

It didn't either; and the soldier, who was very conscientious, was so mortified at his desecration of the Lord's Day, that he broke off playing cards from that moment.

WHO STOLE THE SHEEP?

About February 23, 1862, our command arrived at a point five miles northeast of Bowling Green. During the

2

afternoon a flock of nice looking sheep were seen grazing in a meadow adjoining our camp; and as we had been quite short of meat for several days, we thought of what a delicious stew a piece of mutton would make. That same night a forage squad was made up of small details from several companies, under Capt. Sheets, and, accompanied by Quartermaster Doughty, we visited a mill, a few miles away, where we obtained a quantity of flour and meal. On the return the boys scattered out somewhat, in search of stray chickens and other game. One squad captured a nice hog, and got into camp without being detected; and, although patrols searched the quarters of the entire regiment for it, no trace was found; the hide and refuse being effectually buried out of sight, and the meat divided and safely packed in haversacks. Another squad surrounded the flock of sheep mentioned above, and ran them up and down the meadow three or four times, with fixed bayonets, when, impatient of failure, one of the boys let go a shot from a huge revolver, that brought down one of the sheep, but woke everybody up for miles around. As this occurred a little before midnight, the camp guard was naturally alarmed; and the patrol soon came sailing over the brow of the plateau above camp, in quest of the culprits; who, seeing the mischief they had gotten into, hastened to plan a means of escape. "I have it," said the one who had shot; "we are patrols. Let me do the talking, now; come on!" and they started on a dead run toward the patrols.

"Did you see which way they went?" inquired the shooter, of the corporal of the patrols.

"No, we didn't."

"Well, you go over that way," pointing an opposite direction from camp, "and we will go around this way, and head them off."

Away both squads flew, the Fifty-First boys taking the shortest possible cut into camp; leaving their dead on the field. While they were congratulating themselves on their escape, and about to separate to go to their quarters, they encountered the officer of the day. After questioning them a little, he told them to go on in; but observing the brigade commander standing in front of his tent, on the knoll above, watching the proceedings, he countermanded his order, and sent the boys up to headquarters. The commander exhausted his list of synonyms for thieves and rascals, and then ordered the little band of martyrs to the guard-house, where they stood up until morning; as the prison was an unditched tent, and the rain, which began to fall soon after, rendered any other position next to impossible. In the morning the boys were sent to their own regiment, and confined in a closed tent, while the papers were made out for their court-martial.

Among the incongruous collection that night, of solids and liquids, Herman Buchthal, our German delegate from Co. E, had secured a fine hen. When the patrol swooped down on the squad of foragers, he quickly stuffed it under a cavalry jacket he had on. He had no opportunity that night, nor all the next day, to get rid of it, so it stayed in there till the boys were released on parole at night, that they might sleep in their own quarters. All through the day there was frequent inquiry, "where does that infernal smell come from?" When they learned that it was Buchthal's chicken, they wanted to kill him.

On the second morning, a discovery was made by one of our boys, on duty at brigade headquarters, who, as soon as he was relieved, reported to the company officers of the boys under arrest. The officers proceeded to Col. Harker's headquarters, and in the rear of his tent, under a fly occupied by his cook, they found a nicely dressed sheep hung; very likely the same that had been shot by the foragers. It did not take long to arouse the commanding officer from his sleep, and escort him to the cook's tent; where after a brief parley, in which the company officers used some very uncomplimentary language, an unconditional release was secured for the prisoners; to the great relief of all parties concerned.

TIT FOR TAT.

This was not the end of the joke, however. Colonel Harker had been accustomed, when visiting the various camps, to ignore guard lines; and this privilege had been accorded him as a matter of respect for his position. The next time he rode over on his fine dapple grey, and made an attempt to cross, a sentinel first saluted him as became his rank, and as he neared the line, ordered him to halt.

"Why, what does this mean?" exclaimed the astonished officer, who, although he was a highly-disciplined captain from West Point, very much preferred the easy go-as-you-please style of the Western soldiers.

"It means for you to halt," replied the guard.

"Well, well! I'll see about this!" rejoined the officer, as he drew rein to ride away. At this, the guard brought his gun down to a "ready," as he cried "Halt!"

More astonished than ever, the officer brought up with a jerk, and inquired with uncontrolled anger, what such conduct meant. The soldier gave him no further reply, but at once called out, "Corporal of the guard—beat number —!" Instantly the corporal came running to the post indicated; after a short whispered conversation with the sentinel, he took the horse's bit, and led him clear around the line to the gate, (an imaginary inclosure and opening, familiar to every soldier,) and proceeding to the tent of Colonel Streight, presented the crestfallen rider as "a man that had tried to cross the guard-line." A hearty laugh was Colonel Streight's reply, as he dismissed the corporal, and invited the officer to dismount and go in; where it was fully impressed on his mind that our regiment "had it in for him," as we say in this day, for his arrogant manner toward them; that they were not thieves nor rascals, and that knowing their rights, they would not hesitate to maintain them. From that on, the Fifty-First had no better friend than the little colonel, who was afterwards promoted to be brigadier general, and fell at the battle of Kenesaw Mountain, Ga., June 27, 1864, gallantly leading his brigade in that famous charge.

Why Col. Harker held command over Col. Streight, though, is not yet clear, as Streight's commission dated 2 months and 7 days prior to Harker's.

ARRIVAL AT BOWLING GREEN.

A report by Brig. Gen. O. Mitchell, commanding 3d Div., Dept. of the Ohio, dated Feb. 15, 1862, says:

"The advance guard of Col. Turchin's brigade under cover of artillery * effected a passage of the river (at Bowling Green,) during the night, by means of a large flatboat, which was found by our scouts during the afternoon, at a flouring mill about four miles below the town of Bowling Green. The advance guard, accompanied by a detachment of Col. Kennett's cavalry, supported by three regiments of a reserve from the main body, marched upon the town, and entered without finding an enemy at 5 o'clock this morning."

All could not be accommodated on the flatboat, many having to wade. The stream was deep at that point, but there were places that could be forded. It was found necessary to bundle up our clothes and carry them over our heads on our bayonets. The little fellows fared badly, but they were generally plucky, and plunged through boldly. Occasionally one slipped and flopped under. The boys all yelled, but the next one to him grabbed him and held him up. All got through safely, but all got chilled to the bone; and many a death resulted from disease occasioned by this. The victim usually joined in the jests, and soon forgot his misfortune.

The victory at this place was a bloodless one. Many buildings had been destroyed by fire. The depot was also fired by the citizens, although an effort was made by the artillery to drive them from the place.

Rebel Gen. A. S. Johnston's report, dated at Nashville, Feb. 18, 1862, says:

"The corps under the command of Maj. Gen. Hardee completed the evacuation of Bowling Green on the 14th inst., and the rear-guard crossed the Cumberland at this point yesterday morning in good order."

Col. Streight wrote home February 28, 1862, "We consider the rebellion broke in this part of country. I have no doubt our army will be able to march all over the Southern States within the next three months." We all enjoyed perfect confidence in the same beautiful fiction. We only missed it about three years and a half.

Surgeon Collins had been very ill for some time, and scarcely expected to live; but he recovered at Danville, Ky., though unable for a long time to join the regiment.

THE SUTLER.

The paymaster had not been around yet, and it was pretty hard on the officers. The sutler was delighted and happy, however, as many of them were compelled to buy his stuff, at three or four prices. For their convenience, the "skinner," as the sutler was called through the entire army, issued checks, with the amount printed on them, that were good for so much money on pay-day. And the "skinner" always managed to be on hand on that momentous occasion; and his claim was always satisfied, before the soldier got the pittance that fell to his lot. Naturally enough the sutler was despised by every soldier, and many a trick was played on him, many a raid made on his stuff, when by accident the wagon upset, or an attack was made that rendered it necessary to abandon the supply train. The boys always filled up from the sutler's stock first.

MULE BEEF RATIONS.

While at Bowling Green, we drew rations of meat that had been captured from the rebels, that was issued by our commissary for beef, but that turned out to be nothing less than *mule*. Chaley Cox, of Co. C, got a full ration of it, and devoured it at one meal. Next morning he was very sick, and Lieut. Dooley directed him to strike out ahead. He did so, going about a mile, where he stopped at the farmhouse of Wm. Hawes. There he stayed three weeks, Allen Godfrey, of the same company, being detailed to nurse him. From there they returned to Bowling Green, and securing two large flasks of commissary whisky, they had no difficulty in obtaining a railroad pass; and caught up with the regiment on its way to Shiloh. Several other comrades fared about as badly, but no one died.

We arrived at a point ten miles north of Nashville, on Sunday evening, March 9, 1862. We had expected to be in Nashville ere that, but the large number of troops in advance of us, crossing the Cumberland River, detained us. The weather was lovely. Friday, 14th, found us still four miles from Nashville; not very still, either, for the boys wanted to get to the front, and raised a good deal of racket about it. Next morning we were joined by Colonel Streight, who had been back, sick. We then proceeded to Nashville, at sight of whose terrible destruction we were shocked, as it looked like a cyclone had struck it. We got our first sight of gunboats here, as we crossed the river, and marched into the city; proceeding to the city square, and stacking arms; after which we had the freedom of the city, and the boys all made good use of the opportunity. Acting Sergeant Major Anderson and the writer explored the State House, leaving our illustrious names carved on the drapery of the metalic female at the summit of the long spiral stairway.

The same evening, our regiment passed out through the southeast corner of the city, by the cemetery, in which the grave of the rebel Zollicoffer appeared prominently.

ALL SORTS OF MISFITS.

The boys were in fine condition at this time, many of them having gained fifteen or twenty pounds since enlistment, rendering it somewhat difficult to make their suits fit them comfortably. In issuing clothes, little regard was paid to size; the soldier took whatever the orderly handed him, as his turn came; and it frequently occurred that a little short fellow got a suit four sizes too large for him, while that of the giant squeezed him like a corset. This evil was usually corrected by trading off.

There were also other misfits. Many mistakes were made in the selection of non-commissioned officers, some of whom had no fitness for any sort of responsible service, as subsequent experience proved. Some of these were in time made subjects of discipline, and found their proper place in the ranks. The same might also be said of some of the commissioned officers; but relief could be secured in nothing short of their resignation, and that they were not in a hurry to avail themselves of.

The orderly of one company took a pride in appearing with the visor of his cap over one ear, his hair uncombed, shirt-collar unbuttoned, one shoe open or unblacked, and one pants-leg turned up. His captain gently warned him to "fix up," but he refused to do so, for the reason that if he did, the boys would say he was "stuck up." He made his appearance in this condition on dress parade one day; the colonel spied him, and calling him out in front of his company, administered a scorching rebuke, reduced him to the ranks, and directed his captain to advance one of his duty sergeants to the position.

We had a great many things to learn in order to our becoming good soldiers. Commissioned officers and non-commissioned alike, thought they ought to make lots of fuss, and rip and tear around through the company, when they had anything to do; especially in preparing to march. Everything was new; and many difficulties arose, that in the years that followed became as "easy as falling off of a log." In time everything became as thoroughly adjusted as the finest machinery.

Then began to appear, to us, the first signs of active war; long trains of wagons, loaded with forage, clothing, food and ammunition, great batteries of artillery and long lines of cavalry; all attended with confusion and racket that would have out-babeled Babel. One would not have thought, from the hilarity, the blaring of bands, rattle of drums, the screeching of fifes and yells from thousands of throats, that all these men were on their way to kill other men, or be killed; but all the countless organizations went out in the same way.

THE CANTEEN, PLATE, HAVERSACK AND COFFEE-POT.

The simple use of the canteen was an art that required practice and experience. The first effort usually resulted in about one-fourth of the contents flying up the soldier's nose, strangling him, and most of the balance was dashed inside his shirt-collar, and trickled down into his shoe. The canteen held about three pints, and was the most indispensable article in the soldier's outfit. Its usefulness was not confined to carrying water and other liquids, nor did it cease when it became leaky. It was then but the work of a few minutes, to tear off the cloth cover, throw it into the fire, and pull it out again in the shape of two nice vessels, that might be used as a basin, frying-pan or soup-dish, or as a shovel in ditching his tent.

The tin plate was equally convertible. When corn was too hard for roasting, and too soft for parching, the soldier took his old plate, punched it full of holes from the inside, and the other side made a good grater. With the meal thus grated, griddle-cakes and mush were made, that were simply "out of sight."

We had various sorts of haversacks, and they had as many uses. Things that to the tender recruit seemed very strange, lost their strangeness as his experience broadened; and the educated taste of the veteran removed the objection to the color and smell of the "grub-bag," produced by indiscriminate and conglomerate admixture of hard-tack, sow-belly, sugar, salt and coffee. On the halt, he shifted it to the front, and found in its hospitable depths a princely banquet. We all had splendid appetites, and could digest almost anything.

Coffee-pots became practically obsolete after the first six months. After that a fruit-can, the top being pounded smooth, and a wire bail added, furnished a fine substitute. Camp-kettles and mess-pans had their uses also, during a cessation of hostilities; and alternated between bean soup, coffee, washing clothes and scalding graybacks. Coffee-mills had long been unknown; our coffee being ground by pounding the grains with a bayonet in a tincup, holding one hand over the top, to prevent their flying out.

THE BAYONET. THE PONCHO.

The bayonet had other uses than that for which the government purchased it; such as stabbing pigs, or carrying a side of bacon that had been foraged. Inverted, it did service as a candle-stand: and frequently two of them, on the guns, were driven into the ground, and served as tent-poles. But it was seldom used for puncturing rebels; yet no one ever had the courage to resist a bayonet charge, especially when accompanied by a yell.

The poncho, or "gum blanket," served as a shelter on the march or on picket; placed on the top of the mud, or on brush or straw, it kept us off of the ground; just after pay-day it served as a "chuck-a-luck" board, the squares and figures being marked on it with charcoal; often it did service as a bag or basket for transporting rations; and where two partners had one apiece, they hung one of the ponchos across one end of their "dog-tent" to protect the heads of the occupants.

The generals were slow to adopt the confiscation idea, and the soldiers suffered many privations; for they had not learned to evade the "reggelations." Before two years passed, however, the boys had taught the commanders its marvelous beauties: and as it seriously affected their own

personal comfort, they were not averse to learning. The
chief object at first seemed to be to protect the property of
citizens; that, so far as it consisted of food and forage,
invariably found its way into the rebel storehouses.

There was a natural tendency to pair off into messes.
Often four would mess together, and on going into camp,
the duty of two would be to get wood and water and cook
supper, while the others would put up tents, go for straw,
or other bedding, and otherwise divide up the work. Often
three had to sleep under one cover; and then it required
close "spooning."

One fine device that found its way into the army, was
a combination knife, fork and spoon. It was handy and
very useful; could be separated, and could be closed up,
and carried easily in the pocket.

MULE-WHACKERS.

Our muleteers, of which each company was possessed
of one, besides the regimental headquarters attache, and
over all of whom was a boss, called the wagon-master, was
accorded unlimited indulgence in the most delectable language ever invented. There was an eternal fitness in the
selection of some individuals for this delicate post, their
lungs being provided with sole-leather valves and other
appurtenances that gave to their yawps a peculiar unction
and moral force, without which, applied to the mule teams,
our supply trains would in multitudes of cases never have
reached us. Who will ever recollect Bob Hall, "Mother"
Richeson, Dave Snow, Nick Bates, and a dozen others of
our accomplished artists in that line, without a profound
sense of gratitude? Jack McGrew started in well, but it
proved too much for him; in one year he was discharged
for disability. His lungs were too weak.

Pay-day came to us on Wednesday, March 19, being
up to January 1; that of the officers dating only from their
muster-in as such. This was hard on the officers, as most

of them only got about eighteen days' pay. But the chief mourner was the "skinner."

Twenty cases of smallpox were reported in Nashville, and few cared to go into the city.

GOOD-BYE TO THE BAND.

About March 20, 1862, an order came dismissing all regimental bands, save one to each brigade; and ours was one of the doomed. It was very sad to see the band boys bundle up their "traps," and leave us; but the War Department had decided that they were a useless redundance, and they had to go. How many times, after a hard days' march, had their music inspired us with new life, as they filed off the road to the tune of "Annie Grey," or "Cottage by the Sea!" How those stirring notes braced us up, and enlivened our weary limbs! We can see Jim Todd's long swinging motion, and Jesse Zern's lively step, keeping the rest in time, and Dr. Coe's finely-keyed bugle. And the echoes of "Bonnie Eloise," "Shepherd's," "Bedford," and "Kendall's" come ringing down the years with a sad sweet influence. What new joys come to us, borne on the memories of those early days of the war! Think of Sam Lavey sitting all day long, half asleep, till the order comes to get ready for dress parade. How rapidly he unfolds into new beauty; and when the signal comes to "play," a soft sweetness flows forth from his horn, like apple-jack from a full canteen—smooth as oil! Music had a perceptible effect on everything. Our guns grew lighter; there was no more straggling; the blisters stopped smarting, and the aches faded out like remnants of a painful dream.

Here also our worthy sergeant major, W. M. Cochran, was prostrated by disease, by reason of which he was discharged from the service June 19. It is impossible to tell what might have been his development, with such natural gifts of mind and heart as he possessed.

There was one very popular amusement that began to be introduced into our regiment as the lovely spring days advanced, and that promised to become universal, and to occupy as much attention, time and labor as any other feature of the war. And it was about the only thing wherein the promise was exceeded by fulfillment. This applied to not simply the privates, nor did it stop with the common officers, but with the impartiality of the frogs of Egypt, included everything to the general of the army. This was "skirmishing" for graybacks. The insect mentioned in science as *pediculus corporis*, or, as some call it, *vestimenti*, because it is not simply parasitic on the body, but also on clothing, was no respecter of persons. The first specimen ever seen by the writer, appeared on his socks the next day after having slept with one of the most scrupulous attaches of regimental headquarters, the night before we left Nashville, to move toward Shiloh. The great fecundity of this enterprising little torment was such that it seemed like for every one we killed, a hundred would come to the funeral. One writer tells a story about General Garfield, who, upon the march from Corinth to Decatur, a few months later, was seen out in the rear of his tent, behind a tree, with his shirt spread out over his knees, while his eyes and fingers glanced nimbly over the garment in quest of the festive varmints. Behind two other trees sat two members of his staff, both engaged in the same sanguinary pastime; the crushing of the *pediculi* between their thumb-nails making a sound resembling the snapping of caps. The speediest method of getting rid of them was by boiling the clothes. Cold water washing only seemed to stimulate them; but at times when the camp kettle was not being used for boiling beans or coffee, the boys would give their clothes a bath that would for the time thoroughly eradicate the pest, nits and all. The thumb-nail slew its thousands, but boiling water its tens of thousands.

Wood-ticks were abundant in most of these forests.

They gave no warning. but selecting a suitable spot, bur-
rowed under the skin, creating an itching sensation. If
attended to in time, this little parasite, which somewhat
resembles a bedbug, could be removed with the thumb and
finger ; but frequently he had to be dug out with the point
of a sharp instrument.

We were also annoyed at times by "jiggers." These
were little insects, smaller than a pin-head, that would in
some manner swarm inside of our clothes, and produce an
intense smarting that would set us wild.

DEPARTMENT OF THE OHIO.

On Friday. March 21, 1862, General Buell, commanding the Army of the Ohio, issued the following order :

"The military force in the Department of the Ohio consists of 90
regiments of Infantry, 1 volunteer engineer corps; total 60,877 for duty;
76,614 present and absent. The 6th Division has 12 regiments of infantry, in three brigades, 1 regiment of cavalry, 3 field batteries. These
divisions are now advancing toward the Tennessee River, or taking up
positions between here and there. Halleck has disturbed the equaliza-
tion by withdrawal of troops as they ascended Cumberland River."

This furnished Buell a loop-hole for escape from whatever of odium might attach to his future action, by laying
it onto Halleck. Poor old Halleck ! he had enough to bear
in the results of his own headstrong incapacity, without
having to shoulder the burden of this man, whose capability was of no mean quality, but whose patriotism and
fidelity are sadly doubted. Halleck's action, however, at
Shiloh and in front of Corinth, "prove him wholly unfit
to command an army in the field, and in fact totally void
of that military genius necessary and so essential in the
make up of a military hero."

One week later, General Wood received the following :

{ "HDQRS. DISTRICT OF OHIO,
{ March 28, 1862.

The 6th Division, Brig. Gen. Wood commanding, will put itself en
route on the Columbia turnpike, to-morrow, the 29th. Col. Barnett,
with the reserve artillery, will report at once to Brig. Gen. Wood, and
will accompany the 6th Division."

Then all was hurry and bustle and confusion. Some of the pickets, when relieved, came in with blood-curdling stories of things that were going on "in front," that fairly took the breath of green recruits who took their places. Knapsacks that hitherto had been filled with many little knicknacks and love tokens that had been brought from home, and that had been hauled in the wagons up to this time, were overhauled, and the fancy collection, together with extra quilts and other conveniences, were laid aside, and the load reduced to just what the soldier could carry on his back.

Strict orders were issued forbidding foraging. This was discouraging to the enterprising purveyor, who hungered and thirsted for pigs, chickens, fruit, potatoes, milk, honey and applejack, that he knew was plentiful, and was only saved for the johnnies. In time the veteran learned to circumvent all such orders, and to modify the cruel penalty by a system of division with the officers in command, who allowed the boys to construe orders to suit their needs.

Great quantities of rations were issued, and men and teams in large numbers were detailed to distribute these among the regiments. There was increased activity in all the camps, in preparing food and stowing it in haversacks and mess-boxes; cartridge-boxes were inspected; the sick were sent to hospitals in the city; surplus camp equipage was packed and stored; long trains of wagons were filled with ammunition; ambulances, stretchers, medicine-cases and all the varied constituents of the doctor's department were reduced to first-class condition. There was a general weeding out of the poor material; and those who lacked physical endurance, or "sand," as it was called, quietly disappeared, and rarely turned up in the regiment again. They found a *soft place*, and stayed there. Another class of soldiers was possessed with an ambition to "keep up with the colors." They did not bluster, nor "spile for a fight;" but when discouragements came, they were ready

to "pick flint and try it again;" and when the fight came
on, with pale face, trembling and praying, yet brave and
true and faithful they remained in their places, taking advantage of every means of protection that would shelter
them from the bullets of the enemy.

Marching orders comprehended the transportation of
tents, equipage and seven days' rations, and the information that we were to move in the direction of Savannah.

Many of those afflicted with measles and other kinds
of disease, were sent to Bardstown, where our ever faithful
Mother Streight nursed them back to health again.

"Fall in, Fifty-First!" And amid the rattle of drums
and waving of flags, we got into line for the final stroke
that was to break the back of the Confederacy. The last
wagon was loaded, and was ready to move out as soon as
the troops were out of the way. The 65th Ohio was in the
front, and they stepped off with alacrity, shortly after daylight. Next day the 64th Ohio took the advance of our
brigade, leading us a lively race all day. As we were not
aware of the great necessity for rapid marching, nor was
any one else in Buell's army, not even the general himself,
we considered these antics in the nature of an exhibition
of smartness; so, on the next day, when it came the turn
of the Fifty-First to lead off, there was a general understanding through our regiment, to show those fellows how
to march. We had reduced our luggage to the last ounce;
and the way we sailed from morning till night, was something wonderful. The two Ohio regiments had drawn new
overcoats quite recently, pretty brown ones, and it was fun
to see those boys shed their overcoats whenever we halted,
and then forget them when we started on. Two wagon
loads of handsome brown overcoats are said to have been
harvested that day by the citizens and others.

"Them Fifty-Firsters is tryin' themselves to-day, a'n't
they!" remarked a 64th boy to one of the 65th.

"Yes, the durned greyhounds think ther smart. I'm

jist played out, an' my feet 's that blistered, I can't stand
up. The 13th 's in front to-morrow, 'n' I do hope they'll
have more sense."

The 13th Michigan took the advance next morning,
and the Fifty-First fell to the rear. But there was no more
excessive marching after that; though the term "greyhounds" stuck to our regiment for a long time.

Up to this time Grant had no intimation that Buell's
army was moving from Nashville, 122 miles away, and
Buell was laboring under the supposition that Grant was
on the east side of the Tennessee River. Buell had little
patience with General Nelson, who was nearly consumed
with the fear that the rebels would attack Grant before the
reinforcing army could reach him. Rutherford's Creek,
four miles north of Columbia, was crossed without much
difficulty, but Duck River being forty feet deep, a considerable delay was made. Nelson having found a tortuous
ford by which he could cross his division, pushed ahead;
and by that means arrived at Savannah some hours before
the rest of our army. The chief solicitude expressed by
Grant, was in a letter to McCook, whom he supposed to be
in the advance of Buell's army: "I have been looking for
your army for several days."

THE SIXTH DIVISION.

According to the best authority attainable, General
Wood's command, Sixth Division, Army of the Ohio, consisted at that time of the following:

15th Brigade, Col M. S. Hascall commanding.

17th Indiana, Col. M. S. Hascall.

58th Indiana, Col. M. S. Kerr.

26th Ohio, Col. E. P. Fyffe.

3d Kentucky, Col. T. E. Bramlette.

20th Brigade, Col. C. G. Harker commanding.

65th Ohio, Col. C. G. Harker.

64th Ohio, Col. J. W. Forsythe.

3

51st Indiana, Col. A. D. Streight.
13th Michigan, Col. M. Shoemaker.

21st Brigade, Col. G. D. Wagner commanding.
15th Indiana, Col. G. D. Wagner.
40th Indiana, Col. J. W. Blake.
57th Indiana, Col. W. S. Hines.
24th Kentucky, Col. L. G. Grigsby.

Artillery.
5th Ohio Battery, Capt. C. Bradley.
6th Indiana Battery, Capt. Geo. Estep.
10th Indiana Battery, Capt. J. B. Cox.

Cavalry.
3d Ohio Cavalry, Col Lewis Zahm.

GEN. J. A. GARFIELD TAKES COMMAND.

General Garfield was in Kentucky, when he received orders to report to General Buell; and so long were the orders in reaching him, that he only overtook us at Columbia, while we were constructing a bridge over Duck River. He was at once assigned to the command of our brigade. He continued with us during our fatiguing labors, building railroad bridges and relaying track on the Memphis and Nashville Road, aiding much by his superior knowledge, and also by the inspiration his presence always afforded. He was taken sick in the latter part of July, with malarial fever; and obtaining leave of absence, went to his home.

As soon as we could cross Duck River, the march was resumed with increased activity and eagerness. The distance from Columbia to Savannah is 82 miles, the road being at that time very poor. Over a single narrow road the troops were pushed forward, the divisions taking intervals of six miles, in the following order: Nelson, Crittenden, McCook, Wood and Thomas. On the 1st of April, an exceedingly hot day, Wood's division marched fourteen miles, and encamped in a wood three miles beyond Buffalo River. On Wednesday, the 2d, we had several light show-

GENERAL J. A. GARFIELD.

ers, which did not add materially to our comfort, having been so recently bereft of our tents.

GRANT AND BUELL.

Nothing of importance occurred from that on until we arrived at Waynesboro, at which place the citizens received us with demonstrations of great joy. Heavy cannonading was heard that afternoon, from a southwest direction, creating a ripple of excitement among the troops, who daily expected the first great battle of the war. At Waynesboro the road forked, and a part of the column taking to the left, the main body proceeded directly to Savannah. At the same time, the rebel army left Corinth to attack the Union troops camped at Pittsburg Landing, intending to overwhelm Grant before Buell could join him. On the 4th, Grant telegraphed that the troops need not hasten their march, as transports would not be in readiness, at any rate until the 8th. On the same day, Buell dispatched to Grant,

"I shall be in Savannah myself to-morrow, with one, perhaps two, divisions. Can I meet you there? Have you any information for me that should affect my movements? What of your enemy, and your relative positions; what force at Florence or Corinth? We will require forage as soon as we arrive, and provisions in two or three days after. Has a steamer arrived with a bridge for me?"

Grant replied next day,

Maj. Gen. D. C. BUELL,
    Near Waynesborough:

    Your dispatch just received. I will be here to meet you to-morrow. The enemy at and near Corinth are probably from 60,-000 to 80,000. Information not reliable. Have abundance of rations here, and some forage. More arriving daily. Pontoon bridge arrived to-day.   U. S. GRANT, Maj. Gen."

On the 6th, Grant had learned a part of the lesson his over-confidence in himself subjected him to. There were many more to learn before the close of the war. During the heat of the strife, on that awful day, he telegraphed to "the commanding officer of the advance forces of Buell's army, near Pittsburg:"

*   "The attack on my forces has been very spirited from early
this morning. The appearance of fresh troops in the field now would
have a powerful effect, both by inspiring our men and disheartening the
enemy. If you will get upon the field, leaving all your baggage on the
east bank of the river, it will be more to our advantage, and possibly
save the day to us. The rebel forces are estimated at over 100,000 men.
My headquarters will be in the log building on the top of the hill, where
you will be furnished a staff officer to guide you to a place on the field."

Yet, there we lay, along the bank of the Tennessee
River, hearing the ponderous booming of cannon and the
rainlike whir of musketry, till we were wild with excitement, while our poor boys were being driven back into the
river at Pittsburg Landing—while hundreds of lives were
going out, and the hopes of thousands more were dying on
that bloody field. All this time Buell remained at Savannah, walking or riding about, seemingly as unconcerned
as though it was a matter of very little consequence which
side was defeated; a condition of mind and heart almost
universally attributed to him by the men of his command.
Colonel Streight stormed around at a great rate, and Capt.
Will Scearce became so impatient that he cried like a child,
and railed out against the commanding officer, whom he
characterized as a rebel. Looking up the same moment,
he beheld that individual not forty yards away. He had
certainly heard the remark, but probably had no desire to
resent it then. It was well he did not, as the entire regiment was in accord with that sentiment, and would have
expressed it as forcibly with proper provocation. We had
enlisted *to put down the Rebellion*, and had no patience with
the red-tape tomfoolery of the regular service. Further-
more, our boys recognized no superiors, except in the line
of legitimate duty. Shoulder-straps waived, a private was
ready at the "drop of the hat" to thrash his commander;
a feat that occurred more than once.

All that beautiful Sunday we could hear the crackle of
musketry and the pounding of cannons, but no movement
was made by our command in the direction whence those

sounds came We trudged up and down, along the eastern
bank of the river, or paced back and forth like so many
caged animals. At night the roar of battle ceased, and we
dropped down in the most convenient places we could find ;
the entire surface being covered with a sticky mud, caused
by an overflow. The writer followed the example of Chaplain Gaskins, whose instinct led him into the loft of a log
barn close by, where they found some oats straw, of which
they made a lovely bed. We were all dragged out shortly
after midnight, to march back to Savannah, where we took
a transport for Pittsburg Landing.

PITTSBURG LANDING.

Arriving at the scene of battle, we went ashore under
the shadow of an abrupt bluff, that bathed its northern
slope in the mouth of Snake Creek. The bank was lined
with trembling soldiers, who warned us to not leave the
boat ; that we would all be butchered. Grant's "Memoirs"
says that Buell berated the stragglers along the bank, that
he estimated at 4,000 or 5,000, and threatened to throw a
few shells from the gunboats in among them, to drive them
to the front.

The Landing had no appearance of a town, possessing
but two or three log huts, that Grant used as a postoffice.

There is no question that Grant was surprised at this
place, and badly whipped, too, by a largely superior force ;
and all that saved him was the timely arrival of Buell's
army. The credit of this should also be put in the right
place ; for, while the fact was patent then, and remains,
that Grant made a huge mistake at Shiloh, but for the persistency of such men as Nelson and Harker and Garfield
and the plucky colonels and majors and captains, whose
voices would not be hushed, the day would have certainly
gone against us.

"GRAB A ROOT."

This expression, which became universal throughout

the Union army, is said to have had its origin at this time. Thousands of Grant's men were driven back to the water's edge, where stood hundreds of large trees, whose roots projected from the bank. As the boats approached, conveying Buell's men to their aid, some of the careless and more courageous soldiers made sport of the panic stricken fellows, and as they tumbled over the bank, yelled out to them, "grab a root!" How electrified they were when we arrived. One comrade, who was in Grant's army, says, "I can feel the sensation of joy yet, that thrilled me when the band of the advance got out on the boat and played 'Hail, Columbia.' If ever men shed tears of joy and gratitude, it was then. Wild yells, not simple cheers, but 'tigers,' beat the air, far and wide, till the whole woods on either bank fairly shook with joy."

We were drawn up into line, stacked our great heavy Belgian muskets, and with the rain pouring in almost incessant torrents, impatiently awaited orders to hurry to the front. We had no tents, and very few blankets, and so we laid around sort of promiscuously, ready at the tap of the drum, to fall in and go into the fight.

General Wood's report, covering April 6, says:

"The 51st Indiana was left as guard to wagon train, on a road almost inconceivably bad, with wagons stuck in the mud. About 12 o'clock, midnight, the darkness became impenetrable, and rain began to fall in torrents. It was impossible to see a pace in advance; and it became absolutely necessary to halt until the storm passed. The troops were eager to advance to assist their hard-pressed brethren, and were chafing and impatient. Savannah was reached on the morning of the 7th, and as soon as possible they embarked for the battle-field. The cheerfulness and alacrity with which these troops bore the labor and fatigue of a rapid march, compactly conducted, 140 miles, from Nashville to Savannah, is an earnest of their zeal."

The inevitable, inextinguishable sutler was there; and as if matters were not already as bad as they could be, he had brought with him a quantity of "brandy peaches," the same being a fruit can containing one or two slices of peach and a pint of miserable rotgut whisky. John Burk, of Co. B, a jolly Irishman, managed to empty one of these cans into his stomach, and in fifteen minutes he was a howling hoodlum, going along the line, hugging the boys, and making other demonstrations of joy, until he ran into the colonel, who was riding by ; who rebuked him in not very gentle tones, threatening to "buck and gag" him. The reproof so enraged the Irishman, that he rushed to a stack of guns, grabbed one of them, and before the boys could interfere, his bayonet was within three inches of the colonel's breast. He was put under guard, and kept until morning, when we fell into line for battle ; and being by that time sobered up, he went into action with his company, and the matter was forgotten. Johnny's bad habit clung to him to the end of his service. He got drunk as we started on the "Raid," and fell off of the boat near Paducah. He was rescued, half drowned and badly hurt, and was left at a hospital. It is not known what became of him.

That night was indeed a dreary one. We could only slosh around in the soft mud, with our heads stuck through our ponchos, as our tents were across the river, six miles below. While wandering about in this plight, the writer was met by an equally forlorn comrade, from whatever command will never be known. The rain had slackened, and the following ensued :

"Rough, isn't it?"

"Whew! you bet it is!"

"Let's make down."

"All right ; where'll we make down?"

"O, anywhere—right here's good as any."

"Well, here, hold my things ; I know where there's some hay."

"All right."

The writer, who had a poncho, handed that, with his gun and haversack, to the other soldier, who had a woolen blanket, and started for the bluff at the landing, where he had seen some mules feeding. Securing a good armload of hay, he returned to where he had left his comrade, and they made down their bed, putting the hay on the mud, and spreading the poncho on that; then putting their guns between them, and pulling the woolen blanket over themselves, they tucked their haversacks under their heads, and soon were sound asleep. In about an hour, the rain came pouring down again, filling their bed with water. After enduring it as long as they could, with a grunt of discomfort, each arose, took his own things, and they separated. Neither knew the other's name nor command, and they probably never met again; such, however, was the confidence one soldier had in another.

THE SECOND DAY AT SHILOH.

At 5 A. M., on the 7th, our lines were formed, and we moved forward. Our skirmishers soon met the enemy's pickets, and drove them rapidly for nearly a mile. The character of this onset, with the determined energy shown by the fresh troops, revealed to Beauregard the presence of reinforcements to Grant. The rebel commander says, in his report of the battle,

"At 6 A. M. a hot fire of musketry and artillery opened from the enemy's quarter   assured me of the junction of his forces, and soon the battle raged with a fury which satisfied me that I was attacked by a largely superior force."

The presence of our command was the prophecy of the rebels' defeat, indeed. He had received a special dispatch the night before, of our delay, and counted on our not being able to reach the field of battle in time to save Grant's shattered forces from capture or destruction. The fighting was severe, and toward the close, was purely defensive on the part of the enemy, to hold his main line of retreat, and cover his retiring column.

By 10 o'clock A. M., Monday, our troops had regained the camp from which Grant's army was driven on Sunday morning. Wood's division was pushed on after the rebels, until they had passed their own original lines. Thus the left of Grant's army was saved. Gen. Lew. Wallace had taken the Snake Creek road, that would have brought him in the rear of the enemy, where he would not have lasted a minute; getting back to the right road delayed him considerably; but he got fairly into action in time to save the right wing.

The enemy was not pursued far, on account of the extreme fatigue of our men, and the approach of night. The losses on both sides were very heavy. But the day was ours, and disastrous defeat was turned to glad victory.

Early on the morning of the 8th, Generals Sherman and Wood, with two brigades each, moved forward to discover the position of the enemy. We encountered a large body on Lick Creek, and drove them some distance toward the main army.

UNDER THE HORSES.

When we moved up on the high ground away from the swamp, we were badly crowded, and our sleeping quarters were in too close proximity to those of the horses. On the third night after, one of the animals in moving backward, set one of his feet on the head of the writer, the cork of his shoe cutting quite a gash in the scalp. It was late in the night, and all were asleep; and when Dr. Collins was aroused, seeing the soldier's head and face covered with blood, he supposed he had been shot, and began to hustle around to afford relief. The soldier told him what was the matter, however, and requested that some comrade lead him to the creek; there he washed the blood from his face and head, tied his bandana over the cut, found a secure place to lie, and soon all were asleep again. Such things became common, and we got used to them.

We halted on the morning of the 9th, in a forest of elms and white oaks; and as our baggage was still miles away, on the east side of the river, we skinned the trees

as high as we could reach, using the bark for shelter and
beds, eking out with straw, grass, brush, old clothes, and
everything we could find, that would make our beds soft,
or keep us out of the mud.

AFTER THE BATTLE.

As we passed over the field, and especially near the
"peach orchard," where but a short time before had transpired such horror, such destruction and devastation, and
beheld the multitude of dead and dying men and horses,
and glanced down the long lines of hastily constructed fortifications, which showed the positions of the contending
armies, at different periods in the fight, we almost fancied
we saw and heard it all over again. The cold penetrating
stare of the hundreds of stark, drenched and bloodless
corpses, over which we marched by day, and by whose
sides we dropped wearily down at night, caused a shudder.
The groans of the wounded, and the expiring gasps of the
noble fellows will haunt us through life.

> " No visions of the morrow's strife
> The warrior's dream alarms;
> No braying horn nor screaming fife
> At dawn shall call to arms."

Many corpses lay stretched out in the mud and water,
the rain pattering down in their faces ; some appearing as
though sleeping, while others bore expressions of deepest
agony. One man was thrown backward over a log, his left
hand covering a horrible wound in his body, and the other
with the finger-nails sunk in the flesh, was back of his
head, his teeth and lips firmly closed, his eyes set, indicating an awful death. At the foot of a large tree lay five
rebels, who had evidently been pierced by the same ball—
apparently a small solid shot, each being struck a little
lower than the preceding one, as they filed around the tree.
At another place a large ball had struck two men together,
cutting one in halves, and severing the other's head from
his shoulders. Hundreds of horses were strewn around.

Many of the wounded were disfigured beyond recognition; especially was this true of about one hundred poor fellows, who were scattered through a portion of the wood, that caught fire, roasting them into insensibility. Everywhere lay poor dying mortals, suffering intensely from wounds and hunger and thirst. Our boys immediately contributed liberally from their haversacks and canteens, and our surgeons went over and did what they could for their relief.

THE COLONEL'S LETTERS.

Colonel Streight wrote home, April 10 :

"Three days after the battle, and 2,000 dead traitors unburied. We are in an oak forest, seven miles long and two wide. On our reconnoisance, we saw 35 wounded, still living, who had had nothing to eat nor drink since the battle. Our baggage train is 14 miles from here; we have no tents nor blankets, and sleep as best we can."

On the 17th he wote :

* "Men who were killed a week ago, are yet unburied; many wounded still uncared for. Doctors are scarce, and numbers of wounded great; perhaps 10,000. We have lost several with smallpox. Mumps and jaundice give us most trouble. Over 50 cases now in camp."

And on the 22d :

"Just returned from picket, where we had to remain 36 hours, in a drenching rain, without sleep or shelter. Lieutenants Fox and Williams have resigned and gone home, on account of ill health. Lieut. Slavens died of typhoid fever, at Nashville, and Lieut. Light died at Lebanon. Capt. Denny is also dead, and Lieut. Trent resigned."

Again, before Corinth, May 3 :

"We are preparing for battle. The roar of cannon and rattle of musketry is the music to our march. I have every confidence in my regiment. They will fight bravely, and acquit themselves honorably in whatever circumstances they may be placed. About 500 able for duty."

It is quite impossible to give the names of individuals who were killed, or who died in consequence of wounds received in each battle, or of disease at the various points. The data cannot be obtained, and besides it would require a large volume for these alone.

Proceeding about one mile further, we halted at the place where the rebels had first formed in line of battle, on

the eventful Sunday morning. There we found a great
quantity of clothing, which, in our destitution, we gladly
appropriated. About this time we were further delighted
by the exchange of our heavy Belgian guns for nice little
Enfield rifles.

Next day we rested in a beautiful wheatfield, where
our eyes were greeted by the sight of a squad bringing in
a large number of prisoners; then we were *dead certain* the
war was about over.

From this time till September, we were known as the
20th Brigade, 6th Division, Department of the Mississippi.

Great details of men were made to bury the dead; and
it was indeed a sad duty, to take up the bodies of those
who had fallen, many of whom had lingered during the
long weary nights of neglect, in the pelting rain, and suffering all the pangs of thirst and hunger, and lay them in
trenches like poles in a corduroy road, without covering,
save a few old blankets, that were made to go as far as possible, and dirt, that filled eyes and mouths, and through
which the water soaked from the surface. Yet it was all
that could be done. A little board, with pencil marks, at
the head of each poor body, was all the monument erected.

In General Buell's report, made in August, he says:

"Circumstances attending following the Shiloh fight, subjected the
troops to the greatest discomfort for ten days after. Rains and continual
use of the roads, rendered them almost impassable. The troops lived in
the open air, in miry camps, in frequent cold, drenching rains, and had
to carry provisions two miles from the river. This had a serious effect
on the troops; dysentery of a threatening type prevailing. The arrival
of wagons, and removal of troops to high ground on Lick Creek, remote
from the battlefield, wrought a favorable change. More immediate preparations for advance commenced on the 29th of April. The creek was
bridged at Atkins' and Greer's, and the marshy bottom was corduroyed
three-fourths of a mile. The average distance from Corinth was fifteen
miles. The country was thickly wooded, with dense undergrowth. May
3, Wood's division crossed at Greer's. The enemy's cavalry retired
before us. Work was at once commenced on the roads in front but the
heavy rains of the 4th and 5th, prevented our advance, and destroyed
much of the work both in front and rear. Some skirmishing occurred

on the 6th, between the enemy and Garfield's brigade. A few of the enemy were taken prisoners."

From this till the 17th he had nothing of importance to report.

Just as soon as we got settled down long enough to go into regular camp, and got our tents up and ditched, and the quarters policed, we were ordered to prepare for "battalion drill." Whew! We hadn't had time to get dried out, nor the wrinkles straightened, nor our sore feet healed up; but we had to go. And we faced, and flanked, and countermarched, and formed hollow-square, and wheeled, resisted imaginary cavalry charges, and assaulted forts, through a blamed thorny thicket; leaving the boys breathless and out of temper. This continued from day to day, supplemented by company and squad drill.

"MY WHISKY!"

Major Doughty, our enterprising quartermaster, had "gobbled" a barrel of fine old Kentucky whisky, and was saving it for "medical purposes," in the back of his own wagon. John P. Smith, being on guard at headquarters, discovered it, and reported the same to the boys of Cos. A and F, who resolved to have a few canteenfuls of it; that, properly taken, it would help them to endure the excessive fatigue. By daylight all of the canteens and some of the camp-kettles of the "Shelby drunks" and Co. A contained most of the whisky. The watchful sentinel then called the quartermaster, and told him that something in the wagon was leaking badly. The officer jumped out of bed quickly, exclaiming, "my whisky!" The barrel was taken into the tent, and what was left was put into bottles. A half-pint was given to the guard, as a reward for his faithfulness. The day following was one of hilarity among the soldiers of the right of the regiment; but nobody ever gave the trick away, or it would have been a sorry jamboree for the perpetrators.

On May 8, Gen. Sherman reported to Gen. Grant:

"I went out on the Corinth road. At the forks of the road I found Gen. Wood's division. I ordered Wood to advance the head of his column cautiously on the left-hand road, while I conducted the 3d Brigade, 5th Division, on the right-hand road."

SCARED BY A "QUAKER GUN."

May 9, we were 7½ miles from Corinth, in the vicinity of what was to be Jeff' Davis' "last ditch." On the night of May 6, General Garfield detailed Colonel Streight, with the Fifty-First, to bring up the brigade train and the division supply train. The command was under fire for some time, but there were no casualties. During that week our regiment chopped down the woods in front of us, about seventy acres; though for what reason this work was done, nothing in the Official War Records appears. We had no trouble in moving on the doomed town, for it was already evacuated by the rebels. We were confronted by a mammoth gun, that threatened to blow the Union clear over the north pole; and it was then supposed that General Halleck was afraid that somebody might accidentally run up against the mass of ordnance; and to provide against this, was the cause of cutting away the forest. Five hundred axes were unpacked, and in a very short time our hardy yeomen completed the task. The mammoth gun proved afterward to be a log that had been mounted and painted to resemble a columbiad.

Here it was that Reub. Templin and J. F. McKinley, (Brute,) of Co. C, kept everybody awake during the entire night, destroying rebels that sneaked up on them while on picket. The Government had a herd of cattle to pay for, and there wasn't a ragweed in front of our command that hadn't the top clipped off, as they waved in the misty starlight.

The right of our regiment rested alongside a big pine tree. One day Corporal Gibson was sitting on the trunk of it, writing a letter to his wife. Looking up, he descried

at the end next to the captain's quarters, a huge lizard on
the tree. He commenced writing something about it in
his letter, when Captain Fleece came out of his tent, and
scared the varmint, which ran along the tree and up into
Gibson's pants. It did not stop till it had compassed the
entire length of his body, emerging at his collar. Chaos
ensued; pen, ink and letter flew in different directions;
while Gibson acted like a lunatic, tearing every garment
he had on into shreds, in his eagerness to get them off.
Traces of the lizard's course were plainly visible for years.
Gibson had to draw another suit before he could appear in
public again.

BEFORE CORINTH.

Saturday, May 17, we advanced to within 2½ miles of
Corinth, and a lively cavalry skirmish was had, with considerable loss on both sides, the rebel cavalry falling back
in confusion, leaving many prisoners. During the engagement two companies of rebel infantry deserted and fled to
our lines. They reported that the entire cavalry force was
placed in front, to prevent the infantry from escaping to
our army. Their rations had been cut down to one cracker
a day. We mistook their flight for a charge, and many
shots were fired at them before they could make their intention known. On Sunday, our skirmishers, half a mile in
advance, kept up a racket all day. Several of our boys
were hit by a rebel sharpshooter, perched in a distant tree.
He was finally located, and two half-breed Indians from
the 2d Minnesota were detailed to silence him. Some boys
from our regiment deployed at safe distances, to attract
his attention, while the half-breeds, who were fine hunters,
removing their shoes, crept stealthily through the undergrowth, to within four hundred yards of him, where, at a
signal, they let fly at him; and down he dropped, as they
expressed it, "just like um 'possum!"

Up to the investment of Corinth, the pick and spade

had been unknown in the Western army. But we needed this kind of drill more than any other experience. Labor of any kind was never refused by the Fifty-First ; and we got our full share of it before the war was over. But there were times when untold gold would have been paid for a few picks and shovels, and ready hands would have been abundant to use them. We had given General Garfield an exhibition of our yeomanry, in cutting down the forest ; he gave us an opportunity, on the 19th, to show what we could do in the way of throwing up earthworks. Our division constructed about eight hundred yards in half a day.

May 21, while on picket near what had been a fine brick residence, a rebel orderly sergeant, concealed in the barn, was shot through the breast. We found him there next day, and buried him. He had evidently not been in there long, as his haversack was full of fine biscuits.

The country thereabout was quite swampy, and our engineers had plenty to do. We marched into Corinth on Saturday morning, May 31, 1862. Peaches and apples were nearly ripe, and we anticipated fine times. The most objectionable feature was the extreme heat of the days and the intense cold of the nights. We worried a great deal then over such things, but got after while to taking them as they came.

The water here was very poor, and there was a great deal of sickness in consequence. Water was found twelve feet below the surface, and hundreds of holes, like minia-ture cellars, appeared, with steps cut in the yellow clay sides, to descend by. Frequently a soldier's feet would slip on the moist steps, and he would be precipitated to the bottom, to the furious disgust of the boys below, awaiting their turn, as well as his own loss and discomfort.

May 23, Colonel Streight's message to his home said :

"We had quite a skirmish this morning, while out on picket. The enemy opened on us at daylight, and the boys returned their fire, when I ordered an advance; which resulted in the capture of 5 prisoners, and

GENERAL T. J. WOOD.

several of the enemy killed and wounded. We drove them half a mile, and held our ground against three times our numbers. No one hurt on our side. I really believe that the 51st would whip their weight in wild-cats, arms or no arms. We have a fight every day, but no general engagement."

Pay-day came just before we arrived at Corinth It was very tiresome standing in line, hour after hour, await-ing the slow process of paying off. An "alecky" clerk, a great deal bigger, in his own estimation, than a brigadier general, was in attendance, and seemed to delight in the confusion of the fellows who, though miserable writers, could always be relied on in any kind of duty, and in the hour of danger were up at the front. The sutler got most of what was coming to some, this time; but many sent their little allowance home, where, in many cases, it was sadly needed.

Corinth had at that time some of the homeliest women in America. One writer, who had time to observe all the attractions of that burg, describes them as "sharp-nosed, tobacco-chewing, snuff-rubbing, flax-headed, hatchet-faced, yellow-eyed, sallow-skinned, cotton-dressed, flat-breasted, bare-headed, long-waisted, hump-shouldered, stoop-necked, big-footed, straddle-toed, sharp-shinned, thin-lipped, pale-faced, lantern-jawed, silly-looking damsels."

If a person wanted any article taken anywhere, it was always "brung," or "fotch," or "toted." We could not tarry long enough in Mississippi to get used to its style.

GENERAL WOOD'S REPORT.

General T. J. Wood's report, covering the time from April 29 to May 30, says:

"After bivouacking two weeks on Shiloh, with every variety of dis-comfort, intensified by absence of baggage and transportation and by the most inclement weather, on April 29 we moved forward 3½ miles to Lick Creek. During the halt here, the division constructed corduroy road three days. On this the headquarters of the Army of the Ohio, with the 4th, 5th and 6th Divisions and reserve artillery, advanced be-yond Lick Creek. My division crossed May 3, and falling into the main road from Hamburg to Corinth, camped near Mt. Olivet church. On

4

the 6th, Gen. Garfield's brigade had a rencontre with the enemy, with an interchange of small arms and shells, without casualty on our part. Three prisoners were captured. May 8 was employed in cleaning up and establishing the new camp. On the afternoon of the 10th, the division was ordered to move across the country to the Hamburg and Farmington road, in the rear of Seven-mile Creek, to the right of Nelson's division. We occupied this position one week. Heavy details were made to finish the road across Chambers Creek, where the route crossed it. During this camp, several lessons were given in division drill. On the afternoon of the 17th, this division was ordered to have three days cooked rations in haversacks, to cross Seven-mile Creek, carry tools, and occupy the position on the Purdy and Farmington road. This was accomplished, the troops skirmishing, intrenching and sleeping on their arms all night. On the following morning, 18th, the outposts were strengthened, and there was active skirmishing all day. The advance sentinels (videttes,) were in close range, and the slightest exposure of person was sure to be followed by the sharp crack of a rifle. On the 19th, we moved to the front, on the main Corinth road, with special charge to hold it. We threw up a continuous line of intrenchments, not less than 800 yards, in a few hours. Several successive subsequent days were devoted to the strengthening of our defenses, and making strong abattis. On the 21st a report was received of a movement on foot by the enemy about 10 o'clock that night. I directed Garfield to visit the outpost, and satisfy himself. We expected an attack next morning, and were prepared for it. Deserters reported 70,000 men under the personal command of Bragg, to attack our center. A week passed, but that moment never came. The early morning of the 30th was broken by a loud sound of singular and heavy explosions."

General Buell's report adds :

"On the evening of the 17th I moved my forces across Seven-mile Creek to the Farmington and Purdy road. Some skirmishing attended this movement, which was not completed till some time after dark. The right of Wood's division rested at Driver's house, on the direct Monterey and Corinth road. When two miles from the enemy's works, I ordered to intrench. In front of Wood was an open field, bordered toward Bridge Creek by thickly wooded spurs of high land, on which we were formed. The enemy occupied the woods in our front with strong lines of skirmishers; and till the evacuation, skirmishing, mingled with artillery, was incessant along the whole front. There was some skirmishing on the 29th. About 4:30 P. M. a message was received, that the enemy was evacuating Corinth. There was some rivalry as to which of the three armies first entered the enemy's works."

But he has no word of commendation in this connection, for the soldiers, who through all that exhibition of assininity and incapacity, endured so cheerfully.

After the evacuation of Corinth, we proceeded east. Beauregard well away, and Halleck over his scare, the Army of the Mississippi (or Ohio,) started on a campaign that for thorough exhaustion of body and soul, had not its equal in the history of that department. It occupied about five months; and while begun ostensibly for the possession of Chattanooga, did not stop till the whole army had swept through Tennessee and Kentucky, to the Ohio River, and half way back.

RAILROADING.

June 1, 1862, orders from headquarters of the Army of the Ohio to Brig. Gen. Wood, commanding 6th Division, announce that,

"In compliance with orders from Gen. Halleck, the Memphis and Charleston railroad from Corinth to Decatur is to be put in order by the troops of this command. Your division is assigned to the duty, and will march to-morrow morning, and will furnish the necessary working parties and guards. One brigade should be left to-morrow at camp on the railroad about 9 miles from Corinth, which will place it about half way between the first and second burnt bridges, and it can aid in the repair of both. The remainder should continue its march to Bear Creek bridge, and halt there until the work at that point is completed."

They were to take six days' rations, and draw from Eastport, on the Tennessee River. A squadron of cavalry was to accompany the troops, and great caution was to be exercised against surprise. Brig. Gen. W. S. Smith was detailed to superintend the work. Gen. Crittenden's division was recalled next day, and Wood's pushed forward. Gen. Nelson was directed, June 3, to move in the same direction, and Gen. Wood to leave Bear Creek as Nelson approached. June 6, locomotives and cars were sent up the river to Florence, and Wood was directed to send a force to protect their landing. Our division moved over the road by Farmington, near Burnsville, and so on east, known as the old Alabama road.

June 6, we arrived at Iuka, Miss., a railroad town of 1500, about one mile from the Alabama line. Here are the Iuka Springs, once a popular resort. We remained at that place a short time and recruited up.

A HARD MARCH.

June 9, Wood was ordered to send a brigade to Tuscumbia. A regiment from some other division had been sent to Buzzard's Roost Creek, to encamp and furnish the requisite fatigue parties. Mitchell was in danger, but it was feared that support could not be sent to him in time.

The roads were poor at the best, but the travel of the army made them almost impassable. Miles and miles we marched under a scorching hot sun, the dust so thick we could hardly breathe, our throats parched with heat and thirst, that was illy relieved by the lukewarm nasty water in our canteens; our bodies weak from lack of food, and from lying on the bare ground. We were compelled to go for days and days without change of clothing, or even an opportunity to remove our hot, dirty, sweaty clothing, that reeked with vermin, and blistered our bodies as we threw ourselves on the steaming ground for sleep or rest. Then it rained, and we rejoiced for a while; but when our clothing got wet, we were miserable. We would make a short halt at noon, for coffee, and then on through the mud and rain. At night we dried our clothes by standing before a fire, and turning round as each exposure dried on us.

We began to observe signs of general desertion by the citizens; tobacco-houses filled with great quantities of leaf in process of curing; farm houses, with immense granaries, flocks and herds, left to the mercy of whoever might come. Occasionally an ungovernable hog or sheep would find its way into our mess kettle.

Nature had done much for this section, and was ready to do as much more. But agriculture seemed there a lost art. Thousands of acres lay uncultivated, but the ignorance of the people, and their strong opposition to the use of improved farm implements, prevented its development, and decreased the value of farms and farming to a most alarming degree.

There was evidence here of strained relations between Halleck and Buell, in the confliction of their orders, that resulted in numerous unprofitable and unnecessary movements by the regiments, and also in Bragg's free passage into Tennessee. With the splendid army under Buell, it ought to have been impossible for Bragg to even approach the Tennessee River. In the subsequent examination into Buell's conduct of the Bragg campaign from Corinth to the close of the Perryville fight, Gen. Wood said, "I am satisfied by information received from various sources, that Bragg's army led into Kentucky, did not exceed 35,000 men." Streight said, "From facts I could gather, they (the rebels,) had from 30,000 to 35,000."

AT TUSCUMBIA.

Our next camp was at Tuscumbia, Alabama, alongside the railroad, where we enjoyed the delightful society of millions of mosquitoes and the redolent fragrance of many neighboring marshes. These mosquitoes were enormous, and their bills were longer than those of a plumber. They could easily pierce through two or three government blankets, and the sting was equal to the prodding of a pin, and had similar injurious results. One able writer has said that "they were built to sit lightly, bite deeply, jump high and come again." That day several of the boys were overcome with the heat. The writer only learned in 1893 of his obligation to J. P. Smith, who found him unconscious on the roadside, and put him in a wagon, in which he was hauled into camp; and this affords an opportunity to testify to the faithfulness of our hospital steward, in every duty he was called upon to perform.

Many of the boys fell by the wayside that day, from sheer exhaustion and sunstroke; from which none ever entirely recovered. They were picked up and placed in ambulances and wagons, and carried into camp. Their patriotism, courage and nerve would not let them give up, though; and after a short rest, and a little kind attention, such as one soldier was always ready to give another, they renewed the struggle, and staggered along under the broiling sun, to the end of the journey.

At Tuscumbia occurred the interview between William Alfred Summers and a colored lady, the revival of which by his comrades, was the bane of his life during the rest of his service.

AT TOWN CREEK, ALABAMA.

Sunday morning, June 15, we marched fourteen miles to Town Creek, Alabama. Colonel Streight had command of the forces, four regiments of infantry and two companies of cavalry, and was constructing a bridge. Lieut.-Colonel Spooner had resigned, to take command of the 83d Indiana, and Major Colescott was advanced to that position. The citizens there were very hostile. New potatoes and blackberries were plentiful, and our boys thrived on them. The berries were the finest we had ever seen, and enormous quantities were gathered. Our advance after Bragg was just rapid enough to enable the berries to mature all along the route; so that we had ripe berries all the way to Louisville. Fishing at Town Creek was also fine, and furnished rare sport.

Lieutenant Jonathan Dunbar had command of Co. K here. While drilling the company one day, he wanted to separate the lines; and sung out, "'Tention! company. Rear open—open—open!" But he could get no further; he could not recollect the rest of the command. The boys got ready to obey promptly, but no one moved. Again the doughty lieutenant shouted, "Rear open—open—open!" and again the boys prepared to execute the movement; but no one stirred. When he again repeated it, the irreverent ones snorted. This enraged the officer; and brandishing his sword, he exclaimed, "I have been a Justice of the Peace, Sheriff of Hancock county, and held other offices with credit; but whenever I get out before Company K, I get my finger in my mouth. Company's dismissed!"

"BOB RIDLEY."

A "contraband," in the form of a tall, double-jointed mulatto, came to us here. We called him "Bob Ridley." He made himself useful in a variety of ways. He could harness a team, cook a dinner, dance a jig or convert himself into an orchestra for other darkies to dance to. His knee-joints turned sidewise, and his long spindle-legs had a comical appearance, as he described the most marvelous contortions, keeping time to his own music, made by a combination of his voice and a set of cane reeds, which he manipulated with wonderful dexterity, and some melody. He was also an accomplished sprinter, and won several small stakes in races among the boys of our regiment. He evinced a profound admiration for John P. Smith, and on one occasion put up a dollar on him, in a race. Some one suggested that he might lose his dollar.

"Don't you be 'lawmed. He don't do nothin' but fly!"

"Ridley" was not disappointed.

FORWARD TO DECATUR.

In a few days, three companies proceeded eight miles further east, to Courtland; leaving tents and equipments behind; then seven miles further, where they repaired a small bridge. Their baggage was forwaded to them there. The same night they were overwhelmed by a terrific storm, that destroyed everything perishable. It cooled the atmosphere, though, and made the march next day delightful. The balance of the regiment had come up by this time. Our march of fourteen miles was made with ease, bringing us to Decatur, on the Tennessee River. On the Saturday following we entered the town, and crossed the river, that at this point is nearly a mile wide. Eleven formidable piers remained of the once magnificent bridge, that had been burned by General Mitchell. We crossed on a ferry formed by an old rebel gunboat flanked on either side by a flatboat. John W. Wells, of Co. C, swam across, accompanied by several other expert swimmers. We camped in a cotton field on Pine Creek, in the vicinity of Mooresville, a short distance east of Decatur, and near the Memphis and East Tennessee railroad. Figs were abundant, and china trees furnished us a delightful shade. We also had a splendid spring of clear water. Every one was living better than for some time. Butter was selling at 40 cents, and potatoes, $2. Adjutant Ramsey was absent, sick, and Captain Willis was also at home on sick furlough.

The same evening, after we crossed the river, Co. C was detailed for picket one mile south of Decatur. It was the misfortune of one squad on this force, to be attacked early next morning by a vicious man-eating shoat, which they were compelled to destroy, to save their lives. One of them thrust his bayonet through the ferocious beast, and held it while another comrade almost pounded its head off with a fence-rail. While two of them skinned the animal, another borrowed a kettle from a house near by, filling it at the well, in which they cooked the pork; and, to avoid any possible interruption, as well as to remove suspicion, one of the boys went in and played with the baby, while the rest got breakfast, adding to the variety a nice panful of potatoes from the field on the other side of the fence.

June 30, 1862: We had just returned from a trip up the river six miles, hunting a band of guerrillas. We had failed to find them. Some of our boys were very sick in camp, and Richard H. Ellis and Stephen Hilton, of Co. C, and James H. Parker, of Co. E, died here. Hilton was ordered out on a sort of convalescents' brigade drill, and got as far as the foot of company quarters, where he fell in the dead ashes of a camp-fire, and expired in a few minutes. They were buried by each other just out of camp.

The Fourth of July was ushered in by a federal salute of thirteen guns. About 10 A. M., our brigade, with Gen. Garfield at the head, marched to a beautiful grove near by, where we were joined by the 15th Brigade. Stacking our arms, we rallied on the speaker's stand, a primitive affair, where, after prayer, the Declaration of Independence was read and heartily cheered. Col. J. W. Blake, of the 40th Indiana, spoke briefly, and was followed by General Garfield, in a most powerful, beautiful and stirring address. His rich, full voice, echoing the patriotic sentiments of his great heart, was listened to with eagerness, and responded to at the close, with a yell that made the old woods ring. Then a choir sang "Star Spangled Banner." Other short speeches were made, and the brigade band interspersed a number of fine selections. At noon a national salute was fired by the 6th Ohio Battery. Then followed games, such as throwing balls, wrestling, foot-racing, blindfold race, a man running against a horse, (in which Al. Morrison, of Co. F, and Jonty Peterson, of Co. C, excelled,) jumping, and somersaults. General Garfield offered a prize of $20 for the fleetest sprinter in the brigade. Our Co. A mountaineer, J. P. Smith, took the money in a fair test. He had then to run with the crack racer of the division ; and came off again as easy a winner as before. After the day's sport, we returned to camp.

EXPEDITION TO DAY'S GAP.

The Fifty-First was missionary, as well as vicarious ; and when we learned that in the mountains 25 or 30 miles south of Decatur, in the neighborhood of a point known as Davis' Gap, there were hundreds of loyal Union people, who had refused to join their traitorous neighbors, and many of whom had fled to the mountains to escape rebel conscription, our hearts went out toward them. Some of them came to the Union army, stealing through mountain passes, twenty, forty, sixty, and even ninety miles, aided by a sort of "underground railroad" system like that by which the former runaway slaves made their escape from their brutal masters, through Ohio and Indiana to Canada.

Colonel Streight conceived a plan, which upon careful inquiry, met with a hearty response by every man in the regiment. This plan was submitted to deparment head-quarters, and full authority was granted for its execution. Accordingly, Saturday morning, July 12, we crossed the river, and accompanied by a small detachment from Co. I, 1st Ohio Cavalry, commanded by Capt. Stephen C. Writer, and several Alabama refugees for pilots, we set out for the mountains. The sun poured down upon us furiously all day, and we were all loaded down to the guards with four days' rations and indispensable baggage; for we were not allowed even a mule for transportation. This, with sixty rounds of ammunition, and guns, made us sweat. The boys suffered a little for water, but no one dared fall out; for there were no ambulances, and the chances for bush-whackers were too good to take any risks. At six o'clock that evening, our rear guard was fired into; and we halted and scoured the woods, but without results. Half a mile further on, the pilots came rushing back to us, with the information that the guerrillas were just ahead, and had captured one of the guides and stolen a horse. During this time, Captain Writer's squad had been sent ahead to notify the Union people of our approach, and to give them time to collect at Col. Davis' house by the time we arrived. The cavalry was attacked by several times their numbers, routed, part of them, including the captain, shot, others taken prisoners, and the remainder made their way back to our regiment.

We arrived at Col. Davis' at dark, and Col. Streight knocked at the door. An elderly lady opened the door, to whom the officer said:

"Does Col. Davis live here?"

"He does."

"Is he at home?"

"He is not."

"We are Union troops, who have heard of your suffering, and have come to relieve you."

She still hesitated.

"Do you believe me?"

"I dislike to dispute your word, but—"

At this juncture a young lady came to the door, and asked, "Have you any of the Alabama boys with you?"

They were called up from the rear. While they were coming, she proceeded:

"We have been so often deceived by guerrillas, that we—O, is that you, John?"

And she sprang into the arms of her husband, who had been hiding out for months.

"Thank God! we are safe!" exclaimed the old lady. "Now I can have the old man here in a few minutes. He is just back here in the mountains."

And soon an old man of 73 years, who had lived on that farm 44 years, and was known as a quiet, peaceable, pious man, was led in. He had been driven from home, by threats of rebel vengeance, to seek refuge in the caves and secluded retreats of those dismal mountains.

We got supper, and, wedged in among the rocks, slept till 3 o'clock; a detail in the meantime scouring about to find the wounded man of the day before. What became of him can only be conjectured from the official report.

Sunday night found us with over fifty recruits. They came to us all day Monday, like doves to the windows. In the evening we had speeches by Col. Streight, Adjutant Ramsey and Hon. Chris. Sheets; the latter having been a member of the convention in which Alabama seceded, and prominent among the few who firmly refused to sign the ordnance of secession. He presented the absolute alternative of being forced into an army with which they had no sympathy, and fighting those they loved, for a cause they

hated; or joining the Union army, and contending against
a foe to God and man, and that must be put down before
peace, quietude and prosperity could again prevail. Said
he, "To-morrow I am going to the Union army. I am
going to expose this fiendish villainy before the world!"

During the colonel's speech, in one of his wild flights
he said, "If I had the scoundrelly rebels, I would hang
them so high—hang them so high—their feet would n't
touch the ground!"

HEART-RENDING SCENES.

Tuesday morning, our time being up, we were forced
to return to camp, 31 or 32 miles. About 7 o'clock a company of twenty men were seen approaching, preceded by a
woman. They were received with cheers of delight. The
woman told, with streaming eyes, how she had passed the
guerrillas, to find her husband and son, 34 miles back in
the mountains. She was 55 years old, and rode a poor
old horse; yet she had made the trip in thirty hours; at
the same time hunting for other friends, and cooking their
breakfast. There were few dry eyes in that camp.

The final moment then came to start. The men were
formed in line—150 in all, and the time came to say good-
bye—to leave those families to the merciless cruelty and
outrage that all feared.

"Attention! Forward march!"

A wild shriek—sobs and pitiful pleadings to heaven;
and we moved away from a scene of suffering that it is not
possible to describe.

Darkness came on us seven miles below Decatur, and
we bivouacked for the night; arriving at Decatur about 6
o'clock next morning.

The Alabamians were formed into a battalion, and
were subsequently assigned to the 1st Tennessee Cavalry.
Col. Streight asked for permission to return to the same
place with his regiment, with two weeks' rations and 500

extra stands of arms, and rally the mountaineers; but was refused.

COLONEL STREIGHT'S OFFICIAL REPORT.

{ " HDQRS. 51ST IND. VOL.,
{ Camp near Mooresville, July 16, 1862.

While in command at Decatur, there were several small parties of loyal Alabamians who came into our lines, begging me to give them protection and a chance to defend the flag of our country. The tale of suffering and misery, as told by each as they arrived, was in itself a lamentable history of the deplorable condition of the Union people of the South. Notwithstanding the oft repeated assertion that there was a strong Union sentiment in portions of the cotton States, I had long since given up all hopes of finding the people entertaining it; hence I was at first incredulous as to what they said, and even suspicious that they were spies belonging to the enemy, but as their numbers increased, each corroborating the story of the other, I at last became convinced that the matter was worthy of notice.

About this time (10th inst.,) I was informed by a courier that there was a party of about 40 men some 5 or 6 miles toward the mountain, trying to come to us, and about the same number of the enemy's cavalry were between them and Decatur, trying to intercept and capture them. As my orders were to defend the town only, I did not feel at liberty to send out assistance to the Union men, without further orders; and there being no telegraph communication with you, I at once informed Gen. Buell by telegraph, of the circumstances, whereupon I received the following reply:

' Huntsville, Ala., — 1862.

Col. A. D. Streight, 51st Ind. Vol.:

Send out what force you deem sufficient to assist the Union men in, and drive off the rebel cavalry, and see that they are not playing a trick to draw you out by these reports.

JAMES B. FRY, Col. and Chief of Staff.'

Owing to a storm that was passing over the telegraph lines at the time, the above was not received until near three hours after I sent Gen. Buell the first dispatch. As soon as I received the foregoing instructions from Col. Fry, I at once ordered 3 companies of my regiment, under Maj. Colescott, to cross the river with their arms and full 40 rounds of cartridges. This was done in the least possible time, but just as the 3 companies were in line ready to march, another courier arrived, stating that the Alabama boys had succeeded in avoiding the rebels and had got within our lines; but a short time elapsed before they arrived. Such were the manifestations of joy and gladness exhibited by them, that all doubts were fully expelled from my mind, whereupon I resolved to go to the assistance of those who were left behind, providing I could get permission to do so. Consequently I telegraphed the following:

'Decatur, Ala., July 10, 1862.

Col. J. B. Fry, A. A. G. and Chief of Staff:

SIR: I have the honor to report to you that the party of Alabama volunteers has just arrived, and 40 of them have been mustered into the service of the United States. Their accounts of the hardships endured are sufficient to enlist the sympathies of the hardest heart. They report that there are several hundred who would come but for the danger of passing from the foot of the mountain here, some 25 miles distant. If you will give me one company of cavalry to take with my regiment, I am fully satisfied that I could, by going, say 15 miles toward the foot of the mountains, and then sending out a few of these new recruits to notify their neighbors, within four days time bring back with me at least 500 volunteers. If you will allow me to make the experiment, my word for it I will return safely with my command.

I am, sir, your most obt. servt.,

A. D. STREIGHT, Col. 51st I. V.'

Nothing was heard from the foregoing dispatch till about 2 P. M., the next day, (July 11,) when Capt. Lennard handed me the following communication from Col. Fry to Gen. Wood, with verbal instructions to carry out its provisions:

'HDQRS. Huntsville, Ala., July 11, 1862.

GEN. WOOD: Col. Streight reports that there are several hundred men about 25 miles south of Decatur, who are trying to come on to join our army, and Col. Streight is anxious to go with his regiment to bring them in. You can order an expedition of this kind. In doing so, it will be necessary to send another regiment to take Col. Streight's place near Decatur. It will not be practicable for you to cross cavalry over to send, but the Colonel can take any cavalry that may be at Decatur. Instruct Col. Streight to be cautious, and not expose his command to ambuscade or surprise or to attack from superior force. He should not be gone more than 3 or 4 days, and must take no baggage. He must be careful and not let the people suppose that his presence indicates a permanent occupation, and thus lead them into demonstrations for which the rebels would make them suffer after our withdrawal. Give such orders for the details and precautionary instructions as the case may seem to you to require.   JAS. B. FRY, Col. and Ch. of Staff.'

Upon the receipt of the above, I proceeded to get my command in readiness for the expedition as quickly as possible. Four days' rations were ordered, and one camp-kettle to each company. The haversacks holding only 3 days' rations, we filled the kettles and buckets out of the remainder, and decided to get along as best we could under the circumstances. The guides were selected to conduct us to the Union settlement, who were also to act as couriers to inform their friends of the nature of our mission. There were but 16 men and the captain of Co. D, 1st Ohio Cav., at Decatur, who were also put in readiness to march.

In accordance with these arrangements, we moved off at daylight on the 12th inst., in the direction of a place called Davis' Gap, some 9 miles southeast of Danville, and 25 south of Decatur. The cavalry were thrown out in advance a suitable distance, to give notice of the approach of an enemy, and a strong advance and rear guard was at all times kept in readiness for immediate action. When we had proceeded some 12 miles on our way, being unable to hear anything of the enemy, I ordered the captain commanding the cavalry to proceed with his command in advance with 3 of the guides, and escort them as far toward Davis' Gap as he should deem safe, so as to allow the guides to give the information to the Union people that we were coming. I gave him the most positive instructions to make diligent inquiry relative to the enemy, and to go no farther than he could with perfect safety, and as soon as he arrived near enough to the mountains to enable the guides to get through, he should fall back at once and rejoin me, I at this time having ascertained that it would in all probability be necessary for me to go about 23 miles, instead of 15, the distance I at first expected, but did not expect to be able to get through the first day.

Under these instructions he proceeded somewhat faster than the infantry could march, consequently when he arrived some 22 miles from Decatur, (10 miles from where he left us,) he was probably not more than 5 or 6 miles ahead of my regiment; but it being very hot in the middle of the day, we halted to rest; expecting the cavalry to rejoin us, as ordered. In direct disobedience to my orders, the cavalry spent about an hour's time in scouting about the country after they had escorted the guides to within 3 miles of the mountains, after which they stopped at a Mr. Mentor's house, and ordered dinner; there they spent about 3 hours more. The captain was warned when he first arrived in the neighborhood, that 40 of the enemy's cavalry were within 6 miles of him; yet, with these facts before him, as I have above shown, he spent nearly four hours in the neighborhood of Mr. Mentor's house; a sufficient time to have returned to Decatur, if necessary, much less to rejoin me.

About 5 : 30 o'clock he was attacked by upward of 40 of the enemy's cavalry and guerrillas. Here again his conduct seems to have been very injudicious, for although there were several log buildings that he could have held against any force the enemy could bring to bear against him, yet, instead of occupying them, after exchanging a few shots, in which one of his men was wounded, and 2 of the enemy killed and 2 wounded, he ordered a retreat across the field, which seems to have been accomplished very precipitately, especially when taking into consideration the fact that the enemy did not pursue him but a few rods, and that too on foot. Four of his men got lost from the balance. He proceeded in a westerly circuitous route to Decatur, where he arrived the evening of the same day with 12 of his men.

In the meantime I had arrived to within 2 miles of the place where he was attacked, before the enemy had left, and I think I would have been in time to have done them justice, had I not halted to chastise some guerrillas who had the impudence to fire into my rear guard; but as it was, we arrived just in time to see the chivalry put spurs to their horses and leave hurriedly to the eastward, thus showing conclusively that the enemy did not follow our cavalry. We bivouacked that night 23 miles from Decatur, and within 1 mile of where the skirmish took place.

The next day was spent in ascertaining what we could relative to the extent of the damage done to the cavalry and in notifying the people in the mountains that they could now have a chance to join the Union army. I ascertained the loss of our cavalry in the engagement to be 1 man missing, who when last seen, some 2 miles from where the skirmish took place, was wounded in the thigh (not seriously,) and 1 taken prisoner, 1 horse killed and 1 disabled. Three cavalrymen came in early in the morning without horses, but our boys succeeded in finding the horses and equipments near where they were left. The captain's sword was also found about 100 rods from where the fight occurred.

I soon became convinced that the time set for me to return was insufficient for me to accomplish the object of my mission. The news of the defeat of our cavalry spread over the country like a fire on a prairie, causing great consternation among the Union people and boldness on the part of the guerrillas. The guides became frightened, and it was very difficult to induce them to leave my command. However, after laboring under all these difficulties, we succeeded in bringing back with us 150 volunteers. Several small parties that started to join us failed to get there in time. One party, numbering 34 men, were within 20 miles of us at daylight the morning we left, and although a messenger arrived, giving me that information when we had marched but a short distance on our return, yet I was ordered to return within 4 days time, and could wait no longer.

At 11 A. M. yesterday we took up our line of march for Decatur, and when we had proceeded about 4 miles from our encampment we were informed that the enemy's cavalry about 500 strong, were posted at the crossing of the road, about 1 mile ahead. The country being thickly wooded, I had nothing to fear from mounted men, but supposing that they might dismount and act as infantry, I deployed Cos. A and F on each side of the road in advance as skirmishers, at the same time ordering Co. D forward in the road to form a reserve, and also to deploy 6 men in advance to act as signal-men, 1 company having been previously detailed to act as rear guard. They too were ordered to throw out skirmishers on the flanks, to avoid an undiscovered approach from either of these directions. The Alabamians had previously been placed next to the rear guard. Having advanced the skirmishers and advance reserves some 400 yards, I ordered the whole battalion to move forward, each individual and company to keep their relative positions. In this order we proceeded, but as we approached the position occupied by the enemy, they fled before us without firing a gun.

It now became apparent to me that the intention of the enemy was to harass our march, and as the country was mostly wooded, I concluded to continue the march in the order above referred to, thus avoiding the possibility of running into an ambuscade or of being surprised. The enemy fell back as we approached, for about 2 miles, when they turned eastward. For some time afterward I was expecting a demonstration upon our rear, and made preparations accordingly. We proceeded to march in this manner for 12 miles, frequently relieving the skirmishers by sending out others, without further molestation. It was now getting dark, and we were within 7 miles of Decatur, when we concluded to bivouac for the night. Strong pickets were thrown out in every approachable direction. The boys were allowed to sleep till 3 o'clock next morning, when they were awakened, and as soon as it was daylight we were on our way, and arrived at Decatur at 6:30 A. M., bringing back every member of my regiment who went with us.　　　*　　　*

The misunderstanding, by reason of which the 1st Ohio Cavalry squad got so far in advance of our regiment, cost the "critter-back" fellows a great deal. Coming to a farm-house, they were prevailed upon to eat dinner. They did what good soldiers should never do, laid their weapons aside, feeling secure, and applied themselves to the enjoyment of the hospitality of the mistress. While absorbed thus, they were surrounded by bushwhackers, and had a narrow escape from death or capture. Our advance came up just in time to save them. The captain and a few of his men made their way back to Decatur. The report that the captain died there, is not correct, as is shown.

REPORT OF CAPT. S. C. WRITER, 1ST OHIO CAVALRY.

"Decatur Ala., July 16, 1862.

COL. MINOR MILLIKEN,
　　Comdg. 1st Ohio Cav.:

　　I should have sent you the following official information with regard to my late expedition sooner, but I did not until this morning learn the full details from some of my men who were detained with the infantry regiment which accompanied us at the time of starting.

Late on Friday evening, the 11th, Col. Streight, of the 51st Indiana, informed me that he had received permission from Gen. Buell to march his regiment 24 miles into the hills, and remain four days, for the purpose of recruiting its numbers, as many had already come in, and many more would come in, were they protected from the bushwhackers in their immediate neighborhood, and also received permission from the general to take any cavalry he might find upon this side of the river.

We left Decatur the following morning, at sunrise, and went out six

5

miles. Col. Streight then ordered that I should take five of the new recruits which had accompanied us, and escort them through to Col. Davis', 17 miles farther on, with my cavalry, which consisted of 1 sergeant, 2 corporals and 11 privates, carrying in all 12 guns. I was instructed when I arrived at Col. Davis', to impress any number of horses that they thought they might require to ride all through the country to inform Union men wishing to join our army, that he was there, ready to receive them, they to go on that night, and require a change of horses, it being considered too hard a day's work to use the horses they had that day ridden through.

At the time of parting with Col. Streight, he told me that his regiment would undoubtedly come up with me that night; but if it did not, and I considered it dangerous to remain there alone, to fall back upon his regiment.

I arrived near Col. Davis' all safe, put out pickets, fed horses, and sent forward 3 men and procured horses for 3 others. I supposed at the time I reached Col. Davis' the infantry was 8 or 10 miles back. The place we selected to feed was a farmyard, well fortified by corn-cribs, stables, hen-houses and pig-pens, and might easily have been held, had had any respectable number of men. I suppose I had been there altogether 2½ hours, when I heard an alarm firing from our rear pickets. We immediately mounted our horses, rode out to the pickets, and found the enemy were approaching us with some force mounted, and a very considerable force dismounted, and deploying right and left of the road, under cover of the woods and a rail fence, evidently intending to flank us on all sides and capture us. I then ordered the men to return to the barn-yard, tie up the horses, and take position behind our defenses, and defend ourselves as best we could. The men fired steady and with precision, and staid their advance for the time being; but as their force was being constantly augmented from the woods, I finally gave the order to mount and make our retreat, that being the only way I could then see to save our horses. We retreated toward the woods parallel with their line, they keeping up a constant firing, it being the only route left open to us. While running the gauntlet, 3 men were wounded, one in the thigh, two about the head; the latter 2 not seriously. Two horses were shot and disabled, and left behind.

When we reached the woods, I gave directions that we should turn the enemy's flank, go back by their rear, and join the infantry on the Decatur road, which I then supposed to be about 4 miles back of where we had the skirmish. I then for the first time discovered that 5 of my men were missing, and supposed that they had got scattered from the main body, and would join the infantry that night or in the morning. The country through which we retreated, was a secession, guerrilla neighborhood, and when within 2½ miles of the main road, four more shots were fired upon us, and one of my men had his saber and scabbard shot entirely off the belt. One mile farther on, I was shot, the ball entering the body near the upper point of the hip-bone, traversing down and around the hip, lodging on the inside of the thigh, nearly one-third of the way down to the knee, giving me a gunshot wound in my body of considerably over one foot in length. I then determined to change my course, and come into camp by a by-road, which I did that night by 12 o'clock, having ridden 18 miles after being shot.

Three of my missing men returned this morning, and state that they made their way to the infantry the next forenoon. They report 2 men still missing, one having been taken prisoner, and the other either a prisoner or killed, they were not able to say positively which.

I have lost 3 horses, (2 shot and disabled, and the third taken with the prisoner,) 2 full horse equipments, 2 carbines, 3 sabers and 4 pistols. The enemy had between 75 and 100 men, and report 2 killed and 2 severely wounded upon their side. S. C. WRITER,

Capt. Comdg. Co. I, 1st Ohio Cav.

There appears to be a slight discrepancy in the above reports. You pay your money and take your choice. Captain Writer makes a very long story about a very short squad; but the fact that he was afterward promoted to be major and lieutenant-colonel of his regiment, proves that he was certainly regarded as a brave soldier. The reports, so far as they relate to the cavalry squad, are each entitled to a little salt.

MOVING A LOCOMOTIVE.

While Colonel Streight was perfecting his plan for the relief of the mountaineers, an incident occurred, that ought to have been mentioned before, and that illustrates the capacity of our regiment for anything it might be called on to do. The rebels had run a locomotive over the bridge at Decatur just before it was burned, and left it standing on the track, near the river. Gen. Wood ordered the Fifty-First to move it across the river. Accordingly, the regiment fitted up a flatboat and moved it near the abutment. Strong ropes were then fastened to the engine, a track was built of planks to the boat, and 500 men let the ponderous machine down the bank, floated it across the river, and put it safely on the track, on the other side, without an accident. Just as we reached the south bank, a company of rebel cavalry dashed up to where the engine had stood, and took a few shots at us, but no one was hurt.

Col. Straight to Col. Fry. A. A. G.:

"Decatur, July 9, 1862.

I have succeeded in safely landing the engine Sam Cruse on this shore of the river. When I arrived here yesterday, about 1 P. M., the boat that was to convey the engine was but partially framed. Since then we have completed the boat, launched it, and she has made a successful trip, with her valuable cargo."

ON THE ROAD AGAIN.

We took passage from Mooresville in box cars on the Memphis and Charleston road. The engine was insufficient to pull the train up the grades; and the colonel would order the boys out to "push her up," which they did with a will; jumping on at the top to ride down the other side. In the meantime they busied themselves gathering the fine peaches that grew in volunteer bountifulness all along the road.

Monday morning, August 11, we were at Stevenson, Alabama, with orders to prepare for a four days' scout. We had torn down many houses for timbers, with which we erected fortifications, and were momentarily expecting an attack. Co. C made a detour in the direction of Huntsville, and brought in 200 negroes, who were put to work on the fortifications. This force was supplemented by one of 300 more "contrabands" from other directions, and the work moved along briskly. The soldiers were delighted with this new policy, and the darkies were equally so, the only drawback to the latter's happiness being a dread of having to return to their old masters.

Our regiment yelled at everything they saw or heard. When another regiment passed, they yelled at them; they scared the darkies almost to death, with their yelling; as they tumbled out to roll-call in the morning, they yelled; as they marched out of camp, their voices went up in a muscular whoop, that made the foliage tremble like a leaf;

when they returned, after a hard day's scouting, they were never too tired to hail the end of their task with a joyous yell. If a mule broke loose and ran away, his speed was accelerated by a volley of yells all along the line; and if a dog happened to come their way, they made it livelier for him than could the most resonant can that ever adorned his tail. Indeed, our whole army was blessed with this remarkable faculty. Sometimes a yell would start in at one end of the division, and regiment after regiment, and brigade after brigade, would take it up and carry it along; then send it back to the other end; few knowing what it was about, or caring less.

MISPLACED CONFIDENCE.

Henry Moore and Henry Kirk were natural foragers. At Stevenson they got acquainted with an old fellow named Osborn, who had two bright, good looking daughters. He was an old rebel, and our boys had but little respect for him. The old man had two fine cows, however, and those two soldiers conceived the idea of milking them. They learned that the family were late risers; so they visited the barn quite early each morning, and being used to milking at home, they had no difficulty in relieving the well-filled udders before any of the family were up. The next time the boys called on the ladies, the old man complained to them about the soldiers milking his cows. They sympathized with him, and said it was a shame that the soldiers should do such things; and finally agreed to help him to discover them. Some days after that, Amos Warrick, who had been home, returned, and as he messed and bunked with these boys, they found their bunk too small. Kirk at once thought of Osborn's barn door; and, although it was midnight, they turned out and got the door, and put it in the bottom of their shanty before they went to sleep. Next morning they were quite late in going for their milk, and, though they escaped the Osborns, they did not get back till after roll-call. For this they were put on "extra duty," and were set to "policing" the company quarters. As the company commander, Captain Russell, was getting milk of them every day, the duty was light. While they were at their task, Mr. Osborn came into camp. Finding them at such employment, he asked another soldier the cause of it, and was told that they had been out milking cows. He "caught on" at once, and being directed to their shanty, he found his barn door under their blankets. Thereupon he sailed up to headquarters, and informed Col. Streight of it. As the colonel and adjutant were also flavoring their daily coffee with this same brand of milk, Ramsey put the old fellow under arrest for insulting them with such an accusation, and made him carry a rail for an hour. Kirk and Moore didn't call on the Osborn family after that; and the daily supply of milk was discontinued. Mr. Osborn's cows were not disturbed any more.

Stevenson, July 22, 1862: It was very hot and dry. Capt. W. N. Denny, son of old Captain Denny, of Co. E, was promoted to be major of our regiment.

While out one night, scouting for some cattle that had been brought across the river at that point, the regiment came to a dry creek. There was an old canoe lying there, and the chaplain sat down on it to rest. At the same moment a frog jumped up his pants, causing such a tumult, that the colonel, who rode by just then, supposed he had a convulsion.

"BUCK FEVER."

A detachment of the regiment was sent to Crow Creek, six miles east of Stevenson, to guard a small bridge on the railroad. While there, a regiment of rebel cavalry was reported in the neighborhood, and additional vigilance was observed against surprise. One night, while on picket, a vidette, whose name is withheld by request, saw in the distant gloaming what to him was a stalwart rebel sneaking, half-bent, toward the very spot where the Union soldier stood, under the shelter of a large bush. The vidette was excited, and took what old hunters know as "buck fever." On came the enemy, now and then raising his head to peer about, and get his bearings, then plunging forward among the tall weeds, then stopping to listen. At length the foe had gained the road, on the opposite side of which was stationed the vidette, and as he turned down the track, the sentinel caught his breath, then depressed his bayonet and sprang upon the enemy, that with a yelp of surprise and agony, bounded away in the direction whence it came. It was an inoffensive big "yaller" dog, whose hunger had attracted him to the camp.

The pernicious and disgusting habit of snuff-dipping first attracted our attention here. It is universal among the women of every class in the South, as chewing gum is among the girls in the North. A small vessel, like a mustard or baking-powder box, is used to hold the vile stuff, and is frequently of silver, with gold lining. A small swab about the size of a lead pencil, and made of soft pine, is formed by chewing an inch of the end of the stick until it resembles the brush on the end of a mule's tail. This is moistened so as to make the snuff adhere, then thrust into the mouth, and rubbed along the teeth. It was quite common to see ladies of the best society, calling for an hour, produce from their reticule a fancy box and stick, and take a dip of snuff.

Our boys will never forget the religious services held by the negroes in their camp near the fortifications upon which they were employed. They felt doubtless very much like the Children of Israel did at the crossing of the Red Sea. They believed that their day of deliverance was at hand, though they couldn't conceive how such a marvelous thing was to be accomplished. Their songs were strangely musical, and the weird sounds of voices that responded to the prayers of the white-wooled veterans, who had been for many long years pleading for deliverance from bondage, seemed almost to come from another world. Here is one of the prayers, exactly as it was uttered:

"O, Lo'd, Massa, come to dis e'th; an' when yo' do come, git on de fas'es' hoss yo' kin fin'; an' O, Lo'd, don' run ner gallop, but jest trot all roun' dis e'th, till dese aw sinnehs is converted an' Massa Linkum's sojers whip all de secesh!"

"SYNTAX" AND "PROSODY."

So pressing were the needs of our hospital department, that the entire country through which we passed was laid under contribution for "contrabands" to perform the multifarious domestic and mechanical duties connected with that branch of the service. Among a number taken from the farm of Senator Oates, in Northern Alabama, were two likely young men, who were immediately christened "Syntax" and "Prosody." The latter was possessed of more than ordinary intelligence, and was a kind of preacher among his fellow slaves. He was often called upon to talk at headquarters. One of his favorite subjects was "How de enemy didn' cotch de Lo'd." He said, "Da was a mity conflic 'tween de enemy an' de Lo'd. De enemy was a pressin' ha'd on de Lo'd—pressin' ha'd on 'im. Den de Lo'd fool 'im. De Lo'd come to a blacksmif shop; an' he 'light his mule, an' he say to de blacksmif, 'Slip dem shoes; put 'em 'hind side 'fore.' So he slip 'em, an' put 'em on 'hin' side 'fore; an' w'en de enemy struck de trail, he thought de Lo'd was goin' de oder way. So de enemy was allus goin' de rong drection, an' didn' cotch de Lo'd."

Tuesday morning, 12th, a detachment of our regiment went to Woodville, a little station between Stevenson and Huntsville, where we were joined by a small detachment of cavalry, and another of artillery. As no enemy appeared, we soon interested ourselves in supplying our private commissary department. There was no lack of peaches, corn, apples, chickens, hams, honey, eggs, etc., and it required only courage to go out after them. So, for a brief season we lived fat. It was near here that Col. Bob McCook was murdered by cowardly rebel bushwhackers, and the awful results were seen on every hand, evidences of the hatred of his devoted boys, in the burned and demolished houses belonging to the fine plantations.

"WEASEL." "JONTY PETE." THE TABLES TURNED.

"Weasel" was an attenuated, withered specimen of humanity, with the patriotism and courage of a giant, but lacking mental and physical ability to carry them out. He was frequently made the butt of his unthinking comrades, who would play the most irritating, though never cruel, pranks on him. While waiting for his coffee to boil, some one would divert his attention from it, while another comrade, with a hooked stick would quietly walk off with his coffee-bucket. When "Weasel" turned again, and found his coffee gone, his wrath was unbounded; and he would hurl all sorts of anathemas at his persecutor, whom he threatened to kill, "if possible!" During the Stone River fight, he spied a knapsack that had been discarded by a comrade, and stopping short, he deliberately ransacked it, finding there some tobacco, with which he filled his pipe, and lit it.

"Jonty Pete" was a character. Bold, careless and independent, he would have made an excellent scout. He was in the war for the fun of it, and was indifferent as to the methods of securing his share. He had been banged about all his life, and always bore the air of one expecting a sharp clap of thunder, or that some one would suddenly punch him in the ribs; ready to jump, bullfrog fashion, without taking time to come to a perpendicular. Quiet and smooth-tongued, he was

> "The mildest mannered man
> That ever scuttled ship or cut a throat."

He was one of those fellows who could eat and talk at the same time. He always got his share of rations, whenever he could get up a hot discussion in the mess at meal time. He went from Brownsburg, and deserted at Murfreesboro, while we were building fortifications, just after the battle of Stone River. His name does not appear on any of the company rolls; but in Co. A, 30th Indiana, the record of "Jonathan Peters, deserted Jan. 8, '65," appears, without residence or date of enlistment. It may have been only a coincidence, though, and not our Jonathan Peterson. He was a prime forager, and so persistent was he in this, that he came very near being captured several times. He went fishing one day, and forgot to come back.

The next day after our arrival at Woodville, he and "Weasel" and others were out, and met with excellent success in foraging. A large quantity of milk, honey, butter and chickens was discovered, and they were taking peaceable possession, when an old clay-colored hag appeared on the scene, and proceeded to dispossess the invaders. But they wouldn't be dispossessed; and sent her back to her lines with colors slightly trailing. She threatened them with her "old man," who she said was on "tother side o' the river, tendin' the crap," and who would "make you'ns all know we-uns-all won't be rin over by no nasty stinkin' Yanks." Other boys had brought in several bushels of fine-looking peaches, but they were too hard for use, and lay in piles about camp.

That evening, a snaky-looking old fellow came into camp, cursing the boys all roundly, and inquiring for the "Giner'l." He was directed to Lieut.-Col. Colescott, who was in command, and to him he began a tirade of abuse of the Government and the soldiers; swearing vengeance on the fellows who stole his chickens and other stuff, and had insulted his "old woman." The officer gave the old bushwhacker one look; then he said, "Well, sir, what do you expect? You devils have stolen everything you've got, and have committed murders enough to shame old Satan himself. Now you git! (presenting his revolver,) and be

quiet till you get out, or I won't answer for consequences."
Seeing a crowd of soldiers approaching, he called Sergeant
Wm. Kelly, on duty, and said, "Take this man outside of
camp, before the boys hang him!" This changed the old
fellow's manner; and he made a tumultuous rush for liberty. As he went, some of the unregenerate, who heard
the conversation, rallied on the piles of hard peaches, and
pelted him with them until he was out of sight. The last
seen of him, his long legs were swinging lively, and his
coat-tails snapping merrily in the soft evening air.

A GUERRILLA CONVERTED.

One night Billy Tout and John P. Smith went to the
home of the guerrilla, Willhite, to capture his fine blooded
mare. The guerrilla was absent, but his wife was there,
and with a shotgun in her hand, declared she would shoot
the first man who attempted to bridle the mare. A pistol
pointed at her, however, proved a great persuader; and
the mare was led to Col. Streight's quarters, without blood
being shed. Next morning the guerrilla came into camp,
and the colonel read him a severe lecture on his disloyalty;
and told him he should be hung. At this the fellow turned
pale and began to beg. The colonel asked him why he
was doing thus. He replied that he had been reading a
book called "Helper," and was "opposed to freeing the
niggers."

"If I give you your mare, now, will you go home and
behave?"

The color returned to the cheeks of the wretch, as he
replied, "I'm cussed ef I don't do it!"

He left our camp on his mare; and was for the Union
ever after.

Another night, a negro came into camp, and informed
these same comrades that he knew where six or seven desperate guerrillas were going to stay that night. Our boys
concluded to capture their horses, which the darkey said

were fine ones. It was a daring undertaking, but they were not afraid; so they gave the darkey a dollar and a pocket-knife to take them to the house where the guerrillas were. They reached the place about 9 o'clock that night, and found the men having a good time in the house. Our boys went to the stable, bridled two of the best horses, and mounted them. The darkey, in the meantime, had let the bars down; and when they came out, he got up before one of them. With revolvers in their hands, they whispered to the darkey, "Now lead out for camp, or we'll cut your throat."

"Don' kill me, mastah; I's gwine take you-uns right to you-uns camp!" replied the terrified darkey.

They arrived safely about midnight, without disturbing the pickets. John P. presented the mare he rode to Dr. Collins. A stranger came into camp a few days after, and being attracted by the animal, inquired where she was from. Smith told him that he got her from a man named Fugate, of Warren county, Missouri. The name "Fugate" stuck to John P. all through the service.

THE CHASE AFTER BRAGG.

About the 1st of September, 1862, the style of our organization omitted "Department of the Mississippi;" but it didn't make our load any lighter, nor marching easier.

From Stevenson we went to Battle Creek. It was at this place that our boys first talked with the rebel pickets, across the river; and there was the first place we heard the term "johnny" applied to them.

One peculiarity of the war was the result of a common necessity on both sides. Frequently the only source of fuel or water lay directly between the two armies, and neither of them could have been supplied, but for the expedient adopted by the pickets, and ignored by those in command. As soon as such a contingency was discovered, the pickets would call across to each other, and agree to not shoot nor interfere in any manner with those getting water from the spring, or rails from the fence. Also newspapers, tobacco and other articles were exchanged. When a new relief came on, the truce was continued, unless a special order was issued on either side. Then that side would call out, as they relieved the old pickets:

"Johnny, we've got orders to shoot."

"All right, yanks; hunt yer holes."

"Well, you rebs want to skedaddle in a hurry."

"Go to —, yanks! Let 'er go!"

Whiz went a ball in response to this defi; and a lively fusilade ensued. Rarely any one was ever hit, though, at such a time; and the next relief would likely renew the truce.

Then we advanced to a point above Jasper, and thence over the Cumberland Mountain, where we lost nearly all of our baggage; thence through Manchester, Murfreesboro, Nashville, Gallatin, Mitchellville, Franklin, Ky., and to Bowling Green; marching over 36 miles the last day, and arriving at the last named place at 6 o'clock on the morning of September 11.

We subsisted at this time on quarter rations, because our cracker-line was broken by the rebel cavalry, and at Pelham everything that could not be carried on our backs, was destroyed. The marches were hard, and were only enlivened by an occasional skirmish. Water was hard to get from here on, and much of it was very poor at that. We struck a peanut patch one night, our camp being right over it; and it was fun to see the boys jabbing with their bayonets all over that field, and roasting the nuts in the fire. Nearly every one thought peanuts grew on bushes, like blackberries or currants, and were astonished as their bayonets turned them out of the ground, like so many diminutive potatoes.

Our boys would fight as readily for rations as for anything else. They could stand half-rations, although that

seemed hard in a land of plenty; but when our supply was
clean cut off, and we began to feel the gnawing of empty
stomachs, no amount of travel, nor exposure, nor fighting
was too much. And no tongue can describe the delight
we experienced when the word came that communication
was reopened.

General Sherman's Memoirs, vol. 2, p. 11, says, "To
feed an army of 100,000 men and 30,000 animals, and
keep it in ammunition and other needful things, required
130 car loads, of 10 tons each, per day. These had to be
transported a long distance frequently. Every mile of this
was guarded. Often the line was cut, and then the soldiers had to go on half rations."

During the afternoon of the day before we reached
Bowling Green, we halted for the purpose of butchering
and baking. Flour was issued to each company, pro rata.
The manner of proceeding in the writer's company was as
follows: There was barely enough baking powder, or soda,
to go around, without any wastage. Two experts made up
all the dough on the tailgate of the company wagon, and
gave each comrade a chunk, which he patted out on a flat
rail or board, like a "short-cake," and stuck it up to the
fire to bake. Our beef was salted in a lump, and roasted
on the end of a stick, over a rail fire. Then we marched
all night long, and were so completely fagged out at times,
that we jostled each other and staggered like drunken men.
Henry Welshans and the writer slung their guns on their
outside shoulders, locked arms, and marched together thus,
taking turns sleeping, as best they could; each sleeping as
much as half a mile at a time; while the other supported
and guided him. There were some who "played-off" sick,
in order to get a "pass" to the ambulance. The most were
of the kind that always kept up with the colors; and we
got in on time. At one point we had to double-quick, to
get onto the pike first, so as to be in the advance, which
always made the marching easier. But all the digging and

plowing and harvesting and other labor we had ever done in a month at home, reduced to a single day, would not be more exhaustive than that night march; yet, as we filed off into a cornfield and unslung our knapsacks, and spied the river only a hundred yards away, with one common impulse, we made a rush for it; shedding our garments as we went. O, how soothing was that water! How it restored our overheated blood to its normal temperature, and healed our sore shoulders and shanks, and cooled the great big red blisters on our feet, worn by our new "gunboats," which was another name for the broad comfortable shoes the Government furnished.

There had been a hard rain there the day before, and there was a depth of three or four inches of mud in the furrows; so that we had to pile up cornstalks or brush or rails to keep us out of the mud; with not a sign of straw to soften the irregularities.

There were two, however, who failed to appreciate the blessedness of this beautiful river; who, in truth, had not intentionally put water or soap on their faces nor any part of their persons since they left Indiana. They were Jim Kiley, a red-headed, freckled and brown-skinned boy, and Rinie Houzlot, a young French tough, without any known antecedents. W. C. Clements, of Co. C, and another comrade were detailed to take these two filthy fellows to Green River, and with sand and soap to scrub them. They were probably never so clean in their lives before. Houzlot deserted September 15, '63; as Kiley's name does not appear on the roster, it is impossible to tell whence he came, nor whither he went. So is every one that is born of Satan.

MRS. STREIGHT'S CAPTURE AND ESCAPE.

During the pursuit of Bragg, Mrs. Streight went to Nashville, accompanied by their son John, then a small child, and stopped at the Sewanee House. She desired to go from there by railroad to Bowling Green; but as com-

munication by that route was cut off, it was decided to go
by stage-coach. Accordingly, Sunday evening, September
7, about 7 o'clock, the lumbering old-fashioned stage-coach
drew up at the hotel door, and with Mrs. Streight, Mrs.
Grigsby, wife of the colonel of the 24th Kentucky, Colonel
Shoemaker, of the 13th Michigan, with seventeen other
men and a lady with her two boys, the conveyance was
pretty well filled. They proceeded as far as Tyree Springs,
a summer retreat on the top of the mountain, which they
reached about midnight. When near the summit, they
were surrounded by 250 of Morgan's guerrillas, who fired
upon them. "Don't fire," cried the driver; "there are
ladies in there!" They were taken to the Springs hotel,
placed under guard, the ladies occupying the sitting-room.
When they found they were captured, and had to get out,
the men quickly gave their revolvers to Mrs. Streight, and
she secreted them about her person. They also gave her
important dispatches, which she hid among some clothing
in her traveling-basket. Just then a burly ruffian put his
pistol under her nose in the stage. She slapped it back,
saying, "Keep your revolver out of my face, sir!" He
begged pardon, and disappeared.

As the ladies and children entered the sitting-room,
Mrs. Streight closed the door, and stepped across to a little
stand, opening the drawer, and thrusting the dispatches
into it; then closed it.

After the guerrillas finished searching the men, they
returned to the hotel, and called the ladies out, to claim
their trunks. They found them in an old two-wheeled cart.
Colonel Shoemaker was sitting on that of Mrs. Streight,
on which a card was tacked, bearing the inscription "Mrs.
Col. A. D. Streight." While pretending to grope in the
uncertain light, for her trunk, she put her hand back and
tore off the card. Then she proved her ownership, by fitting her key in the lock. The baggage was taken into the
hotel and searched, but nothing contraband was found.

MRS. A. D. STREIGHT.

Soon the men all went out, but some returned and peeped in. Among them was a doctor, by the name of Joiner, a black-eyed villain, who announced that he, being a doctor, was sent to examine the ladies. He began by, "Ladies, I command you to undress. I was sent here to examine your persons."

"By what authority?" demanded Mrs. Streight.

"By Major Scott and Captain Kirkpatrick!" Stamping his foot, he continued, "I want you to take off your clothes!"

"I won't do it!" declared Mrs. Streight, emphatically.

While he stood stamping his foot, and making demonstrations, one of the strange lady's boys ran to Maj. Scott, and asked if it was possible that he was going to let that doctor compel those ladies to undress. The major replied, "By no means!" and threatened to shoot Joiner if he molested them. When the lad returned, the doctor stood in the doorway, and as the officer's words were repeated, Mrs. Streight stepped suddenly up to the insulting rebel, and putting her hand against his breast, sent him over on his back on the porch, two steps below; while his heels flew into the air like the wings of a windmill. She slammed the door to, then; and the fellows outside, who witnessed the villain's discomfiture, yelled with delight, and shouted at him, "The little Yankee was too much for you!"

The men were then all called away, and a single sentinel put on duty; and the ladies were told to retire. Two or three times during the night, cakes and fruit were sent in to the ladies; but as they bore evidence of poison, they were received with thanks, and quietly put into the fire.

About 5 o'clock in the morning, the guard was taken off. Mrs. Streight, who had not slept during the night, took advantage of this to reconnoiter. Quietly unlocking the door, she went out, locking the door after her, and strolled down the verandah, in search of a chance to get away. The windows were open, and in one room were a

number of men in blue uniforms, who she supposed were
Union soldiers. She told them what she wanted, claimed
them as friends, and offered to pay them well; but they all
refused. Turning back, she saw the stage across the way,
with the driver asleep on top; and her mind was made up.
She went over, awoke him, and requested him to hitch up.
He refused, saying the horses had all been taken. At the
same moment she heard the horses stamping in the barn.
Having been reared on a farm, and being quite familiar
with horses, she found the harness where it had been hidden in a corn-bin, adjusted it to the horses, and led them
to the door. She again aroused the driver, and jerking
out one of the half-dozen revolvers with which she was
burdened, made him get down, hitch those horses to the
coach, rein up and straighten them out; assuring him that
if he uttered a single note of alarm, she would blow a hole
clear through his head. Then she hustled the women and
children and trunks aboard, and in twenty minutes they
were off, on a dead run. Two miles out, they were halted
by a guerrilla, who gave a signal.

"Now, let those horses go," cried Mrs. Streight, "or
I'll get up there and drive."

The old coach flew as it never had before. All along
the route they passed guerrillas, but they sped by so suddenly, that they were gone before they could be stopped.
Several miles were rapidly covered; when, fearing that the
horses might give out before the end of the journey, they
were slacked up. At 12 o'clock, they rolled into Franklin,
Ky., and dashed up to the principal hotel; the horses in a
lather of foam and sweat. Mrs. Streight recognized in
the landlord one of the guerrillas she met the night before.
He slunk away, and the bar-tender assisted the ladies out.
Dinner was ready; and as they were nearly starved, they
all went in. Mrs. Streight bribed a colored waiter to serve
their dinner, and to see that it was not poisoned; and they
stayed there till next morning. By that time the railroad

was again open, and the party went on to Bowling Green; arriving there in the afternoon, a few hours after the Fifty-First went into camp.

Mrs. Streight frequently visited the regiment, and was very kind to the sick boys; and made herself very useful in many ways. She was loved by all the boys, and was revered by all as the "mother of the regiment."

JUST BEFORE THE BATTLE.

Near the close of September, we were at a point fifteen miles below Cave City, Ky. General Wood had just discovered that we were out of provisions, and was greatly troubled thereat, and at a loss for a remedy, "Give me orders," said Colonel Streight, "and I will get them here." "All right," said Wood; "go ahead." The colonel got his men in line along the road, before daylight next morning; and as the wagons came by, the boys climbed into them, the lash was applied to the mules, and away they sped for Cave City; where the wagons were quickly filled, and the command returned before night, accomplishing the mission in a remarkably short time.

It was about the same time that Henry Kirk and Dora Weaver became so conscience-stricken, that they "swore off" on chewing tobacco. It was on the eve of the battle at Perryville, and they felt very much as Mark Twain and his companions did, when hopelessly lost on the boundless plains, in a snow-storm. They were preparing to yield up their young lives on the field of carnage, and only desired to be spared long enough to get the vile scent of nicotine off of their breath. They threw away their last plug and last hunk of natural twist; and putting their arms around each other's necks, vowed to never again defile their lips with the nasty stuff. And they meant it. But humanity is pretty much the same everywhere; and this resolution lasted until Thursday, the lovely New Year's Day, 1863; then, while death was dealing havoc on all hands, and no one could tell what might happen next, these two heroes, excited and desperate, each bit off a huge chunk of cavendish, and applied their jaws with a will in grinding it to pulp.   It was like an inspiration to their almost exhausted natures ; and they have kept it up faithfully ever since.

Passing through a cornfield near the road, the boys were helping themselves to the luscious ears, when they were suddenly interrupted by the appearance of a freckled dame, with a voice like a buzz-saw :

"Hyar! you-all wants to git right out o' thar, now. We-uns is Union, 'n' you-uns-all wants to drap that thar cawn right suddent.   Drap it!"

But they didn't "drap it" till they got into camp.

We began to receive all sorts of rumors here, that increased in improbability as they passed from one mouth to another.   When the authority for some curdling story was demanded, it was said to have come by "grape-vine telegraph ;" and that expression came to be applied to every tale of doubtful origin.

ARRIVAL AT LOUISVILLE, KY.

We reached Louisville, Ky., Sunday, September 28, with Bragg only nine miles away ; we having been 36 days coming from Stevenson.   We had experienced a little smell of powder at Munfordsville, and had witnessed some heavy artillery fighting, with a little lively cavalry skirmishing. The weather was cooler, but we were tired out, and ragged, and nearly destitute of tents and proper outfits ; and were glad our chase was over.   We went into camp on a large common in the lower edge of the city ; where we were soon joined by a number of recruits, fresh from home ; being our share of the 1862 volunteer complement.   It was in the main a respectable lot of young men ; who were immediately subjected to a thorough course of squad drill.   In distinction from the veteran troops, we called the recruits "troopees."

On our entering Louisville, strict orders were given to protect the property of the citizens. The new guard relief was posted accordingly. One comrade, who was on duty when we went into camp, not being relieved for some time after, was late getting to his quarters; and the fires were nearly all out, as fuel was scarce. He was not long, however, in finding a plank, which he pulled from the roof of a shed in the rear of a neighboring building; and dropping it on the ground assigned for his company, he hurried off to get an ax. Just then the colonel rode through the quarters, and espying the plank, asked who brought it there. Of course no one knew; and he was turning away, when a gleam of light reflected from the ax, with which the soldier was returning, attracted his attention.

"Here, soldier; come here. Did you bring this plank here? H–ll! it's ——!" calling the soldier's name.

"Yes, sir."

"Where did you get it?"

"Over there."

"Well, lay down that ax, and carry that plank back, and put it where you got it; then get your gun and guard that place the rest of the night."

The first duty of a soldier, is obedience. He therefore returned the plank to the shed, got his supper on another comrade's fire, then took his traps, and moved camp to the shed. The place was a brewery, and the shed covered two big delivery wagons filled with pigeon-hole boxes used for delivering bottled beer. As soon as he got a little used to the locality, he organized himself into a committee of inspection, and before daylight had examined every bottle in those two wagons. They were all empty, save about nine. At each change of relief one of those bottles had to give the countersign; what was left, was carried into camp, and divided among the boys. Thus was paid the penalty of over-righteous protection, and another illustration given of the perfection of our discipline.

Punishment was sometimes inflicted by officers, who had no sort of qualification for the important duties of the position that had been conferred on them, that was brutal and barbarous. There was very little of it practiced in the Fifty-First, however; for, however scrupulous every soldier was in observing proper discipline, he drew the line within reason. And the few attempts that were made, under very strong excitement, were rewarded in a manner so decisive, that it impressed that event perpetually upon the mind of the officer. One good polishing was sufficient.

ANOTHER CASE OF DISCIPLINE.

The second day at Louisville, Reuben Eaton and the writer, both of whom had brothers in the 79th Indiana, which had just arrived among the reinforcements, got permission to go over and visit them; and returning in the afternoon just in time to miss dress parade, were reported "absent without leave," and placed on the list for "extra duty." They didn't care! First, the writer was ordered to guard a comrade who was punished for a certain misdemeanor, by being made to stand on a hard-tack box on one foot, and when he failed to keep his foot up, the guard was to prod him with his bayonet. The vigilant officer who had imposed the punishment, discovered some deficiency in the execution thereof, and these pages are necessarily graced with the addition that the writer was very suddenly relieved from guard duty, and required to join the display of living statuary, on another box; while Eaton was given the delightful task of prodding both victims. The ridicule of the other companies, who witnessed the spectacle, was too much for the officer; and the boys were soon released.

Governor Morton visited us while at this place, and assisted and encouraged us very much by kind words and assurances of the confidence of our friends at home, that we would ultimately conquer. He also provided for the physical comfort of his soldiers, of whom he was quite proud. Nor was the admiration of all the Indiana boys any less for our noble Governor. Indeed, this was largely shared by the troops of every other State, who regarded us with envy on this account.

Letters and papers from home told of the big scare in the border towns of Ohio and Indiana, and the exploits of the valorous "squirrel hunters" at Lawrenceburg, North Bend and elsewhere. Like the historic Charles, they

"Marched up the hill, and then—marched down again."

They reminded us of the old comedian, Yankee Robinson, who used to sing about how he and his uncle "fit, bled and died" in the Mexican war:

"I got behind a great big log,
    Along with another man;
And every time I raised old Betsy up,
    Down popped a Mex-i-can!"

BATTLE OF PERRYVILLE.

Saturday, October 4, Wood's division marched into Bardstown, late in the afternoon, driving out the rebel rear guard.

Wednesday morning, the 8th, found us at Springfield, having passed through Mt. Washington and Fairfield. We camped in the Springfield fair-ground, till near noon of the 8th. The rebels were not far off, and a fight was expected hourly. We were so tired of marching, that we would have welcomed anything else. It was also fast becoming a positive necessity for Buell to get us into a fight, in order to remove the prevailing suspicion of his treachery, or to prevent outbroken insubordination. It came just in time. We were not favored with our share of the battle at Perryville, that afternoon, but arrived on the scene just in time to see Bragg get decently whipped. Our division laid the night before near Rolling Fork, 12 miles from Perryville. We had orders early in the morning, but did not move till 11 o'clock; and got to Perryville at 4 o'clock; taking our position on the right of Gilbert's force, and on the left of

Crittenden, about opposite the town. From appearances, we were at the extreme left of the enemy. They were trying to flank Gilbert. He had engaged them, and Wood deployed toward the left. Our division was in fine trim for a battle, but the blundering of some one enabled Bragg to get away. He was badly whipped, as it was, but ought to have been captured entirely. Buell was certainly either ignorant of the condition of the enemy, or his alleged superior military talent was directed in the wrong way. It was a pity such a man as "Old Pap" Thomas, or our own "Old Tommy" Wood had not charge of that campaign! Buell had been in the army all his life, and was a very fine organizer and first-class trainer; he simply lacked patriotism and integrity. In proof of the bad feeling described above, we have the statement of General Buell, made in cross-examination, during the investigation of his conduct, in December following, at Nashville:

"They were anxious to move on and relieve the Munfordsville force, and there was general impatience to attack the enemy. It amounted to almost indignation, among both officers and men, from the time we moved with Gen. McCook toward Chattanooga, or about Jasper. We then fell back over the mountains. We knew Munfordsville was threatened, and while at Bowling Green, we heard that Col. Wilder had repulsed the enemy. Then this feeling continued to increase."

The great loss on our side, 916 killed, 2,943 wounded, and 489 missing, was sufficient indication of the valor of those engaged.

BRAGG SKEDADDLES.

At daylight next morning, we advanced to where we could overlook the town, and where we could observe the position of the enemy. We could see them putting a battery in position a little to the right and rear of Perryville. The sun was about half an hour high when we saw them moving off, perhaps a mile distant, going in the direction of Harrodsburg; with baggage train, infantry and cavalry. We laid there till about 2 P. M., when we passed through Perryville, and went to the spring below, where we stayed till next morning, the 10th. Gen. Wood's camp extended from near Reed's Springs to Salt River.

That day, our brigade made a reconnoisance through Harrodsburg, capturing a large number of cavalry, besides a great many convalescents in camp and hospital. Being at least six miles in advance of our army, we moved camp twice that night, and built three sets of fires, in order to deceive the enemy as to our numbers. The following day, Saturday, we proceeded in line of battle to Danville, the Fifty-First passing directly across the cemetery. Then, filing out onto the Lancaster pike, we marched "right in front" through the town, in splendid order. This did not prevent Co. K filling their canteens from some wine-casks which came in their way. We continued on, marching at 12 o'clock the night of the 12th, and engaging the enemy's cavalry and artillery at Stanford, at daylight next morning. The enemy kept the road toward Cumberland Gap, opposing our advance with his cavalry and artillery. We pursued as far as Crab Orchard; a little skirmish near the hamlet of Wild Cat, being the chief fruit of this diversion. Then we retraced our steps; leaving Danville to the right, passing through the village of Hustonville, to Columbia, where we halted a few days, and enjoyed a much needed rest.

AT GLASGOW, KY.

We continued thence to Glasgow; arriving there on Saturday, October 25, going into camp in a cedar forest; and spending the afternoon in butchering. In the night it began snowing, and we awoke next morning to find our blankets covered with four inches of snow, under which we fairly steamed, with the additional heat thus imparted. It continued to snow all day Sunday, so that we couldn't get out to church.

We had captured a lot of rebels on the way; and they must have suffered greatly, as they were destitute of nearly everything; many without shirts and coats, and all bearing signs of severe exposure and disease. They were heartily tired of war; and denounced the military despotism that was being exercised over them. We did all our limited supply would permit, to relieve their wants.

It was very cold, the morning we left Glasgow, and the frost in our guns stung our fingers, as we shifted them from one shoulder to the other. Presently we came to a good sized creek, which General Wood ordered us to cross. As we would have to wade, and the water was very cold, Colonel Streight demurred, saying it would kill the men. General Wood averred it was unavoidable. "I think not," said Streight; "we can build a bridge." "That is impossible," replied Wood; "we have no hatchets, nor nails nor anything." "Give me orders, and I will do it," persisted the colonel. "All right; go ahead," said General Wood. The colonel got the boys out, tore down a house near by, and in a few hours had a good bridge over the stream, on which the command crossed in safety.

We moved thence, by easy stages, to a point 12 miles east of Gallatin, Tenn., after a march, that day, November 7, of twenty miles. According to order, Gen. Wood sent Harker's brigade to try to capture the guerrilla John Morgan's command. Harker's 3d Brigade of infantry, and Col. Lewis Zahm's 2d Brigade of cavalry, reached Gallatin just after daylight, but Morgan had already escaped. We pressed him closely, capturing 18 of his men, with their horses and accouterments. Lt.-Col. Colescott's horse was shot in the nose. It was quite a lively little scrap; the boys running, shooting, dodging, yelling, till we closed in on the handful that remained, and brought them back into town; our regiment resting on the public square, opposite the court-house. Then we moved out to the edge of town, and went into camp.

Col. Streight had the correct idea as to the protection of rebel property; and when we entered a fine blue-grass pasture, he marched us by companies in echelon to within a few steps of the fence, when he turned about and shouted:

"Halt! Stack arms! Unsling knapsacks! Rally on the fence!"

With a yell, the boys hastened to obey the orders with a will that was remarkable. In a few minutes the fence lay in neat piles; and our fuel for that day was assured. Some then went for straw, some for water and forage, and others got breakfast. Most all of us were entirely without rations; but the country was full of stuff, and we had all learned to forage. We did not require a miracle, as Gen. Dumont thought the 72d Indiana would, when that band of innocents run out of provisions. He said, "May be the Lord will shower manna, or blow in quails."

A YANKEE TRICK.

"Fugate" slipped out and went down to a large brick house, and called for breakfast: offering to pay for it. The mistress promptly replied:

"No, sir; we don't feed Yankees here!"

"All right!" and back he went to where the regiment lay. Seeing Sergeant Weaver, who looked pretty lean and hungry, he said,

"Dora, do you want a good breakfast?"

"I was never so hungry in my life."

"Well, get your gun, fix bayonet, and follow me."

Throwing a grey blanket around him, "Fugate" went back to the same house. With a familiar "hello!" which is the Southern sign of recognition, the woman came to the door.

"I am sorry, madam; I was captured here, this morning, by these Yankees; and I would like to have something to eat, before I am hurled off to a Northern prison."

"Come in, sir!" exclaimed the woman, with emotion, extending both hands, and ushering the prisoner into the sitting-room; while the guard kept close after him. While waiting for breakfast, the woman proposed to "Fugate" to get the gun and kill the sergeant, and secrete him; and all would be well. But the prisoner thought it would not be fair to do that; since the sergeant had allowed him to go among his friends. Besides, it would be too dangerous; as the town was full of Yanks. The breakfast of ham and eggs, sweet potatoes, fine bread and coffee, was delicious; and it was fairly divided with the sergeant.

"What company do you belong to!" asked Weaver.

"Captain Woolsey's command."

O, I know them well," rejoined the sergeant; and he told who he was.

Their conversation and actions gave them away before they got through; and it took some pretty stiff fabricating to convince the woman that she was not deceived.

Then the sergeant marched his prisoner back to camp; where they laughed over the ruse, by which they had obtained a good breakfast from a malignant she-rebel, free of expense.

Each day the ties that bound comrades to each other, were more firmly welded. The privations shared, and the scores of mutual sacrifices and self-denials made for each other, created a relation that was never known among so great a number of men before. Possibly Solomon had in his great mind the American soldier, when he said [Prov. xviii : 24,] "There is a friend that sticketh closer than a brother." In their individual affairs, they would stand for their rights against every other individual, and would fight the next man in the line for a single mouldy, wormy, old hard-tack; but in their collective relation, they were true as steel to each other. And they were exceedingly clannish.

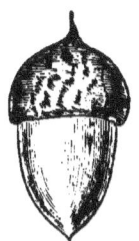

"FOURTEENTH ARMY CORPS"—"ARMY OF THE CUMBERLAND."

Buell was relieved of command by Maj. Gen. Wm. S. Rosecrans. This change occurred October 30, in compliance with General Orders No. 168, War Department, dated October 24, 1862. This order gave General Rosecrans the command of the "Department of the Cumberland," which embraced that portion of Tennessee lying east of the Tennessee River, with a prospective enlargement from Georgia and Alabama. By the same order the troops of the same department were also designated as the "Fourteenth Army Corps." This designation soon gave place to that of the "Army of the Cumberland"—the name which the original portions bore under Generals Anderson and Sherman.

We were glad to be delivered of Buell. We were also much encouraged by the recent emancipation proclamation of President Lincoln, and by the news of the traitor Lee's request for an armistice. Also, we needed overcoats very badly, and Governor Morton had them forwarded to us a month in advance; whereby much suffering was relieved.

We continued to march, till, on Wednesday, Nov. 12, we were at Silver Springs, 18 miles east of Nashville. Our boys were mostly in fair health. We had been to Gallatin again, and had another little brush with John Morgan's guerrillas; routing them, and chasing them several miles. Colonel Streight wrote, on that date:

"I was sent to Gallatin with the 51st and 13th Michigan, and a section of Bradley's Battery; where we cut their forces in two, killed, wounded and captured 30. My boys, as usual, were both brave and lucky; and no one of them was hurt. We are idle now, but the enemy is in force at Murfreesboro."

Dr. Adams' resignation was accepted, and H. R. King was promoted to be Assistant Surgeon. There were 560 men in camp.

On the 24th, we were eight miles east of Nashville. At this place Capt. J. C. McGuire, Co. F. resigned.

At some point, about this time, our command assisted in building a trestle-bridge across the Cumberland River at Gallatin.

"OLD ROSY IS THE MAN!"

There came to the Army of the Cumberland, while encamped about Nashville, just before the battle of Stone River, an old man, a tall, old-fashioned, raw-boned fellow, who sang patriotic songs. He suddenly disappeared; but returned after the battle. He claimed the name of Wm. E. Lock, army poet and balladist, and he had a pass from Abraham Lincoln to travel through the western army, and make and sing patriotic songs. When selling his songs and stamps, and singing on a cracker-box, he would ask the boys to join him in the chorus; which thousands did eagerly. Again he disappeared; and while making his way to the rebel army, of which he was a notorious spy, he was shot and killed, while running the picket line. It was learned afterward, that he was called by Forrest's men "the crazy preacher." The following is a sample of his ballads, and one that was quite popular at one time, especially in the Fifty-First:

"Cheer up, cheer up, the night is past;
    The skies with light are glowing;
Our ship moves proudly on, my boys,
    And favoring gales are blowing;

The flag is at the peak, my boys;
   Her decks are cleared for action;
The time has come—we're ready, boys,
   To meet a traitorous faction.

CHORUS: Old Rosy is the man, old Rosy is the man;
   We'll show our deeds where'er he leads;
     Old Rosy is the man.

The lightning flashes through the West,
   The glorious news repeating;
Of prairie hosts now tramping on,
   And rebel hordes retreating;
Our conquering hosts with steady tread,
   Their crafty foes defying;
O'er many a city, town and fort,
   He set the old flag flying;

CHORUS: Old Rosy is the man, &c.

The Merrimac, all clad in steel,
   Would make the Yankees wonder;
They'd crush our forts, and sink our ships,
   And belch perpetual thunder;
But just as all the rebel crew
   Grew jubilant—defiant!
There came a Yanke cheese-box craft,
Which whipped the mail-clad giant.

CHORUS: Ericcson was the man, Ericcson was the man;
   His little tug, and saucy mug
     Ripped up the traitors' plan.

Old "Stonewall" came to Winchester;
   He thought he'd find us napping;
But rebeldom has yet to learn
   The art of Yankee trapping.
For when he met our gallant Shields,
   His brain soon got to swimmin';
He cursed the day, and cursed his luck,
   And d–d the secesh women.

CHORUS: Brave Shields was then the man ‖:
   His Irish wit, and Northern grit
     Ripped up the traitors' plan.

They thought at Island No. 10
   They'd first blockade the river,
And strike with such terrific blows,
   That all the North would shiver.
But Captain Walk, down through their fire
   His gunboats safely paddled;

Then Pope got at them in the rear,
  And all who could, skedaddled.

CHORUS: Brave Pope was then the man :|:
  From Walk and Pope the rebels slope;
    Brave Pope was then the man.

New Orleans had three mighty rams,
  And fire-ships also handy,
And thirty thousand fighting men,
  To sink poor Doodle Dandy.
But when they came with gentle words,
  For fear they'd speak them louder;
She thought she'd just capitulate,
  And save her blood and powder.

CHORUS: Brave Foote was then the man :|:
  With lawyer But.* and Farragut,
    Brave Foote was then the man.

At Murfreesboro, full of fight,
  Old Bragg drew up his forces,
To make a meal of Western boys,
  And gobble them by courses;
But when he met old Rosy there,
  His appetite forsook him;
The Dutchman might be good to carve;
  But he couldn't catch and cook him.

CHORUS: Old Rosy is the man, old Rosy is the man;
  We'll show our deeds where'er he leads;
    Old Rosy is the man.

A few more blows will close our work,
  And homeward we'll be rushing;
And anxious hearts, that sorrow now,
  With love and joy be gushing.
And when our heads are silvered o'er,
  In telling this day's story;
Some lip of fame will say of us,
  'They saved the Nation's glory!'

CHORUS: Old Rosy is the man, &c."

BATTLE OF STONE RIVER.

Christmas was a beautiful day; and we put it in with
a foraging expedition.   During the day we had some sharp
skirmishing; and Perry Hollingsworth, Co. E, was killed,

---

* Butler.

and two others were wounded. We brought in 18 head of cattle. Next day we struck tents, and advanced to near Lavergne; skirmishing all day. At night it rained, and continued to rain most of the following week.

The first experience of the Fifty-First in this glorious campaign, dates from this skirmish at Prim's blacksmith shop, on the Edmonson pike, on Thursday, December 25, 1862. General Wood's dispatch of that date, says:

"Harker's brigade, which went out this morning for forage, is coming in. He filled his wagons with corn, but had to fight for it. He was attacked in front and on the flanks, and lost 1 man killed outright, and 2 wounded; 1 seriously, the other slightly. The casualties occurred all in the 51st Indiana. Col. Harker estimates the enemy at 600, infantry or dismounted troopers."

Our part of the Army of the Cumberland was organized as follows:

Left Wing, Gen. T. L. Crittenden, *Commanding*.
1st Div., Gen. T. J. Wood, "
3d Brig., Col. C. G. Harker, "
 51st Indiana, Col. A. D. Streight.
 73d Indiana, Col. Gilbert Hathaway.
 13th Michigan, Col. Michael Shoemaker.
 64th Ohio, Col. Alex. McIlvain.
 65th Ohio, Lt.-Col. Alex. Cassil.
   Maj. Horatio N. Whitbeck.

On Dec. 27, '62, Lt.-Col. Garesche', Gen. Rosecrans' chief of staff, dispatched to Gen. Crittenden, at 3:05 P. M.:

"Tell Wood to drive the enemy vigorously, and give them no time to breathe."

How thoroughly this instruction was obeyed, some of the proudest pages of history tell.

The Army of the Cumberland left Nashville with 47,000 men, and had 37,977 infantry, 3,200 cavalry and 2,223 artillery in the battle. It lost 92 officers killed, and 384 wounded; 1,441 men killed, and 6,860 wounded; about 2,800 missing. Lt.-Col. Garesche' was killed by the side of the commander.

7

The monthly return of the Army of the Cumberland for the month of December, 1862, gives the number in Wood's division, 3 brigades of infantry, 10,605; artillery, 395; total, 11,000.

General Rosecrans' report of this campaign, refers to our brigade very favorably:

"From Nov. 26 to Dec. 26, every effort was bent to complete the clothing of the army, provide ammunition and replenish the Nashville depot of supplies, to insure against want. On Thursday, Dec. 26, '62, the movement began. The left wing began its advance about 11 A. M., the 28th, driving a brigade of cavalry supported by Many's brigade of rebel infantry, to Stewart's Creek, saving the bridge, although the rails were fired. This was Saturday night. On Sunday they rested. On Monday at 3 P. M. a signal from Palmer announcing that he was in sight of Murfreesboro, and that the enemy was running, an order was sent to Crittenden to send a division to occupy Murfreesboro. He ordered Harker's brigade to cross the river at a ford on his left, where he surprised a regiment of Breckenridge's division, and drove it back on its main line, not more than 500 yards distant, in great confusion. He held the position till advised, by prisoners captured, that Breckenridge was in force in front; when, it being dark, he ordered the brigade back across the river, and bivouacked.

The battle began next day, on the left, by VanCleve, who crossed at the lower fords. Wood was prepared to sustain and follow him, but was directed to suspend action. Just then McCook was routed. Harker's brigade was sent further down the Murfreesboro pike, to go in and attack the enemy on the right of VanCleve. There our forces sustained an infantry and cavalry attack, leaving us masters of the original ground on our left. Our losses were: *   *   *   *

Losses.	Killed.		Wounded.		Captured.	Total.
	Off.	Enl.	Off.	Enl.		
51st Indiana.		7	2	32	9	50
73d Indiana.	2	22	3	48	36	111
13th Michigan.		17	2	70		89
64th Ohio.	1	23	3	61	17	105
65th Ohio.	2	33	8	92	38	173
6th Ohio Battery.		1	1	8	1	11
Aggregate.	5	103	19	311	101	539

From the Report of James Barnett, Chief of Artillery.

"Capt. Bradley, on the morning of the 31st, moved with Col. Harker's brigade in its advance to check the enemy on the right, and held with it, its position through the day. On the 2d he held a position on commanding ground near to the right of the railroad. When the attack was made on the left, he changed front to fire to the left."

From the Report of Gen. A. D. McCook, Comdg. Right Wing.

"December 30, '62   On arrival at the pike, I found Col. Harker's brigade retiring before a heavy force of the enemy. I immediately ordered Robert's brigade, of Sheridan's division, to advance into a cedar wood, and charge the enemy, and drive him back.   *   Col. Harker, commanding a brigade in Wood's division, performed gallant service."

From the Report of Gen. P. H. Sheridan, Comdg. 3d Division.

"On the 30th Schaefer's brigade was put in action directly to the front and right of Wood's division, on the left-hand side of the railroad. The brigade advanced through a clump of timber, and took position on the edge of the cotton field, close on the enemy's lines, relieving Wood's division, which was falling back under heavy pressure."

General Crittenden's Report.

"My command left camp near Nashville, Dec. 26, '62, and reached the point where the battle of Stone's River was fought just before dusk on the evening of the 29th. The march from Nashville was accompanied by skirmishing. The gallant and handsome things done by the several portions of my command during this march, have been mentioned in detail.   *   It was about dusk, and just at a moment when Wood and Palmer had halted to gather up their troops, that I reached the head of my command. These two generals had their divisions in line of battle, Wood on the left, and Palmer on the right, with the enemy in sight, and evidently in heavier force than we had yet encountered them; it was evident they intended to dispute the passage of the river, and fight the battle at or near Murfreesboro. At this moment I received orders to occupy Murfreesboro with one division, encamping others outside. I immediately gave the order to advance, and the movement commenced. Wood was ordered to occupy the place.   *   At this time it was dark. Gen. Wood had declared that he was hazarding a great deal for very little, to move over unknown ground, and thought that I ought to take the responsibility to disobey the order.   *   I suspended the order one hour. By this time Gen. Rosecrans came to the front, and approved what I did. In the meantime, Col. Harker, after a sharp skirmish, gallantly crossed the river.   As soon as possible I recalled Harker,   *   and he recrossed without serious loss.

On the morning of the 31st, when the battle began, I occupied the front near the pike, Palmer on the right, Wood on the left, and Van-Cleve in reserve, to the rear and left.   *   The right was driven back. The confusion of troops hindered forming. Being soon reinforced by Fyffe's and Harker's brigades, the enemy was pressed vigorously, too far. They came upon the enemy massed to receive them; who, outnumbering and outflanking them, compelled them to fall back. They did so in good order. From this time, the great object of the enemy seemed to be to break our left and front. When the troops composing the center and right wing of our army had been driven by the enemy from our original line of battle, the 1st and 2d divisions of the left wing still nobly maintained their position, though several times assaulted by the enemy in great force.

Gen. Wood being wounded on the 31st, the command devolved on Hascall, on Jan. 1, '63. On the night of the 31st, he rested 500 yards in the rear of the former line, the right resting on the position occupied by Stokes' Battery. On the 2d, Hascall's division laid half an hour in the early part of the day under the heaviest cannonading we endured. Many were killed, but the men would not flinch. That night they encamped a little in advance of the position Beatty had occupied on the river. In this position the troops remained till Saturday night, when the river began to rise; and the rain continuing to fall, all recrossed the river. Sunday, it was learned that the enemy had evacuated Murfreesboro."

Gen. T. J. Woods Report.

"The country occupied by the bodies of hostile troops was favorable for a small force to retard the advance of a larger one.   *   The country between the cultivated tracts is densely wooded; and much of this is interspersed with thick groves of cedar. It is undulating also, presenting a succession of swells and subsidences.   *   On Saturday, Dec. 27, '62, I ordered Hascall to take the advance on either side of the pike.   *   Lavergne was the first object to attain. The enemy was strongly posted in the houses and on the wooded hights in our rear, and opposed us by crossfire.

Sunday, 28th, we remained in camp, waiting for the right and center to get into position.

On Monday, 29th, the advance was resumed. Harker's brigade was on the left of Wagner, in the advance, and Hascall's brigade was in reserve.

Arriving within 2½ miles of Murfreesboro, we found the enemy in force immediately in our front, prepared to resist seriously and determinedly our further advance. I halted the center, and Harker's brigade occupied the wood, in part of which Wagner was posted, and extended the left into an open field.   *   We remained in this position till Tuesday, 30th, the skirmishers keeping up an active firing.

On Wednesday morning, 31st, it was reported that the enemy was moving large bodies of troops to his left. My division was roused at 5 o'clock, got breakfast, and before daylight was ready for action. . * I directed Harker to commence the movement with his brigade.   *   A long wooded ridge within a hundred yards of the stream extends along the southern side of Stone River. On the crest of this ridge the enemy appeared to be posted in force. During the morning some firing had been heard, but not sufficient to indicate troops seriously engaged; but a sudden and fierce roar and rattle of musketry burst on us at this moment, which indicated that the enemy had attacked the right wing in heavy force; and soon the arrival of messengers confirmed the indications. I stopped crossing, withdrew Hascall's and Harker's brigades, and moved to the right and rear, to reinforce the center and right. * The falling back of the right wing, brought our lines into a crochet. The enemy was seen concentrating large masses of troops in the fields; and soon they moved forward to the attack. The artillery in our front line, as well as that in the rear of the center and left, poured a destructive fire on the advancing foe; but on he came, till within small-arm range, when he was repulsed and driven back."

About 10 o'clock, Wednesday morning, 30th, General Wood was struck by a minie ball, on the inner side of his left heel, tearing open the boot, and lacerating the foot; a severe contusion was inflicted also, but he did not dismount till 7 o'clock that evening. After he arrived at Dayton, Ohio, on leave of absence, he wrote, referring to the evening of Monday, 29th, when Harker's brigade was ordered to cross the river, and the order was countermanded:

"Before, however, the order was suspended, Harker's brigade had crossed Stone River, under a galling fire, driven in the enemy's outposts, and seized a strong position, which it held until nearly 10 o'clock that evening."

Gen. Hascall's Report as Division Commander.

"When the command devolved on me, the division was considerably scattered, as Col. Harker's brigade had been in action all day on the extreme right, and had not returned. About 11 P. M. that day, Harker returned with his brigade. * The line was now nearly at right angles with the railroad, Harker's brigade resting on it. In this position we lay all next day, Jan. 1, '63, with nothing to break the silence, save picket firing and an occasional artillery duel. Each brigade was in line of battle; and occupying so much front, kept the men constantly on the alert. Most of the other divisions had reserves, to relieve some. We maintained this position till 8 o'clock on the morning of Jan. 2. At this time the enemy opened the most terrific fire of shot and shell that we sustained during the entire engagement. During the night they had massed several batteries in our front, with a line a quarter of a mile long, and all at once they opened on us. Bradley's battery opened a brisk fire, till Stokes' battery, in their rear, opened with grape, which took effect on Bradley's men, and compelled Bradley to retire. The infantry, however, kept their position, though suffering severely.

Col. John W. Blake, of the 40th Indiana, was so drunk and unfit for duty, that he was arrested and sent to the rear. When next heard from, he was in Nashville, claiming to be wounded, and a paroled prisoner. I recommend his dishonorable discharge."

Report of Maj. S. Race, Chief of Artillery.

"About 6 A. M., Dec. 31, '62, Capt. Cullen Bradley's 6th Ohio Light Battery and Harker's brigade moved to the extreme right, where they were engaged in a most severely contested battle. Before superior numbers of the enemy, the brigade and battery (after repulsing the first attack of the enemy,) were obliged to retire; but not without disputing every inch of ground."

Col. Harker's Report.

"The 3d Brigade, 1st Division, Left Wing, 14th Army Corps, Dept. of the Cumberland, formerly 20th Brigade, 6th Division,   *   left Stewart's Creek about 10 A. M., Monday, 29th ult., marching most of the time in line of battle, with the right of the line in rear of the left of the 2d Brigade, Col. Wagner commanding. Our skirmishers soon came upon the enemy's cavalry, engaging them briskly, and driving them slowly before them. We proceeded in this manner, cautiously feeling our way, until our left arrived at the left bank of Stone River, which was reached about 4 P. M. Up to this time we had suffered no casualties from the enemy's skirmishers. We took up a position near Stone River, about 400 yards to the left of the Nashville and Murfreesboro pike, the 2d Brigade, Col. Wagner commanding, being on the right, and the 1st Brigade, Brig. Gen. Hascall commanding, being on the left, and somewhat to the rear, owing to the conformation of the ground. We remained in this position till about dark, when we received orders to proceed to Murfreesboro. Stone River being fordable in our front, we at once commenced crossing the stream. Throwing a long line of skirmishers over the stream, orders were given to the 51st Indiana, 13th Michigan and 73d Indiana to cross simultaneously, to form on the opposite bank, and to press forward and seize the commanding hights beyond; while the 64th and 65th Ohio, with Bradley's Battery, were directed to follow as rapidly as possible. The skirmishers had barely left the bank of the river, before they were vigorously attacked by those of the enemy, concealed in a thicket and behind a fence in our front. Our skirmishers in no way daunted by this fierce assault of the enemy, pressed gallantly forward, driving the foe, until they came upon the enemy in force. The skirmishers were soon supported by the front line of the brigade. The enemy seemed to have been entirely disconcerted by this bold movement of our troops, and fell back in confusion. In this movement our loss was two killed and three wounded. This slight loss must be attributed to the able manner in which the officers of the brigade conducted their commands. A prisoner taken, reported an entire division of the enemy on my front; and movements along the entire front and flanks indicated that a strong force was near me. I reported this to the general commanding the division; at the same time stating that I could hold the position until reinforced. I soon received orders to recross the stream; which I did; occupying the same ground as before crossing. This movement was so quickly executed, as not to excite the suspicion of the enemy. Too much praise cannot be accorded to the brave officers and men of this brigade, for their bravery and skill in driving a concealed enemy from a strong position, after nightfall, and holding their ground in the face of an enemy three times their numbers.

On Dec. 30, '62, about 8 A. M., the enemy's battery, stationed on an eminence near the right bank of Stone River, opened a severe fire of shot and shell upon my camp. Bradley's battery was ordered into position, to engage that of the enemy. After a severe engagement of 15 minutes, Capt. Bradley succeeded in silencing the enemy's battery. My command sustained no loss in this engagement.

On the 31st, about 8 A. M., I received orders from Gen. Wood, to cross the river with my command. The movement was commenced, in obedience to Gen. Wood's order, but was suspended for a few minutes by an order emanating from Gen. Crittenden. While awaiting further orders, Maj. Gen. Rosecrans passed my command, and gave me direct instructions to proceed immediately to the support of the right wing of our army, which was yielding to an overwhelming force of the enemy at that point. We had hardly commenced moving toward the right, when a Confederate battery located on the south bank of the river, opened on us, killing 1 man and wounding 2. Not stopping to reply to this battery, we pressed steadily forward. On approaching the right, much confusion was visible; troops marching in every direction; stragglers to be seen in great numbers; and teamsters in great consternation, endeavoring to drive their teams they knew not whither. My progress was impeded by the confusion, while the enemy was pouring shot and shell upon us from at least three different directions, wounding several men in my command. The brigade was, however extricated from this perilous position as soon as possible, and pressed on to a position on the extreme right of our line; Col. Fyffe's brigade, of Gen. VanCleve's division, being immediately on our left. After reaching this last position, my brigade marched in two lines, the 51st Indiana on the right, 65th Ohio on the left, the battery a little retired and opposite the interval between; 64th Ohio on the right of the second line, the 73d Indiana on the left, with the 13th Michigan in the rear of the caissons. We marched in this order about half a mile, when our skirmishers came up with those of the enemy, and the fire became brisk in front. About this time a battery from the enemy, situated in a cornfield, and nearly opposite my right flank, opened upon my command with canister. In order to get a commanding position for artillery, and at the same time to guard well my right flank, which I was fearful the enemy would attempt to turn, I moved the command a little to the right. While this movement was being executed, an officer reported a strong force and a battery of the enemy in front. No sooner had I taken position on the crest of the hill, than a most vigorous engagement commenced. * When it had continued twenty minutes, it was reported that the troops on my left had given way, and the enemy was already in the rear of my left flank, and about two hundred yards from it, pouring a destructive cross-fire on my troops. It became necessary to fall back.

My thanks are due to Col. A. D. Streight for valuable information of the movements of the enemy during this engagement.

On Jan 1, the 1st division was moved a little to the right and rear. My brigade occupied a central position in the division, on the front line of battle, and a short distance to the left of the Murfreesboro pike. We were hardly in position, before the enemy drove in our skirmishers. Bradley's battery, with others, opened a destructive fire of case-shot and shell, driving the enemy from our front, and sustaining no loss.

Jan. 2, Bradley's battery being in position on a small eminence on our front, supported on the right by the 64th and 65th Ohio, behind a small clump of trees, and on the left by the 51st Indiana, lying in a skirt of timber; while the 13th Michigan and 73d Indiana were in reserve, 3 batteries of the enemy opened on us. They were promptly responded to by Capt. Bradley and another battery on my right; when the most fearful artillery engagement ensued which I had yet had the experience to witness. The enemy having our range quite perfectly, poured upon us a most destructive fire, causing the battery on our right to be abandoned; but Capt. Bradley continued his well-directed firing, until the enemy's batteries were silenced. While this engagement was going on, Capt. Stokes' battery posted in our rear, opened upon us, mistaking us for the enemy.   *   During the engagement we had 1 man killed, and 11 wounded.   About dark we were ordered to cross Stone River. My brigade was placed in the front line. We were hardly in position, before the enemy opened on us, killing 1 man of the 64th Ohio. During the night we constructed breastworks of rails, and remained on the front till 9 A. M., Jan. 3, when we were relieved and ordered to the rear in reserve, where we remained till about 3 P. M., when we were again ordered to the front, to relieve Wagner's brigade, and occupied a position on the left of the 1st Division. We remained in this position till about 1 A. M., Jan. 4, when we received orders to recross Stone River. We crossed the stream and took position in rear of the main body of our force, and about 500 yards to the left of the railroad, where we remained till the troops occupied Murfreesboro.   *   *   *   *

Capt. Francis M. Constant, Co. G, and 2d Lieut. Alfred Gude, Co. H, 51st Indiana, were wounded.

From Dec. 29 to Jan. 2, inclusive, my brigade occupied some portion of the front, and during each day some portion of the forces under my command were engaged with the enemy, and sustained greater or less losses. For the cheerful manner in which they stood up under these fatigues and exposures, they are entitled to commendation.   *   I must also mention a circumstance worthy of notice, which occurred on Friday, Jan. 2. The enemy's sharpshooters, taking advantage of the woods in our front, and to the right and left, had crept up sufficiently near our camp, with the evident intention of picking off our general and field

officers. They annoyed me exceedingly, firing at every mounted officer
or man who appeared near the front. Desirous of dislodging this concealed foe, I directed the skirmishers to advance, and clear the woods if
possible. Capt. Chambers, of the 51st Indiana, had command of the
skirmishers, consisting of 40 men from his own company, Companies B
and D, 73d Indiana; Companies H, F and K, 65th Ohio; Company F,
64th Ohio. The little detachment numbered only 120 men. The enemy's
force was much larger. Our skirmishers drove them until they were
checked by the enemy's batteries. Thus these brave men not only drove
a concealed enemy from a strong hiding place, but elicited valuable information concerning the position of his masked batteries. This act of
gallantry elicited the praise and admiration of all who witnessed it."

Col. Streight's report agrees with those already given,
except in a few details. It begins at about 4 P. M., Dec.
29, '62, when we arrived on the west bank of Stone River,
half a mile north of the Murfreesboro and Nashville pike,
and two miles from Murfreesboro. Here we were ordered
to halt; and we remained till dark, when we got orders to
cross the river, preparatory to moving upon Murfreesboro.
As we were fully aware that the enemy occupied the opposite bank, and as none of our troops had up to that time
crossed the river, it was necessary to proceed cautiously, to
avoid running into an ambuscade. Companies A and F
were deployed as skirmishers, and ordered to cross in advance, and engage the enemy briskly; and if possible, to
seize the hights on the east side of the river. No sooner
had our skirmishers crossed, than the rebels opened fire on
them briskly, from under cover of a fence but a few yards
distant. Our skirmishers rushed forward on double-quick,
and charged upon the rebels, who instantly fled from their
hiding places. At the same time it was discovered that a
large number was concealed in a field of standing corn on
the hillside; and fearing that they would overwhelm our
skirmishers, the whole regiment was hastened forward at
double-quick. Before the regiment had entirely crossed
the river, information came that the rebels were advancing
in line of battle just beyond the crest of the ridge, about
400 yards to our front. It was at once determined to seize

the crest before the rebels could get there, if possible; and we started on the run forward. The entire ridge seemed to issue forth a continuous flame of fire, yet not a man faltered, but each seemed to strive to reach the desired point in advance of his comrades. The boldness of the movement, and the alacrity with which it was executed, with a well-directed fire, struck terror to the rebels, who fell back in dire confusion. Orders came just then to advance no further, but to hold our position. The colonel ordered the men to lie down, so as to conceal them as much as possible; and in a few minutes the rebels were seen advancing on our position. They were allowed to come within thirty steps, when we opened fire on them with such effect, that they hardly waited for reply, but broke and fled again. In a few minutes reinforcements joined us on our right and left. We remained there, without further molestation, till about 10 o'clock that night, when orders came to retire to the opposite bank of the river. After waiting till the rest of the brigade had recrossed, the Fifty-First followed; at the same time withdrawing our skirmishers in good order. The regiment was marched about 500 yards from the ford, where it bivouacked for the night. Light skirmishing was all that occurred, till the morning of the 31st, when it was evident, from the terrific roar of artillery and musketry, that the rebels were turning the extreme right of our army. We were at once ordered at double-quick to the right and rear; but had only moved a short distance, when we came within range of the enemy's artillery; yet, though several of our boys were wounded, with no chance of striking at the enemy, we moved a distance of more than a mile, with as perfect regularity as if we had been on drill. And even when we came in contact with hundreds of excited, noisy, jangling teams and teamsters, every command was quietly and promptly obeyed, without confusion. After marching about 2½ miles, we reached the extreme right of the army. We had hardly halted, before we were ordered forward in

line of battle across open cotton and corn fields. Companies A, B and F were deployed as skirmishers to cover our
extreme right and front. In this order we proceeded half
a mile, when our skirmishers, approaching the crest of a
ridge in front, were fired upon by a large force of rebels,
concealed in standing corn. Instantly the whole line was
forwarded at a double-quick; our skirmishers soon came
upon the enemy, when a well-directed fire sent them skurrying through the corn like the shoats at Gadara. Again
we were fortunate in wresting from the rebels an advantage
in position. We had a fine chance at them as they were
skedaddling down those long furrows, for about 400 yards;
large numbers of them falling under the superior marksmanship of our Hoosier boys. Shortly after we had taken
possession of the ridge, Lieut.-Col. Colescott, in command
of the skirmishers, sent word to Col. Streight that large
masses of troops were seen moving toward a piece of woods
to our left and front. Streight at once notified Col. Harker, and requested that the 6th Ohio Battery be sent to the
ridge we were then occupying. The battery was soon on
the ground, but not too soon; for by the time it was in position, the rebels had engaged the troops to our left. Capt.
Bradley opened a most withering fire, enfilading them at a
distance of not over 500 yards. They were in column four
regiments deep. Their dead were literally piled in heaps,
by the terrific fire from this battery. The battle had been
raging about three-quarters of an hour, when word came
that the division on our left was falling back. At the same
moment Col. Harker ordered us to fall back; which we did
in good order, taking off all of our wounded. Having no
instruction where to form, we took possession of the first
advantageous ground, expecting to give the enemy battle;
but we were soon ordered to resume the position we first
occupied on the extreme right. Companies H and C were
now deployed as skirmishers. Again we were approached
by the rebels, and had got fairly engaged, when they broke

and fled from the field in great confusion. It was nearly night now, and the contest was ended for the day. Other troops came up, and we were again ordered to the position we occupied the day before; where we bivouacked for the night. Early next morning, we were ordered into position about half a mile to our right and rear, where we remained through the day. Companies A and G, and one company from the 73d Indiana, were sent forward as skirmishers, to drive the rebels from a piece of woods half a mile to our front; which was accomplished in short order. We had nothing further to do that day.

On Jan. 2, Col. Streight took Co. H. with several volunteers from other companies, and drove the rebels from the woods formerly occupied by the 21st Brigade. The contest was very severe for a short time, but our boys finally got the advantage, and what was left of the johnnies, skedaddled. Ten rebels were left dead on the ground, and their wounded were scattered in every direction. This was the last engagement in this campaign in which the Fifty-First participated.

We took 19 prisoners; 1 major and 1 captain. From careful observation made by Col. Streight, on the various grounds over which the Fifty-First fought, he said:

"I am convinced that we have killed not less than 60 of the enemy; and by adding five times that number, the usual proportion of wounded to those killed, we have a grand total of 360. These figures, though seemingly large for the amount of loss sustained by us, I feel confident could be fully verified by the facts. Most of the ground fought over by my regiment has not been covered by other troops, and in nearly every case we have been placed where it was easy to decide which were our killed. The success attending us, in most cases, and our small loss, I think is attributable in a great measure to the advantage taken of the ground.

Feeling grateful beyond expression, for the brave soldierly bearing, and prompt manner in which both officers and men performed every duty assigned them, I feel a great delicacy in mentioning names."

Captains Russell, Chambers and Flinn, and the men under them received mention for distinguished services.

Marion Fitch came to the regiment just as it was going into action on the first day. He had no knowledge whatever of a gun, save the little experience he had in hunting frogs and kildees down on the creek near his home; but he grabbed a rifle, and soon was cracking away with as good will as some of the veterans. Many other "troopees" who were equally inexperienced, made records in that fight.

While crossing the river on the night of Dec. 29, a ball from a rebel rifle passed over the heads of the men in front, striking George W. Holbrook, a recruit of Co. F, square in the forehead. He dropped forward in the river, but his body was recovered and taken back. He was very tall, his hight being 6 feet, 7 inches. He had enlisted but six days before.

During a lull in the first day's fight, John Gasper, Co. C, sat down on a spur of a large tree to rest. On the second day, the fortune of battle brought him to the same spot. Just then a big solid ball struck the same tree, scattering chips in every direction. Gasper gave a big sigh, and an expression of relief.

"What's the matter?" asked a comrade.

"Come mighty nigh bein' shot!"

"How?"

"Why, that ball struck right where I sat yesterday!"

As we fell back, on the 31st, Martin Phillippe, Co. E, was struck by a bullet in the back part of the right calf, the ball splitting, and fitting itself so firmly around the bone, that the ball had to be chipped off. In the Raid, near Rome, Ga., the same soldier had a similar experience, a ball entering the left calf, exactly as in the first instance it entered the right.

As we moved over, on the morning of Dec. 31, to take position on the right, Capt. M. T. Anderson, Co. D, was seriously wounded in the head, by the concussion of a shell. At the same time, Orderly Sergeant David Denny, Co. E, lost the skirt of his overcoat, that was swept away by a cannon ball. Many other comrades received similar little courtesies; and were thankful that they were no worse.

Among the many brave acts of our boys, was the capture of a rebel major, by Corporal Clements, of Co. C, who marched his prisoner to the rear, with 9 others, and turned them into the "bull-pen."

Up to this time, war had been more of a school—a sort of system of experiments, than otherwise. From this time on, we got down to business; and the reports show an enormous increase in the killed and wounded in battle. It was found much cheaper and better in the long run, than to chase around over the country after skedaddling rebels, or to lie in camp, waiting for them to attack us. And, as usual, the common soldiers arrived at this point long before the generals did. It was found that strategy was only the method of cowards. More pluck was needed; indeed that was what conquered the rebellion. And right there comes in the point of comparison between the hobbling tactics of the Corinth campaign and the Bragg chase, with their respective originators and managers. Anybody could figure on the possibilities of a campaign; but it took real soldiers to fight. We had got the poor material weeded out pretty much; and when the order came to go in where the battle raged, every eye brightened, and every form straightened up to its full hight, as the command rang down the line:

" 'Tention, Fifty-First! Load at will!—fix bayonets! —forward!—fire at will!—march!''

Quickly the bayonet flashed from its scabbard, and clicked as it was firmly fixed; then hands flew to cartridge-boxes, teeth tore off the end, the charge was thrust into the muzzle; the rammer slipped nimbly from its place, to drive home the deadly ball, and returned as swiftly to its socket; finger and thumb placed the cap, and all was ready in a moment, and the column was moving forward. They step cautiously, observing meanwhile the alignment; carefully inspecting cartridge-boxes, to see that they are well

supplied with ammunition. Then the balls begin to whiz
about their heads; but they do not falter. Batteries are
pounding away; trees and every other sort of shelter are
taken advantage of; shells fall thick and fast, and general
havoc ensues. Then the colonel again shouts:

"'Tention, Fifty-First! Fire at will!—charge—with
a yell!"

And no power on earth could withstand the awful combination of such a terrific volley, such a withering yell,
and the gleaming of those murderous bayonets! A rebel
flag is shot down. More yells follow; as the miserable rag
is torn to pieces, to be sent home in the next letters.

Thus the battle rages, to the end; and our boys come
up smiling after each sanguinary round.

Jan. 4 '63, was spent in burying the dead; and on the
5th our army occupied Murfreesboro, which was most elaborately fortified.

We were satisfied with fighting, and were glad to rest.
We had had a hard time since Christmas; without tents,
and fighting more or less every day, much of the time on
short rations, and part of the time without any. It had
rained most of the time, too; but amidst all these trials
and hardships, the boys stood it well.

The fall of Murfreesboro, and the complete rout of
Bragg's army, was a terrible disappointment to the copperheads of Indiana, who had planned to openly recognize the
rebel confederacy, and to still further divide the Union by
antagonizing the Northwest and the New England States.
Their scheme was badly frost-bitten.

"INDIANAPOLIS, IND., Jan. 3, 1863—9:20 P. M.

HON. E. M. STANTON, *Secretary of War:*
I am advised that it is contemplated when the
Legislature meets, to pass a joint resolution acknowledging the Southern
Confederacy, and urging the States of the Northwest to dissolve all con-
stitutional relations with the New England States. The same thing is
on foot in Illinois.   O. P. MORTON,
                                  Governor of Indiana."

NOLINSVILLE RECONNOISANCE.

Nothing of importance occurred in the Fifty-First, till the 13th, when a reconnoisance was made from Murfreesboro to Nolinsville. This may be most briefly told in the language of Col. Wagner's report to Gen. Hascall, commanding 1st Division :

"In accordance with orders from Gen. Rosecrans, on the morning of the 13th, at 2 A. M., I marched from camp in the direction of Triune. My force consisted of the 3d Brigade, Col. Streight commanding, the 2d Brigade, (my own,) and Capt. Otis' brigade of cavalry; about 700 strong. The crossing of the river was difficult, detaining us some time. The route was by way of Lizzard and Lane's store, to the pike at Bole Jack. Here we saw some eight or ten mounted men, who seemed to be posted as lookouts, on the hill; only one was taken.   *   We saw nothing of importance, * and moved forward to Nolinsvile, where we camped for the night. Here we ascertained that Wheeler had been joined by Forest, with 1,000 men, making the entire force 3,000, and 7 pieces of artillery. On the morning of the 14th I was ordered to move to Eagleville, 14 miles,   to strike the enemy. Rain prevented, as on the morning of the 15th it was impossible to move.   *   Owing to the rain and cold, the men suffered much. The officers did not suffer so much, yet some complained more than those who waded knee-deep. The men, when they came to a vast pond or creek, raised a shout or a song, and plunged in. The stones of the pike cut their shoes badly."

On the 14th, it rained all day, and we camped that night twelve miles from Murfreesboro. There seems to be a very important omission in Gen. Hascall's report ; for at this point there is information from another and reliable source, that we were suddenly attacked by superior numbers. It was a critical moment, and every one knew we must get out of there as speedily as possible, or we would be captured. Lieutenant Dooley, seeing the situation, and knowing the necessity for prompt action, did not wait for the colonel, lieutenant-colonel or major, all of whom were present ; but rushing to the front of the line, shouted at the top of his voice, "Battalion! forward, double-quick, to the ravine!" The order was as promptly obeyed ; the field officers bringing up the rear.

While skirmishing at Lavergne, along a little creek

on the left of the pike, Henry Moore saw a man dressed in citizen's clothes riding along the fence on the opposite side of an open field. Suspecting him of being a rebel. Henry made up his mind to capture him. So, without orders, he rushed across the field, despite the enemy's bullets, halted the fellow, marched him into our lines, and delivered him at brigade headquarters. The prisoner was a Kentuckian, and boasted of his superior blood. He was so humiliated, that he cried like a baby.

March 8, '63, Lieut.-Col. Colescott resigned, leaving the regiment in command of Major Denny, Col. Streight being in Indianapolis, collecting absentees.

COL. STREIGHT CAPTURES HIS CAPTORS.

March 20, '63, while en route from Louisville to Nashville, the train in which Colonel Streight and a number of other soldiers were going to the front, was captured by 65 guerrillas, who threw the train off by placing obstructions on the track. The engine, tender and two baggage cars were completely wrecked; but, strange to say, no one was hurt. The rebels wanted to parole the soldiers, but they refused to be paroled; believing they could escape before getting into the rebel lines. During the parley, fifty men belonging to the 129th Illinois, came in sight, when the guerrillas ran for their horses. Colonel Streight instantly took command, and they pursued; killing two, wounding a number, and capturing several horses. They then went to work, cleared the wreck away, sent for an engine, and arrived in Nashville next morning all right.

[From the Official War Records.]

" Louisville, Mar. 19, 1863.

Maj. Gen. WRIGHT, *Cincinnati:*

Rebels captured passenger train this afternoon near Mitchellville, Tenn. Col. Streight had men on the train, and gave fight. Were fighting at last accounts. Gen. Judah telegraphs he had sent 200 reinforcements. Train thrown off the track.

J. T. BOYLE,

Brig. Gen., Comdg. Dist. of Ky.

8

THE RAID TO ROME.

ORGANIZATION OF THE PROVISIONAL EXPEDITION.

Then comes the "Provisional Campaign," in which is included the voluminous history of the capture of the regiment, and incarceration in Libby Prison, as well as the romantic escape of some, and death of others.

Van Horne's report of this campaign, says:

"April 7th, Gen. Rosecrans organized a provisional brigade of 1,700 men for independent service, and assigned Col. A. D. Streight to its command, with instructions to repair to Nashville and prepare to make an expedition into Alabama and Georgia to interrupt communications and destroy property of all kinds useful to the enemy. Having obtained a partial supply of unserviceable mules, Col. Streight proceeded to Palmyra, and thence across to Ft. Henry, gathering on the way as many serviceable animals as possible. At Ft. Henry he embarked for Eastport, Miss. He left that point on the 21st, reached Tuscumbia on the 24th, and moved thence on the 26th for Moulton. Leaving that place at midnight on the 28th, he pressed forward through Day's Gap toward Blountsville. While passing through the Gap, his rear-guard was attacked by Forrest's cavalry. The enemy followed him through Blountsville, Gadsden, and on toward Rome. He defeated Forrest repeatedly, but his men and his animals becoming jaded, he lost heavily by capture. With diminished ranks, and in almost utter destitution of serviceable ammunition, (his ammunition had been injured by fording streams,) he moved on, and crossed the Chattooga river, in hope of destroying the bridge at Rome. But in this he failed, as the enemy pressed upon him so closely, that his men became exhausted, and many having been already killed and captured, and there being no hope of accomplishing the object of his expedition, he surrendered to Forrest on the 3d of May. This enterprise was boldly conceived, and there was no lack of bravery and energy in its conduct, but the contingencies were not clearly apprehended, and the actual results did not compensate for the loss of so many men and so much material. But failure though it was, it was the type of enterprises which, undertaken under better conditions, resulted in brilliant success. It was a mistake to start with a half supply of poor animals, depending mainly upon captures to mount half his command at the start. This plan caused delay in starting, and the result was that the enemy was encountered in superior numbers soon after Col. Streight had passed beyond the reach of support. The enemy's partisan leaders in their raids in Tennessee and Kentucky, had citizens of these States for soldiers, could always depend upon the friendship and assistance of a large portion of the inhabitants, and, besides, were themselves thoroughly acquainted with the country, and consequently were hardly ever ignorant of the strength of the forces operating against them, or of the short routes to safety. The conditions of success were very different subsequently, when the national forces undertook to interrupt the enemy's communications and make destructive raids. Such enterprises were given an unheralded start, and were prepared for quick movement, or else had such strength as to defy ordinary opposition. These conditions were wanting in Col. Streight's adventure."

All of which is true, and leads to the moral: You can't jump into the king-row, when it's full. Also, it is easy to stand off and tell how.

The following, which is compiled from the testimony of those who participated in that famous expedition, and from the Official War Records, tells the story more fully; and it also exposes the perfidy of the notorious guerrilla, and sneaking cutthroat, Forrest, to whom Colonel Streight surrendered his command, and who telegraphed to the rebel authorities a very sensational and lying account of the affair, in which he praised himself greatly.

In the spring of 1863, Colonel Streight applied to Gen. Rosecrans for an independent mounted brigade, with which to engage the guerrilla bands of Forrest and Wheeler and other rebel organizations that infested the banks of the Cumberland and Tennessee rivers, and caused a great deal of annoyance to our transportation. This enterprise was favorably received by General Garfield, who was then chief of General Rosecrans' staff, and who presented the matter to the department commander in such manner as to gain his consent to its organization. It was designated as the "Independent Provisional Brigade," designed for special secret service.

On April 7, '63, Colonel Streight received orders from General Rosecrans to proceed with the Provisional Brigade, about 1,700 officers and men, composed of the following:

    51st Indiana, Lt.-Col. Jas. W. Sheets.

    73d Indiana, Col. Gilbert Hathaway.

    3d Ohio, Col. Orris A. Lawson.

    80th Illinois, Lt.-Col — Rogers.

    Middle Tennessee Cavalry, (2 companies,)

                 Capt. D. D. Smith.

They were to go to Nashville, and fit out as speedily as possible for an expedition to the interior of Alabama and Georgia, for the purpose of destroying the railroads and other rebel property in those States. He was to draw about one-half the mules necessary to mount the command at Nashville, and seize in the country through which they passed a sufficient number of animals to mount the rest.

On arriving at Nashville, Colonel Streight organized the following staff:

    Capt. D. L. Wright, 51st Ind., A. A. A. G.

    Maj. W. L. Peck, 3d Ohio, Brigade Surgeon.

    Quartermaster J. G. Doughty, 51st Ind., A. Q. M.

    Capt. E. M. Driscoll, 3d Ohio, A. A. I. G.

    Lieut. J. W. Pavey, 80th Illinois, Ordnance Officer.

    Lieut. A. C. Roach, 51st Indiana, A. D. C.

It is proper, at this point, to introduce the following correspondence, relating to this expedition:

Rosecrans to Hurlburt:

        "MURFREESBORO, April 2, 1863—11 P. M.

Col. Streight, with near 2,000 picked men, will probably reach East-port by Thursday next. Dodge, with the Marine Brigade and the gun-boats, can occupy or whip the Tuscumbia forces, and let my force go directly to its main object, the destruction of the railroads. This great enterprise, fraught with great consequences, I beg you to commend to Dodge's care, enjoining on him to despatch Streight by every means to his destination. Nothing, if possible, should arrest his progress."

Crittenden to Garfield:

        { "HDQRS. 21st ARMY CORPS,
        (Murfreesboro, April 6, 1863.

Brig. Gen. J. A. GARFIELD, *Chief of Staff:*

    SIR—On more than one occasion I have had

some brief conversation with the commanding general in regard to the enterprise proposed by Col. Streight, of the 51st Indiana Volunteers, for cutting the enemy's communications in his rear. This is certainly a most important movement, and if it could be crowned with anything like a reasonable amount of success, would undoubtedly lead to great results. *   My object is to offer some suggestions, supposing that the commanding general should decide Col. Streight's scheme to be feasible.

⁕   ⁕   ⁕   ⁕   ⁕

Garfield to Streight—Assignment:

"April 7, 1863.

COLONEL—By Special Field Orders No. 94, Paragraph viii, you have been assigned to the command of an independent provisional brigade for temporary purposes. After fitting out your command with equipments and supplies, as you have already been directed, in the verbal instructions of the general commanding this department, you will proceed by a route, of which you will be advised by telegraph, to some good steamboat landing on the Tennessee River, not far above Ft. Henry, where you will embark your command, and proceed up the river. At Hamburg you will confer with Brig. Gen. Dodge, who will probably have a messenger there awaiting your arrival. If it should then appear unsafe to move farther up the river, you will debark at Hamburg, and without delay, join the force of Gen. Dodge, which will then be en route for Iuka, Miss. If, however, it should be deemed safe, you will land at Eastport, and form a junction with Gen. Dodge.

From that point you will then march, in conjunction with him, to menace Tuscumbia, but you will not wait to join in an attack, unless it should be necessary for the safety of Gen. Dodge's command, or your own, or unless some considerable advantage can be gained over the enemy without interfering with the general object of the expedition.

After having marched long enough with Gen. Dodge to create a general impression that you are a part of his expedition, you will push to the southward, and reach Russellville or Moulton. Thence your route will be governed by circumstances, but you will, with all reasonable despatch, push on to Western Georgia, and cut the railroads which supply the rebel army by way of Chattanooga. To accomplish this, is the chief object of your expedition; and you must not allow collateral nor incidental schemes, even though promising great results, to delay you so as to endanger your return. Your quartermaster has been furnished with funds sufficient for the necessary expenses of your command. You will draw your supplies, and keep your command well mounted, from the country through which you pass. For all property taken for the legitimate use of your command, you will make cash payments in full to men of undoubted loyalty; give the usual conditional receipts to men whose loyalty is doubtful, but to rebels nothing.

You are particularly commanded to restrain your command from pillage and marauding. You will destroy all depots of supplies of the rebel army, all manufactories of guns, ammunition, equipments and clothing for their use, which you can without delaying you so as to endanger your return.

That you may not be trammeled with minute instructions, nothing further will be ordered than this general outline of policy and operation. You are authorized to enlist all able-bodied men who desire to join the Army of the Union."

Streight to Garfield:

"NASHVILLE, April 9, 1863.

SIR—Your instructions of to-day are received, among which are the following: *   *   *   *   *

The destruction of manufacturing establishments engaged in manufacturing directly for the use of the rebel army, I consider a duty which I would have no right to leave undone, when in my power, even in the absence of any instructions. Every cotton mill, tannery or other manufacturing establishment, and all quantities of corn, bacon, salt, or other supplies for the use or subsistence of an army within rebel lines, is indirectly supporting the enemy. Now, while humanity would dictate that such necessaries of life as were intended only for immediate family use should be spared, yet it is clearly my opinion that all large quantities of anything necessary for the use of an army, as well as factories producing such articles, should be destroyed, whether such be private or public property. I think I fully understand the course you desire me to pursue in relation to this matter; nevertheless I would prefer you send me written instructions.

Second, the rebels not having regular uniforms, would it be violating the rules of war, should I see fit to dress any number of men—say two companies, after the promiscuous Southern style? Something of this kind might be advantageous, should you not think it an improper course to pursue."

He probably got a strong refusal to his latter proposition, as no indication appears, neither in the Official War Records, nor in the conduct of the expedition, of any indorsement of it. His last communication to the chief of staff, was on April 9:

"We can start within three hours from the time of receiving orders, provided Col. Taylor sends the paulins in time."   *   *

As soon as possible, all hands were at work to supply the command with the necessary clothing, ordnance and equipments for an expedition of this kind; and on the 10th Col. Streight received orders from Gen. Garfield, to embark

at once on steamers then at the landing, and proceed down
the river to Palmyra; land there, and march across to Fort
Henry; and to seize all the horses and mules found in the
country. Everything was speedily put on board, although
it was late in the evening before the mules were brought to
the landing for shipment.

As soon as everything was ready, the command started
for Palmyra; where they arrived on the evening of the
11th, and disembarked at once. Colonel Streight sent the
fleet, consisting of eight steamers, around to Fort Henry,
under the command of Colonel Lawson, 3d Ohio, and gave
him four companies from the Fifty-First, as guard. He
had orders to stop at Smithland, and take on a quantity of
rations and forage for Gen. Dodge's command.

As soon as it was light next morning, all hands were
set at work to catch and saddle the mules. It was then
discovered for the first time, that the mules were nothing
but poor, wild and unbroken colts, many of them but two
years old, and that a large number of them had distemper.
Forty or fifty of the lot were too near dead to travel, and
had to be left at the landing. Ten or twelve died before
starting; and such as could be ridden at all, were so wild
and unmanageable, that it took the boys all that day and
part of the next to catch and break them; but in the meantime parties were sent out to gather in horses and mules;
and had succeeded in getting about 150 very good animals,
though mostly barefooted.

On the 13th, the command left Palmyra, and marched
about 15 miles in a southwesterly direction, and camped
on Yellow Creek. The scouting parties did not succeed in
finding many horses or mules. The people had got warning of the movement, and the stock was mostly run off.

Early next morning, the march was resumed, and the
command arrived at Fort Henry about noon on the 15th.
They had scoured the country as far south as it was safe,
on account of the proximity of a large force of the enemy,

under Woodward; and although about 100 of the mules gave out and had to be left behind on the march, yet when they reached Fort Henry, the animals numbered about 1,250. Those collected in the country, were mostly in fair condition, but were nearly all barefooted. Contrary to expectations, the boats had not arrived; nor did they reach there until the evening of the 16th; having been delayed in getting the rations and forage above referred to.

Gen. Ellet's marine brigade and two gunboats accompanied the fleet to Fort Henry; with orders to proceed as far as Eastport, Miss. Gen. Ellet assumed command of the fleet, and the command embarked as soon as possible; but the pilots delared that, at the existing low stage of the river, it would be unsafe to run at night; hence, they did not start until the morning of the 17th; reaching Eastport on the afternoon of the 19th.

Streight to Dodge:

{ "Hdqrs. Provisional Brigade,
{ Savannah, Tenn., April 18, 1863.

I will move up the river at daylight to-morrow morning. We have 130,000 rations on board for you. Will halt at Hamburg, for messenger for you, and if I do not hear from you there, I will proceed to Eastport, where I shall endeavor to open communication with you. Ellet's Marine Brigade and four gunboats are with us."

Streight to Mrs. Streight:

"April 18, 1863.

Steamer Hazel Bell, Tennessee Fleet, 40 miles above Pittsburg Landing. ＊ I am in command of a fleet of some 20 boats, including several gunboats, also a large force of infantry, cavalry and artillery. ＊ I am entering into a most difficult and dangerous service. My command is curious to know where we are going. The general has trusted to my hands a very important command. I hope I will not disappoint him."

Immediately on arrival at Eastport, Colonel Streight left Col. Lawson in command, with orders to disembark, and prepare to march; while he went to see Gen. Dodge, who with his command, some 8,000 strong, was awaiting his arrival twelve miles up Bear River. After an interview with Gen. Dodge, the colonel returned to Eastport about midnight, to discover that a stampede had occurred among the animals, and that some of them had escaped.

Daylight next morning revealed the fact that nearly 400 of the best animals were gone. All that day and part of the next was spent in scouring the country to recover them, but only 200 of them could be found. The rest fell into the hands of the rebels.

The loss of these animals was a heavy blow; for in addition to detaining the command at Eastport to hunt the stock, it caused still further delay at Tuscumbia, to supply their places. Quite a number of the mules drawn at Nashville, had to be left at Eastport, on account of distemper. Several died next day.

Gen. Hurlburt to Gen. Halleck:

"MEMPHIS, April 20, 1863—3 P. M.

The enemy at Tuscumbia has been largely reinforced by infantry. Delay in Streight's coming compelled Dodge to attack. He did so, and drove them from Bear Creek to Caney Creek, with heavy loss. Our loss 100 and one piece of artillery, that was disabled, but saved. Streight is now in Eastport, in communication with Dodge and the gunboats. I reinforced Dodge to-day with 2,000 men, and with instructions that, if he finds the enemy too strong to be dislodged from Tuscumbia, Streight should proceed in rear of Dodge, by Tupelo, and then across the country. I sent cavalry on Friday, to cut the Mobile and Ohio Railroad below Tupelo, and also to push down to the Jackson and Vicksburg Railroad, and cut that. I recommend a strong demonstration on the enemy's left, to relieve the movement on Tuscumbia.   Col. Streight did not come up until four days after the time agreed upon for the movement to commence."

Oglesby to Hurlburt:

"CORINTH, April 21, 1863—12 M.

*   Dodge will move Wednesday morning, to strike the enemy at Tuscumbia on Friday. Streight is to move on this night, to go to his work, if Dodge will not require his support. Dodge will have to remain there two weeks, to cover Streight's operations."

Dodge to Oglesby:

"TUSCUMBIA, April 24, 1863—11:20 P. M.

I have taken this place, without any severe fighting. The enemy steadily opposed our advance. It was a pretty little fight. I shall go forward in the morning, and help Streight in his movement all I can.

They ran cars in here two days ago, and repaired the railroad.   I think the entire force ahead does not exceed 5,000 men.   *   I shall take Florence to-day. Our advance creates great consternation. They are in full belief that this is a flank movement on Johnson, and so informed him. I do not dispute it, and will make him back out if possible."

Colonel Streight to Mrs. Streight:

"TUSCUMBIA, ALA., April 26, 1863.

Leave here to-morrow morning at 1 o'clock for parts unknown. My whole command is now mounted, excepting about 200 men, which I hope to be able to mount to-morrow.   *   I am confident of success, but may fail; in which case I may be taken prisoner; but I trust all will come out right. If I succeed, it will aid our cause more than everything that has heretofore been done by our entire army."

Streight to Garfield:

"TUSCUMBIA, ALA., April 26, 1863.

After numerous difficulties and delays, I am at last supplied with animals to mount all but 200 of my command. I have met with a great drawback on account of mules drawn at Nashville being such poor ones. I shall start at 1 o'clock to-morrow morning for Russellville, and from thence to Moulton, and find what facts I can gather relative to the condition of things on the route. I have strong hopes of procuring the necessary animals to supply me. I wrote you fully from Eastport, and sent it by Capt. Fitch, commanding the gunboats. I learn since, however, that he is still there. Gen. Dodge has let me have nearly 400 animals, and has done everything in his power to aid me; but the people throughout the country here run off most of their horses and mules. This, with the worthlessness of those brought from Nashville, together with what Col. Lawson lost in the stampede in my absence, as referred to in my last, has put me to my trumps; nevertheless I am very hopeful and confident of success. I shall push on as fast as possible, and rest assured that nothing shall be left undone on my part to insure success; though there is something of a force between here and Decatur, variously estimated from 1,500 to 4,000 men. I hope to get two or three days the start of them; and should they chase me too fast, I will turn upon them and give them battle in the mountains. Col. Hathaway joined us on Friday last. He will be of great help to me.   *   *

Gen. Sweeny to Col. Morton, Comdy. 2d Brigade:

{"HDQRS. RIGHT WING,
{ Town Creek, Ala., April 27, 1863.

*   All inquiries of the inhabitants will be answered with the idea that the column is falling back on Tuscumbia for reinforcements, and great pains taken to impress them with that idea; the object being to mislead them as to our intentions. Keep them employed with watching

this column, in order to give time to Col. Streight's command to reach the mountains."

The "Provisional Brigade" left Eastport on the afternoon of April 21, and reached Gen. Dodge's headquarters the following morning about 8 o'clock. From there they proceeded in rear of Gen. Dodge's forces, which were continually skirmishing with the rebels as they advanced, as far as Tuscumbia; scouring the country to the river on the left, and to the mountains on the right, and collected all the horses and mules that could be found.

The command arrived at Tuscumbia about 5 P. M., on April 24. Here Gen. Dodge supplied our men with about 200 mules and six wagons; the latter to haul ammunition and rations. The surgeon was directed to carefully examine the command; and all who were not fit for the arduous trip, were sent with Gen. Dodge to Corinth, and afterward to Chattanooga. This reduced the command to 1,500.

General Dodge was positive that Forrest had crossed the Tennessee River, and was then in the vicinity of Town Creek; and he agreed to advance as far as Courtland, on the Decatur road, and if possible drive him in that direction; but to pursue him, if he turned off toward Moulton.

With this understanding, our command marched from Tuscumbia at 11 o'clock on the night of the 26th, in the direction of Moulton, by way of Russellville. It was raining very hard, and the mud and darkness combined made progress difficult and slow. One hundred and fifty men had neither horses nor mules, and those of fully as many more were unable to carry more than their saddles; hence at least 300 men were on foot.

It was expected that the greater portion of our force would reach Moulton, some forty miles distant, by the next night; but, owing to the heavy rains, and consequent bad condition of the roads, it was impossible. It was therefore determined to halt at Mount Hope, and wait for those on foot to come up. Accordingly, the first night after leaving

Tuscumbia, the entire mounted force bivouacked at Mount Hope, a village in Lawrence county, Ala., having made a march of 34 miles, over mountainous and almost impassable roads. Col. Streight took up his quarters at the house of a wealthy old rebel; whose daughter, however, claimed to be loyal, and did all in her power for the comfort of her guests. She so thoroughly impressed the colonel, that he ordered the quartermaster to pay her for a fine horse taken by one of the boys on foot.

They were continually scouring the country for horses and mules; but so many of those drawn at Nashville were failing, that, although successful in collecting very many, still a large number were without anything to ride.

On the night of the 27th, at Mount Hope, word came from General Dodge that he had driven the enemy; and he directed our command to push on. Our boys had not all come up yet; nor did they until about 10 A. M., next day; when the command proceeded to Moulton, the county seat, where they arrived about dark. Up to this time they had skirmished occasionally with small squads of guerrillas, but could hear of no force of any consequence in that part of country. All of the command but about fifty were now mounted.

The advance consisted of Captain Smith's two companies of cavalry, who charged into the town about sunset, putting to flight and capturing a small company of Roddy's command. In the jail many loyal citizens had been confined for defending the old flag. Many of these had been friends and neighbors of Captain Smith's command, who themselves were refugees from Southern intolerance and malignity. It was with difficulty, therefore, that they were prevented from tearing to the ground the building, whose damp walls and filthy cells had confined their dear ones so long, for no other cause than their fidelity to the principles on which our Union is based, and for which we were then fighting.

The Provisional Brigade left Moulton in the direction of Mountsville, by way of Day's Gap, about midnight on April 28. The two previous days it had rained most of the time, and the roads were terrible; though on the evening of the 28th it bade fair for dry weather; which gave great hope for better times. The command marched on the 29th to Day's Gap, about 35 miles, where they bivouacked for the night. Every man was now mounted; and although many of the animals were very poor, they had no doubt of being able to supply all future demands. During the day a large number of wagons, belonging to the rebels, and filled with provisions, arms, tents, etc., that had been sent to the mountains, to avoid capture, were destroyed. Our command was now in the midst of devoted Union people. Many of Captain Smith's men were recruited near here, and many were the happy greetings between them and their friends.

Nothing could be learned of the enemy, save of small parties who were hunting conscripts. Thus far, progress toward the prime object of the expedition had been slow; the foot soldiers merely keeping along with the mounted force, that was scouring the country for horses. Now, that enough had been secured, the command was ready to push forward the next morning with rapidity. But, alas! the golden opportunity had passed; and many brave souls who responded to the call on that lovely last day of April, were never to see the dawn of another day.

Our command moved out next morning before daylight. The men had been worked very hard, though, in running over the country in search of animals, and being unaccustomed to riding, were by this time illy prepared for the trying ordeal through which they were to pass. They had not proceeded more than two miles, before the rear guard was attacked, and at the same moment the boom of artillery was heard in the same direction. The gap which our force had entered was easily flanked by other passes in the mountains, both above and below. Orders, therefore, were sent to the rear to hold the enemy in check until our command could prepare for action. The head of the column was on the top of the mountain; the column moving through the gap. So, the enemy was easily held in check.

The rebels had moved through the gaps on the right and left of our command, and were endeavoring to form a junction in advance; our forces therefore pushed ahead as rapidly as possible, till they passed the roads intersecting on either flank. It was Colonel Streight's intention to avoid an engagement, if possible; as the ultimate object of the expedition was of such vastly greater importance, than a victory here could possibly be. But the rebels continued to press so closely, throwing heavy shot and shell into the Union ranks, that a battle was unavoidable. The country was composed of open sand ridges, thinly wooded, affording fine defensive positions. As soon as our command had passed the intersection mentioned—about three miles from the top of the mountain, they dismounted and formed a line of battle on a ridge circling to the rear. Their right rested on the summit of a precipitous ravine, and the left was protected by a marshy run that was easily held against the enemy. The mules were sent into a ravine to the rear, where they were protected from the enemy's bullets. Also, a line of skirmishers deployed on the right and left flanks, encircling the rear, in order to prevent surprise from any detached force that might approach from that direction, and also to prevent straggling either of animals or men.

In the meantime, Captain Smith, who had command of the rear guard,—now changed to the front, held his position until the enemy pressed him closely, when he drew them to our lines, concealed immediately back of the top of the ridge. The lines were left sufficiently open to allow Capt. Smith's command to pass through near the center. Two 12-pound mountain howitzers were stationed near the road, concealed. Scarcely had our men completed their arrangements, when the rebels charged Captain Smith, in large force, following closely; when, as soon as he passed through our lines, the whole brigade arose and delivered a terrific volley at short range. Our men continued to pour a rapid fire into the rebel ranks; which caused them to give way in confusion. Their reinforcements coming up, they dismounted, formed, and made a persistent charge. Our skirmishers were soon driven in; and about the same time the enemy opened with a battery of artillery.

The rebels soon attempted to carry the Union lines; but were handsomely repulsed. During their advance, the rebels had run their artillery to within 300 yards of our lines, and as soon as they began to waver, our men prepared for a charge. The 73d and 51st Indiana, on the left, charged first, in order to draw the attention of the battery; then immediately the 3d Ohio and 80th Illinois advanced rapidly, hoping to capture the battery. The enemy, after a short but stubborn resistance, fled in confusion; leaving two pieces of artillery, two caissons, about forty prisoners, representing seven different regiments, a large number of wounded, and about thirty dead upon the field. Among the former was a brother of the guerrilla leader, Forrest. Our loss was about thirty killed and wounded; among the latter Lieut.-Col. Sheets, of the Fifty-First, who died June 21, and Lieutenant Pavey, of the 80th Illinois.

Our command remained on the field some time, anticipating another attack; as the enemy being strengthened by an additional brigade, felt confident of making an easy prey of the devoted little Union army. It was now about 11 o'clock, fighting having continued since 6 o'clock in the morning; the enemy was in heavy force, fully three times our number, with twelve pieces of artillery, under the personal command of the guerrilla chief, Forrest. They were making an effort to get around the Union troops, to attack them in the rear; hence it was decided to hasten forward. Everything was shortly in readiness; and the Provisional

Brigade moved out, leaving a strong guard, dismounted, in the rear, to check any immediate advance the rebels might make while the column was getting in motion. The column had marched only about six miles, when Forrest's guerrillas were seen advancing on the left. At Crooked Creek, which is about ten miles south of Day's Gap, sharp skirmishing began, the rebels pressing so closely, that our command was again compelled to prepare for battle. A strong position was selected, on a ridge called Hog Mountain, about one mile south of the crossing of the creek. The entire force soon became engaged. It was about one hour before dark. The rebels tried first to carry the right of our column; then they charged the left; but with the aid of the two pieces of artillery captured in the morning, and the two howitzers, all of which were handled with fine effect by Major Vananda, of the 3d Ohio, the enemy was handsomely repulsed.

The fighting continued until 10 p. m., when the rebels were driven from our front; leaving a large number on the field, of killed and wounded. Colonel Streight ordered the brigade to at once resume the march; and the movement was made as quickly as possible. By this time the ammunition captured with the two guns, was exhausted; and being very short of horses, our men spiked the guns and destroyed the carriages. The 73d Indiana, Colonel Hathaway, was detailed to act as rear guard; and the command had gotten fairly under way, when information came that the rebels were again advancing.

The best provision was made for those our command was compelled to leave here in a field hospital, in charge of Ast. Surg. Wm. Spencer, of the 73d Indiana, who was furnished with such comforts as the equipment afforded; but no sooner did the vandals come up to our hospital, than they robbed both officers and men of their blankets, coats, hats, boots, shoes, rations and money; and subjected them to the most brutal and humiliating indignities. Not only

was the bread, meat, sugar and coffee taken, but even the
medical stores and instruments were carried off; leaving
our poor wounded boys in a half naked and starving condition. Even combs, pocket-knives and other articles of
use were forced from the helpless sufferers by those gallant
and chivalrous representatives of that most phenomenal
"uprising of the people," whose souls had been fed on the
fallacious conceit that one of their half-caste soldiers was
equal to five Northern pure-blooded freemen. They were,
in villainy. In consequence of such brutality, many laid
there and suffered horrible agony from undressed wounds
and starvation, until death put an end to their misery;
who, by a little kind treatment, might have recovered in a
short time. The loyal citizens would have gladly afforded
all the comfort and relief in their power; but the brutal
rebel guard would not allow the poor sufferers to receive a
cup of milk even, nor a piece of bread, from that source.
The ingenious tact of woman occasionally was too much
for the vigilance of the rebel sentinel; and some of our
boys were the grateful recipients of some kind favor, or of
some article of food smuggled to them. The loyal citizens
were also subjected to gross indignity and inhuman treatment. Mrs. Penn, a widow residing in that vicinity, who
had two sons in Captain Smith's company, seemed to be a
special object of their fiendish barbarity. She and her
daughters were robbed of everything, even their clothing;
and they were driven from home, their house was sacked,
outhouses burned, and mules turned in on growing crops.

Proceeding from Day's Gap several miles, without further evidence of pursuit, about 4 o'clock in the evening
the rear of the Provisional Brigade was again attacked; yet
to avoid losing time, the column was kept in motion; skirmishing, however, all the time. Captain Smith's handful
of cavalry kept the guerrillas at bay for over two hours;
but they were pressing so closely, that Colonel Streight at
length resolved to halt and give them battle.

9

The moon shone very brightly; and the country being
an open woodland, with an occasional spot of thick undergrowth, afforded great advantages for ambushing. In one
of these thickets the 73d Indiana laid down, not more than
twenty paces from the road, which was in plain view. The
rebels came on. The head of their column passed without
discovering the position of our men. At that moment the
entire regiment opened a most destructive fire, causing a
complete stampede of the guerrilla horde. They rallied,
however, and soon a bloody strife raged with all the fury
of desperate and determined foes. Charge after charge was
made by the enemy, and was as often splendidly repulsed
by our brave boys, who drove them back with most terrible
destruction. The clash was terrific; the flashes from rifles
and artillery lighting up the hillsides, rendering the scene
of carnage one of grandest sublimity. It was now about
10 o'clock; and the hearts of our comrades were cheered
by seeing the enemy waver and fall back; unable to con-
tend longer against the terrible fire our men were pouring
into their ranks. Our command was not again disturbed
until it had gone several miles, when the rebels again came
upon the rear guard, attacking it vigorously. Again they
were ambuscaded; which caused them to give up the chase
for the night.

So far, the Provisional Brigade had been victorious;
though they had lost some brave and valuable men. The
enemy had engaged his entire force; yet by bravery and
skill, our forces had repulsed them at every point. Our
artillery consisted of only two small howitzers; the pieces
taken from Forrest's men the morning before, having been
spiked and cut down.

The country from Day's Gap to Blountsville, about 40
miles, being mostly uninhabited, there was nothing upon
which to subsist man nor beast. Colonel Streight hoped,
by pushing ahead, to reach a place where they could feed
before the enemy came up, and by holding him back where

there was no feed, compel him to lay over a day at least to recuperate. The rebels had been on a forced march from Town Creek, Ala., a day and two nights previous to their attacking our men.

Doctors Peck and King were active in collecting and caring for the wounded. Before this was accomplished, however, the command was in motion. In fact, a rebel regiment had already formed and started in pursuit; and our surgeons had to pass along the entire length of that guerrilla regiment. After our doctors had passed the head of the rebel column, it dawned on the johnnies that they were Yanks; and instantly half a dozen started in pursuit of them, yelling at the top of their voices. Dr. Peck got away; but they soon overtook King, whom they made a prisoner.

The march was continued; and about 10 o'clock in the morning Blountsville was reached. Many of the mules had given out, leaving their riders on foot; yet there was very little straggling behind the rear guard.

At Blountsville our command found sufficient corn to feed the tired and hungry animals. Ammunition and rations were hastily distributed to the men, the remaining ammunition put on pack mules, and the wagons burned; as it was now very plain to all, that it would be impossible to take them further. After resting here about two hours, the march was resumed, in the direction of Gadsden. The column had not gotten fairly under motion again, before our pickets were driven in, and a sharp skirmish ensued, between Forrest's advance and our rear guard under Capt. Smith, in the town of Blountsville. The enemy followed closely for several miles, continually skirmishing with our rear guard; but were very badly handled by small parties of our men, stopping in the thick bushes at the side of the road, and firing at them at short range. When our men reached the east fork of Black Warrior River, the ford was very deep; and the enemy pressed them so closely, that they were compelled to halt and stand a fight, before they could cross. After some maneuvering, a heavy skirmish line was advanced, who drove the enemy quite out of sight of our main line; when the troops, except the skirmishers, crossed the river as rapidly as possible. The skirmishers were then quickly withdrawn under cover of the howitzers, and a heavy line of skirmishers thrown out on the opposite bank for that purpose. It was about 5 P. M. when the last of the command crossed the stream; and they pushed on toward Gadsden, without further interruption, except by small parties, who were continually harassing the rear of the column, until about 9 o'clock next morning, May 2, at which hour the rear guard was furiously attacked at the crossing of Black Creek, near Gadsden. After a short but sharp fight, the rebels were repulsed. The bridge was then burned; and it was thought this would delay Forrest long enough to enable the Provisional Brigade to reach Rome, before the guerrillas could again overtake them; as the stream was very deep and unfordable at that point. But among a lot of prisoners captured by our men that morning, was one named Sansom, a low-browed brute; who, in common with others, as was the custom, was immediately paroled; and who, as soon as he was set at liberty, made his way direct to Forrest, and piloted him to a ford, where the whole rebel force soon crossed. Sansom, the perjured scoundrel, was with Forrest, when our command surrendered; and notwithstanding his oath of parole, was fully armed and equipped; and boasted that it was a bullet from his gun that killed Col. Hathaway, of the 73d Indiana.

Our scouts reported that a large column of the enemy was moving on the left, and parallel with the route of our forces, evidently with the intention of getting in front. It became necessary, therefore, for our command to march all night; though neither men nor animals were in a condition to do so; and to add still more to their embarrassment, a portion of the ammunition had been damaged in crossing

Will's Creek, which at that time was very deep fording. Our command remained at Gadsden only long enough to destroy a quantity of arms and commissary stores found there, and proceeded. Many of the animals and men were entirely worn out; and unable to keep up with the column, gradually they fell behind the rear guard, and were taken prisoners.

It now became evident to Colonel Streight, that if he would save his command, his only hope was in crossing at Rome, and destroying the bridge over the Coosa River; as that would delay Forrest a day or two, and give our men a chance to rest and to collect horses and mules, without which it was impossible to proceed.

The rebels followed closely, and kept up a continuous skirmish with the rear of the column, until about 4 P. M., at which time our command reached Blount's farm, about fifteen miles from Gadsden, where it was designed to obtain forage for the animals. It was impossible to continue the march through the night, without feeding and resting; although to do so, was to bring on a general engagement. Accordingly, the command was dismounted, and a detail was made to feed the horses and mules; while the balance of the command formed in line of battle on a ridge southwest of the farm.

Meanwhile, the rear guard, in holding the enemy in check, had become seriously engaged, and was driven in. The enemy at once attacked our main line, and tried hard to carry the center, but was gallantly repulsed by the 51st and 73d Indiana, assisted by Major Vananda, with the two howitzers. The rebels then made a determined effort to turn the right of our line, but were met by the brave boys of the 80th Illinois, assisted by two companies of the 3d Ohio. This action lasted nearly three hours; the rebels charging from right to left repeatedly; but so determinedly did every part of our noble brigade maintain its position, that the enemy recoiled in greatest confusion; our boys

pouring a perfect hail-storm of lead into their retreating
columns. Our heroes won the day, by their indomitable
courage and desperate fighting.

The enemy, with the exception of a few skirmishers,
then fell back to a ridge half a mile distant, and appeared
to mass his force, as if preparing for a more determined
attack. It was becoming dark ; and Colonel Streight concluded to withdraw unobserved, if possible, and conceal
the command in a thicket half a mile away; there to lie in
ambush, and await the enemy's advance. In the meantime, Captain Milton Russell, of the Fifty-First, was sent
forward with 200 of the best mounted men, selected from
the whole command, and directed to proceed to Rome, and
hold the bridge until the main force could come up.

The engagement at Blount's Farm, which was hence-
forward to possess special historic interest, revealed the
alarming fact that about all of the remaining ammunition
was worthless, on account of having been wet. Much of
that carried by the men also, had become useless, by the
paper wearing out and the powder sifting away.

It was in this engagement also, that the gallant Col.
Gilbert Hathaway, of the 73d Indiana, fell with a mortal
wound, and in a few minutes expired. The Union army
possessed no braver nor more valuable officer than he. To
our devoted brigade, his loss was irreparable. His men
almost worshiped him ; and when he fell, it cast a heavy
gloom of despondency over his entire regiment, that was
difficult to overcome. Those of them who yet remain, will
remember how cheering and inspiring was his presence in
their midst ; how his coolness steadied them, amid greatest
excitement ; and his voice of encouragement, was a herald
of victory.' His character so frank and open ; his bearing
so modest, and so full of simplicity, conciliated and capti-
vated all hearts, and made every one who knew him his
devoted friend.

Charles McWilliams and George Bilheimer, of Co. C,

were detailed immediately after the Stone River fight, in the 8th Indiana Battery. When the Fifty-First started on the Raid, McWilliams was returned to the regiment, and was given a position under Major Vananda, in charge of the battery. In this battle, he had his head shot off by a rebel cannon ball, while faithfully performing his duty.

Affairs were now rapidly approaching a crisis. Every one felt that the next twenty-four hours would decide the fate of the provisional expedition. The brigade was now within sixty miles of Rome, where it was designed to cross the Coosa River; and if they could reach there before the rebels could intercept them, complete success was assured. Once on the opposite side of the river, and the bridge destroyed, Forrest would be effectually beaten. Much was, therefore, hoped for from Captain Russell's demonstration.

The Provisional Brigade had been in ambush but a short time, when the enemy, who by some means had been informed of their whereabouts, commenced a flank movement, which was discovered just in time to check. It was then decided to withdraw as silently as possible, and push on in the direction of Rome. As a large number of men were dismounted, their animals having given out, and the remainder of the stock was so jaded, tender-footed and run down, their progress was very slow; yet, as everything was depending on their reaching Rome, before the rebels could throw a force sufficient to prevent our brigade crossing the bridge, every possible effort was made to urge the column forward. They proceeded without interruption, until they reached the vicinity of Center, when a scout brought the intelligence that a force of the enemy was in ambush but a short distance ahead. Immediately a line of skirmishers was advanced, with orders to proceed until fired upon, and then to open a brisk fire on the enemy, and hold their post till the command had time to pass. The plan worked admirably; for, while the skirmishers engaged the enemy, the main column made a detour to the right, and struck the road three miles further on. As soon as the main force had passed, the skirmishers withdrew, and fell in the rear of the column. They were then hopeful that they could reach Rome before the enemy could again overtake them. Colonel Streight's principal guide had thus far proved all right; and he assured the commander that there were no difficult streams to cross, and that the road was good; the command therefore approached the Chattooga River at the ferry, without any information as to the real condition of things. Captain Russell had managed to ferry the last of his command across about an hour before; but the rebels had seized and taken the boat away before the main force could reach there.

It was then ascertained that there was a bridge, seven or eight miles up the river, near Gaylesville; and securing new guides, the command pushed on as rapidly as possible in order to reach the bridge, before the enemy should take possession of it. In doing this, our men had to pass over an old coal chopping for several miles, where the trees had been cut and hauled off for charcoal; leaving innumerable wagon roads in every direction. The men were so nearly worn out and exhausted, that many were asleep; and in spite of all that could be done to prevent it, the command got separated, and scattered in different directions. It was nearly daylight, when the last of the command had crossed the river. As soon as the brigade had crossed, the bridge was burned, and the iron works at Gaylesville, where the rebels were manufacturing munitions of war, was also destroyed. The illumination was magnificent. Time now was precious; and the brigade hastened toward Rome. It was evident, however, that they could never reach there, without halting to rest and feed the animals. Large numbers of the mules were continually giving out; in fact, it is probable that not a score remained, of the mules that were drawn at Nashville; while nearly all of those collected in the country, were barefooted, and many of them had such sore backs and tender feet, that it was impossible to ride them. In order, though, to get as near as possible to the force that had been sent ahead, they struggled on until 9 A. M., when they halted and fed the animals. The men, being unaccustomed to riding, had become so completely fagged out, and had lost so much sleep, that it was almost impossible to keep them awake long enough to feed.

In the meantime the vanguard, under Capt. Russell, arrived in the vicinity of Rome, about 8 o'clock the next morning after the battle of Blount's Farm ; having ridden their badly jaded horses all night. By this time the town was full of armed men. Forrest had dispatched a citizen of Gadsden to inform them of the approach of our men ; and a large number of troops had been hurried there from Atlanta, Kingston and Dalton ; besides, the citizens were put under arms, and several pieces of artillery had been placed in position. The floor of the bridge was torn up, and piled with straw saturated with turpentine, ready to ignite at a signal.

The Provisional Brigade had halted but a short time, when word came that a heavy force of rebels was moving on their left, on a parallel route ; and were then nearer to Rome than our men were. About the same time our pickets were driven in. The command was immediately called into line, and a strong effort was made to rally the men for action ; but nature was exhausted, and a large portion of them actually went to sleep while in line of battle, under a severe skirmish fire. After some maneuvering, Forrest sent in a flag of truce, with a demand for the surrender of our troops. The regimental commanders had expressed a conviction already, that unless our force could reach Rome and cross the river, before the enemy came up with them again, they would be compelled to surrender. A council of war was called, and the condition fully canvassed. It was learned meanwhile, that Captain Russell had been unable to take the bridge at Rome. The ammunition was ruined, horses and mules exhausted, men overcome with fatigue and loss of sleep; and, confronted with at least three times their numbers, in the heart of the enemy's country, the situation seemed so utterly hopeless, that it was decided to surrender on the following terms:

1. Each regiment to be permitted to retain its colors.

2. The officers to retain their side-arms.

3. Both officers and men to retain their haversacks, knapsacks and blankets; and all private property to be respected, and retained by the owner.

These terms were fairly and fully agreed to by Forrest; and our brigade stacked arms, and were prisoners of war. The surrender occurred at noon, Sunday, May 3, 1863.

OPERATIONS ELSEWHERE.

At the same time operations were going on elsewhere, which indicated the unusual importance that was attached to this expedition; yet how little was really known of its wonderful character and experiences.

Dodge to Oglesby:

"May 3, 1863.

Finding it impossible to obtain stock to mount Col. Streight's command, I took horses and mules from my teams and mounted infantry, and furnished him some 600 head, mounting all but 200 of his men. I also turned over all my hard bread, some 10,000 rations, and he left me at midnight on the 26th ult., with the intention of going through Russellville, Moulton and Blountsville, to Gadsden, then divide, one force to strike Rome, and the other Etowah Bridge.   *

That night I communicated with Col. Streight, and ascertained that he was all right.

Col. Streight reached Moulton Tuesday night, and commenced crossing the mountains Wednesday, having got nearly two days start of them. They supposed he was making for Decatur, and only discovered Wednesday that he was crossing the mountains toward Georgia.   *   I have no doubt he would have succeeded, had he been properly equipped, and joined me at the time agreed upon. The great delay in an enemy's country necessary to fit him out, gave them time to throw a large force in our front. Although Col. Streight had two days start, they can harass him.   If he could have started from Bear Creek the day I arrived there, my movements would have been so quick and strong, that the enemy could not have got their forces together. The animals furnished him were very poor at the start. Four hundred of them were used up before leaving me, and those furnished him by me, were about all the serviceable stock he had, though I hear he got 200 good mules the day he left me, in Moulton Valley."

Oglesby to Hurlburt :

"JACKSON, TENN., May 3, 1863.

＊ Col. Streight left Tuscumbia Sunday night, 26th ; moved to Mt. Hope on Monday, and to Moulton on Tuesday. He was supplied with very poor animals; 400 of them broke down between Palmyra, on the Cumberland River, and Tuscumbia. With those Dodge turned over to him, he had 1,600 on leaving Moulton, Tuesday night, April 28. At that time no enemy was after him, as Dodge had engaged them up to that time. Roddy and Forrest then heard of Streight's movement, and supposing it a flank attack on Decatur, instantly fell back to that place. Streight thus had two days start, but his men were so badly mounted, he would have to lose some time to pick up 200 animals at Moulton. From there he proposed to go by the way of Blountsville, and strike the Coosa River. Dodge supplied him with rations to last him to Coosa Valley, where it is supposed he can help himself."

Hurlburt to Rosecrans :

"MEMPHIS, May 5, 1863—1 P. M.

The following is just received from Dodge :

'The rebels came up with Streight, between Moulton and Blountsville, eight miles south of Somerville. Streight ambushed and whipped them badly. The rebels sent word from Decatur to Chattanooga that Streight was making for that place. Forrest and Roddy are on his track. I think Streight is far in advance of them. I will keep free south of Corinth, to enable Streight to get back.' "

Rebel A. A. G. to Pegram, Comdg. Cavalry Brigade :

"KNOXVILLE, May 4, 1863.

A cavalry force of the enemy, estimated at 4,000, has moved from Corinth, Miss., across Northern Alabama, and on the 2d, destroyed the depot at Gadsden, Ala., and was threatening Rome, Ga. Gen. Forrest was pursuing them, and it is thought that they may endeavor to return through East Tennessee, to their own lines. [Rebel Gen. Maury, commanding Knoxville, was warned to intercept them.]

From Rebel Gen. Bragg's Report :

"TULLAHOMA, May 5, 1863.

Forrest, falling back on the 28th, discovered a heavy force of cavalry under Col. Streight, marching on Moulton and Blountsville. Gen. Forrest pursued this force with two regiments, fighting him all day and night at Driver's Gap, at Sand Mountain, with a loss of 5 killed and

50 wounded.   The enemy left on the field 50 killed and 150 wounded; burned 50 of his wagons; turned loose 250 mules and 150 negroes, and pursued his way toward Blountsville, Gadsden and Rome. Ga. On May 3, between Gadsden and Rome, after five days and nights of fighting and marching, Gen. Forrest captured Col. Streight and his whole command. about 1,600, with rifles, horses, &c."

Hurlburt to Rosecrans:

May 6, 1863.

Dodge reports by letter to me that Col. Streight left Tuscumbia on Sunday night, 26th;   *   *   If his animals hold out he will succeed, as the enemy cannot follow him fast, the mountains being between them. All things being favorable, he has done his work by this time. Grierson, with his regiments of cavalry, has destroyed the railroad east and south of Jackson, and gone into Gideon, the enemy having gathered near Okolona, to intercept his return. I have sent, two days ago, five regiments to break them up, and draw attention from Streight."

Rebel Bragg to Cooper, A. I. G.:

"TULLAHOMA, May 7, 1863.

Between Rome and Gadsden, a party of 1,600 of the Federal army surrendered to Gen. N. B. Forrest, after several days' fighting, in one of which he forced them to burn their wagons, and turn loose a large number of negroes. Shall I send them as prisoners of war to Richmond, or deliver them to the Governor of Alabama?"

Reply of Cooper:

" RICHMOND, May 8, 1863.

The slaves captured by Gen. Forrest should be sent for safe-keeping, with sufficient guard, to the nearest camp of instruction."

" RICHMOND, May 13, 1863.

Send at once to this city, all captured officers and men."

PRISONERS OF WAR.

Let us now go back to where we left our unfortunate command, in the hands of heartless, jubilant victors.

Notwithstanding Forrest's most sacred promise, made in the terms of surrender, no sooner were our troops turned over to the rebel authorities, than a system of robbing was instituted, which soon relieved our boys of everything of any value in their possession. Blankets, knapsacks, haversacks, overcoats, money, side-arms, colors and everything

followed each other as fast as the brutal guards came to
them. The following is a specimen of the paroles issued
to each prisoner:

PRISONER'S PAROLE.

I, ... of Co. .... of the
United States Army, captured by BRIG. GEN. FORREST, solemnly swear
before Almighty God, the Sovereign Judge, that I will not bear arms
against the Confederate States Government, nor help, aid or assist, either
directly or indirectly, any person or persons, in making war against the
same, until regularly exchanged as a prisoner of war, and that I will not,
at any time, communicate to any person, information received within
the Confederate lines, detrimental to the same.

Sworn and subscribed to before me at   ⎫
.... ⎬   (Prisoner's name.)
.... A. Inspr. Genl. ⎭

The next day the command was marched under guard
to Rome. The citizens were delighted to see the boys, and
thronged the streets to greet them. The prisoners stayed
in the town till Tuesday morning, May 5, under orders of
Forrest; enduring every insult that such a low, ignorant,
unprincipled, ill-born people only could invent. The vile
creatures crowded around the cars, the women flaunting
themselves in the most indecent manner; and all boasting
of the superior chivalry of the South.

INCIDENTS OF THE RAID.

Many humorous incidents of the raid, as well as sad
ones, are revived. Sergeant Wm. P. McClure, of Co. H,
drew a most obstreperous mule, that had an ugly habit of
"tilting up behind," and by a simultaneous and dextrous
movement to the right or left, would land his luckless rider
on his head. Nobody therefore would risk his neck on the
beast; so, to utilize him, half a dozen camp-kettles were
strapped on the saddle, and he was turned loose. He made
the grand rounds of the camp at lightning speed; then,
thrusting his head into a brush-heap, he laid down and

brayed in a most mournful way. The kettles were taken off, and two boxes of cartridges (1,000 rounds in each,) were substituted. With these he started off on the march all right; but it rained that day, and the mule slipped off of the road, and was precipitated to the bottom of a deep gulley, heels up, where he died in a short time.

While the command camped at Buzzard Roost, Will Jordan and Caleb Smith, of Co. A, went across the railroad after night, for water. Clambering down the steep bank of the stream, Jordan took hold of a bush, to steady himself while he filled his bucket. The bush pulling out by the roots, he was thrown into the stream, which was very deep, and he would have drowned, had not Caleb fortunately found a pole and reached down to him.

One day "Mother" Richeson and Alex. Ward, of Co. G, got into an altercation, and kept it up until the other boys prevailed on Captain Wallick to make them step out in front of the company, and "have it out." On the Captain's invitation, they both stepped promptly to the front, and, with their haversacks and accouterments on, went at it like tigers, till they had it out. From that moment no one ever heard a word from either of them. When they arrived at Columbus, after they were paroled, a number of the boys, including our two heroes, took a "French furlough" and started for home in advance of the rest. After two or three days one of them took sick, and had to be left with a farmer; the rest proceeding on their way. When they had traveled two or three miles, discussing their sick comrade on the way, they concluded they had not done right to desert him; but no one was willing to go back, till the former enemy declared he could not go home and leave him. So he went back; and after three weeks' nursing, the sick comrade was restored, and the two went to their Indiana home together. They were ever after close friends.

One of the sad incidents of the fight at Day's Gap, was the wounding of Wm. Jelf, of Co. C. After the first fire, the command arose to make a charge, when the rebels fired again, and he fell. At the same moment, Lt.-Col. Sheets and another man fell, immediately behind him; and all were supposed to be mortally wounded. Calling John P. Smith to him, Jelf delivered to him a silver watch, with a small chain attached, with a request that if he got through safely, he would take them to his mother. As John P. anticipated search and robbery by the rebels, in case they were captured, he tore the chain loose, throwing it away, and concealed the watch on his person. Soon afterward, securing a pone of corn bread, about the size of his hand, he carefully cut out a circular piece of the top crust, then removed just enough of the inside to receive the watch, replaced the disc of crust, and on examination, after capture, so innocently exposed the corn pone, as to entirely elude discovery; and so he carried that watch through all the vicissitudes of subsequent imprisonment and exchange, to Jelf's home in Indiana, where he delivered it in good condition, to Jelf's mother. Charles Cox, who was among the last who saw Jelf, gave him a canteen of water, and left him with the citizens to die. Jelf recovered slowly; and when John P. returned to camp at Indianapolis, he was almost the first person he met.

"For God's sake! Will," said John P., "go to your mother as soon as you can. I have just been to see her, and I told her you was dead!"

Jelf hastened home; and the meeting was to his grief-stricken mother, as though he had been raised from the grave; rejoicing her crushed heart beyond measure.

When Captain Russell's advance guard came to the Chattahoochee River, his guide and Corporal Gibson, of Co. A, started in to ford or swim their animals across the stream. The guide reached the other shore all right; but Gibson's horse would not go forward, after his hind feet touched bottom. It began turning round and round; and Gibson slipped off, to let it raise and get out. But being weighted down with his accouterments, gun, overcoat and heavy boots, he could not swim himself, but was pulled under, and began a struggle for life. Captain Anderson, who was second in command, saw Corporal Gibson's peril, and springing from his horse, rushed onto the old scow at the ferry, and with the aid of the young man in charge, pushed off toward where the unfortunate comrade had gone down. Placing himself at the forward part of the scow, the captain watched for the reappearing of the corporal ; when plunging his arm full length into the water, he succeeded in catching the drowning man by the hair, raising him out and taking him to shore. The boy was hastened off to the nearest point for brandy, while the corporal was rolled on the bank. He was then rubbed vigorously for an hour and a half, when he was again able to ride. By this time the detachment had all been ferried over, and they moved on. But for Captain Anderson's prompt action, Comrade Gibson would certainly have been lost.

STARTING FOR RICHMOND.

All are agreed as to the barbarity of the rebel authorities, and the inhuman treatment by the citizens of Rome, and other places through which our men had to pass ; the jeers and taunts of women, who spit on them, and offered such indignities as only degraded females of the viler sort would be guilty of. And Forrest's fiends felt "perfectly at home" there.

After paroles were presented to the men, in accordance with the stipulation of surrender, every one was searched for valuables. A number of gold and silver watches were taken, and a large amount of money. The commissioned officers were not searched so closely, but their swords were taken, and most of their money.

Hospital Steward Smith was ordered to accompany 54 sick and wounded of the brigade, in the custody of Dr. Curd, the Medical Director of Georgia, to Richmond ; and

Peter Phillippe, of Co. E. was detailed to assist him. All of these were sent to Libby, and confined there until they were exchanged.

The command was first taken to Atlanta; where they remained two days. By the time they arrived there, they had been prisoners three days and nights, yet had received nothing to eat. On the morning of the fourth day, quarter rations were issued for three days; which were instantly devoured. That night about dark, the prisoners boarded a train; and at daylight next morning were at Knoxville, Tenn. The trip thus far was unmarked by any event of sufficient importance to mention. At Knoxville, the prisoners changed cars and guards; and a most fortunate and merciful change it was.

A detachment of the 54th Virginia rebel regiment was camped near the railroad; and they kindly divided their rations with our starving boys. This was a most gracious thing for them to do; and proved that even out of Sodom some good might come. And while it went far to modify the hardships incident to this journey, it also united the hearts of otherwise enemies by an inseparable bond. This band of hardy and big-hearted mountaineers was detailed to conduct the prisoners from Knoxville to Libby and Belle Isle. They saw at a glance the wasted condition of our poor comrades, from fatigue and hunger and exposure and outrage; and they opened their big hearts and their haversacks; and for the first time in many days our boys enjoyed the rare pleasure of rest and plenty of food. This hearty and unexampled kindness continued till the prisoners were delivered to the rebel authorities at Richmond.

Before taking the cars, quarter rations were issued for two days; and our boys received no more till they arrived at their destination: five days. At points along the route, ladies presented the boys with bouquets; and at Farmersburg, Va., the guards allowed the boys to go into the negro quarters, and buy food; and many a half-starved soldier

10

got a nice corn pone, accompanied by a hearty "God bless you, sah! wish we-uns cud feed ye all!"

The rare treatment by the 54th Virginia boys was not forgotten; and when, on the final surrender of the traitor Lee, his misled and dishonored followers came to us up in East Tennessee, the 54th boys were received with genuine joy, by the remnants of the old Provisional Brigade, and supplied with the best of everything the camp afforded.

THE LOSSES COMPARED.

It is quite impossible, with the data at hand, to report the exact casualties in the command; but from the best information obtainable, there were 15 officers and about 130 enlisted men killed and wounded. It was a matter of real astonishment to all, that so much fighting should occur, with so few casualties on our side; but our command acted purely on the defensive, and took advantage of the nature of the country as much as possible. From actual personal observation made by Colonel Streight and others, when the enemy had been driven from the field, and from reports of surgeons, left with the wounded, there is no doubt that our men killed more rebels than we lost in killed and wounded together.

Previous to the surrender, our command had captured and paroled about 200 prisoners; and had lost about the same number, in consequence of the animals giving out, and the men breaking down from sheer exhaustion, falling into the hands of the enemy by necessity. But in no case were Forrest's guerrillas able to capture a single man in a skirmish or battle.

ARRIVAL AT RICHMOND.

Arriving at Richmond, the officers were taken to the old pork house of Libby & Son, that was used by the rebels as a military prison; and none of them saw their men any more for months; in some cases not for years.

At Belle Isle, a few old rotten tents were given to the

boys, and quarter rations again issued. The day's allowance was scarce enough for one meal. The lieutenant in command was a low, vile, drunken wretch; who had only abuse for his captives.

Belle Isle was a barren, sandy tract of land, several acres in extent, situated in James River, opposite Richmond, Va. The prisoners had no barracks nor shelter of any kind, except in winter, when a few old worthless tents, too ragged to keep out snow or rain, were furnished. The prisoners made excavations in the dry sand with bones and sticks, or with their fingers; and into these the poor fellows would huddle for warmth. Lost to all sense of pride and cleanliness, energy wasted, minds almost gone, they would lay for days together, till the sand worked into their skin. They had been already robbed of their hats, shoes, coats, pants and socks; and when they came to this lousy island, had but their underwear to cover their nakedness. This was nothing, however, to the misery occasioned by their want of food. This became so great as to deprive the men of their reason; and many a poor comrade shared the fate of Tilman McDaniel, of Co. C, who in his delirium, staggered over the "dead-line," and was shot down by the inhuman rebel guard.

As Sergeant McClure, Co. H, was "counting off" his company for rations, one day, he became dizzy from weakness, and fell to the ground in a semi-conscious state.

"What's the matter?" inquired his alarmed comrades.

"I'm starving to death!"

His cousin, Noah P. McClure, Co. E, took from his waistband a $2 greenback secreted there, and purchased a couple of small loaves of bread. In a few hours after eating some of this, and drinking some water, he was able to sit up.

Next day the number of prisoners was increased by a great many from the 11th Corps, and the misery of all was correspondingly augmented. Quarter rations continued,

and the severity of the brutal guards became more intoler-
ant. But God was merciful to our boys; and relief came.

BACK TO GOD'S COUNTRY.

In a few days an order came for the removal of the lot
of prisoners to which our boys belonged, to City Point, 35
miles distant, for exchange. The march was a weary one
to all; but all were buoyed by anticipation of speedy deliverance. The first night they bivouacked within ten miles
of City Point. Next day, the remainder of the journey was
made; and the hearts of our delighted boys swelled with a
sense of gratitude and unspeakable joy, as they beheld the
old stars and stripes floating aloft.

As each comrade stepped on board the Federal transport, he was handed coffee and bread and meat. Soon the
happy soldiers were sailing down James River, and thence
up Chesapeake Bay to Annapolis, where the vessel touched,
and then proceeded to Baltimore; where the boys took the
Baltimore and Ohio Railroad for Columbus, Ohio.

There was evidently a mistake made at Belle Isle, in
selecting our boys for exchange; and the government ship
did not leave City Point a moment too soon. After it had
gone ten miles, a small steam-tug came splashing alongside, and signaled the vessel to stop. A rebel officer, with
a very pompous air, sprang on board, and presented a dispatch from Jeff Davis to the master of the ship, ordering
the return of our entire command to Belle Isle. To this
the captain replied:

"These men are in my charge now; and I am not
subject to Jeff Davis' orders!"

The pompous rebel sprang back to the tug; and the
ship was soon beyond recapture.

At Camp Chase, Columbus, O., the boys drew clothing,
and fixed themselves up to go home. Some of the Fifty-
First boys were too impatient to wait for furloughs, and
started in advance. They had one or two days' visit, and

returned to Indianapolis before the regiment arrived there. The command finally separated at Camp Chase, and were furloughed from their State capitals.

At the expiration of their furloughs, the Fifty-First boys returned to Indianapolis, where they were employed for some time in guarding rebel prisoners at Camp Morton, the present site of the State Fair Ground.

It is quite impossible to give any further account than has already been given, of those who were wounded on the Raid. Most of those who survived, doubtless made their way back to Tuscumbia, and remained with Dodge's forces until otherwise disposed of.

Dodge to Rosecrans:

"CORINTH, May 17, 1863.

Surgeon Abbott, of the 80th Ill. Inf., has arrived here with some of the wounded from Tuscumbia. The wounded I left there were badly treated, and one Wm. Cooper, of Roddy's command, shot a prisoner by the name of John Chambers, who died of his wound. He was a member of the Alabama cavalry, and had just been discharged. It was a cold blooded murder.

IN LIBBY PRISON.

· The officers of our command were, as has been said, placed in Libby Prison, a military bastile constructed from an old pork house owned by a man named Libby, and his son. It was situated but a few yards from the Lynchburg canal, was three stories high, 165 feet front, and 105 feet deep. The ground floor was separated into several apartments, one being the prisoners' hospital, and the others used by the commissary department and the officers of the prison. The upper stories were each divided into three rooms, 105 by 55 feet. At each extremity of these rooms were five windows, heavily barred. In the cramped limits of these six rooms 1,100 Union prisoners were confined for many months; being compelled to cook, eat, wash, bathe and sleep in this narrow space.

Ten thousand stories might be told, of the varied experiences of these men, who had yielded up all that life and home and earth offered to them of happiness; stories that would chill one's blood with horror, and again would cause it to boil with indignation, at the inhuman conduct of the rebel authorities, whose fiendish accomplishments even eclipsed the cruel barbarity of the carboneri of Italy.

As the 4th of July approached, these prisoners began preparation for a celebration. How to obtain a flag for the occasion, was the question of greatest moment; for a real Fourth of July celebration, without the stars and stripes, would be like the play of "Hamlet" with Hamlet left out. Finally, a Connecticut officer, observing that some of his

comrades wore red flannel, and others white cotton, suggested that each contribute a strip from his shirt, while a navy ensign should furnish the blue field from his garment. It was adopted with great applause. Soon a respectable standard was constructed, and on the national anniversary it was swung from a beam in the upper west room. Col. Streight was selected to deliver the address; and he took the stand beneath the flag, and began his speech, when a prison official made his appearance. Catching sight of the stars and stripes, he stopped the proceeding, and ordered that "hateful rag" taken down; informing them also that Fourth of July celebrations were not tolerated in that part of country. No one obeying his order, he was compelled to mount and pull down the flag himself. Tom Turner, the superintendent, regarded it as quite a trophy, and was very curious to know how it was brought there. He said he was going to present it to one of his lady friends, and wanted its full history.

SAWYER AND FLINN.

Early in June, two men, claiming to be Union officers, and wearing the uniform of a colonel and major, presented themselves to Col. Baird, commanding the post of Franklin, Tenn., and stated that they were Colonel Anton and Major Dunlap, and that they were authorized, by an order from Adjt.-Gen. Townsend, at Washington, and another from Gen. Rosecrans, to inspect outposts. Their conduct excited suspicion, and it was soon concluded that they were spies. This supposition was proved to be correct, as upon inquiry at department headquarters, it was ascertained that there were no such inspectors in the national service. A drum-head court-martial was at once ordered by Gen. Rosecrans, and enough evidence was adduced to convict them. Their object was to gain such knowledge of the post as to enable Forrest to dash in and capture it. Learning that a court-martial was ordered, they weakened, and confessed

that they were Col. Lawrence A. Williams and Lieutenant
Dunlap, of the rebel army. The former had been in the
army of the United States. They claimed they were not
spies, but the proof was positive, and the prisoners were
hung June 9th, in accordance with the following order :

("HDQRS. DEPT. OF THE CUMBERLAND,
{ Murfreesboro, June 9—4:40 A. M.

Colonel J. P. Baird, Franklin:

The general commanding directs that the two spies,
if found guilty, be hung at once, thus placing beyond the possibility of
Forrest's profiting by the information they have gained."

FRANK S. BOND, Major and Aid-de-Camp.

"FRANKLIN, June 9—10:30 A. M.

To General Garfield, Chief of Staff:

The men have been tried, found guilty, and executed
in compliance with your order.   I am, ever yours,

J. P. BAIRD,
Colonel Commanding Post.

This summary disposition of two very dangerous rebel
accessories, fired the hearts of the leaders at Richmond,
and determined them on revenge. And their method was
retaliation of the most unreasonable and cowardly kind.

Two days after the national celebration in "Libby,"
that was so suddenly and ungraciously nipped in the bud,
July 6, 1863, all of the officers of the rank of captain, 78
in number, were drawn up in line in one of the rooms, and
an order was read from the rebel Gen. Winder to Major
Turner, in which the latter was directed to select two captains of the United States army, from the number he held
in confinement, for immediate execution. Some reports
have this order for execution of two captains in retaliation
for the execution of two rebel spies by order of Gen. Burnside, in Kentucky. It does not matter which story is true,
in this relation. The information fairly electrified those
whose fate was concerned. When they first got into line,
they stepped out gaily, with expectation of exchange; but
their spirits fell, and a stern resignation took the place of

hilarity, and a brave resolution to accept whatever might befall them in the glorious cause they had espoused, lit up every countenance.

On a small table in the center of the semi-circle, was placed a box containing the names, written upon separate slips. At one side stood the brutal Turner, at the other, the white-haired chaplain of the 9th Maryland, who had been designated by the prisoners to draw two slips from the box; which should determine who were doomed.

Solemnly the chaplain first offered prayer. Then, as each stood breathless, one was drawn, each feeling that his life depended on what was written on it. It read:

"Henry W. Sawyer, 1st New Jersey Cavalry."

All eyes turned toward him, and a slight commotion ensued, but not a sound was heard. Again the old chaplain thrust his hand into the box. All was silent as death. Then again he read:

"Captain John Flinn, 51st Indiana Infantry."

The ceremony ended, the doomed men were conducted to Winder's headquarters for an interview with him. He shamefully cursed and abused them, and notified them that they would be executed within ten days; after which he ordered them placed in the dungeon, to be kept there until the day of their execution. It did not take long to communicate this matter to President Lincoln. Immediately, Brig. Gen. W. F. Lee, a nephew of the rebel leader, R. E. Lee, and Capt. Winder, a son of the rebel commandant at Richmond, both prisoners of war, were placed in close confinement, as hostages for Flinn and Sawyer, and the rebel authorities were notified that the moment our officers were executed, Lee and Winder would meet a similar fate. This prompt action had the desired effect. The execution was indefinitely deferred, though Flinn and Sawyer were kept in the dungeon a long time. It is said that so great was the shock to Captain Flinn's entire nature, that his hair turned white almost in one day.

OTHER SUFFERERS.

The experience of Capt. E. M. Driscoll, 3d Ohio, and Lieut. C. W. Pavey, 80th Illinois, was even worse than that of Flinn and Sawyer. They were selected in retaliation for the death of two rebel recruiting officers, who were executed for violation of a standing order of General Burnside, while in command of the Department of Ohio. They were confined in the dark, damp, filthy dungeon, 147 days, in torture and agony of both mind and body. Nearly every day they were visited by a brute named Dick Turner, a sort of commissary officer in the prison, who with curses and abusive epithets would taunt and insult them. Their rations were half a pound of coarse corn bread and James River water. They were not allowed to communicate with any one; and no one can realize the intensity of their suffering. They survived it, however, and lived to return to their homes; though with wasted bodies and health gone forever.

Lieut. E. N. Reed, 3d Ohio, was severely wounded in the hip, during the Raid, and fell into the hands of Forrest's guerrillas, who suffered him to lay several days with no medical attention whatever. In this pitiable condition, he was thrown into a wagon, and hauled many miles, over a rough, mountainous country, to the railroad at Huntsville, Ala., where with other prisoners, he was packed into a dilapidated old stock car, and taken to Richmond, where for many months he endured untold suffering; when, for a mere imaginary breach of prison rules, he was thrust into the dungeon, with no bed but the bare floor, and without a morsel to eat, he was kept for 48 hours. At the same time his wound was running so as to require frequent washing and dressing. Surviving his wound and the terrible treatment, he was sent to Charleston, S. C., and thence started for Columbia; but before boarding the train, he escaped from the guard, and found refuge in an old house in the suburbs. While concealed there, awaiting a chance to get through to the Union lines, he took yellow fever, and soon after, with no friend to minister to his dying wants, his great spirit was added to the long line of "unknown."

REDUCING THE RATIONS.

For a few weeks, the inmates of "Libby" continued to receive the rations of bread, beef and rice established in that miserable institution, in as fair quantity and quality as our officers, from recent experience, expected. Colonel Streight wrote at this time as follows:

"RICHMOND, VA., July 12, 1863.

You will see by this I am still a prisoner. I have no idea when I will be exchanged, consequently am making the best I can out of my present misfortunes. My health is good; so is that of the prisoners generally. I have received no letter from you since I left Murfreesboro."

But with the increase in numbers, the rations began to decrease, both in quantity and quality, till the amount was not sufficient to sustain life. Many succumbed, and were sent to the hospital. Then the colonel wrote another letter, and one of a very different character:

"LIBBY PRISON, RICHMOND, VA.,)
August 31, 1863. /

Hon. James A. Seddon, Secretary of War:

SIR— I take the liberty of addressing you on behalf of myself and fellow prisoners in relation to our situation.

About six hundred of us are confined here, with an average space of twenty-eight square feet each, which includes our room for cooking, eating, washing, bathing and sleeping. Our rations consist, as nearly as I can judge as to quantity, of about one-fourth pound of *poor* fresh beef, one-half pound of bread, and one-half gill of rice or black peas, for each man per day.

Scorbutic diseases have already appeared, proving fatal in one instance, (Major Morris,) and impairing seriously, if not permanently, the health of many others.

Our sanitary condition would have been much worse than it now is, but for the large purchases of vegetables and other provisions, amounting to nearly one thousand dollars per day, which we have been allowed to make. But as nearly all our money was taken from us when we entered the prison, the daily expenditure of this large sum has at length about exhausted what was left us. We have also been notified that we would not be allowed to receive any portion of the money taken from us here, *nor to receive such sums as have been sent to us from home since our imprisonment;* though before writing for these monies, we were express-ly assured by your officers having us in charge, that we would be allowed to receive them.

It will be perceived from the above statement, that our immediate prospective condition is, to say the least, that of semi-starvation. The rations furnished by your Government, may be as good, and as much as it can afford under the circumstances, but in that case it does seem that we should be allowed to purchase the necessary amount to sustain us. It cannot possibly be that it is intended to reduce to a famishing condition six hundred prisoners of war. Humanity cannot contemplate such a thing without feelings of the deepest horror. Saying nothing of our rights as prisoners of war, even criminals, guilty of the blackest crimes, are not, among civilized people, confined for any length of time on insuf-ficient food.

I wish further to state to you, that previous to my surrender, I made a stipulation with General Forrest, to whom I surrendered, that all pri-vate property, including money, belonging to my officers and men, should be respected. This stipulation, in the handwriting of General Forrest, over his own signature, is now in the hands of General Winder, having been taken from me here. Notwithstanding this, my officers (ninety-five in number,) have been notified with the balance, that their money has been turned over to the Confederate authorities.

For the purpose of avoiding further loss of money, or misunderstand-ing, and if possible to obtain relief from the unhappy situation in which we are placed, you are most respectfully requested to state in your answer to this communication, the manner in which we will be allowed to obtain the necessary food and clothing to render us comfortable.

I have the honor to be, Sir,
Your most obedient servant,
A. D. STREIGHT,
Colonel of Fifty-First Indiana Volunteers."

This letter had the effect to improve things for a little while, but other cruelties were added in time.

Writing letters home was for some months the chief source of comfort. But even this was denied them. The following order was issued by the ignorant brute in charge of the prison:

"OFFICE C. S. MILITARY PRISON, }
Richmond, Va. }
Hereafter prisoners wont be allowed to write no letters to go to the so called United States of more than six lines in length and only one letter per week.
By command of
THOS. P. TURNER,
Major C. S. A."

Becoming desperate in consequence of these cruelties, and long confinement, a plan was conceived and set in operation, for the general delivery of prisoners at Richmond. The scheme was deep, bold and daring, and was known as the "Council of Five." The plan, with additional details, was to escape from "Libby," release about 15,000 Union soldiers in Richmond and on Belle Isle, seize the arsenal, make Jeff Davis a prisoner, cross James River, burn the bridges after them, and escape down the Peninsula. The plan was perfectly feasible, and would have been executed, but for a traitor in the prison, who communicated the plan to the rebels, and thus checkmated the game.

Half a block from "Libby" was confined over 7,000 enlisted men; on Belle Isle about the same number. Col. Streight was the acknowledged leader. He originated the "Secret Council of Five," and was chosen commander-in-chief. It was a sworn secret organization, and so perfect was its development, that nothing short of treachery could have defeated its plan. Suddenly, one night, a battery and two regiments of rebel infantry were drawn up in front of the prison. The artillery was trained on the building, and the infantry stood in line all night. This was continued some days. Our enlisted men were soon after sent to Andersonville, and iron bars were put up at the windows of "Libby." Pickett's division was also ordered to the vicinity of Richmond.

This plan being abandoned, each officer set about to devise some other means of escape. A number succeeded in bribing the guards, and getting away.

ANDERSON AND SKELTON.

Capt. M. T. Anderson tried it in a way quite original, and, it is a pleasure to add, eminently successful, though full of danger.

The day he entered the loathsome prison, he began an inspection of every accessible part of the building. In one of the board partitions he found a knothole, through which he saw several half-starved Union prisoners, from whom he learned that they were to be exchanged. One of them also told him it would doubtless be a long time before another exchange would be made; and he added, "If there is any word you wish to send to your friends in the North, you do not care to have the prison authorities know, write it on a piece of paper, and if I can secrete it in any way until I reach the Union lines, I will send it to your friends." He tore the tissue leaf out of his pocket Bible, wrote on it his father's address, and a request that when he sent for provisions and clothing, to send also a good sum of greenbacks sewed up in the lining of the pants. Soon after that all of Streight's officers were moved to the third floor, having access, however, to the second. After months of fruitless hoping and waiting, Anderson became convinced that his escape from the upper rooms was a moral impossibility, as he came near losing his life several times, by being shot at by the guards while climbing down from an upper window. He must try strategy; and he spent one entire night formulating a plan. He would feign sickness, and get an order to go down to the hospital, which was on the ground floor. Keeping his own counsel, he became alarmingly ill before the morning roll was called, and by 9 o'clock, the hour for "sick call," he was seemingly in such a condition, that the surgeon sent him down stairs at once. After keeping his bed about four days, under treatment, he sat up an hour on the fifth, and on the ninth stayed up all day. Then he began to operate his plan.

Underneath the hospital was a basement and a cook room. Two large doors opened from this basement to the sidewalk, where a sentinel was constantly on duty. Another, but very small door, opened out of the cook room to the sidewalk directly at the southeast corner. This was decided on as the place of exit. A suitable companion was the next desirable thing; and one was found to his liking in Lieut. J. F. Skelton, of the 17th Iowa, who had been an inmate of the hospital some time, and was quite familiar with the surroundings.

It was a noticeable fact that the guards were the same every other day; the same sentinel being placed on the same beat. Skelton was well acquainted with one of these guards, and introduced the captain to him. Anderson lost no opportunity to talk with this guard, and soon brought him to the precise point where he wanted him. For a sum specified, he agreed to allow the two prisoners to pass over his guard line. Everything seemed favorable, for the very next morning a large box of provisions and clothing came to Anderson. A pair of pants was included; and as soon as practicable, he examined them. On ripping the lining, great was his joy to see a liberal roll of greenbacks tumble out; the key to liberty. The preliminaries were quickly arranged, and the night set for the attempt. The cook, who was a Union prisoner, was sworn to secrecy. To open the small door without exciting suspicion, was the next important move. It was to be done in the forenoon, after the delivery of the beef, which was brought in quarters. It was the duty of the cook to cut up the beef, which made a great deal of noise, and was quite favorable to the work of opening the prison door; a very delicate task, with a sentinel just outside on duty. This door was fastened by four heavy oak bars spiked across it with 40-penny nails, with smaller spikes around the facing but a few inches apart. Almost every day, the prison inspector, brutal Dick Turner, visited that place at that hour; so that great caution was necessary. With a large meat cleaver, an old chisel and a hatchet, the large spikes were carefully drawn, then cut off, leaving about an inch of nail from the head, and as soon as cut returned to its place. One by one the spikes were all drawn and doctored, and late in the afternoon the door was ready to swing on its hinges. Gathering some dried beef, cheese and crackers, the two were soon ready to step forth from the jaws of death into freedom. At about 9:35 they said good-bye to one or two trusted friends, who were informed of their plan, and silently removed the bars and spikes. Opening the door an inch or two, the guard was signaled, and at once responded. A few hurried words could only be whispered, for fear of detection.

"Are you ready?" asked the guard.

"Yes."

"Then give me the money."

"Here it is," said Anderson.

"Is it all here?"

"Yes, every dollar."

"Come on, then," the guard whispered. At the same instant the next sentinel called the corporal of the guard; and our boys, whose hearts now throbbed with a horrible dread, felt that after all they had been betrayed. Every second seemed an hour. But their fear was relieved when the guard whispered, "The corporal will not be here long; then the coast will be clear." To the anxious comrades, who were both under 23 years of age, this was sweeter than music. Hope revived rapidly; and in a few minutes more they were assured by the sentinel that again all was ready. At 10 o'clock they knew the hour of the night would be called, at which moment the sentinels on the south side all faced westward, and those on the east side faced northward, as they took up the cry; and it was decided to make the break just as the clock struck. The greatest danger was from a sentry guarding some boxes on the canal bank directly opposite the little door. But quicker than it can be told, they had jumped over the guard-line, passed within a few feet of a number of armed rebels, who would not have hesitated a second to shoot down an escaping Yankee prisoner, and walked quickly down Canal street, whistling as they went, yet each moment expecting a rebel bullet, until two blocks had been traversed; then turning onto Main street, they elbowed their way among the crowds of rebel soldiers, paying no attention to any one, and animated by no thought other than to get as far away from the foul pen as possible.

Captain Anderson had a faithful friend in George, a colored boy, who had gone out east of the village of Rockets, and carefully examined the ground, the result of which he had detailed to the captain; so that when they neared the outer works, the fugitives had no difficulty in recognizing the location, and in finding a path leading off to the right of the road. Following this as well as they could in the dark, they soon came to a small stream. Turning east up this stream, they waded and stumbled over rocks and logs for hours; and just where they passed the picket lines they never knew. By that time it was pouring down rain. They did not dare to strike a match to see the small compass Skelton wore on his watch chain. On they pressed; though cold and wet, without overcoat or blanket, they did not complain, for they were now free, and traveling toward God's country. In consequence of their limited knowledge of the country and the blackness of the night, they lost the road, and wandered about until daylight, when they found they were only six miles from Richmond. To attempt to travel by day, meant certain capture, so they hid in what they thought was a thick clump of underbrush, but which proved a sparse thicket, and less than a mile from a large rebel camp. Rebel soldiers were constantly passing, and many came within fifty yards of where they lay. Closely they studied a little map the captain had copied from one loaned him by the hospital steward, but they could not locate their position. So, hour after hour they waited and watched, hoping some slave might pass that way, knowing that Union soldiers could always trust the black man. At length they were rewarded by the approach of a large covered wagon, driven by a negro. When they halted him, to their astonishment a white man jumped out, and inquired, "What you-uns want?" They knew no white citizen there

11

was likely to be their friend, so they quickly answered that they were in search of a runaway slave; that he had been tracked to Richmond, and into that neighborhood, where all trace was lost. They also named a good sum offered for his capture and delivery. This satisfied the old Virginian, who promised to do all he could for them; and with their profuse thanks, he drove on.

Immediately after dark they struck the Williamsburg pike, leading to Bottom's bridge, where they hoped to cross the Chickahominy. The night soon became black as ink, and while groping along they suddenly found themselves tripping over the guy-ropes of the headquarter tents of the rebel force guarding Bottom's bridge. This was not a very healthy situation, but crawling on their hands and knees, they finally got clear of the camp, and fortunately soon got back on the road; but it was pouring down rain, cold, and so dark, that to travel was out of the question. So, they went into an adjoining woods, and stood up against a tree, occasionally walking around it to keep warm. They decided then to lay their course at the first streak of dawn, by map and compass, due north to the White Oak swamp. This they reached, and all day long, Sunday, December 13, 1863, they toiled through that dense swamp, often waist deep in mud and water, and having to part the underbrush and briars to get through at all. About sunset they suddenly emerged, covered with black mud, clothes in tatters, shoes torn from their feet, and they filled with briars and snags, and bleeding, to find themselves on the Chickahominy River. It had concerned them much how they would cross that stream, knowing it was deep and swift. Here Providence seemed to favor them; almost in front of where they stood was a large tree uprooted, reaching entirely to the eastern bank, on which they crossed with ease. Tired, hungry and footsore, they again camped on the cold, damp ground in a clump of bushes, and not daring to build a fire to dry their clothing, they had to keep moving to prevent

freezing. The night was one of storm, wind, rain and
sleet, and sleep was impossible. At earliest dawn of day,
after a few mouthfuls of food, they proceeded; but had not
gone far when they spied a rebel scout approaching them.
To run was to excite suspicion; so, they determined to defend themselves with their clubs, and die ere being taken
back. But the scout passed by with a single glance. Then
crossing the road, they struck for the pine woods, and for
four hours they ran, through forest and swamp and field,
keeping a due easterly course. About 10 A. M., on coming
out of a ravine they discovered a colored girl sweeping up
leaves. They questioned her as to roads and localities, but
she could give them no information. They learned with
amazement, however, that they were only a hundred yards
from a large house, where her master lived. He had just
left her, and was coming back soon. When they told her
they were Yankee officers escaped from Richmond, she was
greatly alarmed for their safety, telling them to hurry on,
as "Massa he got bloodhounds, an' he cotch lots o' Yankees from Belle Isle. He take you back ef he see you."
They started on briskly, and she said, "You better run; I
won't tell massa." Away they went, on double-quick, till
many miles lay between them and Mr. Bradley. On their
run, looking down from a ridge they saw not over a quarter of a mile away a troop of rebel cavalry. They had not
been observed fortunately, and they rolled off a few miles
more, till they were brought to a halt by a swamp over 400
feet wide, 300 of which was quicksand or quagmire. They
were an hour and a half crossing it; but once over, felt safe
from Bradley's hounds and the troopers. Late that night
they reached Haw Creek. At a negro cabin they asked for
food, and were gladly supplied; but as it was unsafe to stay
there, they returned to the woods; though they could not
sleep because of pain and cold. The captain had traveled
barefooted nearly all day, and his feet were bleeding and
swollen. Their suffering was inexpressible; but death was

COLONEL STREIGHT AND CAPTAIN REED.

Colonel Streight and Captain Reed, of the 3d Ohio, tried it. One day one of the guards poked a note through a window, telling the colonel he was a fool to stay in there; adding "You may come out to my post to-morrow night, with a friend, and if you will give me $100 and your watch, I will let you escape." With the aid of a rope made of a blanket, at the time appointed, the two officers descended from a second-story window, handed the guard the money and watch, and passed outside. They had only gone a few steps, when, without challenge, they were fired upon by a squad of rebel soldiers. It was simply a scheme to catch them, and they were led back and placed in a dungeon, in which they were kept for thirty days. It was a dismal, dark hole, about eight by ten feet, in the basement. Protestations, threats nor prayers had no effect. Clevises, such as were used to shackle negro slaves, were placed on their wrists, and they were allowed nothing to sit or lie upon. Each request to the superintendent, Turner, was answered by, "Oh, no; you were not very well pleased up stairs; I think this will please you first-rate." One day the notorious John Morgan visited the dungeon; and having a sort of admiration for Streight, he said, "This is no place to keep a white man; take them out of here." So they were released from that terrible place, and returned to their old quarters.

Soon after Captain Reed was released from the horrid dungeon, he was selected and sent to Salisbury, N. C., in irons, and there placed in close confinement, as a hostage for the safety of a rebel officer in the hands of the United States authorities. From Salisbury he made several efforts to escape, and on two occasions got within a few miles of our troops in East Tennessee; but was each time hunted down with blood-hounds, and taken back to prison. While being transferred to Macon, Ga., he procured a gray suit, and in this he slipped from the car, passed along the line of guards, until he selected one on whom to practice his trick. He pretended to engage the guard in conversation; but, supposing him, from his dress, to be a citizen of the town, he ordered him outside of the lines. The captain walked away, looking back very angrily; and losing himself in the crowd at the depot, he found a place of safety, where he remained concealed, until a dark stormy night enabled him to secure a small row-boat, in which he went down the river into Charleston harbor, and finally to Sullivan's Island, where he was again under the folds of the old flag. Returning home, he was appointed Major of the 174th Ohio, and was killed in battle near Murfreesboro, December 7, 1864.

TWO TUNNELS.

The "Council of Five" did not despair of escape on account of failure. A league was organized, each member of which was sworn to not divulge anything to even his most intimate friend. A few bricks were carefully removed from the back of the fireplace, and an opening was made through the wall, coming out below the joists on the opposite side, into the cellar. This work was necessarily done all at night, and all traces were removed before morning. Two or three trusty men would be at work, and the rest sat around and sang, making so much noise that the sounds of the workmen could not be detected. Then a tunnel was begun near the south wall, with the intention of running through to the sewer under Canal street. On account of the water seeping in from the sewer, which threatened to flood the cellar, that tunnel was abandoned.

Colonel Streight then planned another tunnel. The building was situated on a hillside, the basement being on a level with Canal street, and the first floor on a level with Carey street, on the other side. Across Carey street was Carr's warehouse, and adjoining it a stable. From a window the colonel got his bearings, and by a little calculation by triangulation, at which he had acquired a readiness in many years' experience "lumbering" among the forests of New York, he got the distance to the stable, into which the tunnel was designed to lead. A stone was removed from the foundation in day time, after which the work was prosecuted by night. In digging, it was necessary to dispose of the dirt. This was carefully distributed in the cellar, and covered over with straw, a large quantity of which was stored there for beds. The men in the secret dug by regular turns. The man in the tunnel would fill a little sack, then pull a cord connected with a comrade in the cellar, who would drag the sack out and empty it. This continued till the tunnel was completed. On returning to the room, the bricks would be replaced, and ashes scattered about the place to prevent suspicion. Toward the last it was thought best to keep a guard on duty, to prevent surprise.

One day Lieutenant White, of West Virginia, was on guard at the tunnel, when some rebels came into the basement for supplies of some kind, having with them several negroes to carry packages. One of the negroes strolled off toward where White was; and he crawled under the straw, leaving his shoes sticking out. Imagine a barefooted darkey in winter, who sees a pair of shoes lying around loose, and one can conceive the eagerness with which he seized the lieutenant's feet. He dropped them as suddenly, however, and jumped back with a startled expression. His companions inquired what was the matter.

"I see a awful big rat back dar!" he replied.

He had instinctively grasped the situation. He afterwards assured the prisoners that they need have no fear of him. "I's not gwine tell on you-uns."

In some way an acquaintance had sprung up between the officers and Mrs. Abbie Green, a citizen of Richmond, and a "true blue" Union lady. Through her colored man correspondence was carried on, and she was fully apprised of everything that transpired, and was prepared to hide the officers when they should escape. This correspondence was carried on between Mrs. Green and Captain Wm. W. Scearce, of the Fifty-First, whose middle name was Waller, and over which signature he conducted the correspondence.

The tunnel was about sixty feet in length, the diameter being just large enough for a large sized man to go easily through; though in one place, where it curved around a rock, it was smaller. The time consumed in digging was about three weeks. When it was about half completed, a small hole was dug up to the surface of the street, in order to ascertain whether the tunnel was going exactly in the right direction. Into this hole an old shoe was thrust, the toe sticking up a few inches above the street. So accurately had the diggers calculated, that the shoe was in a perfect line to the center of the stable. It was finished on the night of February 8, 1864; and at about 9 o'clock the night of the 9th, the prisoners commenced passing out. Colonel Streight was one of the first to go out that night. When he came to the curve around the rock, he stuck fast, and had to be pulled back, take off his clothes, and draw them through after him with a string. Soon a knowledge of the hole spread among the prisoners, and each one was resolved to go out. Of the 700 or 800 who jammed and pushed around the entrance, only 109 succeeded in getting out. The discovery of the delivery was made at the daily morning count, which consumed nearly four hours. The guards were immediately placed under arrest, as they were supposed to have been bribed. A thorough inspection was made, and the hole was discovered. Couriers were hurried in every direction, pickets doubled, and a posse from the prison galloped off after the fugitives, 55 of whom were recaptured and taken back.

A history of the adventures and sufferings of the 54 who reached the Union lines, to say nothing of the experiences of those who were recaptured, nor of the hundreds

who did not get even a sniff of free air, would form a large
and very interesting volume. It is impossible to give here
more than a general outline of a few ; which, however, are
fair samples of the rest.

STREIGHT, SCEARCE, McDONALD AND STERLING.

Colonel Streight and Capt. Will Scearce were joined
by Major McDonald and Lieut. Sterling, of the 101st Ohio.
Coming up out of the tunnel inside of the old stable back
of Carr's warehouse, they went through an arched gate to
Canal street, passed around the building within a few feet
of the sentinels, and proceeded according to the direction
of Mrs. Green, to the house of a negro woman, where Mrs.
Green found them, and conducted them to the house of
Mr. Quarles, where they met Mrs. L. A. Rice, who gave
up her rooms to them, and provided clothing and food.
They were visited by several Union men, who furnished
them with money, revolvers and ammunition, and recon-
noitered the rebel lines, to ascertain the best place to pass
out. They stayed there one week ; then, accompanied by a
guide, and well provided, they started for the Union lines,
directing their course a little east of north. That night
they crossed Chickahominy River, in full sight of the rebel
pickets. The weather was cold, and they suffered greatly,
as they dared not build fires. On the fourth day they arrived at Pamunkey River, which was flowing with ice.
Streight crossed it on a fallen cedar tree, found a boat on
the other side, and returning, rowed his companions over.
Being pursued, they concealed themselves in a dense pine
thicket. The next night, with their feet badly swollen and
nearly frozen, they reached Mattaponi River, which was
also full of heavy ice ; they found a boat, however, and got
across with little difficulty. They built a fire to heat the
sand, and buried their feet to keep them from freezing.
The fifth night they traveled over a very rough country,
through brush and briars. Toward morning they met a

negro, who told them they were near Rappahannock Station. Next morning they were pursued by soldiers, citizens and hounds; and when the blood-hounds overtook them, they fed them and urged them on. That day two of the party gave out, and had to be supported and almost forced along. They would say, "For God's sake let me lie down and die!" Next day it rained very hard, and they found refuge and shelter in a negro hut, where they were feasted on the best the plantation afforded. Next day they made a raft of rails, which a number of negroes carried a quarter of a mile, cheerfully, for that purpose. Before starting the darkies had gathered all the ropes and lines they could find, and these were used in tying the rails together. In this way they crossed the Rappahannock. The Potomac was then only fifteen miles further. Here a negro directed them to the house of a German who owned a boat. They stayed all night with him, and finally, after another hairbreadth escape, from rebel soldiers, who fired on the crew, succeeded in getting to Blackstone Island, about 2 o'clock in the morning of Feruary 28, 1864. Dr. Williams kindly cared for them; and next day Commodore Parker, of the Potomac squadron, conveyed them to Washington. Eleven days and nights of perilous wandering, hungry, half naked and cold, in marshes and thickets, crossing ice-bound rivers, and in constant fear of capture or horrible death, were at last ended in liberty and home.

For seventeen years after Colonel Streight's escape from Libby Prison, no word was heard denying his leadership in the construction of the tunnel through which 109 officers made their exit from that foul and horrible den. It remained then for a few copperhead newspapers and a fake show to undertake to injure him by publishing infamous lies, glorifying others and divesting him of the glory with which popular history has surrounded him. In 1880, Colonel Streight delivered a lecture before the Union Veteran Association, of Indianapolis, in which he described the

Raid and incarceration in Libby Prison, depicting that hell upon earth in its true light, and telling of the awful sufferings inflicted upon the prisoners of war, and the barbarity and inhumanity of the rebel authorities. A garbled report of this was published in a prominent paper in that city, with an accompanying editorial, belittling the accomplishment of the tunneling out ; saying, "a rat might have done as well or better ;" and it even virtually, if not actually, ridiculed the idea that Colonel Streight had anything to do with originating the tunnel, and saying that he was barely an accidental beneficiary. In reply to this, Capt. Wm. Wallick, of the Fifty-First, and Major John D. Simpson, of the 10th Indiana, both of whom escaped with Colonel Streight, published the following in the Indianapolis *News:*

THE ESCAPE OF "THE RATS."

To the Editor of the Indianapolis News:

If the Union soldiers who, after long and weary months of confinement and misery in Libby Prison, with incredible labor dug out to freedom, are at this distant day to be classed with vermin and moles, it seems to me that it makes little difference who projected the work or who participated in it. I notice with astonishment and mortification, from a publication in the *Indianapolis Journal,* that "a rat might have done as well or better." I was a Libby prisoner, and I helped dig in two tunnels, one of which was never completed. It seemed to me then that we were digging for life, and we hoped we had the prayers and kind wishes of Union-loving friends at home. But if any rat might have done as well or better, as the *Indianapolis Journal* thinks, what matter who was the head rat? It is a prominence not to be coveted ; a leadership not to be envied. When prominent Republican editors revile and burlesque the sufferings of unfortunate Union soldiers, it matters little who was prominent and conspicuous in miseries, or most active and efficient in escaping them. Better be an unknown and obscure Union soldier than a disgraced and defamed rat. I was one of the unfortunate rodents who, under the direction of Gen. Streight, assisted in digging out of Libby Prison. I have carefully read the synopsis of his lecture to the Veteran Club ; and I indorse its accuracy in all substantial particulars. There were two tunnels ; I dug in both ; one was not completed. Some confusion has no doubt arisen from confounding the operations of the two tunnels. This I know: Gen. Streight was the commander-in-chief in Libby of the Council of Five, the friend and helper of everybody. He was of the Council upon whose discretion, sagacity and secrecy everything depended. We all looked up to him and loved him. So much depended upon secrecy and stillness, our hopes for liberty and life and one more sight of home and friends, that the men who worked and dug were as silent as rats, and as industrious. They dug and worked, or, as the *Journal* probably would have it, "gnawed" away in darkness and utter silence. Death was the penalty of failure, and with bated breath, they dug on, rarely whispering and often not knowing who were their helpers, caring or knowing little or nothing as to who was "head rat," satisfied that it was better to dig on desperately rather than "die like a rat in a hole." I always considered Gen. Streight the projector and superintendent of the last tunnel, through which he escaped; and I, with others, was willing to work under his direction.

One word more: Gen. Streight has never claimed any special merit in the tunnel business, wonderful achievement as it was. He always insisted upon giving to the boys full credit, and disclaimed for himself anything like the prominence he really had. His lecture before the Veteran Association, of which a mere synopsis is printed, has been called for earnestly a thousand times. He has been importuned and earnestly besought to make it by the old soldiers and citizens for years. It is the plain unvarnished narrative of an honest, frank, noble old soldier, of whose achievements the tunnel work and subsequent escape was a very small part. He deserves the thanks, the gratitude and the honors of his countrymen; and the pitiful attempt to defame and defile him merits the scorn, denunciation and contempt of every honorable man believing in justice and fair play. WILLIAM WALLICK,
Late Captain Co. G, 51st Ind., Peru, Ind.

ANOTHER RAT SQUEAKS.

To the Editor of the Indianapolis News:

I have read with deep regret the shameful and uncalled for attack of the *Indianapolis Journal* upon Gen. A. D. Streight, and feeling keenly the injustice done him, I lose no time in adding my testimony to the truth of his statement made in a lecture before the Union Veteran Association of Indianapolis. I carefully read the synopsis of that lecture, and know it is true. His plain and simple statement, told in the frank and open manner of a soldier, awakens touching recollections, for I was a fellow "rat." It happened that I was a prisoner of war from Chicamauga in 1863, arriving home on a blessed Christmas day in 1864. In Libby Prison I was early a member of the Secret Council of Five, made a member by Gen. Streight, who was the commander-in-chief of that organization. I was also one of the working party, "gophers"—that's a better word than "rat"—who dug the now historic tunnel out of Libby. I was adjutant of the "Lower Chicamauga" room, which was commanded by Capt. Smythe, of the 19th U. S. Infantry,   who was afterwards adjutant general of a picked command of the Secret Council of Five.   *   As to Gen. Streight,   *   he was compelled to accept to a great degree our leadership, for nature had evidently fitted him for it. He never despaired, even when in a dark, filthy cell, the manacles of treason welded on him. Men naturally leaned upon and trusted one whom nature had endowed with unconquerable will and exhaustless resources. Rebels hated him, watched him, plotted to starve, sicken, murder him, simply because he, despite himself, seemed the originator of all plans to escape, the head of all schemes for relief, the support of the living and the comfort of the dying.   *   Gen. Streight seemed absolutely essential to the success of our enterprise. I have always regarded him as its soul.   *   *   *

Very respectfully,
JOHN D. SIMPSON,
Late of 10th Ind. Inf.

After the war Mrs. Abbie Green went to Washington, where, on account of her heroic acts, a government position was given her. She faithfully discharged her duties to the last, and her good deeds will live in the hearts of friends, a more lasting monument than a marble shaft. Her funeral took place Tuesday evening, March 19, 1884, in Washington City, and was the occasion of many words of highest praise by all the journals of that city. She was born and educated in New Hampshire, inheriting a strong will and fixed purpose in all she did. Force of circumstances drifted her into the South, and the war found her in the rebel capital. But her heart was ever true to the Union; and she conceived the idea of rescuing Union soldiers from Libby Prison; which she accomplished to the jeopardy of her own life. The *National Republican* said, in speaking of her death:

"Gen. Streight and several prominent Union officers who were incarcerated in Libby owe their safe deliverance from that den to Mrs. A. H. Green. Many others, homeless and friendless, have been taken care of by her."

CAPTAIN RUSSELL AND OTHERS.

Failing to escape through the tunnel, Captain Russell and many others became discouraged, having given up all hope of exchange of prisoners. Plans for escape, in case of removal, were discussed, however; and it was with real gladness that word was received to get ready to march. At 1 o'clock, on the morning of May 7, 1864, the rebels began

counting our men out at the narrow door, like so many
hogs, the rebel commissary pitching a pone of corn bread
to each as he passed out. They were marched to the Danville depot, and there packed into old stock cars, over sixty
prisoners and five guards in each car. The weather was
very hot, and water so scarce, that they received but two
half pints during the entire journey of 24 hours. During
the trip, some of the boys cut holes in the floors of the cars,
and got away. The scoundrel in command of the guard
was called Captain Tabb, and the prisoners united in de-
nouncing him as a low, cowardly and unfeeling dog; a fit
agent for the masters he served. At Danville, they were
crowded into two frame buildings, where they had less than
half the space allowed in "Libby." They remained there
five days, when they were again jammed into cars, 60 or 70
in each, and started for Macon, Georgia. Before leaving,
they were furnished with a pound and a half of corn bread
and one-half pound of bacon; and that was all they got
till they arrived at Augusta, three days after; beside, they
were not permitted to buy of the hucksters who thronged
the train at each stopping. Arriving at Macon, May 16—
just one year from the time they entered "Libby," they
were placed in a stockade. At once squads were organized
to tunnel out; and several large ones almost succeeded,
when the folly of one of our own officers exposed the plans,
and placed a check upon their operations. In July, they
were removed to Charleston, S. C., where they were kept
three months, under the fire of our own guns. During the
fall, the yellow fever made its appearance among the prisoners; in consequence of which they were mostly removed
to Columbia, and placed in an old field, with only a single
guard-line around them. Captain Milton Russell took this
occasion to bribe a guard, with a silver pen-holder and gold
pen, to let him pass his "beat" one dark night. With a
rebel "ten dollar" bill the captain purchased a quart of salt
and some matches; he also baked his five days' rations of

corn-meal; and for a haversack, he tied the lower extremity of an old shirt with a string, and the sleeves together, to swing over his neck. Three days after, the same rebel soldier guarded the captain and several others outside the lines, to gather wood for fuel. At the first opportunity, the pen-holder changed hands, and the captain made a bee line for a pine thicket, through which he traveled four or five miles, when he reached a swamp. He waded into it several hundred yards, and found a large pine log, lying out of the water. Scarcely had he crawled onto it, before he heard some one walking in the water; and he thought of blood-hounds. Instead, however, it was Lieut. Frank A. Lakin, 18th Indiana, with whom he had been confined in various prisons, over a year. As soon as it was dark, they started, going through Lexington, and marching all night, entered another pine thicket; stopping near a pond, they raked some leaves together, and slept till near sunset. Then, washing in the pond, and drying on the leaves, they ate the corn-bread, which was the first morsel either had tasted for 24 hours. At dark they started again, and went all night. Next morning they caught a lamb, and killed and dressed it. That evening they passed through a sweet potato patch, which they relieved of half a bushel, and a little farther on they borrowed a big wash-kettle to cook them in. Two more nights they traveled without anything to eat, and were on the road the third night, when they came to a large plantation. Approaching a negro cabin, they peeped through the chinks, and saw an old negress spinning. At their knock the wheel stopped suddenly, as the old woman cried out,

"Who dat?"

"Friends."

"Whah you want?"

"We are Confederate soldiers, and nearly starved."

"Gemmen, ye can't fool dis chile. You's Yankees; case I see de buttons on dat jacket."

The officers owned up, and soon a bountiful supply of corn-bread and sweet potatoes was prepared. She also set before them a fine fat 'possum, nicely baked, which disappeared in a very short time. All the darkies came in to see them, bringing provisions. One volunteered to guide them ten miles. At the end of ten miles, he turned them over to another negro, who went five miles, and as it was near daylight, another took them half a mile to a dense pine thicket, where they lay concealed all day. At night the darkies came to them with corn-cake, fresh pork, sweet potatoes, cabbage and coffee; a feast the poor tramps did ample justice to. Going on till they came to Broad River, they plunged in, and though the water came to their necks, they succeeded in crossing. They now felt safe, and talked of the happiness of going home. But the following night they were discovered by blood-hounds, and surrounded by 25 of the rebel chivalry, armed with shot-guns, knives and clubs. The rebels seemed to think they had done the most gallant deed of the war; and swore that they would never submit to Yankee rule. The prisoners were marched to Anderson court-house, 17 miles distant, where they were kept five days. The negroes also were anxious to see the prisoners. One of them had a violin, on which he played some lively airs. Lieut. Lakin, being a musician, played "Yankee Doodle," which delighted the darkies. As they departed, they insisted on leaving the violin with the prisoners. This aroused the curiosity of the prisoners; and making examination, they found inside of the instrument, $39 in rebel currency. The prisoners were sent back to their old quarters at Columbia, which were known by the name of "Camp Sorghum," that was acquired on account of the rations issued there, consisting of two-thirds of a pint of coarse corn-meal, grain and cob ground together, unbolted, and a gill of sorghum molasses for each man.

In a few days Russell was ready for a second escape. With his share of the money taken from the old violin at

12

Anderson, he purchased salt and matches, and bribed a guard. Creeping for some distance beyond the guard-line, before rising, he started off on a dead run to some bushes; almost coming in contact with another man; both of them being scared almost out of their wits.

The other man was Frank Lakin!

They started at once for Knoxville, but near Anderson they met a negro, who told them of General Sherman's movements, and assured them that he was "bound to take Augusta." The negro was to start for Augusta next morning with a big wagon, and proposed to conceal them under a load of fodder, and take them there. Near Augusta, the fugitives left the wagon, crossed the Savannah River, and arrived at Millen next day; being directed continually by the negroes along the road. After many mishaps, escapes from blood-hounds, wet to the skin, tattered and torn, sore and nearly exhausted, they came to a railroad, where they found a hand-car, on which they started at full speed for Savannah. After going six miles, they had to abandon it, as the track was torn up. They had then eaten nothing for four days, save two ears of corn, and they reeled like drunken men, and fell by the side of the road, so fatigued that sleep soon overcame them. About daylight they were aroused by the drums in Sherman's camps. They forgot empty stomachs, weary limbs and sore feet; and springing up, they started with light hearts for the Union camp. In two hours they reached the picket line; and language fails to describe their feelings, as they again beheld the glorious old stars and stripes.

On the 12th of February, there were intimations from the rebel authorities at Columbia, that the Union prisoners would be there but a few days longer. On the 14th, about 600 were marched to the Charlotte depot, packed in stock cars, and consigned to Charlotte, North Carolina. In the confusion attending this transaction, Lieut. A. C. Roach and several others of the Provisional Brigade, whose names could not be learned, got separated from the crowd, and were reported "lost in transportation." They made their way to the Union lines; being aided in their dangerous undertaking by the darkness of a misty, moonless night. As their previous experience was similar to that of Captain Russell, their stories would be repetitions, possibly with as great a variety of personal horrors and sufferings as there were individuals.

The foregoing orders, reports, dispatches and communications, with those also that follow, are all taken from the Official War Records and from Colonel Streight's letters to his wife, and are intended to verify what has been said relative to the great Raid.

Brig. Gen. Wistar, on Peninsula, to Secretary Stanton:

"YORKTOWN, Feb. 14, 1864.

Two escaped Union officers have reached my pickets from Richmond. They report 109 more on the road. A general delivery of one prison-house was effected by digging a tunnel under the street. Gen. Dow could not stand the fatigue of the trip, and consequently did not come. My cavalry are in motion, scouring the Peninsula, to cover the escape of the rest. Several colonels, among them Col. Streight, are on the road; but the path is hard."

Wistar to Chief of Staff Dept. Va. and N. C.:

"YORKTOWN, Feb. 15, 1864.

Col. Streight is concealed in Richmond, but at large. His friends desire the papers to state his successful arrival here, for obvious reasons. Please arrange it immediately with the Associated Press agent."

Colonel Streight to Mrs. Streight:

"WASHINGTON, D. C., Feb. 29, 1864.

I have succeeded in making my escape from the enemy. Am much tired and worn out, but my general health is good, and I will soon be all right. I shall remain a short time here.   *   I cannot describe my feelings of gratification at once more being at liberty. I trust I will never again be a prisoner in the hands of our barbarous enemies.   *   I cannot tell you now of the many narrow chances I run of being recaptured. My feet are very sore, and my legs are stiff and much swollen, but I will be all right shortly."

A great many *wise* things were said, and many were the predictions made, by envious would-be leaders, about

the foolhardiness of the great Raid ; many ready to say, "I
told you so ; and each one of these great minds had a plan
by which they would have "whaled the daylights" out of
Forrest and Roddy, if they had been in command of that
expedition ; and they would have torn a hole in the map of
Alabama and Georgia big enough to empty the Gulf of
Mexico into. Yet, with all deference to those able fellows,
it is not at all likely that any one of them could have done
better, if as well, under similar circumstances. Doubtless,
however, there were *one hundred enlisted men in the Fifty-
First*, any one of whom, had he been assigned to the same
great duty, and been given *carte blanche* in the matter, to
exercise his own judgment in preparing for and conducting
the expedition, and had the support and co-operation that
was promised to Streight, would have made a magnificent
success of it. The great pity is that "human foresight is
not nearly as good as its hindsight."

One of the most remarkable papers preserved from the
rebel archives, is the resolution adopted by the rebel Congress, that is intended to compliment the notorious military
trickster and colossal liar, N. B. Forrest, but really magni-
fies Colonel Streight's expedition beyond all its friends
ever claimed for it :

"*Resolved by the Congress of the Confederate States of America,*
That the thanks of Congress are again due, and are hereby tendered, to
Gen. N. B. Forrest, and the officers and men of his command, for meri-
torious service in the field, and especially for the daring, skill and perse-
verance exhibited in the pursuit and capture of the largely superior forces
of the enemy near Rome, Ga., in May last.   Approved Feb.
17, 1864."

Forrest must have been a very insignificant officer, to
have been honored with no greater force than he is credited
with, or we must believe that the rebel Congress was very
ignorant and gullible, and accepted fully the extravagant
language of Forrest's lying report.

The following correspondence, which is also taken from
the Official War Records, explains itself :

Maj. Gen. B. F. Butler to Secretary Stanton :

"When Col. Streight was here I had conversation with him in regard to the transfer of himself and regiment to this department. The long residence of himself and officers in Richmond, and their knowledge of the city, will render them invaluable here at some day, which I hope is not far distant. May I ask that Col. Streight's regiment be sent here?"

Canby, A. A. G., to B. F. Butler :

"WASHINGTON CITY, April 5, 1864.

The Secretary of War directs me to acknowledge the receipt of your communication of the 28th ult., requesting that Col. Streight and his regiment might be transferred to your department, and to inform you in reply that he cannot consistently grant your request at present."

SEVENTY-THIRD INDIANA REGIMENT.

[From Adjutant General Terrell's Report, Vol. 2, p. 684.]

"On the 10th of April, 1863, the regiment was assigned to Col. A. D. Streight's 'Independent Provisional Brigade,' organized and mounted for the purpose of penetrating the enemy's country, and cutting his communications. Embarking at Nashville on steamers, it moved down the Cumberland, and up the Tennessee River, disembarking at Eastport, Miss. The brigade was mounted by impressments from the country, and moved by land by Tuscumbia, Ala., in company with Gen. Dodge's division of the 16th Army Corps. On the 28th of April, the brigade left Tuscumbia, on its perilous expedition. Gen. Dodge's division was to have co-operated by a movement eastward, but failed of success. On the morning of the 30th of April, at Day's Gap, Ala., the brigade, numbering 1,500, was attacked by 4,000 cavalry, under Forrest and Roddy. The 73d occupied the left flank of the line formed, and gallantly repulsed a fierce charge of the enemy, some of whom charged within twenty feet of its colors. The whole brigade then charged the enemy's line, and drove him from the field, capturing 2 fine pieces of artillery. The brigade at once pushed southward, to execute its mission; but the enemy, having collected his scattered cavalry, overtook and attacked the brigade late in the afternoon, at Crooked Creek, Ala. A spirited engagement was kept up until night closed the battle, with a loss to the 73d during the day of 23 killed and wounded. The enemy, however, was repulsed with a heavy loss.

On the 2d of May, the brigade was again attacked, at Blount's Farm, Ala. The 73d bore the brunt of this fight, and here the gallant Col. Gilbert Hathaway fell mortally wounded, while at the head of and cheering on his men. On the 3d of May, Col. Streight being nearly out of ammunition, and exhausted by five days' incessant traveling and skirmishing, and surrounded by superior forces, surrendered his brigade to the enemy, at Cedar Bluffs, Ala., on most honorable conditions, which, after surrender, were basely violated by the enemy. The men were soon forwarded north and exchanged. The officers were kept in close confinement nearly two years, with the exception of a few who were specially exchanged or escaped.

The men of the regiment were kept in parole camp for several months, and then sent to Tennessee."

THE DETACHMENT "AT THE FRONT."

Just before the Fifty-First started on the Raid, the writer of this book was detailed as assistant to Capt. John W. Aughe, of the 40th Indiana, A. A. I. G. on General Wagner's staff, and arrived at Murfreesboro on Saturday, April 11, 1863. He remained there till the exchanged portion of the regiment returned to the front, at Chattanooga, when he rejoined his company. In consequence of this, his experience embraces all that was common to the men of Wagner's brigade, which included many more of the Fifty-First, as will be seen further on.

In the latter part of June, Wagner's 2d Brigade, 1st Division, 21st Army Corps, to which the detachments of the Fifty-First in the field were attached, broke camp at Murfreesboro, and proceeded to Chattanooga, by way of Manchester and Pelham, down the beautiful Sequatchie Valley, and over Walden's Ridge. The private notes of the writer detail his own personal experience in entering Chattanooga and establishing the first picket lines, and in witnessing and participating in the famous battles of Lookout Mountain, Chicamauga and Missionary Ridge, and are of little interest in this particular connection. A few of these, however, are deemed necessary in order to "complete the roundness of the organic unity" of the Fifty-First, as Van Horne's history attributes to the Department of the Cumberland as the cause of the 4th Corps going to Texas.

August 30, 1863, found Wagner's brigade on Walden's Ridge, a rocky range extending from the north side of the Tennessee, about 8 miles northwest from Chattanooga, to the head of Sequatchie Valley, 80 or 90 miles northeast. Here all the Fifty-First boys, except the writer, with Capt.

Haley in command, started for Indianapolis, to join the regiment; going with a wagon train to Stevenson, 50 miles, and thence by railroad. In a few days more Wagner's brigade advanced upon Chattanooga, the battery shelling the town. Next day the town was deserted by the rebels. Captain Aughe, Inspector, and Hartpence, his assistant, rode 8 miles up the river, to a ford, where Colonel Wilder was crossing with his mounted infantry; coming down on the other side to the city. In this way the Fifty-First was represented among the very first to enter that city. And further, the first picket line established in front of Chattanooga by the Union army, was located in person by this same inspector and assistant, on Wednesday afternoon, September 9, 1863.

A WAR TROPHY.

Henry Watterson, now editor of the Louisville *Courier Journal*, was at this time publishing the Chattanooga *Rebel*, and had his office in a little dingy second-story room on the east side of Main street. He had come there from Cincinnati, where he was a sort of dramatic editor on the *Times*. The *Times* was a Republican organ, and Watterson was a Democrat, with political aspirations; so he packed his kit, and moved to Nashville, and then to Chattanooga, where he started a regular sensational blood-thirsty rebel sheet. When the Union forces entered that city, he hastily loaded his office in a wagon, and went along with the rebel army, printing his little paper at irregular intervals. In his hurried departure he forgot a few unimportant articles, among them a composing-stick, a little steel box-like instrument used by printers to set type in. The writer, familiar with its use, captured it as a trophy of war; and observing the unities, every line of this book, up to this point, has been set in that stick.

MOSES.

We had with us an old negro, an ideal "Uncle Tom."

He cooked for one of the headquarters messes, and did odd chores. He was a good old man, and very religious; and said he had been a Baptist preacher. He could not read a word, but had learned a great many passages of Scripture, after a style, by hearing others read or quote them. Oft-times the boys would gather around him in the evening, and start him off on the subject of religion. He would take it up with great earnestness, and became eloquent as he warmed to it. The following is a sample. It was taken verbatim at the time of delivery, and read to the old man; and he declared, "dat's kerect, an' jes' as it wus delive'd unto me:"

"Foh God so lub'd de wul, dat He made de wul in six days, an' all things dar-in. Now God am a jes' God, an' He will do jestice by ebery one ob He chillun, fum de smalles' to de greates'. Ef day will ony come to Him wid insinceriousness ob heart, He will hoveh 'em in de holler ob His han' as a hen 'd hoveh her brood. Foh He so lub'd de wul, dat He made de wul in six days, an' all de things dar-in. Now, ye caint see dis as I sees hit, case ye ain't been whah I's been. I's been away up yandeh, on de oder side ob de riber Jawdan, an' I's tasted ob de hidden manual, an' I's had my name wrote down in de Lamb's Book ob Life. Foh I seed de Lo'd write it down on He ve'y knee. I went ober de riber, an' I crost on de benches whah was put ober by de angels in de wite roves. Dere I seed de Lo'd, He who is de ony fo'gotten Son. Now ye caint see dis, case ye is all sinnehs, an' is in de dawkness ob sin, an' I kin see all ye sins. Foh de light shines in de dawkness, an' de dawkness comperhendest de light not. An' I hab eahs to heah, an' to heah not. I heah not wot de debil say, but I heahs wot de Lo'd say; an' I heah de sweet music ob His voice, an' de fine singin' ob de angels in de wite roves; an' dey sing dese words:

'Now, de ve'y nex' blessin dat Mary bah,
'Twus de blessin' ob two;

To think dat her son Jesus
  Could read de Bible thoo.
He could read de Bible thoo,
  Like Amanuel an' glo-ri be,
Fatheh, Son-an' de Holy Ghos'
  Thoo all eternitee.'

Now, I's not got no book lawnin', nur cain't read 'bout
dis in de Bible; but it's dar. Jes' look yeh Bible, an' dar
it is — dar yo'll fin' it. An' dar He say, too, 'Behol'! lo,
hab I come down in dis sin-'based wul, into de vulgah ob
dy Book, written to do dy will, O. God!' Now, ye is all
sin-based, an' de light is not in ye. De debil done got ye
a'ready. Ye run afteh de lus' ob de debil, an' afteh de
weemen, an' afteh gol' an' fine clo's. But de debil git ye,
sho'. Foh in de great jedgment day ye will hab to gib a
incount ob all de deeds w'at's in de body; an' de good will
be casted ober on de right side, an' de bad will be casted
on de lef' side. Now, I's a Babtis', an' I knows de road.
Well, I's wande'd fum de paf, but I knows whah it is. I
was 'ticed by de weemen, an' de lus' ob de debil, an' I fo'-
got to look on de Fatheh. Oh, weemen is de fruit ob all
evil! I knows it fum sperience. Now, right ober heah da
wus a man whuh lub a woman, an' wanted to git married
to her; an' dey wouldn' let him go home; an' so he jis'
got desput, an' went an' shot hese'f thoo wid a pistil, case
dey-all wouldn' let 'im exert (desert) an' go home. Dat's
on 'count ob de weemen. 'Pend on it, ye mus' let dese
bad things 'lone, an' look on de Fatheh, an' pray to Him.
Foh He is a jes' God, an' a good God, an' ye mus'·pray to
Him an' His on'y fo'gotten Son. Foh God so lub'd de wul,
dat He made de wul in six days, an' all things dar-in.''

THE MORGAN RAID.

When the Fifty-First and the 73d Indiana regiments
reported at Indianapolis for duty, they were sent to Camp
Carrington, and placed under the command of Capt. D.
W. Hamilton, of the 7th Indiana, then in command of the

camp, who proceeded to form the two regiments into companies, all together forming one regiment of 500 able for duty. The infamous "Democratic Mass Convention" was held there, and the guerrilla John Morgan thought it an auspicious time to make a raid through Indiana and Ohio, and our command was there in time to join in the chase after the chivalrous mob, and to aid in holding the copperheads in check. The two arch-traitors, Tom Hendricks and Dan Voorhees, had matured the scheme of having a grand rally at the capital, on June 24, 1863, release the rebel prisoners at Camp Morton, seize the arsenal, arm the rebels, kill Governor Morton, and then march to meet John Morgan, who was then in Kentucky, and had started on his infamous raid. On the night of June 23, Capt. Hamilton was ordered to take the regiment at midnight, and march as quietly as possible to the arsenal grounds, located on Market street, just north of the old State House, which was surrounded by a high board fence, where the soldiers could not be seen by those on the streets. There they laid on that 24th of June, and through the cracks of the fence, saw that traitorous mob gather· by thousands, in the State House yard, and listen to the speeches of their leaders, display their butternut breastpins and other traitorous emblems, and swagger and strut, and heard them perfecting their murderous plans. Our boys could only communicate in whispers or in pantomime. While these speeches were being made, two of our boys who had been at home, had returned, and not finding the command in camp, started out in search, taking their guns with them. In the rounds they brought up in the State House yard, with fixed bayonets. While going through the crowd, one of them saw a butternut breastpin on the breast of one of the traitors, and with one clutch snatched it off, at the same time knocking the miscreant down with his fist. This of course created a great commotion. The immense crowd of cowardly curs, seeing guns with bayonets, and supposing that they were surrounded by an army, were struck with horror. The panic which ensued, cannot be described. They made one wild tumultuous rush east, falling over each other in trying to scale the low plank fence that enclosed the yard; the pressure being so great, that the posts were broken off near the ground, and the fence thrown flat, from Market street to Washington.

While this wild scene was being enacted, the speakers on the stand turned deathly pale with fear, and being near a window of the State House, slipped quickly through it, ran along the corridor north to Market street, across that street; then turning east, they sneaked along the fence behind which our boys were concealed. Our boys were wild to get over the fence after the fleeing scoundrels, and it was all Capt. Hamilton could do to restrain them, running up and down the line with drawn sword, making all sorts of gestures, but not daring to speak out. So those two chief traitors narrowly escaped, though well deserving death.

The butternut breastpin was given to Capt. Hamilton, who retained possession of it in 1894.

The great mob of traitors hurried to their trains, but recovered from their scare too soon; for, thinking that the danger was over, they began firing off their pistols. This was the signal for what is known in history as the "Battle of Pogue's Run."

In a day or two after this, Captain Hamilton received an order to take the regiment and proceed by railroad to Louisville, Ky., and report to General Boyle, as guerrilla John Morgan was said to be near that city with his raiders. When the regiment arrived there, they found the citizens greatly excited. General Boyle sent our command out on the Bardstown pike about two miles, with orders to throw out strong pickets, and hold the pike at all hazards. They held the pike, but Morgan failed to put in an appearance. After lying there one day, our boys were directed to cross the Ohio River to New Albany, and proceed to Edwards-ville, five miles below that city. There they were held till Morgan had plenty of time to cross the river. Our command was anxious to pursue him, and harass his flanks, but was not permitted. After Morgan had got under fair headway, our command was ordered to Jeffersonville, to report to General Manson. Here they were put on a transport, and steamed up the river, in company with five other boats loaded with Union troops. The aim was to travel up the river as fast as Morgan was going on land, while Gen. Hobson pressed him in the rear; also to prevent him from recrossing the river, which he was making a great effort to do, since he had learned of Dan Voorhees failure to materialize with his 100,000 "butternut" traitors, promised to the South.

Right here, it may be confidently said that this raid made more Union men of Democrats, than anything that had occurred since the war began.

Proceeding to Portsmouth, Ohio, our men were taken from the transports, and put on cars and run back into the country, to intercept Morgan, and strike him on his flank; but he had passed the point where they aimed to strike, and Hobson's men were just coming up. Taking the cars again, they returned to Portsmouth. Next morning word came that Morgan had surrendered; and thus the chase ended.

Smallpox, or varioloid, having broken out among the Fifty-First, General Manson ordered Captain Hamilton to re-embark and proceed at once to Cincinnati, and report to General Burnside. This was done, and General Burnside ordered our command to go to Madison, and there go into quarantine. The sick were sent to a hospital a few miles below Madison, and the rest of the regiment returned to Indianapolis.

Captain Hamilton was then directed to take command at Camp Morton, and to use the Fifty-First to guard rebel prisoners in that place. In a few hours Morgan's men began to arrive, and were added to those already confined.

During their stay at this place, the Fifty-First showed their appreciation of Captain Hamilton's interest in their welfare, by presenting him with a handsome sword. The captain had the sword in 1891, still nicely preserved, and he prized it very highly. The 73d boys gave him a fine horse and saddle, which he preserved till old age took the faithful animal to the pastures green prepared for all good horses.

The origin of "Whar's Morgan?" was in a little incident that occurred one night, in Southern Indiana, during this chase after the guerrillas. C. P. Cox and Allen Godfrey were together, and the former having tarried too long at the apple-jack, about midnight he was stretched out on some brush, feeling like he could clean out the whole rebel army, and calling out,

"Fry, Fry! whar's Mawgan? I can whup 'im!" This became a by-word, and was afterward communicated to the entire corps.

SIEGE OF CHATTANOOGA.

In the latter part of September, 1863, the troops at Chattanooga began to experience distress for food. Their "cracker-line" was disturbed by rebel guerrilla bands. It was pitiful, to see the hungry boys, whenever the wagon trains came in from Stephenson, with a meager supply for that great army, watching for every bit of cracker as big as their finger-nail that might be dropped in unloading, and holding their hats under the wagon to catch whatever might fall; following forage wagons for squares with the hope that an ear of corn, or a few grains even, might be jolted out. Horses and mules were dying daily from starvation, while hundreds that survived were unfit for service. It is estimated that 10,000 animals died during this siege. A secret conference was held one night, at Gen. Wagner's headquarters, of the corps and division commanders, at which the writer was present. It was then discovered that in no command was there a mouthful of food, except what was in the men's haversacks, save that of General Wood, and that was only three days' rations. This condition was relieved at long intervals, by half or quarter rations, according to the success or failure of our supply trains in getting through. This continued till the capture of Lookout Mountain and the valley reopened transportation.

BATTLE OF MISSIONARY RIDGE.

The battle of Lookout Mountain was witnessed by the members of the Fifty-First at Chattanooga, and was a magnificent spectacle. They did not participate in it, however, nor in the bloody struggle at Chicamauga. They did take part in the most important event of the campaign, the famous charge on Missionary Ridge, and Wood's division won for itself special glory on that day. On this account, it will not be inappropriate to insert a description of that battle, as it appeared in the Nashville *Union* of Sunday, November 29, written on the 26th, the day after the fight:

"The operations of the army in front of this place, during the last three days, have been not only of a brilliant, but of a decisive character. Hitherto we had struggles—bitter, stubborn and bloody; but when the tragedy had ended, the combatants retained their organizations, and too frequently their positions. But not so in this instance. With the exception of the Mississippi campaign, this is the first time that a rebel army, with comparatively trifling loss to our own, has been demoralized, broken, crushed.

Sherman, having arrived at a point opposite the mouth of the Chicamauga, and four miles above the town, the orders were issued, and the plan of attack made known to the corps commanders, and each directed to execute his portion strictly in accordance with it.

The first object was to deceive the rebels.   *   Sherman made a feint of moving up the north bank of the river, as if to attack Longstreet, and relieve Burnside, while the Eleventh Corps was moved into Chattanooga. Simultaneously with these movements, and on the eve of the 23d, our lines, opposite the rebel right and right center, were extended three-quarters of a mile, and beyond the outer line of rebel rifle-pits, which were captured, with three hundred prisoners, by a brilliant and unexampled dash of Hazen's and Willich's brigades of Wood's division, of the 4th Army Corps. Our loss in this skirmish was slight, while the positions gained were of the highest importance. From thence the foot of Missionary Ridge was plainly visible, and the nature of the ground readily ascertained. The enemy was completely deceived by the happy combination of strategy.

From Fort Wood, on the east of Chattanooga, the movements of the rebels could be distinctly seen with glasses. The movements in this direction had been completed at dark, and the rebels lay upon their arms for the night, confidently expecting, if not a general engagement, at least a severe skirmish at daylight of the 24th. But they were seriously disappointed. No sooner had darkness set in, than Ewing's and Osterhaus' divisions of Sherman's corps, and a part of Cruft's division of the Fourth Corps, which had been supposed to be engaged in other duties, filed along the foot of Lookout Mountain, and took up a position to make an attack on the following morning.

The rebels did not discover the arrival of these reinforcements until about midnight; and by that time it was too late to reinforce their left. At 7 o'clock in the morning, Geary's division crossed the creek, and began the ascent of the mountain. Their progress was at first seriously resisted; but an incessant shower of shot and shell from our batteries on the hights so gallantly won by Hooker some weeks ago, soon had the effect to drive them, and to enable our columns to swing around and sweep the whole western slope, from the ledge to the foot.

The rebels, for at least two miles, resisted every foot of our progress, from behind rifle-pits, rocks and trees; but having been driven to a point nearly opposite the railroad bridge, when Osterhaus commenced ascending the Ridge, the rebels finding themselves utterly overpowered, fled precipitately and in confusion. The guns from our batteries played upon them with terrific effect; and hundreds threw down their arms, and surrendered themselves prisoners.

In the meantime Sherman had crossed the river on the night of the 23d, near the mouth of the Chickamauga, and on the 24th he occupied and fortified one of the knobs at the northern terminus of Missionary Ridge; and Howard's 11th Corps had been moved to the left, to effect a junction. This was accomplished with slight skirmishing, and comparatively little loss, and our lines were rendered solid from left to right.

During the night of the 24th, Ewing's division crossed from Lookout Mountain, and joined Sherman.

The morning of the 25th found both armies preparing for action. It was apparent that the conflict would be no longer delayed. Ere the sun disappeared, the great struggle—not for Chattanooga merely, but East Tennessee, would be decided. In proportion to the importance of the stake, would be the stubbornness of the struggle.

At 10 o'clock in the morning, Sherman made a feint on Tunnel Hill, an important position from which Missionary Ridge could be raked at any point within cannon shot. The charge lasted an hour, in which a number, say 150, were killed and wounded. General Corse fell dead gallantly fighting at the head of his column, and Col. Loomis received a slight wound. Our forces then fell back to the rifle-pits.

Believing this to be a real assault, the rebels continued to mass their forces in that direction; and to confirm their opinions, large bodies of troops were moved from the camps at Chattanooga, through an opening into the Tennessee Valley, in full view of Bragg's headquarters, as if intended to reinforce Sherman; and then having reached a thick growth of timber, they were countermarched and placed in the woods, opposite the rebel center.

At noon a second attack on Tunnel Hill was ordered, and Matthias' brigade charged up the hill. Having nearly reached the summit, they were met by a superior force of the enemy, and a fight of three quarters of an hour ensued.   *   A flank movement on the part of the rebels, at length compelled them to break, and a disorderly rout ensued. The rebels pushed on with vigor, and captured 200 prisoners, who were afterward retaken

After this movement, a thundering sound from the Parrots and Rodmans in Fort Wood, announced the commencement of the contest in the center. Our columns, which had hitherto been concealed behind the underbrush which skirts the eastern side of the Chattanooga valley, now pushed out, presenting a bold and solid front to the enemy. This movement was designed to break the rebel center, and the task was assigned to Generals Baird, Wood, Sheridan and Johnston, whose divisions were posted from left to right, in the order named,   *   *

Opposite the center were posted forty pieces of cannon, in eight commanding positions, and it was made the duty of one brigade to charge upon and capture each battery. The interval between the timber and the front of the mountain was soon passed, but the ascent was a matter of great difficulty. The sides of the hill were exceedingly steep, and covered with loose rock, and many places with briars and underbrush; and as a consequence, one could scarcely reach the summit uninjured. But our brave heroes neither halted nor faltered, though exposed to the fire of the whole line of infantry, on the summit of the ridge, and all the batteries in front of them, and a raking fire from Tunnel Hill which did frightful execution. Steadily, however, they proceeded; each brigade vieing with its rivals in the effort to be the first to place the old standard upon the spots desecrated by the rebel ensign.

They were half way up. The deadly missiles thickened around them; but onward they went; they nearly reached the top; the artillery could no longer be used against them; the bayonets of the rebels were fixed, and a hand to hand struggle commenced.

At length a shout was heard, and a thrill of horror ran through the rebel ranks; the heart of every loyal man beat high; *the 79th Indiana regiment had planted its banner upon the summit of the ridge!*

The strong arms of the assailants were nerved to renewed efforts; their bold spirits incited to greater deeds of daring. Further suspense was but momentary; one long, loud and hearty shout arose; and all was over. Missionary Ridge was ours!"

LIEUT.-COL. COMPARET' TAKES COMMAND.

At some time in November, 1863, Lieut.-Col. John M. Comparet', of the 15th Indiana, then at Chattanooga, was ordered to proceed to Nashville, and prepare for the field the Fifty-First, which had been sent there some time previous, but was unfit to go to the front, because our officers were mostly in Libby Prison yet.

The weather was cold when Lt.-Col. Comparet' started from Chattanooga, accompanied by Lieut. Benj. Owens, of Co. E, 57th Indiana. The road had been opened as far as Bridgeport, Tenn. There they took a car for Nashville; where, in company with the adjutant of the post, the new commander went out to see the boys. Walking leisurely through the camp, the officer, who was not very tall, overheard one of the boys inquire, "Is that little cuss going to command the regiment?" He paid no attention to this, save to be amused; and seeing the condition of things, he took immediate command, and proceeded to put the regiment in order, so as to be prepared to march at a moment's notice. They were first fitted out in all things pertaining to a campaign — a train of wagons and mules, ten teams, and the men properly equipped. Soon a telegram came from Gen. Jos. Reynolds, General Thomas' chief of staff, directing the new commander to proceed to Knoxville, with supplies for General Burnside. The order stated the number of wagons, and included a squadron of cavalry; but it was countermanded, and the regiment was finally ordered to Chattanooga, there to join a brigade to which it would be assigned. The command started immediately: making fine marches by way of Murfreesboro, Shelbyville, Tullahoma and Bridgeport, thence over Walden's Ridge. The boys were in fine condition, and all as merry as a picnic party. Sometimes the woods and hills re-echoed with the

13

strains of "John Brown's Body," "Rally Round the Flag,"
etc. The march was divided into rests of from ten to fifteen minutes each hour, and 1½ hours at noon, with good
camps at night.

One day one of the boys came walking into camp with
a nice pig impaled on his bayonet. It was not long before
a poor widow, who lived near by, made her way to regimental headquarters, and reported the case. The soldier
was ordered to carry it back, and pack it for her. "And,"
continued the kind-hearted little lieutenant-colonel, "if she
hasn't any salt, get some!" The order was obeyed, too.
When the boys came to realize the character of their commander, they stood up to him faithfully.

The command made an average of 20 miles per day,
and reached Chattanooga just after the battle of Missionary Ridge; about December 10. In a few days after, they
were ordered to join their corps. There were a number of
convalescents of the various regiments there, and they had
formed in their various brigades. These, with the Fifty-
First, were all ordered to report to Col. Bernard Laiboldt,
of the 2d Missouri, who was directed to guard a supply
train. Colonel Laiboldt took command, and soon got his
forces strung out on the road, and started east. The first
halt was at Cleveland, camping for the night. About 1
o'clock that night, Hospital Steward Smith went to Comparet' and advised him that they were about to be attacked.
He had been out visiting in the neighborhood, and got his
information from the family of guerrilla Wheeler's quartermaster, who thought J. P. was a spy for rebel Gen. Joe
Johnson. Smith was sent to Colonel Laiboldt with the
information; and Col. Comparet', without waiting, got the
regiment in line, with skirmishers out, ready to receive the
enemy. It commenced raining about the same time, but
the boys kept their places all night; cooking breakfast by
detail; and vigilant watch was observed for the encounter.
But the johnnies failed to appear.

Soon daylight came, and with it the order to march. Rain and mud! No wonder that the old veteran now has rheumatism, and his life is shortened many years. Long exposure, sunstroke, rain, mud, cold, ice, etc., were more than enough to bring down those of the best health to the grave.

BATTLE OF CHARLESTON.

On the night of December 26, they reached Charleston, on the Hiawassee River, and camped along a ridge of cedar brake. The rain had subsided, and the next morning was ushered in with beautiful sunshine; cheering the hearts of all the boys. It soon became apparent, however, that a fight was near at hand. Comparet', who was standing by Laiboldt, heard firing down the valley, and called the commander's attention to it. He then ran over the bridge, to where the Fifty-First was, and threw the regiment into line, to cover and protect the train. There were with the detachment 100 wagons, loaded with supplies; and to secure them, Colonel Laiboldt ordered the teamsters to take the entire train down the bank into the bottom, and make their way out as best they could.

The valley was a beautiful one, about 400 yards wide, and a mile long; a most magnificent view of which might be had from where the regiment was.

The guerrilla Wheeler, with 1,500 men was approaching, with the confident expectation of easily capturing our supply train. Soon the rebels came in sight. Wheeler had divided his forces, throwing some on our right. Comparet' immediately dispatched Co. A to that part of the field, so as to confront their movements; also Co. B was sent to the left. Word was sent to Colonel Wilder's camp, then at Calhoun. All of his command was out scouting; but Col. Eli Long, in command of the 2d Brigade, 2d Cavalry Division, came to their assistance with a few men. In addition to these, all of our own headquarters orderlies and clerks were put in; and they made a handsome line across

the valley. The bugle sounded the charge; and the result
was great. Our brave boys routed the enemy, taking 131
prisoners, including 5 officers, one a division inspector and
one a surgeon. The number of killed and wounded could
not be ascertained. Colonel Long's loss was 2 killed, 12
wounded, and 1 missing. Our immediate command went
through the fight without a casualty, save a few saber cuts.

To solve a seeming difficulty, it is deemed necessary to
state here that Charleston is situated on the south side of
Hiawassee River, a few miles east of where that stream
empties into the Tennessee, and at a point where the little
river is crossed by the Knoxville Railroad. Calhoun is on
the north side of the Hiawassee, and is the next station on
the same railroad. The fight was at Charleston.

Wheeler commanded in person, and anticipated a rich
prize, with little trouble or loss.

[Extract from Col. Eli Long's Report.]

"On the morning of the 28th [December] a wagon train which had
arrived at Charleston the evening before under escort   *   of Gen.
Sheridan's command, and commanded by Col. Laiboldt, was attacked
by Gen. Wheeler with about 1,500 rebel cavalry. As soon as I was made
aware of the attack, I mounted the small portion of my command not
on duty (less than 150 men,) and as soon as the train had crossed the
bridge, moved over the river. Col. Laiboldt was now sharply engaged,
and soon had the enemy's lines wavering. I then drew sabers and
charged, driving before me a force of some 400 or 500; pursued them to
Chatata Creek, capturing 121 prisoners, including 5 officers, and many
stands of arms. The enemy lost several killed and quite a number
wounded; among the latter 2 colonels. The main rebel column retreated
out the Dalton road.   *   *   *

Our command then resumed its line of march; going
into camp in the neighborhood of Calhoun. On the way,
Laiboldt stated to Comparet' that he had sent Wheeler a
message, saying:

"This day have you been whipped by a d— Dutchman.   LAIBOLDT, Colonel commanding."

Next day the command took up its line of march for
the Tennessee River, and arrived at Loudon on New Year's

day, with four inches of snow on the ground, and still falling. They camped in the outskirts of the village, in the neighborhood of a church building. A detail was made of men and wagons, and they soon had the snow removed, and the boys all in fine spirits. They stayed there about five days; long enough for the boys to get acquainted, and leave behind them regrets. The commander complimented the Fifty-First boys on their good behavior, and said they were always gentlemen, and showed a disposition to encourage neighborly feeling. They made themselves such a name, that their return was gladly hailed.

The command crossed Tennessee River on the morning of January 6, 1864, and marched toward Knoxville; where the train was turned over to Burnside's ordnance officer.

The Fifty-First, now joined with Newton's brigade, of Sheridan's division, continued with that command to Dandringe, where our boys had a fight on Sunday evening, December 20. After the siege of Knoxville was raised, it went to Strawberry Plains, in the vicinity of the French Broad River, where among other hardships, spoiled flour was issued, which had the effect to make the boys deathly sick, and set them to vomiting in a few minutes after eating the bread made of it.

Lilly's 18th Indiana Battery was also in the fight at Dandridge, and did fine execution.

Then orders came to retrace their steps. Longstreet had fled the country, and having seen him off, our boys were needed elsewhere. They had a bad morning to start on; during the night before it had rained, and froze as it fell; so that everything was covered with a coat of ice.

THE FIFTY-FIRST VETERANIZES.

They then reached Knoxville, on their return to Loudon, for winter quarters. While at Knoxville, the Fifty-First took a notion to re-enlist. The order from the War Department was out, but was not distinctly understood; no one had seen it — only heard of it. Lieut.-Col. Comparet' sought information of General Sheridan, who commanded the corps. and who was camped but a short distance away ; but found him no better posted than himself. So it was concluded to wait patiently till the order came.

Arriving in London, on Friday, January 7, 1864, the Fifty-First was camped promiscuously about. The second day, in the afternoon, the regiment was ordered into line ; and while on the march, General Sheridan rode along and directed that all who desired to re-enlist as "veterans," in accordance with the order promulgated by the War Department, the provisions of which he proceeded to explain, to report under heavy marching orders. This was just about to be executed ; the call was made ; when almost the entire regiment stepped out. The quartermaster was dispatched to the general, stating that if the regiment had an opportunity, it would rather go as an organization ; and it would be better. The request was granted ; and the next morning, Sunday, the regiment marched out of camp, with flags waving and bands playing ; creating great excitement all over the camp. They were met at the river by an aid, and requested to visit headquarters ; which was complied with. The general stated that it would be impossible to let them go for a day or two, on account of rations. On Tuesday morning, however, they started for Chattanooga ; and on arrival there, reported to be mustered into the "veteran" service. The non-commissioned officers, of which the regiment had a good staff, and also the officers, all manifested great interest in carrying out the orders, and in getting up the rolls in good style and condition. It was a big task, but ready hands made quick work of it.

At this point, Hartpence, who had been released from the inspector's department at his own solicitation, rejoined the regiment, and was one of the most active workers ; his ready pen having the honor of filling out all the "veteran discharges" in his own company, beside much other more important work. Captain Anderson, who had returned to the front a few days previous, also rejoined the regiment here, and was very useful in assisting the commander.

The next thing was the pay, accompanied with which was to be a thirty days' furlough home. To the writer, who had been right at the front continuously for nearly two years and a half, without a sight of "God's country," the thought of going home was inspiration enough, without the additional honor that attached to the title of "veteran."

There were probably as many motives for re-enlistment — in addition to that of patriotism, pure and simple, as there were individuals. With a few it was a "fad," that they followed as naturally as many did the introduction of the steel collar. To the writer it came at a time when his heart was brimming with gratitude to God for the recovery of his brother, who was so badly wounded in the battle of Missionary Ridge, and who he had promised, in the event of such recovery, to devote his life to the great cause of the Union. Some hesitated till the example of others carried them over the ripple. Others held out to the very last; and only yielded when they saw the boys pack their traps, and start off. There was a sort of heroic display in that, they could not resist; and hustling their stuff together, they joined the jolly crowd, as they swung off to the tune of "Johnny comes marching home."

Those who remained behind, consoled themselves with the assurance that they "knew when they had enough;" and in response to the "good-bye" of the "veterans," they said, with an attempt at cheerfulness, "Our turn 'll come before long."

Loaded in cattle cars, reeking with vile odors, we mingled the delectable perfume with our songs and cheers, and were happy. There were few things that fell to the lot of soldiers, which we had not experienced; and it would have taken a great deal more to deter us from our purpose now. Had duty called in an opposite direction, not one of that crowd would have hesitated. That was the sort of stuff "veterans" were made of. It had required those years of severe testing, of disappointment, heart-break, fatigue and deprivation, and all the sympathy for each other in mutual suffering, to bring them up to that high standard of perfection : and there was in it a rare exemplification of "the survival of the fittest." They could always be relied on. And the Government recognized that fact. We were not alone ; our experiences in camp, on the march, on the field of battle, on picket, in bivouac and in prison, were similar to those of many thousands, who in the nobility of their young manhood, underwent all those things necessary to make them veterans. No extra coloring is needed, nor is there any exaggeration in this narrative. Indeed,

"The half has never yet been told;"

nor will it be, by the boys whose heroism and nobility of manhood stands unexampled in the history of the world. Think of private soldiers, just out of school, or half way through their apprenticeship in a printing office or a carpenter shop, becoming such adepts in the art of war, as to command great armies, and by their masterly conduct of a campaign, to astonish the whole world with their wonderful accomplishments ! Quite frequently there were privates in the ranks, who were much more capable of handling a regiment or a brigade, than some of those who through influence were assigned to such commands.

A MERITED TESTIMONIAL.

The following paragraph, which is full of encouragement to all the brave boys to whom it applies, is from Van Horne's History of the Army of the Cumberland :

"There were now in the Army of the Cumberland a large number of re-enlisted troops. During the winter and spring there re-enlisted 85 regiments of infantry, 3 of mounted infantry, 16 of cavalry, 18 batteries of artillery, and 26 detachments of all arms, and 8,136 recruits in the aggregate were added to these organizations while on furlough. The importance of the re-enlistment of these troops can not be overestimated.

Without them and the "veterans" of the other two co-operative armies, the Atlanta campaign could not have been safely undertaken; the war would have been greatly postponed, and its issue might have been different. The slow movement of the draft, and the provisional measure of short enlistments could not have furnished such troops as were demanded in the spring of 1864. Without the veterans, aggression could not have been entertained, and the feeble armies, during the summer, might have been compelled to relax their grasp upon the heart of the rebellious states. It is then the plainest duty of the historian to mention the regiments and other organizations, whose members, in whole or in part, re-enlisted as "veteran volunteers," and ever after bore the grandest name which the war originated."

Then follows a list of regiments and batteries whose organizations were continued under re-enlistment; and the Fifty-First takes its place in the front rank.

As a badge of honorable distinction, "service chevrons" were furnished by the War Department, to be worn by the "veterans." This chevron consisted of a red strip of worsted braid, about 12 inches long and seven-eighths of an inch wide, on which a strip of blue worsted braid, the same length and half an inch wide, was sewed; this was doubled in the shape of a V, and tacked on the left coat sleeve.

Lieut.-Col. Comparet' called on the paymaster, and told him that if he would give us drafts on Louisville or Indianapolis, we could draw our money there, and the men could be paid at the end of the journey. All went well till we arrived at Louisville. Captain Anderson had been sent ahead to procure the funds, but the colonel had neglected to sign the drafts, which were drawn in his name. This was corrected, however, immediately on our arrival at Louisville, and the money was drawn. Anderson was made custodian of the funds, assisted by Lieutenant Scearce and Captain Haley. While the officers were getting things in order, so that there would be no interruption, when we got to Indianapolis, some Jews got among the boys, and incited some of them to compel the payment of the money there; and when the colonel entered the barracks where the regiment was, two stepped forward, with bayonets fixed, and demanded their money. Several other soldiers rushed to the officer's defence, and taking possession of their guns, put them under arrest. It was pouring down rain; but it was determined to get away from there at once. So, "attention" was called, and out into the rain we glided, down to the river, and across to the depot. The train was there, waiting for us; but we had to wait for our treasurer. He joined us as the engine backed down; and soon we were on our "winding way" to the Hoosier metropolis. Colonel Comparet' had telegraphed to Governor Morton that we would be there at 1 A. M., and we arrived on time. It was cold, and snow covered the hills. The engineer gave us a good run. While the boys waited for orders, Lieutenant Murray visited the "Soldiers' Home," a large frame structure arranged for the accommodation and convenience of the Indiana soldiers on such occasions. He returned soon, reporting that all was ready for us. The boys got in line and marched to the "Home," where they met a very warm reception. Everything was cheerful: great stoves, red hot; the boys were served with hot coffee; then laid down and rested till morning; when they got out, washed up and got ready for business. In the meantime, Comparet' and Anderson had gone to the Occidental Hotel, on the southeast corner of Washington and Illinois streets, and secured a room; where the officers in command of companies were summoned to meet at 7 A. M., with their pay-rolls. Then payment was begun, Anderson and Murray disbursing the money. The money for each company was handed to its commander, and he in turn disbursed it to the men. As the paying-off proceeded, the colonel busied himself with getting furloughs and transportation. Soon the boys were paid off, and had their furloughs; and the colonel had so dated the papers, as to give the boys three days more than they were entitled to.

Governor Morton had inaugurated a system of "recep-

GOVERNOR O. P. MORTON.

tions," which contributed very much to the gratification of
the loyal heart of the people, and the encouragement of
returning soldiers. On the arrival of a regiment, or any
regular organization of troops, a public dinner was prepared, and the regiment to be received was escorted, with
appropriate music, and other demonstrations, to the Capital grounds, or some public hall, where patriotic speeches
were made, praising the brave boys, and welcoming them
home. These occasions were always enlivened and greatly
enhanced by the presence of large numbers of ladies, who
did their best to serve the gallant boys with the delicious
things on the tables, meanwhile engaging with them in animated conversation. Songs were frequently introduced,
and clubs and choirs often favored the soldiers with fine
programs of patriotic selections, alternating with a cornet
band. On these occasions the venerable Col. James Blake
uniformly presided, and acted as chief marshal. The influence of that scene is not forgotten by the comrades, nor
how greatly the bronzed veterans were recompensed for all
their hardships and privations, in these evidences that the
toilsome marches and hard-fought battles were appreciated
and valued by loyal hearts at home. Many a one returned
to duty with fresh courage and renewed determination to
perform his part faithfully and well, till the last armed foe
expired.

Next day we had a reception, tendered by Governor
Morton; after which we turned over our arms and accouterments and regimental colors, and marched back to the
"Home" parade ground, where we formed a hollow square.
In this Lieut.-Col. Comparet' took a position, and made a
ringing speech to the boys; complimenting them on their
gentlemanly conduct, and the success that had attended
their present trip thus far, and admonishing them to preserve the excellent reputation they had won. The fellows
who had threatened him at Louisville, then came forward,
and in a very contrite manner, acknowledged their error,

and begged his pardon; which was readily granted, and

> "All went merry as a marriage bell."

The work was done, and the Fifty-First scattered for home; while other regiments, that had been there three days, were not yet disbanded.

RETURN TO THE FRONT.

Few of us realized before how strong were the ties that bound the soldiers to their homes. It required no ordinary courage and unselfish patriotism, to part with the loved ones, with no assurance of meeting them again on earth. And it required all the integrity of a true heroine, to send forth from the pleasures of home and the joys of domestic life, for the toils and privations and hardships of war, the men and boys who were dearer than life itself. Its results were ofttimes more than human heart could endure. Dr. Kirkbridge, in his report of the insane asylums of Pennsylvania, at that time, notes an enormous number of female patients, whose insanity was caused solely by the loss of relatives in war. This was doubtless equally true of all the loyal States. To the encouragement received from the loyal women, may be credited very much of the noble determination that characterized each veteran.

We had learned patience in many ways, during the long delay of the consummation of our enthusiastic hopes. We had learned to endure the sorrow and trial and hardship and exposure and mean insult and indignity; for we felt that this was essential to the grand baptism and new birth which our Nation was to experience.

> "As flake by flake the beetling avalanches
> Bind up their imminent crags of snow,
> Till some chance thrill the loosened ruin launches,
> And the blind havoc leaps unarmed below:
> So grew and gathered through the silent years,
> The madness of a people, wrong by wrong;"

Till, in a moment of despair, every element of loyalty and patriotism and humanity

"Leapt up, with one hoarse yell, and snapt its bands!"

A wag remarks that, according to his recollection, it was not exactly a "one-horse yell," neither, nor was it precisely in the nature of a "snap," especially for the rebs.

When our time expired, we all came together at Indianapolis, and repaired to the seat of war; being already assigned to duty at Chattanooga, under command of General Steedman, to whom Lieut.-Col Comparet' reported.

A TRAMP ACROSS THE COUNTRY.

On their arrival at Nashville, it was found impracticable to go farther by railroad; the road being cut in several places, and menaced by a number of guerrilla bands. So, without much delay, they proceeded on foot over the same route taken only a few months before. The march was not so agreeable as on the first occasion, there being a great deal of rain, sleet, snow and mud. When they came to Walden's Ridge, the wagons had to be unloaded, and their contents carried to the top.

On his leaving home, W. B. Gibson's old mother had put into his knapsack four or five pounds of maple sugar. While engaged in getting the wagons up the mountain, he laid his knapsack where he thought it was perfectly safe. He certainly must have left his sugar-poke exposed, however, as when he returned, it was gone. Some person had stolen it. O, how he swore! He could do that beautifully then. John P. Smith called him over to where Comparet', Al. Harris, Lon. Smith, himself and some others were at supper, and asked him what was the matter.

"Some un taken my sugar; 'n' I can whip him on less ground 'n he can stand on!" ·

John P. dipped up a cupful of something out of a kettle, and offered it to him. As soon as he took one sip, he exclaimed:

"There's my sugar now, Johnny!"

But he didn't whip anybody, for the sugar was neatly

surrounded by a gallon or more of hospital brandy, and the whole crowd got happy as lords over it. Which proves that maple sugar will intoxicate.

Charley Cox didn't want to march; and wasn't in a hurry to get back anyhow. He had plenty of money, and wanted to have a good time. So, he obtained a fine flask of liquor; and by a judicious distribution of it, secured a pass to Rowlett's station on the Louisville railroad. He overcame the difficulty presented by the bridge guards, by showing a big "official" envelop, which he had picked up somewhere, and which the officer had not time to examine. At Rowlett's, he exchanged his blue suit for that of a colored citizen, (a former slave of Cox's father,) walked 12 miles east to his father's home, stayed one day and night, returned to Rowlett's, traded back with the darkey, took the next train for Nashville, got with John Parker, hired citizens' suits for both, and "bummed" around there for a week; then they put on their own suits, got aboard a train, and were in Chattanooga by the time the regiment was fairly settled in camp there.

Immediately on our arrival at Chattanooga, our regiment was detailed to inaugurate the National Cemetery at that place, and to remove the dead comrades from where they had been placed, in the vicinity of Chicamauga and Missionary Ridge battle-fields. It may not be generally known, but is nevertheless true, that the Fifty-First broke the ground and, from plans furnished by the War Department, laid off that cemetery, which is acknowledged to be one of the finest institutions of that character in the land.

THE "THIMBLE SOCIETY."

One of the most gratifying experiences of our army life, and one that served wonderfully to soften the asperities of our unnatural existence, was the occasional receipt of substantial tokens of love and patriotic admiration from the loyal girls at home. Sometimes it was a box filled with socks, handkerchiefs, needles, pins. thread. mittens, cakes, butter, letter paper, envelops, ink and such other articles as the boys so badly needed ; inclosing also a letter from the sender — mother, sister, aunt or sweetheart. Then a shout would go up, as all the fellows of his "mess" would gather around the happy recipient, to see the box opened, and perhaps get a taste of its contents. A great deal of literature was sent in this way to the boys in hospital ; and many a grateful heart blessed the thoughtful women and girls up in "God's country," for the magazines over which the sufferers spent many a lonely hour.

In the battle of Missionary Ridge, Walter Hartpence, of the 79th Indiana, and a brother of the writer, was very badly wounded ; and it was the good fortune of the latter, to be permitted to combine with his military duties, that of nursing the wounded comrade and brother. One day a bundle of magazines was received and distributed among the boys of that ward, which was in the cottage directly north of the old Baptist church in Chattanooga, and that was occupied by General Wagner while he was commander of that post. Among these magazines was a copy of the *Atlantic Monthly*, and on it was written, in a delicate hand, "From the 'Thimble Society,' Buffalo, N. Y., Nettie Marsh, Vice Pres." On the fly leaf of the same, or another of the same lot, a little pencil sketch informed the reader that the "Thimble Society" consisted of twelve young girls in the city of Buffalo, whose object was to aid in any way they could in contributing to the comfort of suffering soldiers. A brief letter of thanks was returned from the boys. also describing their condition and hopefulness. At the same time a similar letter was addressed to Miss Hattie Brown, whose name appeared on another magazine, but having no reference to the "Society." The following is the reply :

"BUFFALO, Jan. 27 '64

Dear Friend :
        I received your letter with mingled gratitude and surprise. Little thought I as I wrote that small article in the *Atlantic Monthly*, I

should ever receive an answer to it. We were all gratified to hear that our work had done some good to the poor suffering soldiers. My friend Hattie Brown received a letter from you a short time ago, and we had a fine time reading them at the Society, which met at the President's, Miss Jennie White's house. The Society send their thanks for the dollar that you so kindly sent us, and which helped to increase the weight of our money box. There is to be a great "central fair" here, for the benefit of the "sick and wounded soldiers." It is to commence on Washington's Birthday, and last a week. I suppose it will be a grand affair.   *
If you ever receive this letter, and think it worth while to answer it, will you describe a battle to me? What do you think of this war? Do you think it will ever end? I most sincerely hope it will.   *   Our society is called the "Thimble Society."

"*Thimble Society*" *Members.*

Jennie White, *President.*	Nettie Marsh, *Vice President.*

Carrie Burnham, *Treasurer.*

Sarah Burrows,	Della Litchworth,
Julia Burrows,	Julia Vougt,
Hattie Brown,	Minnie Vougt
Emma Butman,	Kittie Wilber,
Minnie Wilber.	

Your friend,

NETTIE."

"WHAT'S IN A NAME?"

One of the humorous features of our camp life, that was formed from long familiarity with each other, was the substitution of nicknames; and so complete was that in many instances, that the real name of the individual was scarcely known to any person except the orderly sergeant, whose duty it was to call the roll and make details. In Co. C, for instance, Stephen Hilton was known as "Billy Cat," Joseph Brown as "Wolf," Charles Newnam as "Squirrel," John Wells as "Goose," Howard Pike as "Fish," David Thompson as "Weasel," W. F. Hadden as "Big Jig," and J. T. Dinwiddie as "Little Jig;" J. F. McKinley answered to "Brute F.," and Jonathan Peterson was contracted to "Jonty Pete." The same thing existed in all the other companies. "Boss" Ferguson would hardly have known who you meant, if he was addressed as Sebastian, the good old Spanish name his mother gave him; nor would Jeremiah Richeson respond to anything else than "Mother."

The name of "Eyesickle McGunsky, Co. B," appears among a list of men from the Fifty-First, buried in Crown Hill Cemetery, at Indianapolis, but careful search through the Adjutant General's Report has failed to show such a name. It is most likely a nickname by which the comrade was known, and was so reported.

And there was "Petty" — Pettigrew, of Co. G, a veritable "son of the sod," who was always ready to buoy the drooping spirits of a homesick comrade. He was always ready for a bit of a joke, too, no matter at whose expense. While passing through Pulaski, the streets of which were lined with people of every shade of color, he indulged in a little pleasantry, directed at Comrade Black, of the same company; which the women and children took up, and created such a happy excitement, that every one forgot his fatigue and discomfort; while the darkies on the sidewalks jumped and danced, and shouted, "God bress Massa Linkum an' his sojers!"

"Little Jig" was a good soldier; but he had a way of doing and saying things that was strictly original. When he received notice from the orderly that he was detailed as ordnance sergeant at brigade headquarters, he caught his breath; then replied:

"Well, I jist wisht you'd hush! I ain't no such a thing."

"Yes; get on your things, and report."

"Naw, I won't do no such a thing. What do I have to do?"

"Just take charge of the guards of the ammunition train."

"Jig" reconsidered his decision, and went. Next day we got hasty marching orders; and the colonel began to hurry up all hands, to get out on the road as soon as possible. At the ordnance camp, the teamsters were having a "picnic" with a lot of intractable mules, that persisted in tying themselves up in all sorts of shapes. "Jig" was an

14

artist in that line. He had a strong voice, beautifully adapted to that calling; and the rhythmic vernacular, as it found its way into the inner consciousness of those mules, was electrifying in its effect. Going at once to the relief of the muleteers, he soon evoked order out of chaos, and started the happy drivers on their winding way.

But his new position soon brought him to grief. Bob Hall, who was at the time wagon-master, got into trouble at the very next piece of bad road, and having a poor hand with one of the teams, ordered "Jig" to get up and drive.

"I'll not do it, fer you nor nobody else."

Just then the colonel came along; and not thinking of his being a sergeant, nor the indignity offered in such a requirement, seconded the demand of the wagon-master. He met with a like refusal, which was steadily adhered to; and another driver had to be found for the unruly team. The result was, the sergeant was reduced to the ranks as soon as he came to camp. This was a very unjust act on the part of the colonel; as it humiliated and discouraged a good and efficient soldier, while it only stimulated the petty tyranny of the wagon-master.

In March, 1864, Col. Streight was enjoying his "leave of absence" following his escape from the rebel prison, and was making speeches in Indiana.

Our reorganization at the time of our final return to Chattanooga, was with the 2d Brigade, 2d Division, 4th Army Corps, which included the following regiments:

Maj. Gen. Gordon Granger, *Commanding Corps.*

Maj. Gen. Phil. H. Sheridan,   "   *Division.*

Brig. Gen. Geo. D. Wagner,   "   *Brigade.*

  100th Illinois, Major Charles M. Hammond.

  15th Indiana, Col. Gustavus A. Wood.

                Major Frank White.

                Capt. Benj. F. Hegler.

  40th Indiana, Lieut.-Col. Elias Neff.

  51st Indiana, Lieut.-Col. John M. Comparet'.

57th Indiana, Lieut.-Col. Geo. W. Lennard.

58th Indiana, Lieut.-Col. Jos. Moore.

26th Ohio, Lieut.-Col. Wm. H. Young.

97th Ohio, Lieut.-Col. Milton Barnes.

About April 30, 1864, the Fifty-First was transferred to the "Separate Brigade of the Etowah," Brig. Gen. Jas. B. Steedman commanding, including the following:

15th Indiana, Col. G. A. Wood.

29th Indiana, Lieut.-Col. David M. Dunn.

44th Indiana, Lieut.-Col. Sim. C. Aldrich.

51st Indiana, Lieut.-Col. J. M. Comparet'.

68th Indiana, Lieut.-Col. Harvey J. Espy.

8th Kentucky, (5 comp's.) Capt. John Wilson.

3d Ohio, Capt. Leroy S. Bell.

24th Ohio, Lieut.-Col. Armstead T. Cockerill.

About the 1st of May, many of the boys were beginning to get interested in the development of vaccination, that had been ordered about a month previous; the writer had a splendid case, which subsequently proved to have been accomplished with impure virus, and had to be burnt out with lunar caustic. John Gasper and James Griggs, of Co. C, also, who were vaccinated from his arm, came near losing their left arms, which swelled up to two or three times their usual size.

A STORM IN CAMP.

On the 24th of May, while nearly everybody was laid up with vaccination, we experienced a most terrific wind and rain storm. The elements got on a regular tear; and for a day or two it was hard to tell which end of the world was up, or for one to swear to his identity at all.

The day had been beautiful — one of unusual loveliness. Old Sol had risen in all his majestic splendor, and kissing the bright dew-drops on the millions of tiny plants, strode up to the meridian like a fresh adjutant in his new uniform on dress parade. Up to this stage everything was

"o. k." Lying extended on our home-made couches, our
feet elevated at an angle of 90°, our right hands chiefly
employed in brushing away the festive blue-tail fly, that
persisted in pestering our vaccination—earth all this time
trying to observe its regular motions, we did not anticipate
trouble.

Have you seen the enraged tiger spring from his lair,
as though he would crush everything visible, imaginable
or hypothetical, beneath his ponderous paws, or tear it into
shreds with his merciless fangs? That is a feeble comparison to the occasion referred to. With an overwhelming
savage power, yet with awful grandeur, it came, bursting
suddenly from the silent valleys and the rugged hights of
Lookout and Walden. Great black ugly threatening clouds
loomed in the hollows of the air, the lightning flashed, the
thunder bellowed; while a dense mass of inky frowning sky
hurled itself down on us without a moment's warning; and
away went our earthly possessions. As the winds jostled
against each other, they lifted the sacred curtains and loose
boards of our sanctums sanctorum, carrying off the entire
stock, credits and assets, with the mad fury of a demon.

It was beautiful and grand; but we were not in a mood
to absorb its spirit, nor to even contemplate it unbiased.
It might have been an amusing sight to a disinterested witness—one gust of wind after another skurrying through
our dog-tents, ripping off the roof, emptying bucketfuls of
water over books, papers, blankets and guns, with boards,
bricks, camp equipage, etc., flying around in wildest disorder. But it wasn't to us. Our guns, which had just been
brightened up for inspection, came lumbering down across
our necks, rapping us into a most distressing condition of
impatience.

Then it suddenly disappeared, and there was a great
calm. The sun came out in splendor, brightening nature,
that had just washed its dusty face, with a pretty, dazzling
smile that was really fascinating. But this did not much

ameliorate our forlorn condition. All was rack and ruin. Herculaneum and Pompeii in all their glory were not arrayed like this.

Such experiences were common, however, and we had to just get used to them. We all became philosophers.

June came on us so hot that it seemed like Fahrenheit was fairly exhausted. The flies tortured us by day, and the gallinippers by night. It was a rare pleasure to get out in the cool of the dawn, and stroll off toward Missionary Ridge, with its masses of giant trees waving their shaggy heads in the winds, their vernal hangings glittering and glistening in the bright morning sunshine, their aged and battle-scarred trunks heaving and sighing mournfully, as though they were telling of the many young lives that had gone out beneath their ample spread, whose blood was thus mingled — patriot and traitor — to fertilize the lovely wildwood flowers, with whose delicious perfumes the whole air was redolent.

COL. STREIGHT RETURNS TO THE REGIMENT.

About the latter part of June, 1864, Colonel Streight returned to the front, and reported for duty ; and turning over the command to him, Lieut.-Col. Comparet' reported to his own regiment, whose three years' term had expired, and who were awaiting orders for home. Comparet' had greatly endeared himself to the Fifty-First, and it was with sincere regret that we bade him farewell. In speaking of his connection with our regiment, years afterward, he said : "All the time I was in command of the regiment, was one of pleasure and joyful event. Our marches and camp life will always be remembered by me, and the men, as a body, were gentlemen, and were obedient in all respects." And in his farewell remarks to them, he said, with deep feeling :

"My dear and gallant old comrades, these events form a bright page in the volume of your historic regiment, and of your lives in the defence of your country and your flag.

May your memory never wither, and may the name of each
be enrolled as the heroes and defenders of our Nation."

RAILROAD GUARDS.

During the summer of 1864, a detachment from the
Fifty-First was sent to the depot yard in Chattanooga, to
take charge of and guard all railroad passenger trains running to Knoxville. The first detail was commanded by
Lieut. Roman Salter, of Co. K. This detail was relieved
June 13, by another, commanded by Lieut. J. N. Brown,
of Co. G, and including W. R. Hartpence, "Doc" Chitester, Francis M. Piper, John Charles, Wm. Tout, Amos
Warrick, and a number of others, whose names got away.
Hartpence acted as conductor of the train, while the lieutenant looked after the ladies and children, and examined
passes. This lasted till November 8, when the detachment
was relieved, and ordered to report to the regiment. This
experience was one of great danger and risk ; and the boys
witnessed a great deal of the inside life of loyal Tennessee-
ans and their disloyal neighbors. Their hearts were often
touched by scenes of sadness and distress. Knoxville was
at that time in a state of desolation ; having been overrun
by both armies. It was surrounded by green ponds, and
almost devoid of herbage, and presented a most disgusting
appearance. The boys were always glad to get away from
it. Along the route, however, were several pretty little
villages, that were inhabited by loyal people. Athens and
Cleveland will especially be remembered, for their uniform
kindness and hearty encouragement.

A very sad incident occurred on one of these trips. A
rebel soldier's wife, who had obtained permission to visit
her husband, (who was a prisoner,) at Chattanooga, got
on at Knoxville, with her two little children, one of whom
was not more than four months old. On her return, the
older, who had been sick, grew worse, and was once laid
out as dead. But through the attention and kindness of

those on board, it was kept alive until their arrival at the "refugee-house" in Knoxville. It died there at 4 o'clock next morning. The sorrowing mother came to the conductor before the departure of the train, telling him of her distress, and thanking him and his comrades for their tender consideration in her time of trouble.

A serious accident occurred one day, which it was for some time feared would prove fatal. While passing under a bridge, when the train was making fast time, Will Tout, of Co. A. was struck on the head by one of the heavy timbers, and almost knocked from the car. It seemed likely at first, he would lose his mind. Happily, he recovered, and was restored to duty in a few weeks.

Our mail was greatly disturbed at this time, having to be sent around by way of Huntsville, on account of the Nashville and Chattanooga Road being torn up by Wheeler's critter-back guerrillas.

ANONYMOUS CORRESPONDENCE.

Among other innocent amusements to relieve the dull tedium and torture of this sort of life, was that of answering "anonymous correspondents." One specimen of this is certainly enough for the average reader. Following the popular idiocy, Lieut. Newt. Brown and Hartpence yielded to the influence of a double-rigged invitation from a couple of ladies of Newport, Ky. Here is a verbatim copy of the first response from the ladies:

" DELECTA AMICA :
Brave Hoosier soldiers, far from home, I read with anxious care
Your wish for correspondence with luscious maidens fair.
As you've thrown down the gauntlet, now I'll take up the pen,
And we'll see, my bonnie vet'rans, where this flirtation ends.
They call me free and forward, but I love the soldier brave
Who fights beneath the stars and stripes, his country for to save ;
Yet I pity the condition of those who are so vain
As to make love to all the world, a lady's heart to gain.
'Tis not so hard to please our sex, if you're at all inclined.
Send on your shadows, soldiers brave, and I will send you mine ;
I know that you will love me when you my photo see.

So give all other maids the slip, and only write to me.
'Tis true, upon my finger a ring of gold I wear:
A token from a soldier who is youthful, brave and fair;
But my heart is large enough for three, and all this world may know
That from this hour I ever sport three strings unto my beau!
In hight, I'm five feet four or so; of age, but twenty-three;
Complexion fair, dark eyes and hair, and heart still fancy free.
Though myself a Buckeye girl, I rather like the Hoosiers too:
So success to your vet'ran comrades, and a double health to you.
Now, my unknown soldier friends, you must admire my charms;
And if any ill befall you, just come unto my arms;
I'll cherish you and love you, though fortune frown or smile.
But, Oh! *avoid the frail fair ones* who would your hearts beguile!

Toujours votre ami,

PAULINE C. LAVANT.

Newport, Ky.

P. S.   Sub rosa, boys, don't forget;
And a speedy answer you'll not regret.

P. C. L."

Of course the boys wrote immediately, and sent their pictures — the lovely ferrotypes they took in Chattanooga; which required a diagram to explain who they were; and that settled it.   They never got an answer; and would not have dared to come home through Kentucky by daylight, after that.   Whatever became of "dear Pauline," is not known; but "the years as they pass slowly by" make sad havoc of human aspirations and conceits; and Pauline's disgust when she saw those pictures, and discovered that these soldiers were only a small-sized lieutenant and brevet corporal, instead of major generals, possibly faded out long ago; and she may have spent her days spanking the babies of a red-headed street-car driver, or teaching school.

COPPERHEAD LETTER.

We were encouraged about this time by the removal of a lot of generals whom we had distrusted, and had just begun to appreciate the worth of their successors.   We were all eager to complete the war; and only feared that some foolish "peace-at-any-price" compromise would be made, that would subject us to the contempt and ridicule of the world.   We did not want a declaration of peace, without

the obliteration of every vestige of the so-called Southern
Confederacy, and the utter and permanent subjugation of
every rebel. More than all, we desired the humiliation of
the miserable copperheads that poisoned and paralyzed society at home, and the complete eradication of the scurvy,
malignant horde. As an illustration of the influence that
was wielded by that infamous party, we copy an ingenious
and cowardly letter received by Frank M. Brown, of Co. G,
the original of which is preserved:

"NEW WAVERLY, CASS CO., IND. }
June 27, 1864. }

    The d—d tories have nominated two men for president Fremont and
Lincoln so you can have your choice I feel sorry for you I think you
have lost your senses since las harvest when you were here You feel very
bad because I will not do as your brother Sam has done turn traitor to
my party take some abolition paper & cry "down with the butternuts &
copperheads" & curse all my brothers because the could not see just as I
do that is what constitutes a union man now-a-days. I am happy to inform you that I will never do either. You say you are sorry that I will
vote against the soldiers after being one myself. I don't know what you
mean by voting against the soldiers for the Democrats tried to raise the
soldiers wages to $16 in gold this winter or paper enough to buy 16 in gold.
That would be death on you all for then you could buy whisky enough to
kill all of you. Is that what you mean by voting against the soldiers?
or do you think that if I would vote for Lincoln the war would last as
long as he was president so you could all stay in the army & not have to
work, for they say in their platform that they will never compromise
with traitors or rebels. It will take a long time kill them all off. They
want to give the "niggers" all the land in the south & it will take all the
land & property in the north to redeem the greenbacks & pay for the
war. They want to amend the constitution to free the "niggers" & they
say "Old Abe" has already done that. Jeff Davis wanted to amend the
constitution so that the north would have to send their "niggers" back.
*Now which is the worst Abe and Jeff. I say one is as much of a traitor
as the other & whoever supports either of them are traitors to the constitution & want to tear down our government.* The Democrats are the
only Union party that we have in the United States & whoever says they
are traitors are d—d liars I care not who they are where they come from
or what they call themselves If the Democrats were traitors as you say
they are they would not pay taxes to carry on this unconstitutional war
& wait till they can elect a man of their own but they would refuse to
pay them & if they went to force them they could wipe out the d d abolition torys. But they wait patiently. Thank God we will soon elect
one & then we will see who looks through the bars of Fort Lafayette &

those military dungeons We will do with them just as the did with our party. Vallandigham has come home to Ohio hurrah for him !

from   JAMES NOLAND."

THE FIGHT AT DALTON.

It has been impossible to ascertain the dates of return of officers to the regiment ; and notice can only be given by the incidental mention of their names. Most of those who had not resigned, made their appearance about the opening of the Atlanta campaign.

August 15, 1864, we had a lively set-to with the rebels near Dalton, Georgia, that being the beginning of our part in that memorable campaign. Wheeler's mob of 3,000 rebel cutthroats had surrounded that town, with its little garrison of 300 men, who were huddled together in a large brick house, and commanded by the indomitable Colonel Laiboldt, of the 2d Missouri. General Steedman was with the command, but deferred to Colonel Streight, who had command of the brigade ; Capt. W. W. Scearce being in command of the Fifty-First. There were with us the 68th Indiana, 78th Pennsylvania, 108th Ohio and 14th U. S. Colored. Leaving the train just before daylight, our command slipped quietly over the rugged hills and through almost interminable thickets, until we were in sight of the enemy's pickets. Then forming a strong double line both of skirmishers and reserves, we swept over them like a gust of wind. Our boys fought like tigers ; and the devoted garrison, whose spirits were beginning to flag, were thrilled with joy at the prospect of deliverance.

The day before, a soldier from some Kentucky regiment, who had just been discharged, and had stopped at Dalton on his way home, had volunteered to aid in holding the town. He was out on the skirmish line ; and being too closely pressed, he sought refuge in a house whose mistress had protection papers from General Steedman. Here the Union soldier thought himself safe ; and he would have been, but for the perfidy of the ungrateful she-rebel, who informed the enemy of his concealment. They took him out and shot him in four places, and left him lying in the road.

Our boys were infuriated at report of this, and were resolved on revenge. The word was passed along the line. The colored boys mounted a hill in their front, to where the first lines of rebels were lying. Here they met a slight check, and wavered a little; it was their first fight. Just then the story of the murdered Kentuckian came up their line. They rallied in a moment, and poured into the rebels a most galling fire. The word was given to "charge," and with a tremendous bound and unearthly yell, they pounced like wounded tigers on their prey. When the rebels cried for mercy, the colored boys hissed back at them, "Remember Fort Pillow!" as they drove their bayonets through the vitals of the perfidious wretches. The mingled shouts and shrieks rang out on the fresh morning air, like the wail of lost souls in the perdition of those who hate God and virtue.

One of the darkey soldiers, describing their charge, said, "As I wuz gwine up de hill, a reb drap 'ight down in de weeds, 'n' 'gin to holler 'O, Lo'd hab mussy on me! I surrendehs, I surrendehs!' But I did'nt see no surrendeh. I jis' plug 'im in de mouf; and den th'ee fo' fi'd on 'im. Dey jis' keep on fi'n' on he; thought dey nevah git done. Spec' da wa'n't a bit o' bref in dat dar reb w'en he struck de groun'. O, I tell ye 'twus life o' death to we-all. I jis' knowed dey nevah take we-uns no pris'nehs. Dey jis' finish us up 'ight dar!'"

Wheeler's cruel and soulless method operated on this occasion like a boomerang. He hastened to get away as soon as possible; being closely followed by our skirmishers.

George W. Scearce of Co. K, was promoted to be 2d lieutenant, in March, and took command of Co. A just before this fight, when that company had no officers. As we approached the town, the skirmish line, consisting of Co. A, was confronted by a force of rebels around a dwelling.

The skirmishers charged the house, but were repulsed, and Wade Harrison and Mason Morris were taken prisoners. The skirmishers, being reinforced immediately by Cos. D and F, under command of Captain Anderson, renewed the charge upon the rebel stronghold, finding it evacuated, on account of the flanking by the troops on our left. In this charge, Levi Todd, of Co. F, was mortally wounded and died on the 17th.

The next day, as we were leaving Dalton, a man was seen in the distance, running and waving his hands. On his coming up to the command, it proved to be Wade Harrison. He went to Lieutenant Scearce, saying, "I guess I won't carry a gun for a while," as he exhibited a parole. "All right," said the lieutenant, you can stay with us and cook flapjacks and make coffee."

In the charge by Co. A. Sergeant A. C. Weaver was seriously wounded in the left heel. He was carried back by David Alley and Sergeant Montgomery, to an improvised hospital in a farm-house, which was already so full of wounded Union and rebel soldiers, that he was laid on the portico, drenched with the rain that fell just as the battle closed. He did not have his clothes changed till three or four days after, when he was taken to the general field hospital at Chattanooga.

In the general engagement, Lieutenant Holman, Co. G, who was then a sergeant, saw a Union soldier lying on his back, his clothing torn from his breast, which had been pierced in several places by a bayonet passing clear through and out at his back. The dastardly act appeared to have been done after the poor fellow was killed by a bullet.

The Official War Records furnish the following reports, which are slightly abbreviated for this work.

Report of Col. Wm. Sirwell, 78th Penn. Inf.

"Maj. Gen. Steedman directed me to report to Col. Streight. Sunday noon, August 14, 1864, on reaching Chicamauga Station, on the Chattanooga and Atlanta Railroad, I reported to Col. Streight. He placed me in command of the 78th Pennsylvania, 108th Ohio and 68th Indiana, with instructions to move forward on Dalton as speedily as possible. At Tunnel Hill I disembarked, marched across Tunnel Hill, then taking the railroad marched perhaps three miles. Here I received orders from Col. Streight to halt, it being 2 A. M., and so dark, imprudent to go farther. At daylight Gen. Steedman ordered me to move forward rapidly as possible. At this time the 14th U. S. Colored troops were sent forward, and took position on the left of my command, and sent forward one company to skirmish and to protect their flanks. Due preparation being made, the troops began to move forward, meeting the enemy in strong force, said to be about 3,000, driving him three miles, through Dalton, where the entire command halted in a very heavy rain."

Report of Capt. W. W. Scearce.

"CHATTANOOGA, Aug. 20, 1864.

The regiment having received orders on the 14th, embarked on board the cars at 5 P. M., August 14, and arrived at Tunnel Hill at midnight. Here the regiment disembarked, and was ordered to accompany the artillery through the country to the gap in the Rocky Face Ridge, where it arrived at about 3 A. M., and lay in line of battle on Col. Morgan's (U. S. Col. Inf.,) left until after sunrise; we then moved beyond the gap, and took a position on the right of the 29th Indiana. These two regiments formed the reserve, and occupied a position to the right and rear of the front line. After the charge made by Col. Morgan's regiment, I was ordered to throw out two companies, to protect our flank on the right. The skirmishers soon became warmly engaged; the right of the line, having advanced some distance beyond the main line, suddenly found themselves upon a large body of the enemy concealed in and about a large house. The enemy rushed upon them, and demanded their surrender, but I sent a timely support, that saved the line, and after more severe skirmishing, the enemy withdrew, and my command, with the rest of the force, marched into Dalton. The strength of my command was 380. My loss was 4 wounded, 1 mortally, since died, 1 captured."

Extract from Gen. Steedman's Report.

"Early in the morning of August 14, the enemy's cavalry in considerable numbers, attacked a herd of cattle near Calhoun, Ga., dispersing a portion of the guard and driving off a large number of cattle. At 3 P. M. I received information that rebel Gen. Wheeler, with a strong force, was moving toward Dalton. At 6 P. M. a demand had been made by Wheeler for the surrender of Dalton, which had been refused. I did not reach the bridge north of that place till after midnight. I was told our forces were overpowered and captured. At daylight I advanced my command; we soon became engaged with the enemy's skirmishers.
Heard firing, and learning that the garrison was still holding out, moved forward rapidly, and soon cleared the town of the enemy; but being without cavalry, could not pursue. The enemy's loss could not be less

than 200. He left 33 dead and 57 badly wounded on the field. My loss was 1 officer and 8 men killed, 1 officer and 29 men wounded, 1 officer and 23 men missing. ⁂ Troops engaged, 2d Missouri, 29th, 51st and 68th Indiana, 108th Ohio, 78th Pennsylvania and 14th Colored."

From Gen. Thomas' Report.

" Early on the morning of the 15th, Maj. Gen. Steedman, with two regiments of white and six companies of colored troops, arrived at Dalton from Chattanooga and immediately attacked the enemy, driving him off toward Spring Place, after four hours' fighting. The enemy's loss was heavy, and he left his dead and wounded on the field. Our loss was 40 killed and 55 wounded. We captured 50 wagons and 2 surgeons."

Rebel Gen. Hood was almost as big a liar as Forrest. In his book " Advance and Retreat," he claims the above victory for himself; and says :

"On the 13th I demanded the surrender of Dalton, which, the first instance, was refused, but was finally acceded to at 4 P. M. The garrison consisted of about 1,000 men. As the road between Resaca and Tunnel Hill had been effectually destroyed, the army was put in motion the next morning, in the direction of Gadsden."

The 24th was made memorable by the arrival of a big boat-load of onions ; the very recollection of which brings tears to one's eyes.

" How sublime a thing it is to suffer and be *strong!* "

THE NORTH ALABAMA CAMPAIGN.

In the latter part of August, 1864, Gen. Jas. B. Steedman, commanding the District of the Etowah, organized an expedition to meet the advance of the rebels through Northern Alabama. The organization of the Post of Chattanooga then, from which the expedition was made up, was as follows :

Col. T. R. Stanley, *Commanding Post.*

1st Brigade, Col A. D. Streight *Commanding.*

| 51st Indiana, | 14th U. S. Colored, |
| 11th Michigan, | 2d Ohio. |

2d Brigade, Lieut.-Col. Dunn, *Commanding.*

29th Indiana,	68th Indiana,
Detach't 5th Iowa,	18th Ohio,
" 10th Iowa.	

3d Brigade, Lieut.-Col. Hurlbut, *Commanding*.

39th Iowa.   57th Illinois.

The following is the report of Captain Stansbury, 19th Inf., A. A. A. G., to the general commanding:

"CHATTANOOGA, Sept. 13, 1864.

The troops were loaded upon the trains, and the trains left the depot at this place at 7:30 A. M., September 1, and reached Whiteside's Station at 10 A. M., the same day. Here, in obedience to the railroad authorities, the command was delayed 2 hours and 45 minutes, awaiting the arrival of three engines and the cabooses. We left Whiteside's Station about 12:50 P. M., arrived at Bridgeport, taking on the train at that point the 39th Iowa, and reached Stevenson at 1:10 P. M. At this point the command was again delayed 1 hour and 45 minutes by the local agent, Mr. Irish, for the purpose of changing engines and conductors. Mr. Irish also took the responsibility of cutting up one of the sections of the train, and joining the cars belonging to it on the other four sections. By this some of the regiments were scattered upon three or four trains, and the horses of the artillery separated from the pieces. The expedition reached Murfreesboro at 10:30 P. M., and was disembarked from the train at that point. After several hours' rest, to give the troops an opportunity to cook their rations, the command moved out on the La Vergne pike at 2:30 A. M., and marched to that point, reaching there at 9 A. M. Here a messenger was dispatched to Gen. Rousseau, and awaiting his reply, the command rested in camp. At 5 P. M., no word having been received from Gen. Rousseau, the command was got in readiness to move, when it was reported to the general commanding that a column of the enemy was moving down the Lebanon pike, in the direction of the town. The command was immediately moved into position, and the 18th Ohio deployed as skirmishers. The enemy advanced within sight of the skirmish line, but seeing, or learning our force from the inhabitants, fell back, refusing attack. The command then moved up the pike toward Murfreesboro, crossing Stewart's Creek, and taking up position at the church two miles from the creek. Here, on the next morning, the 3d of September, the enemy again tried to cross, but finding us in their front again retired and moved up toward Lebanon. At the time the enemy fired upon our pickets, Gen. Milroy had sent word of his coming up with cavalry, and the command waited until his arrival before moving. At 9 A. M. Gen. Milroy arrived, and the line was formed. The command moved forward in line for one mile, when it was found that the enemy had left our front. Pursuit was commenced and kept up as far as old Jefferson Crossing of Stone's River. The command then halted and rested, and then moved over to the railroad, where it had been destroyed by Wheeler. The trains arrived here during the night, and at daylight of the 4th of September the command was again embarked on the train and moved to Murfreesboro. At 9 A. M. Gen. Milroy sent word that the enemy was crossing the Salem pike, five miles from town, and the command was at once moved in that direction. While on the march, word was received that the enemy had gone in full retreat, and Gen. Milroy was in pursuit. The command was moved back to Murfreesboro, where it remained till 10 A. M., September 5, when we moved upon the trains toward Tullahoma, repairing some 300 feet of track near Christiana. On arriving at Tullahoma, a request was received that the general should move his command to Huntsville and Pulaski. Arrangements were made to comply with this request, and the expedition arrived in Huntsville upon the trains at 8 : 30 A. M. of the 6th of September. Rations were drawn here by the men, and the expedition proceeded to Pulaski, arriving there at 8 : 30 P. M., where it remained all night. On the morning of the 7th the command was moved to Athens, and disembarked about 12 M. Here word was received that Generals Rousseau and Granger were making for the same point, and we awaited their arrival. In the meantime Col. Streight, commanding First Brigade, was sent with his own and the Third Brigade to Rogersville. Generals Rousseau and Granger arrived at Athens September 8, at 4 P. M., and about 6 P. M., at the earnest solicitation of Gen. Steedman, the whole command of cavalry was set in motion to support Col. Streight. The cavalry camped at Elk River on the night of the 8th of September. At 4 A. M. September 9, that command moved and overtook the infantry under Col. Streight's command at Shoal Creek about 3 : 30 P. M. Col. Streight had overtaken Gen. Wheeler's rear guard, and skirmished with it, driving the enemy and crossing the creek, where he awaited the arrival of the cavalry. At this point it was determined by Gen. Rousseau to remain for the night. On the morning of the 10th of September, after a long delay, the cavalry started in pursuit, and the infantry of this command awaited developments. In the meantime foraging parties were sent out, and meat sufficient for two days' rations collected from the rebel citizens of the country. A portion of the command was moved down to — Ferry, where some of the boats of the enemy were concealed. Some skirmishing was had, and the guards of the boats driven from their cover, one being killed and several wounded. Orders to move up to Florence prevented any attempt to gain possession of the boats. These orders were afterward countermanded, and the troops moved back to their camps. Gen. Rousseau announced here that Wheeler had crossed the Tennessee River at 4 P. M. On the morning of the 11th the command started for Athens, reaching Elk River at dark, and Athens at 9 A. M. on the 12th of September. The command started at 11 A. M., September 12, for Chattanooga, arriving there at 11 : 30 P. M."

Rebel Capt. Lester, 7th Alabama Car., to Wheeler:

"Friday morning, Sept. 1, 1864.

The enemy passed through Rogersville at 1 P. M. yesterday, on the Florence road from the direction of Athens, the force between 2,000 and 2,500, consisting of 4 regiments of white infantry and 1 negro regiment,

1 regiment of cavalry, about 250 men, and 2 pieces of artillery, commanded by Gen. Streight. Gen. Rousseau is reported in Athens with 2 brigades of cavalry. The Yankees expect him to reinforce them to-day."

Gen. Miller, Comdg. Nashville, to Gen. Sherman :

"NASHVILLE, Sept. 8, 1864—11:30 P. M.

Dispatches from Gen. Rousseau, at Athens, state that Wheeler is in the vicinity of Rogersville. Col. Streight has gone toward Rogersville, with 2,500 infantry and 2 pieces of artillery."

Gen. Granger to Gen. Whipple :

"ATHENS, Sept. 8, 1864.

Have just returned from the pursuit of Wheeler with 1,300 cavalry and 2 pieces of artillery. At 11 A. M. to-day, I met Col. Streight at Elk River. I advised him to move down and attack Wheeler, and gave him one of my best regiments of cavalry, about 450 strong, and ordered the 10th Michigan Inf., 300 strong, which had marched down with him, to report to him. I advised Streight, that if Wheeler crossed the river, or if he forced him over the river, to destroy the ferries, and guard the fords."

The Post of Chattanooga. Sept. 30, 1864. consisted as follows :

Col. T. R. Stanley, *Commanding.*

29th Indiana, Capt. Samuel O. Gregory.

44th Indiana, Capt. Jas. F. Curtis.

51st Indiana, Capt. W. W. Scearce.

68th Indiana, Lt.-Col. H. J. Espy.

8th Kentucky, Lt.-Col. Jas. D. Mayhew.

"BOUNTY-JUMPERS."

In the summer and fall of 1864, the people became intensely excited over the draft. Extraordinary efforts were made to fill the quotas, by securing volunteers. Large local bounties were offered, and the places where the draft was yet to occur also strove with each other. Liberal bounties were also offered by the Government, a considerable installment of which was paid on the muster of the recruit.

This unprecedented liberality of the Government and local authorities, while it served its intended purpose, by promoting genuine enlistments, also opened the way for a vast amount of swindling on the part of speculators, and

15

systematized fraud by organized conspirators. The worst class of men from Europe and British America, deserters from the rebel army, thieves and toughs thronged the recruiting stations, with a well-assumed display of patriotic ardor. They were regularly enlisted, and received their advance pay and clothing. In a few hours their uniform would be laid aside, they would present themselves at the next recruiting station, and again go through the process of enlistment, muster and pay under other names, in many instances enlisting several times in the various districts in the same State. These fellows would in the eye of the law "fill the quotas" of wards and townships. The muster-rolls exhibited a lot of fictitious names, that, when ordered to report for duty, made no response. One officer reported 389 men, of whom more than 200 had deserted almost immediately after receiving their bounties. Especially in the States where larger bounties were paid, an investigation showed that thousands of names on the muster-rolls were but the various aliases of scoundrels, some of whom had enlisted as many as twenty times, receiving in bounties as much as $8,000.

A likely fellow named Pat, was tempted by a large bounty to enlist. Some time after, an officer met Pat's mother, and inquired how he was getting along.

"Oh, foine ; he is doin' well, and has got some kind of an office. He is sendin' me a lot o' money," was the reply of the proud mother.

"What kind of an office has he got?"

"Och ! I don't know ; but I belave they do call it the leaping of the bounty."

Pat was finally caught, and made to serve a long term in the penitentiary for "leaping of the bounty."

General Hovey, commanding the district, and General Carrington, commandant of the draft rendezvous, set to work to detect and arrest this class of deserters. A large prison was prepared for their reception at the "Soldiers'

Home," and a strong guard was placed about it. A number of them were collected, manacled and paraded on the streets of Indianapolis, to the tune of "Rogue's March." They were then sent to the different commands in the field, where they generally embraced the first opportunity to desert again.

A court-martial was convened, and a large number of the worst bounty-jumpers were sentenced to imprisonment for from six months to five years at hard labor. They had their heads shaved, and wore a heavy ball and chain, and were drummed out of the service at the expiration of their sentence.

Among the worst of those tried by court-martial, were John Doyle, Charles Billingsly, Thomas Ryan, alias John Reagan (on the roll of Co. C, 51st Indiana, as "Patrick Ryan, mustered in Oct. 21, '64; deserted March 28, '65,") and Thomas Murry, who had heard in New York that a "soft snap" was offered in Indiana, and had gone there to secure it.

Charles Billingsly enlisted in the 7th Indiana Battery, from which he deserted, and enlisted again. He was taken to Chattanooga and tried by court-martial, was released on parole, and deserted and went to Louisville, where he was caught. He refused to tell how often he had deserted, but substantially admitted a number of times. He confessed to the murder of a woman and her child, and was known to have used the names of Cooper and Miller as aliases.

Thomas or Patrick Ryan, or John Reagan, enlisted in the Fifty-First, and deserted, bribing the guard to let him pass out of the camp. He had received $433.50 in bounties. When arrested, he declared that he had never been in the service, nor enlisted in any regiment; but he was fully identified by Colonel Streight and others. He then declared that he had not "jumped the bounty" more than once before; but it was known that he had admitted to his associates that he had "jumped" thirty times.

Thomas Murry said he came from London about one year previous to his arrest. He enlisted in the 11th Indiana Cavalry, at Lafayette, and was sent to Indianapolis, to Camp Carrington, from which he deserted the first night after his arrival, and was arrested in a sleeping-car on the way to Chicago.

They were sentenced to death, and the sentence was approved by President Lincoln and by General Hovey, in command of the District of Indiana. The sentence of John Doyle was suspended by President Lincoln, for ten days; and was afterward changed.

On the 23d of December, 1864, the other prisoners mentioned were shot to death at Camp Burnside, situated immediately south of Camp Morton, north of 7th and east of Delaware street. The execution was announced to take place at 10 o'clock, at which hour about 2,000 soldiers of the Veteran Reserve Corps were drawn up, forming three sides of a square, the north side, next to Camp Morton, being left open. As usual with that class of felons, a Romish priest accompanied the condemned prisoners, and recited a lot of Latin mummery, so full of comfort to murderers and rascals of that sort, and behind them came a detail of soldiers bearing coffins on their shoulders. They marched to the east line, filed north, and at the north line, on the bank of the State ditch, about six feet high, turned west and marched to the middle, halted and faced the soldiers and several thousand people. The detail of soldiers moved off and formed two lines, about ten paces from the prisoners and facing them. The rear rank of the firing party was the reserve. One-half of the guns were loaded with balls and the others with blank cartridges, handed to the soldiers by the officer in charge, without their knowing which were loaded. The first five on the right were ordered to fire at the first prisoner on the right, the second five at the second prisoner, and the third five at the third prisoner. All were ordered to aim at the hearts of the prisoners, who were dressed in citizens' clothes. During the reading of the order of the court sentencing them to death, the prisoners manifested little or no interest in the document nor surroundings. Ryan looked about over the crowd with an air of indifference, occasionally glancing over his shoulder at the bank in his rear, as if he were expecting something from that quarter. At a sign, a non-commissioned officer stepped forward, loosened the cords about the arms of each prisoner, removed his hat, tied his feet together and set him down on his coffin. He then tied a white cloth over their eyes, and they awaited their doom. The firing party advanced five paces, halted, and in perfect silence brought their guns to an aim. Ryan, in the center, threw his head back, as if he were trying to see under the bandage. The order to "fire" was given by waving a handkerchief. The hammers of the guns fell so unitedly, that no individual sound was distinguished. As the white smoke curled away from the guns, Ryan fell squarely back on his coffin, and died apparently without moving a muscle.

This ended a strange and fearful scene, which had not before been witnessed on Indiana soil. One of the most impressive features was the presence of about 100 "bounty-jumpers," then in confinement at the "Soldiers' Home," who were sent out that they might be impressed with the enormity of the crime they stood charged with. They were placed inside of the line of soldiers, where they had a full view of all that occurred. This was a terrible lesson to the "bounty-jumpers," and contributed greatly in breaking up the infamous business in Indiana.

About the 1st of November, 1864, during the last levy, Colonel Streight was at home, and received recruits to the number of 300 drafted men and substitutes. To these were added a number of "bounty-jumpers," who were chained together, and marched through the principal streets of Indianapolis, headed by a large negro, ringing a bell, and bearing on his back the inscription "Bounty Jumpers."

By order of General Carrington, Lieutenant Scearce took command of the entire detachment, and on November 6, he reported them at Chattanooga. Orders had been issued, that any guard permitting one of the chain-gang to escape, should take the convict's place. On the way, one of the convicts, although manacled, managed to get a car window open, and hurled himself through it while the train was in rapid motion. Before he touched the ground, however, the guard had observed his escape; and rushing to the rear platform, jumped off into the darkness. Alighting aright, he groped about till he found his prisoner, marched him to the next station, and on the next train caught up with the detachment at Nashville. The chain-gang was turned over to the provost marshal at Chattanooga, and immediately sent to the front. The drafted men and substitutes were distributed among the companies of our regiment.

In many cases such dishonorable means had been used to obtain substitutes by brokers, and by even some of the State agents, who in their zeal to line their own pockets, overlooked the noble and patriotic object of enlistments, that old soldiers felt the disgrace of having these fellows dumped unceremoniously into their ranks; and were not slow in evincing their resentment. They knew that patriotism had not sent them there; and that unjust and unfair discrimination had been made against themselves. There were, however, some who, after the first scare incident to exposure in line of battle, became properly infused with the quality of good soldiers, and were always found ready for duty at every call. But they never quite attained that fraternity acquired by long comradeship; and to this day there remains a strained condition in their relation with veterans.

Our army was also recruited by "100 days" men; the veterans called them "100 years men," and regarded them with derision at first. Some called them "Wide-awakes," also, referring to a political club during the first Lincoln campaign. These boys were treated kindly, however, and many of them made as good soldiers as their time allowed. They needed experience; and some of them got a little of that up in East Tennessee, under Burnside. Many a "100 days" boy went out, never to return.

Captain Hamilton was assigned to the command of Co. C, to fill the vacancy caused by the death of Captain Sheets, and while Lieutenant Dooley was in Libby Prison. Captain Sheets had been commissioned Major, but had not been mustered in his new position. Our new captain was a jolly fellow, and the boys soon learned to like him.

"DOG-TENTS."

The introduction of shelter-tents occurred about this time, and was a very funny era in our soldier life. There was such a sudden shrinkage from the "Sibley" and the "wall" and the "Bell," to the diminutive "pup-tent," that our proportions could not contract rapidly enough to fit it. Besides, it seemed ridiculous to call such a thing a tent. The first time we occupied them, the boys acted like a lot of lunatics; imitating all sorts of animals, barking like dogs, squalling like cats, braying like mules, cackling like hens, and crowing like roosters. As soon as dark came, one soldier, hidden away in one of these little quarters, would yell out:

"Who stole the doctor's whisky?"

Away over in another part of the regiment came the answer:

"Jim Landon!"

"It's an infernal lie; and I'll shoot the scoundrel that says so! Curt., get out and see who that is," shouted the grizzled old fifer; addressing the last sentence to Welshans, the drummer boy. But it was useless to try to find the culprit; and the victim would retire under a volley of subdued yells from all directions.

The soldier would put up his "dog-tent" regardless of

the location, spread his brush and straw, and then adapt
his body to the surface, adjusting the conformation of his
anatomy to the irregularities of the ground, roots, etc.   A
Fifty-First boy dreamed one night that he was in a hard
battle, where volleys of musketry were interspersed with
the crash of batteries.   Suddenly a monster shell struck
directly in front of him, while he was on his back loading;
the ball plowed its way under him, and lodged directly beneath him.   He felt it under him plainly, and knew that
in another second it would explode, hurling him into space
and scattering his remains in a thousand directions.   He
sprang like a cat from the place of danger, and — awoke,
to find himself in a thick briar-patch, with his tent torn to
pieces, and a drizzling rain falling.   He had made his bed
over some large roots, and in turning had got his back on
one of them.   His imagination did the rest.

About the 1st of October, 1864, great excitement prevailed in all the camps of Indiana soldiers; and among the
division and brigade commanders there was considerable
planning to relieve all Indiana soldiers from detached duty,
and to furlough them home.   Thousands of furloughs were
issued for a period of fifteen days, which were afterward
extended to thirty days.   These were in usual form, but
the indorsement included "(To vote)".   To facilitate this,
transportation was furnished to any point in Indiana.   The
Presidential election was at hand, and the copperhead legislature of Indiana had made it impossible for her soldiers
to vote in the field.   And the traitors hoped for much in
that fact; but the loyal managers circumvented that.   The
presence of the boys at the polls had a wholesome effect on
the copperheads; and the honor of Indiana was saved on
this occasion, as it was in the field, in the memorable campaign that followed.

THE HOOD CAMPAIGN.

At 4 o'clock, on the morning of November 13, '64 the furloughed men arrived at Bridgeport, Ala., where the rest of the command had been since October 18, guarding the Tennessee River fortifications, about half a mile below the town. Three gunboats lay near us, in the river, their dark sides and turrets looming above the banks, like so many huge monsters. Hood had left Sherman to wend his way to the sea, and was swinging around toward us. We felt wonderfully encouraged by the glorious victory at the polls, and regarded it the precursor of more glorious conclusions with rebels in arms. We were eager for it. Nor had we long to wait. The 23d Corps, under Schofield, at Resaca, was directed to concentrate at Pulaski, and was on its way, in the rear of the 4th Corps. On November 5, Schofield, with the advance of the 23d Corps, arrived at Nashville, and was ordered to join the 4th Corps at Pulaski, and to assume command of all the troops in that vicinity.

On November 14, the Fifty-First got orders to prepare for marching. Hood was expected to make an attack on Chattanooga or Pulaski; and our regiment was a part of a large force lying convenient to either point, and ready to rush promptly to either, when Hood should make his appearance. We had had very heavy rains at Bridgeport, and the river was booming. About all we could do was to drill the recruits, which in the dreadfully muddy condition of our camp, was very unpleasant. Most of the original officers were preparing to be mustered out on December 14, at expiration of service, and the non-veterans expected to go at the same time.

Bundling up in a hurry, we proceeded to Nashville at once, where, after a tedious wait till 8 o'clock that evening, we started for Pulaski, landing there in mud knee deep, with a fine prospect of a battle before morning. Fortunately for us, Hood was delayed. According to his report, he had contemplated a grand flourish, that would astonish the world. Going on from his defeat at Atlanta, he says:

"From Villanow, the army passed through the gaps in the mountains and halted at Cross Roads, 9 miles south of Lafayette [about half way between Chattanooga and Rome].

After halting two days at Cross Roads, I decided to make provision for twenty days' supply of rations in haversacks and wagons; to cross the Tennessee at or near Guntersville, and again destroy Sherman's communications at Stevenson and Bridgeport; to move on Thomas and Schofield, and attempt to rout and capture their army before it could reach Nashville. I intended then to march upon that city, where I would supply the army and reinforce it if possible, by accessions from Tennessee. I was imbued with the belief that I could accomplish this feat, afterward march northeast, pass the Cumberland River, and move into Kentucky. In this position I could threaten Cincinnati, and recruit the army from Kentucky and Tennessee."

And so on, for quantity. What a wonderful dreamer! Like "Weasel," he would have done something awful and desperate — "*if possible!*" There was in Hood a gorge of crust with a grudge of filling. He was the victim of misplaced self-confidence; and discovered, long before he was through, that he had bitten off more than he could chew. Hood went to Gadsden, where he met Beauregard; and on weighing their combined brain, concluded that they "were not competent to offer pitched battle to Sherman," nor to even follow him, lest the movement might be construed into another disgraceful retreat, "which would entail desertions." After two days' deliberation, Beauregard told him to go into Tennessee. Hood proceeded to Guntersville, where he intended crossing the river; but learning that Forrest, on whom he depended largely, was near Jackson, Tennessee, and could not cross the river, he pushed on to

Florence. This move gave us a chance to straighten up at Pulaski, and to have things ready for their reception. Special rations of sourkrout, onions and a superior quality of bacon were issued to us, and we were happy and defiant. Our regiment had recently been recruited, and numbered now 951. Capt. Will Scearce was in command of the regiment; and felt like making up for his sad experience in "Libby." He ordered the erection of "shebangs" from the wreckage of houses torn down for fortifications, putting up comfortable bunks, and supplying the boys with everything the country afforded. Patterson, the "skinner," was there, to fret our souls; but even he proved a blessing in the end. For, when we had to move, the call was so short that he had not time to load his stuff in his wagons; so he told the boys to help themselves; which they did.

Hood, with his army replenished, and rested up, then crossed the Tennessee, and on November 21 was in motion. His army consisted of 45,000 infantry, and 12,000 to 15,000 cavalry. His hope was "by a rapid march to get in rear of Schofield's forces, before they were able to reach Duck River." The available force of Thomas was less than half that of Hood, comprising only about 12,000 under Stanley, 10,000 under Schofield, about 4,000 cavalry under Hatch, Croxton's brigade of 2,500, and Capron's of 1,200; in all about 30,000. The forces engaged in battle, were at least three rebels to one Union.

Hood commenced his move northward from Florence, on parallel roads; and on the 23d a portion of his force took possession of Pulaski, with but little resistance. As he advanced, Thomas and Schofield, who were directly in the way of his march, covering the approaches to Nashville, retreated slowly and in good order in that direction. The whole Union force was not yet concentrated; and the chiefs at both Washington and Richmond seemed persuaded that it was not likely to be in time to save our little army. But Thomas was sufficient for the occasion. He wisely deter-

mined to fight the decisive battle of the campaign with all
the troops his department could furnish, and as near his
base as possible.

As we approached Columbia, Cos. C and I, under command of Captain Hamilton, were thrown out as skirmishers in the neighborhood of the railroad round-house. The
rebels attacked them, and firing was kept up all night. In
the morning our skirmishers were driven in, when Cos. B
and K, commanded by Lieutenants Arnold and Scearce,
were sent to reinforce them. They drove the rebels back,
and burned several residences the johnnies had taken refuge in. While doing this, Sergeant Hurst, of Co. B, went
to a well to get a drink, when he was shot dead. He was
taken back and buried in the camp. We held the skirmish
line during the day, falling back leisurely. Just at nightfall, Charles Eaves, of Co. K, received a severe gunshot in
his thigh. He survived it, however.

On the 26th, the enemy invested Columbia. Schofield
commanded the Union rear-guard. An effort was made to
cross to the north side of Duck River that night, but failed
on account of a severe storm and intense darkness. A severe artillery duel was kept up all the next day, and after
nightfall our forces accomplished a crossing. The 28th was
passed quietly, but on the morning of the 29th things had
a very critical appearance. Hood was crossing the river
above, and was aiming to cut off our retreat to Franklin.
Great apprehension was felt that we would be unable to
elude this movement; and every hour of delay in crossing
our supply train, was fraught with most painful anxiety.

As night came on the enemy's line was extended until
a corps of infantry was in order of battle facing the pike
on which we had finally got straightened out and were now
slowly moving. One of the severest tests of the soldier's
integrity, was in marching with a wagon train. This was
one of those occasions, our regiment bringing up the rear,
at that. There was not more than half enough room on

the side of the road to march comfortably; and we were
continually being called upon to help lift a wagon out of
the mud, carrying rails for a long distance often for this
purpose, prying and heaving, in the cold and rain, already
fatigued from loss of sleep. But the boys plodded on patiently; not realizing the imminent danger that impended.
It would have been a simple thing for the enemy along the
pike to press forward a few steps, and sweep our troops,
artillery and train from the road in utter confusion and
rout; yet no interruption was offered by the enemy. The
rebels were more intent on getting to Nashville before that
place could be reinforced from other points, probably, and
believed that they could attend to us afterward. It was
known that Hood had been crossing all of his cavalry, and
that they were also conveniently posted so that they could
have dashed in on us at a dozen points, destroyed our supply train, and captured the entire force guarding it. The
troops in our advance had a considerable fight with some
of this cavalry, and succeeded in driving them off; night
coming on just as the rebel infantry came up to join in.

A NARROW ESCAPE.

That was a night of exquisite agony and anxious fear,
to those who knew the state of affairs: but the unapprised
were very differently affected. We could see in the sky the
glare of camp-fires, that always was a cheerful sign to the
weary tramper, and supposed the advance of our division
was going into camp a mile or more ahead. The boys were
therefore making a little more noise than usual in jollying
each other about what we would have for supper. As the
night advanced, some became very sleepy, and occasionally
one would sit down to rest till the rear-guard came up and
started them on again. Pickets were stationed at short intervals all along the roadside, within ten steps of where we
were passing; but, as we thought they were our pickets,
and the pickets thought we were their troops, no alarm was

felt nor created. Occasionally we were accosted by some one who had already been in camp, with,

"Hello! what rijment?"

"Same old rijment" was the reply.

Then an officer rode along the line, and in a hoarse whisper said :

"For God's sake, boys, don't open your heads ; there's the whole rebel army !"

This announcement was to us like the opening of the eyes of Elisha's servant, among the mountains of Syria. There it was, sure enough, spread out all over the hillside, for miles, and the fellows who were inquiring "what rijment?" were the pickets who had just gone on duty. We didn't utter a sound ; and there was no more straggling that night. Hundreds of the wagons had already halted, and were being parked at Spring Hill ; the teams were put in motion again hastily, and we did not stop till we had put a good mile between our pickets and the rebels'. As we filed off then to the right, across the fields, each soldier took a rail, with which to construct fortifications ; and we soon had a good line of defence along our entire front. It was one of the times when the boys hankered for picks and shovels. They usually didn't.

Next morning we started quite early, and soon were skirmishing with Forrest's cavalry. About 2 miles above Spring Hill, at a place where a long grassy slope led up to a wooded cove, a body of cavalry numbering about 500 made a feint of attacking us. Some of them dashed in and set fire to two of our wagons, and then fled. At this juncture Lieutenant Baldwin, of the 6th Ohio Battery, brought up a gun, and in half a minute had sighted it and sent a shell whizzing into the enemy's midst, the explosion being so exceedingly well-timed as to unhorse more than a score of the "critter-back" johnnies, and sent the rest skurrying into the woods.

Report of Rebel Gen. J. B. Hood.

[Abbreviated from "Advance and Retreat."]

"The Federals at Pulaski became alarmed, and by forced marches reached Columbia, on Duck River, just in time to prevent our troops from cutting them off. The enemy having formed line of battle around Columbia, Lee's corps filed into position with its right on the Mt. Pleasant pike; Stewart's formed on Lee's right, his own right flank extending to the Pulaski pike; and Cheatham established his left on the latter pike, with his right resting on Duck River. Headquarters were established at the residence of Mrs. Warfield, about 3 miles south of Columbia. The two armies lay opposite each other during the 27th. The Federals being entrenched, I determined not to attack them in their breastworks, if I could possibly avoid it, but to permit them to cross undisturbed to the north bank of Duck River that night, as I supposed they would do; to hasten preparations, and endeavor to place the main body of the Confederate army at Spring Hill, 12 miles directly in the enemy's rear, and about mid-way on the only pike leading to Franklin; to attack as the Federals retreated, and put to rout and capture, if possible, their army, which was the sole obstacle between our forces and Nashville — in truth, the only barrier to the success of the campaign.

[Strange, that such a little thing as an army should be "the only obstacle" to their success! That seemed to be the chief trouble at Atlanta, too. In fact, the disgraceful and humiliating failure of the entire Southern slaveocracy, and the removal of the stain and stench of the inhuman system on which it was based and fed, was due to the same "obstacle" — the loyal army.]

I was confident that after Schofield had crossed the river, and placed that obstruction between our respective armies, he would feel in security, and would remain in his position at least a sufficient length of time to allow me to throw pontoons across the river about 3 miles above his left flank, and by a bold and rapid march, together with heavy demonstrations in his front, gain his rear before he was fully apprised of my object. As I apprehended unnecessary and fatal delay might be occasioned by the appearance of the enemy on the line of march to the rear, I decided to bridge the river that night, and move at dawn the next morning, and to leave Lee with the bulk of the artillery to demonstrate heavily against Schofield, and follow him if he retired. I resolved to go in person at the head of the advance brigade, and lead the army to Spring Hill. Col. Presman and his assistants laid the pontoons during the night of the 28th, about 3 miles above Columbia. I passed over the bridge soon after daybreak, and moved forward at the head of a Texas brigade, with instructions that the remaining corps and divisions follow. Gen. Forrest had crossed the evening previous, and moved to the front and right. During the march the Federal cavalry appeared on the hills to our left; not a moment, however, was lost on that account, as the army was marching by the right flank, and was prepared to face at any instant in their direction. The troops moved in light marching order, my object being to turn the enemy's flank by marching rapidly on roads parallel. When I had gotten well on his flank, the enemy discovered my intention. The cavalry became engaged near Spring Hill, but the trains were so strongly guarded, that they were unable to break through them. No attention was paid to the enemy, save to throw out a few sharp-shooters in his front. I well knew that to stop and lose time in reconnoitering would defeat my object, which was to reach the enemy's rear, and cut him off from Nashville. I also knew that Schofield was occupied in his front, since I could distinctly hear the roar of Lee's artillery at Columbia, whilst a feint was made to cross the river. Thus I led the main body of the army to within 2 miles and in full view of the pike from Columbia to Spring Hill and Franklin. I here halted about 3 P. M., and requested Gen. Cheatham, commanding the leading corps, and Major Gen. Claiburne to advance to the spot where, sitting upon my horse, I had in sight the enemy's wagons and men passing at double-quick along the Franklin pike. As these officers approached, I spoke to Cheatham in the following words, which I quote almost verbatim, as they have remained indelibly engraved upon my memory ever since that fatal day: 'General, do you see the enemy there, retreating rapidly to escape us?' He answered in the affirmative. 'Go,' I continued, 'with your corps, take possession and hold that pike at or near Spring Hill. Accept whatever comes, and turn all those wagons over to our side of the house.' Then addressing Claiburne, I said, 'General, you have heard the orders just given. You have one of my best divisions. Go with Gen. Cheatham, assist him in every way you can, and do as he directs.' Again, as a parting injunction to them, I added, 'Go and do this at once. Stewart is near at hand, and I will have him double-quick his men to the front.'

They immediately sent staff officers to hurry the men forward, and moved off with their troops at a quick pace in the direction of the enemy. I dispatched several of my staff to the rear, with orders to Stewart and Johnson to make all possible haste. Within about one-half hour from the time Cheatham left me, skirmishing began with the enemy, when I rode forward to a point nearer the pike, and again sent a staff officer to Stewart and Johnson to push forward. At this juncture the messenger returned with the report that the road had not been taken possession of. By this hour twilight was upon us, when Gen. Cheatham rode up in person. I at once directed Stewart to halt, and turning to Cheatham, I exclaimed with deep emotion, as I felt the golden opportunity fast slipping from me, 'General, why in the name of God have you not attacked the enemy, and taken possession of that pike?' He replied that the line looked a little too long for him. I could hardly believe it possible that

this brave old soldier would make such a report.   After leading him in
full view of the enemy, retreating in great haste and confusion, I would as
soon have expected midday to turn to darkness, as for him to disobey my
orders.   Darkness soon closed upon us, and Stewart's corps, after much
annoyance, went into bivouac for the night, near but not across the pike,
at about 11 or 12 o'clock.   It was reported to me after this hour that the
enemy was marching along the road, almost under the campfires of the
main body of the army.   The Federals with immense wagon trains were
permitted to march by us the remainder of the night, within gunshot of
our lines.   One good division could have routed the enemy which was at
Spring Hill, making it an easy matter to capture Schofield's army that
afternoon and the ensuing day.''

The best move in my career as a soldier, I was thus destined to be-
hold come to naught.   The army, after a forward march of 180 miles, was
still, seemingly, unwilling to accept battle unless under the protection of
breastworks.

[That's right.   He should not have been surprised at
it, though, as it was a well known characteristic of the entire rebel army.]

I hereupon decided, before the enemy would be able to reach his
stronghold at Nashville, to overtake and drive him in the Big Harpeth
river at Franklin, 18 miles from Spring Hill.''

The danger we passed through that night will not be
easily forgotten.   It was like awakening from a horrible
nightmare, and the boys shudder as they look back on our
situation then.   Nor was the danger past when we arrived
at Spring Hill.   There were 800 wagons, including artillery and ambulances, that had to pass singly over a bridge,
and it was 5 o'clock A. M. when the last wagon crossed.

BATTLE OF FRANKLIN.

The head of the column reached Franklin at daylight,
November 30, but the rear-guard did not arrive until late
in the afternoon: finding the 23d Corps occupying some
hastily constructed works: our troops joining their right,
in a line running southeast, both flanks resting on Harpeth
River.   Wood's division crossed on the railroad bridge, so
as to be ready to support either flank, in case the rebels attempted a turn.   The line rested on a slight elevation, and
constructed breastworks, with additional abattis in places.

16

The cavalry was posted on both sides of the town, on the north bank. The artillery of the 23d Corps crossed to the north side, while that of the 4th Corps remained on the south side, some batteries being in the line, and others in reserve. The position was a good one for defence.

Schofield's object in making a stand here, was simply to detain Hood until the trains could be crossed safely over Harpeth River, and well on their way to Nashville. That of Hood was to overwhelm Schofield, compel the sacrifice of his artillery and stores, and then to secure possession of Nashville. His men were encouraged by the immediate prospect of looting that city, and then making a complete sweep to the Ohio River. He hurried up his troops, therefore, and massed them behind a screen of thick woods in a line almost parallel with the Union line, and extending to the river, on the east, where Forrest crossed his guerrillas, but was held in splendid check by Wilson's cavalry. This was done so rapidly that Schofield was almost surprised.

The enemy advanced with two corps heavily massed on the Columbia road, and one corps in reserve, meeting with little resistance; Wagner's two brigades, in their immediate front, having been instructed to check them without involving our army in a general engagement. Slowly our skirmishers retreated to their works, exchanging a sharp fire with those of the enemy; then came a terrific outburst of artillery, and the entire line of rebel skirmishers rushed forward, quickly followed by the massive lines of Cheatham and Stewart, four deep. They met the first resistance in these two brigades, that withstood them with great persistency, till compelled to retire. It was about 3:30 P. M. when the rebel skirmishers began moving, and the battle from that on was a succession of ferocious assaults, bloody hand-to-hand struggles and horrid scenes of carnage and destruction that beggar description. With terrible yells of confident victory, the thirsty rebels came on; our lines falling back in most perfect order, indicating the presence of

veterans, without whom the rebels would have swept everything before them. No other troops of like proportion in
numbers, could withstand such charges. They were like
the sturdy, well-rooted oak in the grapple of a cyclone. At
length one of Cheatham's divisions gained the outworks
held by Wagner, and forced him back on the stronger lines
held by Cox and Ruger. The rebels then reformed their
lines, and again rushed on; and after a most desperate and
bloody contest, penetrated the second line of defenses, capturing two guns. The impetuosity of this charge swept
both Union and rebel forces clear over the fortifications.
In a moment thousands of Union and rebel soldiers were
mixed in an almost inextricable mass, each side demanding
the surrender of the other. The situation had become critical in the last degree. Bayonets and swords and pistols
were freely used, and guns were clubbed. This contest did
not last more than twenty minutes, but it resulted in half
of the entire loss on both sides; and with the clashing of
arms and the yelling of the combatants, it was an accumu-
lated pandemonium. At this supreme moment, Opdycke's
brigade, of Warren's division, which had been in reserve,
was ordered forward, with Conrad's brigade, in support.
Opdycke's voice was immediately heard, ringing clear and
loud above the tumult. Passing down on the north side of
the Carter House on foot, with a revolver in each hand, he
shouted to his command:

"First brigade, forward to the works!"

His brave men responded promptly to the call. On
they went, with firm and steady step; with crushing weight
they fell upon the exultant rebel columns. Having emptied his revolvers, Opdycke seized a musket, and fought till
victory was gained, and the rebels not only checked, but
driven back with fearful slaughter.

The break through the center of the Union lines was
closed, and the assault repelled from one end of the line to
the other. By this our works and guns were recovered,

and 400 prisoners and 10 battle-flags captured. Again and again, in four successive assaults, Hood flung his hungry men, as if with the energy of despair, on the now compact Union lines; but all in vain. The recaptured artillery, 8 pieces, were again turned on the rebels, while sheet upon sheet of flame sprang with certain aim from the veterans, whose soldierly instincts led them unbidden to anticipate the wishes of their brave commander. And as he dashed into the breach, each gallant comrade shouted, "We can go where the general can!" Four regimental commanders fell in the charge, but other officers of equal ability and zeal were ready to take their places. From that time on, we held the line, until the entire place was evacuated in excellent order during the early hours of the next morning. It was midnight before the sounds of musketry and artillery had ceased.

That battle stands without an equal in the history of the world, in the number and vigor of its oft-repeated repulses — bloody, ferocious, impetuous and terrible; and its effect was most plainly visible upon every part of the rebel service. Cleburne, who was a dashing officer, and one of Hood's most capable division commanders, doubtless with a desire to repair his gross mistake at Spring Hill, led his repeated assaults with the expression of frenzied vengeance and valor, his men following him to the very points of the Union bayonets, and falling with him upon the parapet in front of Opdycke's brigade. The moral effect of this fight on the rebel rank and file, may be judged by the following, from an old rebel soldier who fought under Pat. Cleburne on that awful day:

"We were awake early the next morning to discover that the Yankees had crossed the river during the night, and were probably well on their way towards Nashville. We were glad they were gone. Hood seemed to be stupefied at the disaster that had befallen us. He allowed his discouraged army to remain in camp by that bloody battlefield. The repeated disasters we had encountered under Hood had dampened our ardor. The unwise rambling of our men over the battlefield of Franklin broke their spirit. We could not fight at Nashville. We lost that fight because the specter of Franklin, livid, with distorted features, with blood-streaming wounds, with ghastly, horror-stricken eyes, stalked among us. It was in the columns as we marched; it rode astride of the Napoleons; it sat by our camp-fires; it stood in the trenches at Nashville, and it lay in the rifle-pits o' nights."

The Union losses were great, but were not to be compared with those of the enemy. This is more wonderful, when it is remembered that, beside the rebels having near or quite three times our numbers, our troops had had no rest in the 48 hours preceding the battle. They were not too tired to do the honors of the occasion. Cheatham was correct in thinking our line was "too long for him."

Hood's Report of the Franklin Fight.

"Within about 3 miles of Franklin, the enemy was discovered on the ridge over which passes the turnpike. It was about 3 P. M. [Nov. 30] when Stewart moved to the right of the pike and began to establish his position in front of the enemy. Cheatham filed off to the left of the road; the artillery was instructed to take no part in the engagement, on account of the danger to which women and children in the village would be exposed; Forrest was ordered to post cavalry on both flanks, to capture those who attempted to escape; Lee's corps was held in reserve. The two corps advanced in battle array about 4 P. M., and soon swept away the first line of the Federals, who were driven back upon the main line. At this moment resounded a concentrated roar of musketry, which recalled to me some of the deadliest struggles in Virginia; the contest continued to rage with intense fury. Just at this critical moment, a brigade, reported to be Stanley's, gallantly charged and restored the Federal line, capturing at the same time 1,000 of our troops. Still the ground was obstinately contested, and at several points on the immediate sides of the breastworks, the combatants endeavored to use the musket on each other, by inverting and raising it perpendicularly, in order to fire; neither being able to retreat without almost a certainty of death. It was reported that soldiers were even dragged from one side of the breastworks to the other by reaching over and seizing the enemy by the hair or collar. The struggle continued till 9 P. M., when followed skirmishing till 3 A. M. the ensuing morning.   *   Our loss in killed, wounded and prisoners was 4,500."

According to Van Horne, [vol. ii, p. 202,] the Fourth Corps alone expended one hundred wagon-loads of ammunition in this battle. Hood buried 1,750 men on the field. He had 3,800 so disabled as to be placed in hospitals, and lost 702 captured; an aggregate of 6,252, exclusive of those slightly wounded. General Schofield lost 189 killed, 1,033 wounded, and 1,104 missing; an aggregate of 2,326.

Gen. T. J. Wood's division retained its position, near the railroad bridge, until the rest of the troops had withdrawn; then, destroying the bridges, they followed as the rear-guard of the army, the Fifty-First Indiana bringing up the extreme rear, with Wilson's cavalry on its flanks, and with which they were able to beat back the head of the rebel column. With the exception of a little skirmish at Brentwood, a little more than half way between Franklin and Nashville, they gave us no trouble on the way.

When we arrived at Nashville, about 1 P. M., Thursday, December 1, '64, the Union line of battle was formed on the hights immediately surrounding that city. A. J. Smith's corps from the Army of the Tennessee, which had arrived just the day before, held the right, with its flank touching the river below the city. The 23d Corps, under General Schofield, was assigned to the left, extending to the Nolinsville pike; Gen. T. J. Wood, commanding the 4th Corps, occupied the center, opposite Montgomery Hill. Wilson's cavalry was directed to take position on the left of Schofield; which would make safe the interval between his left and Cumberland River above the city. Steedman took up a position about a mile in advance of the left center of the main line, and on the left of the Nolinsville pike.

And "Old Pap" Thomas directing it all.

On the 3d, General Thomas moved all the remaining cavalry to Gallatin and across the river to Edgefield, and then Steedman covered the space between Schofield and the river.

At the same time Hood approached the city, drove in our outposts, and on the 4th established his main line, with his salient on Montgomery Hill, directly facing the Fifty-First, and within 600 yards of our center. His main line occupied the high ground on the southeast side of Brown's

Creek, and extending from the Nolinsville pike—his extreme right, across the Franklin and Granny White pikes, in a westerly direction to the hills south and southwest of Richland Creek, and down that creek to the Hillsboro pike, with cavalry and guerrillas extending from both flanks to the river. Artillery opened on him from several points on the line, without eliciting any response. With this disposition of his troops, Hood began to intrench vigorously, and continued so to do up to the morning of the 15th, with little or no change.

JUST BEFORE THE BATTLE.

Friday, December 2, the paymaster visited us, and we received two months' pay, with the addition, to "veterans," of the installment of bounty due. We were also cheered by the wonderful good fortune that had attended us during our retreat from Pulaski, and by the announcement that heavy reinforcements were coming. Each day we looked for an attack, and increased vigilance was observed to prevent surprise by Hood, who had sworn to eat his Christmas dinner in Nashville or in hell. He found it convenient, however, to place the Tennessee River between himself and his "only obstacle" before he hung up his stocking.

We had many good singers in our regiment; and there was no trouble to scare up a full orchestra on any occasion, when opportunity offered, and the instruments could be obtained. But our voices we had with us all the time; and when in camp or on the march, it was no uncommon thing for one to start a song, and then for the whole regiment to join in the chorus. Indeed, it became necessary at times, when crossing a bridge that was a little shaky, to make the boys stop singing, and break step, because the swinging motion given to the bridge by keeping time, threatened to tear the structure down. But let us get into camp early on a pleasant afternoon, with no enemy in close proximity, with wood and water and good rations plenty and handy—

just as we were then; listen to the boys, as they broiled a
slice of bacon or beef on a forked stick. or boiled a fruit-can
pot of coffee. No one had to be led up to the piano, nor
apologized about a sore throat, nor waited for an invitation
or somebody to lead off. Each one was a master; and the
less melody or mellowness a voice possessed, the greater
reason it seemed for cultivating it. A thought would come
into a comrade's mind, of how pretty the old flag looked as
it floated out in front of headquarters, and instantly, .

"O, say, can you see, by the dawn's early light,
What so proudly we hailed in the twilight's last gleaming?"

rang out loud and clear; mingling its patriotic incense
with the delicious fumes of the coffee and bacon. Then,
as the moon came out and moved serenely across the clear
sky, some love-sick swain, who had just received a letter
from his sweetheart, would break forth in

"Roll on, silver moon; guide the traveler on his way;
While the nightingale's song is in tune.
For I never, never more with my true love will stray
By the sweet silver light of the moon."

And how sadly true this proved with many. Or another,
filled with a hopeful longing for the sweet Hoosier girl that
occupied the bulk of his heart, would launch out with

"O——h! that girl, that girl, that pretty little girl;
The girl I left behind me!"

And wind up with an attempt to reproduce it with his feet.
or land the toe of his bootee into the anatomy of some
good-natured comrade, to whom he would confide the fond
assurance that she was the nicest girl in Indiana, and tell
him enough of the contents of her last letter to prove it.

Over in the next company you might hear

"Dearest love, do you remember, when we last did meet,
How you told me that you loved me, kneeling at my feet?
Oh, how proud you stood before me, in your suit of blue;
When you vowed to me and country ever to be true.
Weeping sad and lonely:
Hopes and fears how vain!
Praying, when this cruel war is over,
Praying we may meet again."

While another, snugged down in his dog-tent, stretched out on the flat of his back, contemplating the "grand and awful time" in which we were living, his sweet rich voice would breathe the noble sentiment of

> "A thousand years, my own Columbia!
> 'Tis the glad day so long foretold;
> 'Tis the glad morn, whose early twilight
> Washington saw in days of old."

Another took his pipe from his lips long enough to hum,

> "Maxwelton braes are bonnie, where early falls the dew;
> And 'twas there that Annie Laurie gave me her promise true."

when he was probably broken into by

> "Brave boys are they! gone at their country's call;
> And yet, and yet, we cannot forget, that many brave boys must fall."

Down the quarters strides a little fellow, with his cap to one side, who rings out with

> "Say, darkies, hab you seed de massa,
> Wid de muftash on his face?
> He pack his trunk dis mawnin' mighty airly,
> Like he gwine to leab de place."

Instantly he would be joined by a hundred jolly fellows in the chorus:

> "Ole massa run, ha! ha!
> De darkies stay, ho! ho!
> It mus' be now de kingdom's comin',
> An' de yeah ob jubilo!"

These were all popular songs of those days, and were sung in all the theatres and opera halls all over the world. One of the most popular was "Babylon has fallen," which came out about the time the negro was introduced in the solution of his social and commercial relation to the rest of humanity It took like hot cakes, and was used much in retaliation for such venomous and insulting songs as "Bonnie Blue Flag," which was sung by all rebel women whenever occasion offered:

> "Don't you see de black cloud rising ober yender,
> Whar de massa's ole plantation am?
> Neber you be frightened; dem is only darkies,
> Come to jine an' fight for Uncle Sam!

CHORUS: Look out, dar, now; we's gwine to shoot!
    Look out, dar; don't you understand?
Babylon is fallen! Babylon is fallen!
    An' we's gwine to occupy de land.

Don't you see de lightnin' flashin' in de cane-brake,
    Like as if we's gwine to hab a storm?
No! you is mistaken; 'tis de darkies' bay'nets,
    An' de buttons on dar uniform.—*Chorus.*

'Way up in de cornfiel', whar you hear de thunder;
    Dar is our ole forty-pounder gun;
When de shells is missin', den we load wid punkins;
    All de same to make de cowards run.—*Chorus.*

And nowadays, when you want to stir the old boys, as nothing else will, just start

"Bring the good old bugle, boys; we'll have another song:
Sing it with the spirit that will start the world along:
Sing it as we used to sing it, fifty thousand strong,
    While we were marching through Georgia.
CHORUS: Hurrah! hurrah! we bring the jubilee!
    Hurrah! hurrah! the flag that makes you free!
So we sang the chorus from Atlanta to the sea,
    While we were marching through Georgia.

How the darkies shouted, when they heard the joyful sound!
How the turkeys gobbled, which our commissary found!
How the sweet potatoes even started from the ground!
    While we were marching through Georgia.—*Chorus.*

Yes, and there were Union men who wept with joyful tears,
When they saw the honored flag they had not seen for years:
Hardly could they be restrained from breaking forth in cheers!
    While we were marching through Georgia.—*Chorus.*

Sherman's dashing Yankee boys will never reach the coast!
So the saucy rebels said; and 't was a handsome boast.
Ha! they not forgot, alas! to reckon with the host?
    While we were marching through Georgia.—*Chorus.*

So we made a thoroughfare for freedom and her train,
Sixty miles in latitude, three hundred to the main;
Treason fled before us; for resistance was in vain,
    While we were marching through Georgia.—*Chorus.*

General Sherman heard that so often, that he came to almost hate it; and the writer has seen him turn with an expression of disgust, as band after band, followed by every variety of drum-corps, each shifting hastily, and sometimes awkwardly, from no matter what they were playing, to the air of "Marching through Georgia;" which each of course intended as a personal compliment to "old Tecump." In Boston, where, at the National Encampment of the G. A. R., he stood in review for seven mortal hours, listening to the endless din, 250 bands and more than a hundred drum-corps passed him; the dying notes of the last band fairly dove-tailing into those of the next, playing that same tune. It is said that the old general got so mad, that he swore a big oath that he never would attend another Encampment, until every band in the United States had signed an agreement to not play that tune in his presence. That was his last National Encampment. When next it was played in his presence, it was as a dead march accompanying his funeral cortege.

The most popular of all the army songs, however, was "Johnny, fill up the bowl." It ran as follows:

"In eighteen hundred and sixty-one,
        So bold! so bold!
In eighteen hundred and sixty-one,
        So bold! so bold!
In eighteen hundred and sixty-one,
The war had then but just begun;
And we'll all drink stone-blind:
        Johnny, fill up the bowl!

In eighteen hundred and sixty-two,
        So bold! so bold!
In eighteen hundred and sixty-two,
        So bold! so bold!
In eighteen hundred and sixty-two,
They first began to put us through;
And we'll all drink stone-blind:
        Johnny, fill up the bowl!

In eighteen hundred and sixty-three,
        So bold! so bold!
In eighteen hundred and sixty-three,
        So bold! so bold!
In eighteen hundred and sixty-three,
Abe Lincoln set the niggers free;
And we'll all drink stone-blind:
        Johnny, fill up the bowl!

In eighteen hundred and sixty-four,
  So bold! so bold!
In eighteen hundred and sixty-four,
  So bold! so bold!
In eighteen hundred and sixty-four,
We all went in for three years more;
And we'll all drink stone-blind:
  Johnny, fill up the bowl!

In eighteen hundred and sixty-five,
  So bold! so bold!
In eighteen hundred and sixty-five,
  So bold! so bold!
In eighteen hundred and sixty-five
We'll all be glad to get home alive;
And we'll all drink stone-blind:
  Johnny, fill up the bowl!

While this was being sung, some one would chime in with "So, ball! so, ball!" Next time, another would ring out, "Sow-belly! sow-belly!" and another, "S'boy! s'boy!" and so on; till every change was rung on the refrain. As to this intoxication, however, it was a fantastic fiction; the only flowing bowl the average soldier ever had "filled up" for him by "Johnny," or by anybody else, being a rusty old tin-cup, with a gill of the nastiest kind of commissary whisky, so loaded with quinine, that the victim would howl with agony before the contents fairly touched his stomach; and he seldom repeated it.

All this time, our mothers and wives and sisters and sweethearts at home were doing their part. In addition to the packing and forwarding of nice boxes of creature comforts, lint and bandages, they were wielding a powerful moral influence, which held the cowardly copperheads in check. One letter told about a young fellow, who, having served three years, and also through the "hundred days" service, was present at a copperhead meeting in the town where he lived. On their way home, four of the copperheads gave notice that they were going over to "clean him out." Accordingly they went; but he was prepared for them, and shot two of them; killing one, and badly crippling the other. The soldier boy was arrested, tried and acquitted. The ladies paid his attorney's fee; and that night gave the grandest party that was ever known in that locality, in his honor. There was a world of cheer to us at the front, in reports of such doings at home, which assured us that our interests were regarded with sacred devotion by our noble women.

Picket duty in front of Nashville was attended with unusual danger, as the rebels were continually on the alert for any surprise, and would shoot at anything that had the appearance of a Yankee. Corporal Calvin Dickerson, on picket on the 9th or 10th, received a shot that went clear through both legs, just below the knees. He was a non-veteran, and his time would have expired on the 14th.

Lieut. Geo. W. Scearce declared it was the hottest job he ever undertook. He was ordered to take Co. K, join the skirmishers in front, take command, and drive off the rebels, who were building fortifications right in our front. On reconnoitering, the lieutenant reported to Col. Streight that the rebels were too many for him. Colonel Streight then sent his orderly, George Gregg, with orders for them to lie down, and fall back under cover of darkness. This was the only thing that could be done, as there was a continuous sheet of flame blazing along the entire line as they went up. Great was the surprise, when the men reported in camp that night, on discovering that not a single man was hurt. The suspense during the hours they lay on that bare moor, waiting for night, was something terrible.

In the reorganization of our brigade, we were placed with the 8th Kansas; and the Fifty-First still lacking in commissioned officers, Lieutenants Slemmens and Schultz. of that command, were assigned to duty in our regiment, the former in command of Co. A, and the latter of Co. F. They were both brave and efficient officers, and won the confidence of our own brave boys whom they led in the storm of battle that soon came.

THE BATTLE OF NASHVILLE.

General Thomas had been waiting impatiently for an opportunity to attack Hood, and punish him for his temerity. He had hoped to be ready for battle on the 7th, but on account of delay in remounting the cavalry, he was not ready until the 9th; and then, there came a heavy rain, accompanied by a cold wave, that covered the hills around Nashville with a coat of ice, that prevented any military movements on either side, and rendered a battle an utter impossibility. Reconnoisances on the 11th and 13th, made it plain that infantry could only move with extreme difficulty, while horses had to be expressly shod for the slippery surface. A knowledge of this fact — that was also manifest to every veteran in the ranks, prompted General Thomas' refusal to comply with an order from General Grant, in the far-away city of Annapolis, Maryland, to attack without waiting longer for weather or reinforcements. For this, Grant ordered his removal from command, naming Schofield as his successor. On the 13th, Gen. John A. Logan, who was at St. Louis, was also ordered to relieve Thomas; and on the 15th, Grant reached Washington, on his way to take command in person. To the old boys who had been fighting and marching under "Old Pap" Thomas so long, and who they had learned to regard as "the noblest Roman of them all," these orders appeared spectacular and useless.

The morning of the 14th was indeed a bleak one for that latitude. Everything was covered with ice an inch thick, as far as the eye could reach, and walking was still extremely difficult and dangerous. The week previous had been well employed by General Thomas in reinforcing both cavalry and infantry; and he was also well informed as to the disposition of the enemy. By noon the weather had so moderated and the ice thawed, that the commander determined to attack the next morning; and at 3 P. M., he called his corps commanders together to announce to them his plan of operation, and to instruct them in the specific part he desired each should take. After thorough deliberation, the following special field order was issued:

" As soon as the state of the weather will admit of offensive operations, the troops will move against the enemy's position in the following order:

Major-General A. J. Smith, commanding detachment of the Army of the Tennessee, after forming his troops on and near the Harding pike, in front of his present position, will make a vigorous assault on the enemy's left.

Major-General Wilson, commanding the cavalry corps, Military Division of Mississippi, with three divisions, will move on and support General Smith's right, assisting as far as possible in carrying the left of the enemy's position, and be in readiness to throw his force upon the enemy the moment a favorable opportunity occurs. Major-General Wilson will also send one division on the Charlotte pike, to clear that road of the enemy, and observe in the direction of Bell's landing, to protect our right rear until the enemy's position is fairly turned, when it will rejoin the main force.

Brigadier-General T. J. Wood, commanding Fourth Corps, after leaving a strong skirmish line in his works from Lawrens' Hill to his extreme right, will form the remainder of the Fourth Corps on the Hillsboro pike to support General Smith's left, and operate on the left and rear of the enemy's advanced position on Montgomery Hill.

Major-General Schofield, commanding Twenty-third Army Corps, will replace Brigadier-General Kimball's division of the Fourth Corps with his troops, and occupy the trenches from Fort Negley to Lawrens' Hill with a strong skirmish line. He will move with the remainder of his force in front of the works, and co-operate with General Wood, protecting the latter's left flank against an attack by the enemy.

Major-General Steedman, commanding District of Etowah, will occupy the interior line in rear of his present position, stretching from the reservoir on the Cumberland River to Fort Negley, with a strong skirmish line, and mass the remainder of his force in its present position, to act according to the exigencies which may arise during these operations.

Brigadier-General Miller, with troops forming the garrison of Nashville, will occupy the interior line from the battery on hill 210, to the extreme right, including the inclosed work on the Hyde's Ferry road.

The quartermaster's troops, under the command of Brigadier-General Donaldson, will, if necessary, be posted on the interior line from Fort Morton to the battery on hill 210.

The troops occupying the interior line will be under the direction of Major-General Steedman, who is charged with the immediate defence of Nashville during the operations around the city.

Should the weather permit, the troops will be formed to commence operations at 6 A. M. on the 15th, or as soon thereafter as practicable."*

General Thomas modified this order by directing Gen. Steedman to make a strong feint against the enemy's right, so as to lead Hood to bring still more of his troops to that wing, and to divert his attention from the dominant movement against the enemy's left. It was Thomas' intention then to mass the Union forces against the enemy's reduced left, to overwhelm it, break his line, roll it back upon the center, and if possible crush both. This was his plan for the first day's fight; on the second he proposed to break down Hood's right, and either envelope and capture his army, or shatter and rout it so thoroughly as to completely destroy its organization, and send it in ignominious flight beyond the Tennessee. How nearly prophetic his calculations were, the history of that campaign tells.

The weather and ice, that had prevented offensive operations on our part, also barred all activity of the rebels; who, deeming it impossible to successfully assault the army intrenched before Nashville, meditated a movement around the city. Hood evidently had no idea of General Thomas' intention; and must have been greatly astonished when he beheld on that cheerless morning of the 15th, the threatening attitude of the host that confronted him.

At 4 A. M. on the 15th, the provisional division formed from various organizations of Sherman's army, commanded by General Cruft, moved forward and relieved the 4th and 23d Corps, and occupied their exterior line of works. Gen. T. J. Wood formed the 4th Corps with the 2d Division on the right, commanded by General Elliott; 1st Division in the center, commanded by General Kimball; and the 3d Division, commanded by General Beatty, on the left. The formation was in double battle-line; the first deployed, and the second in column, by division, opposite the intervals in the first. The front was covered with a line of skirmishers, and a similar force remained in the works in the rear.

As the sun arose, a dense fog was formed, that hung

over the two armies till nearly noon, when it lifted, revealing to the rebel commander the handwriting on the wall — that the time of his defeat and humiliation was at hand.

When the combination to turn Hood's left was completed, General Thomas sent a message to General Steedman to advance, in semblance of actual assault. This was done, and the charge on the enemy's works was gallantly made. Hood was so deceived, that he drew troops from his center and left to strengthen his seemingly endangered flank. Soon after this action, the forces on the opposite flank moved forward on the Harding and Hillsboro roads; both movements being attended with success almost phenomenal. Then Schofield and Smith advanced their lines.

The action of the 4th Corps was, if possible, even more successful. On it depended the most important results; and true to its record, it performed the part assigned in a manner that evoked the highest praise.

In the preparatory alignment, the Fifty-First advanced to the summit of a low rocky ridge overlooking the Montgomery farm, forming in echelon, in the edge of a woods pasture that ran down and across a broad ravine 300 or 400 yards in width. On the crest of Montgomery Hill stood the residence of Widow Montgomery, a substantial brick.

As the sun began to penetrate the fog, a beautiful and grand scene was presented to us, as far as the eye could reach, of the forces moving out, the double line of soldiers gradually dwindling, till they seemed like a thread of blue yarn, with here and there a patch of red, where the colors appeared.

As we stood on that point, awaiting the formation and alignment of troops on our left, our attention was attracted to the Montgomery residence, from the windows of which some rebel sharpshooters were exhibiting a superior marksmanship by sending well-aimed bullets among our boys, a number of whom received these tokens in various parts of their bodies. Some of those whose term of enlist-

17

ment had expired on the 14th, had a little delicacy about exposing themselves, and were excused. There were many exceptions, however; some of whom received wounds more or less severe. The fun of those sharpshooters came to be very monotonous to us; and a gun from the 6th Ohio Battery was run up, an officer, Capt. A. P. Baldwin—then a lieutenant, and since the war a citizen of Akron, Ohio— hastily sighted and pulled the lanyard; when bang! whiz! went a shell, crashing through the Montgomery house, at the precise point where the rebel sharpshooters had been observed a moment before. The shell, exploding at the same instant it struck the building, tore a hole several feet in diameter, and effectually silenced those sharpshooters. The writer met Captain Baldwin at the great G. A. R. National Encampment in Washington City, in September, 1892, and without knowing who the comrade was, was narrating this incident; when that officer quietly extended his hand, while a tear of proud recollection stole out, and he said, "That's right; I fired that gun!"

Then came the signal to advance; and wheeling the companies quickly into line, we started off on a quick-step, that very soon increased to a run. Down the grassy slope we sped, and up again on the other side of the shallow ravine; the rebel bullets whistling merrily about our heads. The ascent was more abrupt and difficult in some places, the approaches being covered with abattis and sharpened stakes firmly driven in the ground. Occasionally one of our boys was hit; and dropping down, he was soon found by the ambulance corps, and carried to the rear. Schofield having been sent to the right, to fill the interval between Smith and Wilson, as the 4th Corps advanced, it swung to the left, in order that our division might have an easier ascent. Then came the command to "charge with a yell!" And such a yell as we gave! The command was needless, so far as the Fifty-First was concerned; for we anticipated it. Captain Scearce was in command; Captain Anderson

being next in order of rank; John Young, of Co. G, color-
bearer; Will Shockley, of Co. C, with the regimental flag.
On and up we rushed; every fellow trying to gain the rebel
works first — shooting, loading, yelling; all inspired with a
single thought — of crushing every obstacle. About half
way over, Captain Scearce, impatient to plant our flag first
on the enemy's salient, dashed up to John Young, who was
pushing forward with long and rapid strides, two or three
paces in advance of the line, and grasping the flag-staff,
the officer put spurs to his horse, leaving the regiment behind, but taking with him the plucky color-sergeant, who
did not propose to relinquish the colors, but was determined
to plant them there himself. So violent was the struggle,
that the captain was pulled from his horse; and before he
could remount and overtake him, "Jug," as he was familiarly called, had driven the staff into the soft dirt on the
top of the rebel works. But it did not remain there long;
for the troops swarming over the fortification only a second
later, swept colors and color-bearer to the very summit; and
the Fifty-First Indiana Veterans had taken Montgomery Hill!
while the johnnies fled in dire confusion. And the record
now reads, "Wood carries Pos. A (Montgomery Hill,) at 1
o'clock."

As we charged into the yard of the Montgomery residence, two boys of Co. C, were shot in the legs, by fleeing
rebels, who immediately paid for it with their lives. On
our occupation of the rebel works, we at once moved to the
left a short distance, and began throwing up breastworks,
when we were ordered to move over in front of the works,
a little to the right. The rays of the sun had softened the
ice so that it crushed beneath our feet, rendering walking
easier, and enabled the cavalry and batteries to move with
less difficulty. An increasing slope ran to the woods now
occupied by the rebels. Over this our line moved in one
steady, imposing column. The crest of the hill in front
partly sheltered us from the enemy's artillery. A dense

volume of smoke rose from the valley, shrouding the hills and the rebel lines in our front, and uniting with the heavy fog that had not yet entirely left the hilltops. The roar of rebel artillery was becoming fainter, while the crash of our guns increased each hour. The 4th Corps halted for a moment, to enable Smith to connect, when suddenly the rebels could be seen breaking pell-mell from their works, cavalry, infantry and artillery skurrying and sweeping in various directions. A wild cheer rang from our lines, and the batteries redoubled their iron storm. Soon a column was seen emerging from the woods on the rebel flank, and the stars and stripes at their head showed that Smith had swung around the force in his front. Instantly the 4th Corps jumped to their feet, and pressed forward, driving the rebels steadily. The fighting from this time on was all in our favor. We drove the enemy several miles. General Wood had put the reserve of each division on his right, and then engaged the enemy with the entire corps. Three batteries were brought into play. Advancing to a fortified hill on the west side of the Granny White pike, and near the center of Hood's main line, two batteries were placed so as to throw a converging fire upon the hill, which was furiously bombarded for an hour, when General Kimball was ordered to charge with his whole division. At the same time General Elliott carried the intrenchments in his front, and our division crowned the hill. With loud cheers the 4th Corps ascended and leaped over the intrenchments, capturing a large number of prisoners, several pieces of artillery and several stands of colors. In this general advance, our line became slightly involved with that of Smith's, and we were directed to move to the Franklin pike, 2½ miles distant, and facing to the south, to drive the enemy across it. The order was taken up, and the corps moved as directed; but night came too soon for it to reach its destination, and we bivouacked on the east side of the Granny White pike, on a line parallel with the road.

At nightfall the Union lines were readjusted, so as to run along the Hillsboro pike, excepting the 4th Corps, disposed as mentioned above ; Schofield on the right, Smith in the center, and Wood on the left, with the cavalry on the right of Schofield.

By these movements Hood was entirely crowded out of his original works, and compelled to take a new position along the base of the Harpeth hills. So promptly did each part of the Union army respond to the action of the rest, that the rebels were continually deceived and kept dodging about, wondering what we would do next.

The result of that day's operations, was the capture of 17 pieces of artillery, over 1,200 prisoners, several hundred stands of small arms and 40 wagons. The Union casualties were unusually light, and insignificant compared with those of the enemy ; also, the behavior of General Thomas' troops was remarkable for steadiness and alacrity in every movement.

During a lull in hostilities in the afternoon, the commissary sergeant having to go to Nashville to draw rations, the sergeant-major was directed by the commander of the regiment, to bring up some beef that had been delivered just before the advance was made, but had no one to issue it to the companies. On arriving at the place, he found meat enough to load ten men, but no detail to carry it forward, nearly a mile, to where the regiment was. So he pressed in half a dozen white fellows and nearly as many darkies, who said they had come out to see the fight, but who were really only a lot of thieves, in quest of plunder ; ready to rob the dead soldiers, who had just been paid off. Like those fellows mentioned in the Scriptures, each one had a powerful reason for being excused, but the sergeant-major was insensible to distress ; drawing his revolver, he declared he would make a ghost of each one before he could turn around, if they didn't grab onto that meat and hump toward the front instantly. With white lips and trembling knees, they laid hold of the beef, and bore it to within a few yards of the regiment, that was again in line expecting a charge by the rebels. At that moment, the rebels, who had reached the summit of the slope overlooking the pike, made a stand, and a lively little skirmish ensued. Two or three crashing volleys rent the air; when with eyes rolling in an agony of terror, the citizens begged to be permitted to return to town. With a significant word of instruction *to go back to the city*, they were released; and dropping the meat they split the air like a flash of greased lightning, and in a second more were out of sight. The meat was distributed to details from each company, while the fight was in progress, and the overshot bullets made the work one of extreme danger. It was a hard fight, and a number of the Fifty-First boys were wounded; but they all stood right up to the work, and fought like true heroes. Here it was that Sergeant Frank Brown, with seven men of his company, captured a rebel battery of four guns, and turned them on the enemy.

It was between 9 and 10 o'clock that night, when the Fifty-First, after countermarching, flanking and obliquing up and down the Granny White pike enough to bewilder the most accomplished backwoodsman, laid down in a nice grassy meadow. Spreading our dog-tents on the grass, we threw our overcoats or blankets over us, and after a word of gratitude to the gracious Father who had protected us through the bloody experiences of the day, we drifted off to dreamland.

In the morning of the 16th we felt refreshed, and were ready for battle at an early hour. The whole army arose with an assurance of victory. Congratulations from President Lincoln and the authorities at Washington sped their way with lightning rapidity to General Thomas, and were hastily communicated to his army; this added to the inspiration of accomplished victory, and the defeat of this one of the two great armies on which the existence of the rebellion depended, seemed a foregone certainty. At home, the reaction from the uneasiness that had obtained, to the ecstasy of hopefulness, was one of the most marked revulsions of opinion and feeling during the war.

During the night Hood had drawn back his center and right to a stronger position, moved his right wing over on Overton Hill, his line extending along the base of the Harpeth or Brentwood range, and his artillery massed at such points as were most available for effective use. He had straightened his line and shortened it nearly one-half, and his troops spent the night in strengthening and extending the fortifications previously constructed by him. He was therefore prepared to receive us: and we were on hand ere they had their breakfast dishes washed.

Each corps of Thomas' army was prepared both for attack and pursuit, and was ordered to move forward rapidly at 6 A. M., until the enemy should be met. At that hour the 4th Corps advanced promptly as ordered toward the Franklin pike, about two miles, nearly due east, part of the way by right of companies, but frequently forming in line of battle. This was very tiresome, and sufficient of itself to exhaust the troops; who, however, affected even a cheerfulness that was wonderful. The weather was somewhat improved in temperature, but the thaw was succeeded by mud, that rendered walking extremely difficult. The enemy's skirmishers were soon encountered, and speedily driven back, and we gained the Franklin pike. Here the corps was deployed — Elliott's division across the pike and facing south, Beatty's on the left, and Kimball's in reserve behind Elliott. We then advanced rapidly three-fourths of a mile, where we met a strong skirmish line behind barricades, their main line being plainly in view, half a mile beyond. Simultaneously, General Smith on the right, and General Steedman on the left, advanced, but found the enemy had fled. Steedman then pressed forward and took position on our left, across the Franklin railroad. Owing to the irregularity of the surface, the country being very hilly, and covered with dense forests, most of the cavalry was found impracticable. For the same reason, it was hard also to move artillery; but the guns at all points available kept up a measured fire, shelling the woods.

The Brentwood hills, rising 350 feet above the level of the country, consist of two ranges, one running southeast, the other southwest, terminating on opposite sides of the Brentwood Pass, through which the Franklin pike runs. These hills formed Hood's background. Overton Hill, the northernmost summit from which these ranges trend, commanded the Franklin pike, running along their base, and was intrenched around the northern slope, the approaches being obstructed by abattis and felled trees. This made the position a very strong one; and as we came into full sight of it, it became apparent that one of the most desperate struggles awaited us.

The assaulting column consisted of Post's brigade supported by Colonel Streight's brigade. General Steadman also directed Col. Thompson's brigade of colored troops to co-operate in the assault. At 3 P. M., the assaulting columns moved up the steep ascent, covered with a strong line of skirmishers, to draw the enemy's fire, and cause him to expend his limited ammunition, as well as to annoy his artillery. It was very dangerous clambering among the long lines of sharpened stakes, which were firmly planted in the ground; and many, who were crowded against them, were almost impaled on their points. Our instructions were to move steadily till near the intrenchments; then dash right up, leap the parapet, and sweep everything before us. An obstacle was presented, however, that raised a doubt as to the completeness of our success. The rebels had four large guns posted at the top of the hill, supported by six lines of infantry. Our boys were exhausted, and under ordinary circumstances would have been glad to delay the battle a few hours. But they felt that the end was near; and were eager to begin the fray, and have it over. As we moved up, the rebels on the summit got such range of us that they slashed the canister and solid shot into us with a prodigality that was appalling. We were compelled to lie down.

While in this fearfully exposed position, an incident occurred that will haunt the writer as long as life remains. 1st Lieut. Peter G. Tait, of the 89th Illinois, while standing a little in advance of his regiment, which lapped the right wing of the Fifty-First, was struck by a cannon ball near the center of his body, tearing a great hole in the left side. As he fell, he threw his right arm around to his side, when his heart and left lung dropped out into it. The heart continued to throb for twenty minutes, its pulsations being distinctly seen by his agonized comrades, who stood there and saw the noble life fade out in heroic self-sacrifice. The ball buried itself in a log immediately in the rear; doubtless thereby saving the lives of others who were in direct range of the deadly missile.

Then our artillery got in position, and opened a vigorous fire, giving roar after roar, with quick repetition, and the command was given to forward the whole line. Col. Thompson's brigade of colored troops came up at the same instant, and a part of their right lapped the left of our regiment. We reached the crest with comparative safety; but in another moment the enemy rose, and poured into us a fire of grape, canister, schrapnel and musketry, so terrific and destructive, that we were compelled to fall back, with great loss, leaving our dead and wounded, white and black, mingled indiscriminately in the dense and almost impenetrable tangle of felled trees. The colored troops fought as bravely as any here, and suffered equally with the whites. There and then was gallant Joe Fleece, of Co. A, pierced through the heart with a rebel bullet. Another was John W. Wells, of Co. C. He was a brave and faithful soldier. There was no better type of the American soldier than he, :far as patriotic ardor, honesty and sobriety required;

and he was without a spark of braggadocio. There, also, were stricken down in their noble young manhood, killed instantly, eight others of our own regiment, besides 86 others — according to the memorandum made that night by Hospital Steward Fitch — who received more or less severe wounds, most of whom died in consequence, within the next few weeks or months. Lieut. John Welton, of Co. E, was shot so badly in one of his legs, that it had to be amputated there. Capt. M. T. Anderson was shot in the side, the ball passing clear around his back, lodging in the hip opposite, whence it was extracted. He fell from his horse waving his sword and cheering the boys on. Lieut. Geo. W. Scearce was wounded in the thigh, at the head of his company ; and many others, whose records ought to be in this category, but which it has been impossible to obtain, received wounds while performing deeds of valor equal to any that have been mentioned. Captain Anderson was granted a medal by the War Department, for conspicuous gallantry in this fight, in accordance with the act of Congress approved March 3, 1863. Co. G lost Joseph Brown, a noble young man. He was shot through the head, when within twenty feet of the rebel works. Sergeant Holman and another comrade went to him, but he was unconscious. They carried him back and placed him in an ambulance ; and that was the last they ever saw of him.

The following names of killed and mortally wounded, in that bloody charge, are all that can be obtained from the Adjutant General's report : Joseph Fleece, Ephraim Tull, Co. A ; John Musson, G. E. Tiffany, J. S. Hurst, Harry Troup, Co. B ; John W. Wells, Samuel Patterson, Co. C ; Alva E. Sowers, Wm. Smith, Ira G. Thorn, Timothy Whitmore, Co. E ; George Walker, Co. F : John L. Keith, Wm. W. Bruce, Perry Hollingsworth, Bernard Hollingsworth, Daniel T. Myers, Co. H : David Welty, Co. I ; David A. Harvey, David S. Strain, Adam Wolf, Co. K.

How we got there — or stayed there — or got away at

all, alive, no one will ever tell. Showers of lead — whole sheets of blue liquid lead — seemed to pour over those rebel earthworks. But we got back. O, yes; we had to. Some of us ran backward most of the way, because we didn't like the idea of being found with a hole in our back. In this way the writer discovered a badly wounded comrade of Co. H under the lee of a large stone chimney, where a hut had stood, and to which he had managed to crawl for safety. Calling another comrade, they made a chair of their hands, carried the wounded boy back, and placed him in an ambulance.

Captain Scearce, commanding the regiment, had his horse shot under him. In falling, the captain's foot was caught under the horse; from which he soon extricated himself, and hobbled back.

Sergeant-Major Hartpence sustained a slight wound on his head; a rebel bullet having pierced his hat, cutting a gash in the scalp, and passing out through the hat-band. It was a close call, for which he was properly grateful. He prizes that little scar more than any other token it is possible for him to obtain.

Many incidents of individual bravery might be mentioned. It is said that Fred. Tellsman, of Co. H, did not stop till he had scaled the 8-foot parapet; where he was confronted by a rebel lieutenant, who in a very obscene and profane manner demanded his surrender. Fred. only replied less politely, consigning him to a locality hotter, if possible, than where he was, and facilitating his departure thereto by emptying his rifle in the johnny's bread-basket. Then jumping to our side again, he came off in safety.

The 8th Kansas went up alongside of our regiment; and never did a little band of heroes fight more valiantly. Surgeon Nathaniel Clark distinguished himself by charging into the midst of the fray with his medicine-case, and by his heroic attention to his men, quite a number of whom were wounded.

The original order of this assault was, as has been repeated, for the Fifty-First to advance to easy supporting
distance; but by some error in giving or repeating it, the
order was changed to a charge, which was made with knapsacks on; rendering it that much more distressing. The
great wonder is that it was not much more disastrous; and
it seems like a rare providence that the error was made; for
had we remained at the point to which we were ordered at
first, we would have received the entire contents of that
rebel battery. As it was, we got down into the ravine, or
depression, under the battery just in time to feel the wind
produced by the crash of schrapnel and grape two or three
feet above our heads.

Furious as was the repulse, we fell back in splendid
order, about 300 yards, to the northern edge of a field, bordered by a forest. Here Captain Scearce ordered the regiment to reform, and calling the sergeant-major to him, directed him to go to the left and call the members of each
company to their places in the line, while he performed a
like service upon the right. The facility and promptness
with which every requirement was obeyed, was the more
remarkable for the fact that the companies were mainly of-
ficered by sergeants; in fact, it was said of the boys of the
Fifty-First, that they didn't need commanders — they commanded themselves. In three minutes the regiment had
reformed, and the command was given to "unsling" knapsacks and "forward! — charge!" We didn't need anything
more. Away we went, more determined than before; more
impetuous, and more eager to decide the issue. Although
received with a heavy fire, the onset was irresistible. One
crash followed another, as we swept through the network of
felled trees and over the parapet, routing the six lines of
rebel infantry supporting the battery, clubbed the gunners
off of their pieces, captured the guns and turned them on
the flying johnnies, and took half of the entire command
in front of us prisoners. At the same moment, the troops

on both of our flanks swung around the brow of the hill, and joined with us in deafening shouts of victory. The defeat of the rebels at this point was the most complete of all they had sustained, because it destroyed even the very organization by which they might have hoped to retrieve their fortune. That part of their army was forever gone — was a thing of the past; and it was a common sight to see a dozen or more johnnies —officers and privates — totally demoralized, going to our rear, in charge of a sinlge guard.

The charge then became general, and the enemy was hurled from every position, in utter rout and demoralization, hopelessly shattered; and in wildest confusion they fled along the Franklin pike and through Brentwood Pass, closely followed by the 4th Corps for several miles; the frequent discharges of our artillery increasing the confusion of their most disorderly retreat. All along the line of retreat small arms and accouterments were strewn thickly; while no effort whatever was made to carry off the wounded or dispose of the dead, who were tenderly cared for by our men. They stood not on the order of their going, but went.

The 4th Corps bivouacked that night a mile from the village of Brentwood; while Knipe's and Hatch's divisions of Wilson's cavalry corps moved rapidly down the Granny White pike, to reach Franklin if possible in advance of the rebel army. They came upon the rebel cavalry about a mile further on, posted across the road and behind barricades. They charged upon the rebels, scattering them in every direction, and capturing a large number of prisoners.

Surgeons Collins and King and Steward Fitch made a sad and weird picture, that night, as with lanterns in their hands, they searched among the trees and bushes for the brave boys of the Fifty-First who had fallen on that day; binding up an arm here, giving a draught of water there, and wiping the death-damp from the brow of an expiring hero, whose life had been preserved through so many dangers, to go out on this last field of battle.

When James Ferris, Co. H, opened his knapsack next day, he found in it two ounce balls, that were evidently shot there by rebels when we fell back after our first attack on the parapet on Overton Hill. The balls had both gone through eleven thicknesses of oil-cloth poncho, doubled up between the folds of his knapsack, besides all the clothing in one side.

The drafted men exceeded our most ardent expectation. They went right in, after the first scare was over; and when the old flag waved in triumph over the enemy's works, they raised the yell as proudly as any veteran. One fellow was so well tickled and so enthusiastic over his part of the accomplishment, that he said he felt like he could "lick a ten-acre field of wild-cats," or eat up a regiment of greasy johnnies, greybacks and all!"

The action of this day announced the overthrow of the rebellion in the West. The rebel army on whose existence and activity that section of the rebellion depended, was in disorganized and demoralized flight.

The authorities at Washington were momentarily apprised of our action, by a system of signals and telegraph. General Grant, on his way to take personal command, got no farther than Washington, and Logan stopped at Louisville. The President and the Secretary of War rained congratulations on General Thomas and his army. The following message, sent before the issue of the second day was known, was also received in the afternoon, and communicated to the troops that evening:

"WASHINGTON, Dec. 16—11:20 A. M.

MAJ. GEN. THOMAS:

Please accept for yourself, officers and men the Nation's thanks for your work of yesterday. You made a magnificent beginning. A grand consummation is within your easy reach. Do not let it slip.

A. LINCOLN.

General Thomas replied to this the same night, in an able communication, recounting the accomplishments of the 16th by his army, in which he said:

"Brigadier-General Wood's corps, on the Franklin pike, took up the assault, carried the enemy's intrenchments in his front, captured eight (8) pieces, and something over 600 prisoners."

That something remarkable had been done, was recognized by the civilized world. Indeed, historians have told the story of this two days' fight with expressions of wonder and astonishment. But the rest of the world has been at an equal loss to understand how two millions of men (or boys,) from every department of civilized life — the farmer from his plow, the mechanic from his bench or forge, the merchant from dallying over calicoes and ribbons, or sugar and coffee, the printer from his composing-stick, or the book-keeper from his desk, could be thrown together, skillfully drilled and disciplined in the short space of two or three years, so as to become the admiration of the most accomplished and celebrated militarists of the world. God was in it all, and the truths of His Word, that had in all the generations of their immediate ancestry been liberally sown in the hearts of His freemen, fitted them in advance for the grand work of purging our Nation of the sin of the South — and incidentally of confirming in the minds of the haughty chivalry of that section for all time, the superiority of the free Northerner over the native Southerner, in everything that goes to constitute true American manhood.

We resumed the pursuit early next morning, 17th, and met with comparatively little resistance. Disorder continued to mark every foot of the route. At Hollow Tree Gap, four miles north of Franklin, the cavalry overtook the rebels' rear-guard, and carried their position, capturing 413 prisoners. The enemy continued their flight to Franklin, where they attempted to defend the crossings of Harpeth River, but were again defeated and driven from the town, leaving their hospitals, containing over 2,000 wounded, of whom 200 were Union men, taken at the battle of Franklin. Five miles below Franklin the rebels were so pressed by our cavalry, that they made another stand; but only to fly with greater rapidity when Wilson's cavalry charged upon them. At this point they abandoned nearly all of their remaining artillery. The few cannons they retained, were afterward thrown into the Tennessee River, whence they were recovered.

The 4th Corps reached Franklin a little after noon ; but the river, which was easily forded by the cavalry, had risen so rapidly that we were delayed some time to extemporize a bridge. Steedman followed us, and the other two corps were in the rear. Trains followed, with rations for 10 days, and 100 rounds of ammunition to each man.

As we passed Franklin, our hearts were sickened at sight of the long lines of graves and other evidences of the work that was done there on our recent visit. Great trees and brush, that we had converted into abattis to protect us from the furious charges of the enemy, were fairly whittled and splintered like kindling. At one place, where the rebels had made three successive charges, and as often met a withering repulse, the earth was plowed up as though a mammoth harrow had been dragged over it. On every hand were clusters of new graves, where each regiment had buried its dead. Hundreds of horses, great heaps of equipage and arms were lying all around in lavish profusion. The earth, as far as we could see, was literally covered with remnants of that doomed army. That was an awful day, and a still more awful night which followed. As with the historic Senacherib,

> " Like the leaves of the forest, when summer is green,
> That host with their banners at morning was seen ;
> Like the leaves of the forest, when autumn hath blown,
> That host in the evening lay withered and strown."

Sunday morning, December 18, '64, was cloudy and gloomy enough, but our boys felt light and happy ; for we had been blest with victory from the first. We were without tents ; and many letters home had to be written under the shelter of an overcoat. The roads had become exceedingly bad, from the late heavy rains and their use by the rebels, and pursuit was greatly retarded in consequence. The 4th Corps joined Wilson's cavalry at night, at Rutherford's Creek.

On the morning of the 19th we attempted to cross the creek, whose deep swift current formed a better rear-guard for the enemy than his cavalry; and several efforts were made through the day; but all were fruitless. The rain continued, also, causing great distress among the boys, who were almost destitute of protection. Next morning Hatch's men constructed a float from the debris of the railroad bridge, and advanced rapidly to Columbia; to find that the rebels had lifted their pontoon bridge. The 4th Corps also crossed during the day by various expedients, and camped that night near Columbia. The weather now changed from excessive rain to extreme cold; and this retarded the throwing of pontoons. We had a little skiff of snow on Friday, 23d, and had a hard time crossing Duck River that afternoon. Forrest had left a small force to dispute our crossing. Our regiment was in advance that day, and it devolved on us to settle the matter. We deployed on the bank of the river, without a shadow of protection; while the johnnies stationed among the rocks on the bluff opposite, where they had constructed a sort of honey-comb defense, fired down at us from the apertures. It was one of the severest tests our boys ever experienced. We had the material of two "skeleton-boats," consisting of light framework and heavy canvas. The canvas was spread out on the shore, and the framework fitted together on it, by a system of mortises and hooks; then the canvas was gathered up at the sides and ends and secured by ropes tied in eyelets and drawn tightly to the frame. This made a boat capable of conveying twenty men across an ordinary body of water. But the exposure required to launch these two boats was awful. Robert A. Condiff, of Co. A, was killed, and ten others were wounded. The passage of the boats,

18

too, was attended with extreme danger; as the water was 15 to 25 feet deep, and the rebels on the bluff could shoot right down through our boats, and sink us.

Corporal Charles Salter, who was in the front line, received a shot that cut a gash in his scalp, parting the hair a little to one side of the center, making a lovely cowlick. He was crazy for a few hours; but got all right again in a few days.

The sergeant-major had another narrow escape here. While carrying orders to the skirmishers, he was selected by several johnnies, whose leaden compliments brushed his hat-rim on either side, and chipped the bark of a little tree a few steps in his rear. He made no response, save to softly murmur a line of "Willie, we have missed you," at that time a popular song.

Captain Hamilton was in command of the skirmishers, consisting of ten men from each company, and took charge of the first boat; the sergeant-major having the honor of commanding the second. Fortunately for us, the 6th Ohio Battery forwarded a gun, that in a moment was raising merry sheol among the rocks, driving the rebels out; thus enabling us to cross in safety. The whole command then crossed, clambering with great difficulty up the almost perpendicular bank, and went into camp near by.

The skirmishers pushed ahead through the town after Hood's rear-guard. In this movement, Corporal Will Jordan, with 5 of Co. A's detail, overtook 18 rebels, who were conducting 2 Union prisoners to their train. Jordan was in advance; and yelling out to an imaginary force behind, made a rush, captured the entire rebel guard, who readily surrendered. The skirmishers also surrounded the hospital, capturing all the attendants.

The pontoon train came up later, and the entire army crossed that night and next day.

We met with a very cordial reception by the citizens of Columbia, and while the remainder of the command was crossing the river, a number of us were invited to partake of their hospitality. And the wives and daughters of the most respectable portion of the population entertained us in a very agreeable manner, till an order to "carry up the line" compelled us to go. The young ladies of the town also made an arrangement for a social party that evening; but the Fifty-First was drawn into the court-house square, and strict orders given to stay there. The writer was sent out on three roads, to relieve the pickets, on two of which our men had been thrown out a mile and a-half, and the other nearly a mile. When he returned, got his own supper and made down his bed on the court-house floor, he was ready to sleep, although the place reeked with the foul stench of blood from those who had lain there before, and swarmed with graybacks.

"AFTER THE BALL."

December 24, we continued our pursuit of Hood; our immediate command taking the road running due south, and leading through Lynnville and Pulaski. We camped that night just below Lynnville, and had a hard march all the next day; passing through Pulaski, to 5 miles beyond. The cavalry had a brisk engagement in the evening. We remained in the same camp all the next day. At this time the pursuit was abandoned, as it had been ascertained that Hood's infantry forces had effected the passage of the Tennessee River at Bainbridge, a few miles east of Florence. On the 27th, we marched twelve miles in a southwesterly course, over an almost impassable road; and the next day we proceeded twelve miles farther, to the village of Lexington, Alabama, only a few miles from the Tennessee River. We were interrupted by nothing save heavy rains, which made marching and bivouacking very unpleasant. On the road we moved very slowly, but that did not prevent our foragers from getting over a great deal of contiguous territory, that abounded with all the luxuries of the season; so that we were kept supplied with fresh cured shoulders and hams, turkeys, chickens, honey, molasses, dried apples and peaches, corn meal, etc., which we relished greatly after a long abstinence from anything but the roughest kind of food.

The results of this victory over Hood cannot be estimated in figures, nor scarcely in any other way. The Union army captured 13,189 prisoners of war, including 7 generals, 16 colonels, nearly 1,000 officers of lower grades, 80 serviceable pieces of artillery, 70 stands of colors, (battle-flags,) many thousands of small arms, and untold quantities of wagons, pontoons and other material. Besides all this, 2,207 deserters from the rebel army came in and took the oath of allegiance. The number of rebels killed and wounded cannot possibly be ascertained with any degree of exactness; but from the best data to be obtained, exceeded 18,000. If to all of these are added the desertions not reported, more than half of Hood's army failed to recross the Tennessee River. General Thomas reported his own loss in killed, wounded and missing, as not exceeding 10,000, a large portion of this aggregate being slightly wounded.

Hood's Report of the Battle of Nashville.

        *   *   "I therefore determined to move on Nashville, to entrench,   *   to await his attack, and if favored by success, to follow him into his works.

[If Thomas had followed Grant's direction, doubtless he would have furnished the opportunity.]

        *   I ordered the army to move forward on the 1st of December;   *   Lee's corps in advance, followed by Stewart's and Cheatham's, and the troops bivouacked that night in the vicinity of Brentwood. On the morning of the 2d the march was resumed, and line of battle formed in front of Nashville. Lee's corps was in the center and across the Franklin pike; Stewart occupied the left, and Cheatham the right;   *   Forrest's cavalry filled the gaps to the river.   *   Stewart and Cheatham were directed to construct detached works   *   to protect their flanks against an effort to turn them. The works were not completed when, on the 15th, the Federal army moved out and attacked both flanks, whilst the main assault was directed against our left.   *   Finding that the main movement of the Federals was directed against our left,   *

Cheatham's corps was withdrawn from the right, and posted on the left of Stewart.　*　In this position the men were ordered to construct breastworks during that same night. The morning of the 16th found us with Lee's right on Overton Hill. At an early hour the enemy made a general attack along our front;　*　about 3 P. M. the Federals concentrated a number of guns against a portion of our line, which passed over a mound on the left of our center, and which had been occupied during the night. This point was favorable for massing troops.　*　The enemy availed himself of the advantage, massed a body of men —apparently one division— at the base of this mound, and　*　made a sudden and gallant charge up to and over our intrenchments. Our line, thus pierced, gave way; soon it broke at all points; and I beheld for the first and only time a Confederate army abandon the field in confusion.　*　I was seated on my horse not far in rear when the breach was effected, and soon discovered that all hope to rally the troops was vain."

[It must have seemed like a "division" to Hood, when the Fifty-First with the 8th Kansas and 14th Colored came swarming over that parapet, and made such havoc among Lee's men. Those regiments never failed to impress their audience whenever they had a chance. Wood's 4th Corps whipped Stewart's corps on the 15th, and Lee's corps on the 16th, and made its usual splendid record. Hood was certainly a chump of the most pronounced character, however, or he could not have added, as he did, the following:]

"Just previous to this fatal occurrence, I had matured the movement for the next morning. The enemy's right flank, by this hour, stood in air some six miles from Nashville, and I had determined to withdraw my entire force during the night, and attack this exposed flank in rear. I could safely have done so, as I still had open a line of retreat.　A number of guns in the main line were abandoned, for the reason that the horses could not be brought forward in time to remove them. The total number of guns captured amounted to 54.　*　*

It will be of interest to note how deeply concerned Gen. Grant became for fear we should finally reach Kentucky. He ordered Gen. Thomas to attack on the 6th of December, and evidently became much worried about our presence in front of Nashville."

[But he finally came to comprehend the situation, and closed his report in as few words as possible.]

" After the fight at Nashville I at first hoped to be able to remain in Tennessee, on the line of Duck River, but after arriving at Columbia, I became convinced that the condition of the army made it necessary to recross the Tennessee without delay, and on the 21st the army resumed its march for Pulaski, leaving Maj. Gen. Walthall with Ector's, Strahl's,

Maney's, Granberry's and Palmer's infantry brigades at Columbia, as a rear-guard under Gen. Forrest.   *   *   *   *

[Here again the Fifty-First Indiana "Division" drove the heroes who couldn't fight without some kind of breast-works to rest their guns on.]

From Pulaski I moved by the most direct road to the Bainbridge crossing on the Tennessee river, which was reached on the 25th, where the army crossed without interruption."

In another place he explains the sudden disappearance of his army, by the statement that thousands were fur-loughed for a short period; which simply meant for good, so far as Hood was concerned; for on Jan. 13, '65, he sent the following to the rebel "Secretary of War:"

" I request to be relieved from the command of this army.

J. B. HOOD, General."

The wonder is, what army; as Thomas had relieved him of his own. Following this, he says:

"9,000 out of 14,000 who left Tupelo to repair to Johnson's standard in North Carolina, deserted, and either went to the woods or to their homes."

When the pursuit ended, General Thomas ordered his forces into winter quarters; but immediately Grant tele-graphed his disapproval of this disposition, and Thomas at once issued orders to Generals Schofield, Smith and Wil-son to concentrate at Eastport, Miss., and Wood to hold his corps at Huntsville, Ala., in readiness for a renewal of the campaign.

SOME REFLECTIONS.

We read in books, of the genius of mighty warriors, whose names have been heralded throughout the world, coupled with an exaggerated account of their achievements. If you could have slipped unobserved among the companies of quiet soldiers, in any of those veteran regiments, whose eyes gleamed with a brightness and significant earnestness that told of the ardent, eager heart glowing underneath the blouse, and if you could have reclined with them on those rugged hillsides during the lull in hostilities, and heard the simple expressions of those hardy patriots, who drew inspiration from their rusty bacon and mouldy hard-tack, and criticised the movements of the armies in undertones, lest their words might seem to be mutinous, or might affect the fidelity of a weak comrade ; or, if you could have gathered from the humble privates the results of their intuitions — the things they had learned by the long years of experience, the flankings and the feints, the tricks and the schemes by which they had been defeated, and by which they had overcome the foe ; you might be able to appreciate the fact, that there was oftener wisdom and judgment in the ranks than on horseback. There is no doubt that very many battles that were lost by those who were called brave and efficient commanders, might have been saved by men who carried only muskets. The history of the war of the rebellion furnishes abundant evidence in proof of this.

Instinctively the veterans of General Thomas' army recognized his superior leadership, and from the first their hearts beat in lively sympathy with his. They believed in his capability, his loyalty to the great cause for which they had sacrificed everything dear to them on earth ; and to question his integrity, either by accusation or innuendo, was bound to subject the offender to their dislike, if not to their odium ; which even time rarely extinguished. In the beginning of this campaign, General Thomas had been unjustly censured and criticised by certain authorities at the national headquarters ; even an order was issued, transfering the command from him to Schofield, and indirectly to Logan. Providentially, as it proved, he was not relieved ; but his soldiers felt the humiliation, and in ten thousand forms of expression, have never ceased to denounce those who were responsible for it. On December 21, Thomas wrote a letter to Halleck, who was then toasting his shins in comfortable quarters in Washington City, while Thomas and his army were enduring the rigors of one of the severest winters ever known in that locality. It is in reply to one from Halleck, urging him to "make every possible sacrifice to accomplish the great result," and urging "a most vigorous pursuit;" and is very interesting reading:

"IN THE FIELD, December 21, 1864.

MAJOR-GENERAL HALLECK, *Washington, D. C.:*

Your dispatch of 12 M. this day is received. General Hood's army is being pursued as rapidly and as vigorously as it is possible for one army to pursue another. We can not control the elements, and you must remember that, to resist Hood's advance into Tennessee, I had to reorganize and almost thoroughly equip the force now under my command. I fought the battles of the 15th and 16th insts. with the troops but partially equipped, and notwithstanding the inclemency of the weather and the partial equipment, have been enabled to drive the enemy beyond Duck River, crossing two streams with my troops, and driving the enemy from position to position, without the aid of pontoons, and with but little transportation to bring up supplies of provisions and ammunition, I am doing all in my power to crush Hood's army, and, if it be possible, will destroy it. But pursuing an enemy through an exhausted country, over mud roads completely sogged with heavy rains, is no child's play, and can not be accomplished as quickly as thought of. I hope, in urging me to push the enemy, the department remembers that General Sherman took with him the complete organization of the Military Division of the Mississippi, well equipped in every respect, as regards ammunition, supplies and transportation, leaving me only two corps, partially stripped of their transportation, to accommodate the force taken with him, to oppose the advance into Tennessee of that army which had resisted the advance of the army of the Military Division of the Mississippi on Atlanta, from the commencement of the campaign till its close, and which is now in addition aided by Forrest's cavalry. Although my progress may appear slow, I feel assured that Hood's army can be driven from Tennessee, and eventually driven to the wall by the force under my command. But too much must not be expected of troops which have to be reorganized, especially when they have the task of destroying a force, in a winter's campaign, which was able to make an obstinate resistance to twice its numbers in spring and summer. In conclusion, I can safely state that the army is willing to submit to any sacrifice to oust Hood's army, or to strike any other blow which may contribute to the destruction of the rebellion.   (Signed,)   GEO. H. THOMAS,
Major-General."

"Old Pap" Thomas had fulfilled the highest possible expectations of his loyal followers. Letters of congratulation and cheer poured in on us from all over the North. The terrible fear of disaster by our friends, and which the copperheads hoped and prayed for, was removed; and we

GENERAL G. H. THOMAS.

were very proud of the campaign. Any army might well be proud of it; and when, on the 30th, General Thomas announced its conclusion, he paid his valorous command the highest compliment, and congratulated us on our eminent success. This chapter would scarcely be complete without the glowing tribute offered to the memory of our beloved commander by Major J. A. Ostrander, at the G. A. R. National Encampment at Indianapolis, September 4, 1893:

"The country is proud of the great names and great deeds of Grant and Sherman and Sheridan. So am I. But there is one other immortal name that has been written on the marble of a tomb for a quarter of a century, whose lightest mention will swell the hearts and straighten the bowed backs of the old Cumberland Army. Though the years of his life were told to a generation that has passed, new times and new men clasp glad hands with the lingering veterans to keep the Philip Sidney of our troubled days a living, loving memory.

You remember him, men of the Cumberland. Nay, you can never forget. You saw him that wild day at Stone River, when our right had been crushed and driven in, and the flushed victors, following the stars of the Southern cross swept down like a resistless Alpine flood to engulf the doomed center, and a day of disaster and the year were passing together. You remember how that human tide of victory wavered, paused, rolled back, because— 'the hand of the master compelled it to pause.'

Thomas was there!

You saw him in the cold chill of that terrible September evening at Chicamauga — where the army that had faced fearful odds, since the morning sunlight of yesterday, was broken and drifting back to Chattanooga, a hopeless, helpless rout — gather around him the fragments of the wreck, and firm as the eternal hills on which he leaned, roll back the billows of war that beat against him until the sun went down.

'Mid the gusts of wild fire, when the iron-clad rain,
Did ripen brown earth to the reddest of stain,
In that moment supreme, to their bridles in blood,
Like a rock in the wilderness grandly he stood,
Till the red sea was cleft,—
                    Thomas was there!'

You remember that glorious day at Mission Ridge, when with armies for audiences, the thunderbolt of the Cumberland gored the tempest of war, rolled in desolation up the fire-crowned hights, burned through the lines of gray veterans, and sent them reeling in defeat across the Chicamauga, while æons of victory, moving the rock-ribbed hills, told in gladness the story that the leaguer was raised and the red field was won.

Thomas was there!

You remember Nashville. That fragment of an army facing a foe that all the legions of the mighty West had battled for a hundred days—the hurried gathering of numbers from detachments, hospitals and convalescent camps—the impatience in high places, that the great soldier was slow; forgetful that never man was surer,—sturdy resistance to the clamor that would hazard victory; and then, when all the toils were laid and time was full, a great rebel army swept from existence, as though earth had opened and swallowed it up.

Thomas was there!

On the banks of Stone River, by the waters of Chicamauga, where the Tennessee rolls northward from the land of sun; by the rock-bound Cumberland, in bleak December days; from Mill Springs to Nashville; wherever Cumberland men fought and rebel armies went down, Thomas was there; and where he was, perched victory.

Where others were falling, he stood faithful among the faithless.

When sacred pledges were 'false as dicers' oaths,' his plighted word meant what it said; and the first flash of his naked blade was in deadly menace to the recreants who had betrayed their country for a price; told in blasted honors, that stand pilloried of time.

Build monuments to him, Virginia of the new South! He was your greatest son! Honor his memory, grateful Americans; he was easily the peer of any! What Wellington was in tenacity, what Frederick was in courage, what Washington was in purity of purpose—that Thomas was in all. Great in stature, great in heart, great in loyalty, grand in deeds.

> 'And when his statue is placed on high,
> Under the dome of the Union sky,
> Write only this, for time to read,
>   'The Rock of Chicamauga.'

A soldier of the antique type. He spoke little of his honor; but kept it stainless as the snow. Mankind is better, nobler, that he lived."

ADDENDA.

The official report states that it was Mrs. Acklen's residence, instead of Widow Montgomery's, that confronted us on Montgomery Hill, [see page 257]; also, cannons were thrown into Duck River, while the rebels were crossing, instead of Tennessee River [see page 272].

The Fifty-First was assigned to the 1st Brigade, Nov. 17, '64, and by reason of seniority, Colonel Streight assumed command. The brigade then consisted of the following regiments:

89th Illinois, Lt.-Col. Wm. D. Williams.

51st Indiana, Capt. Wm. W. Scearce.

8th Kansas, Lt.-Col. John Conover.

15th Ohio, Col. Frank Askew.

Lt.-Col. John McClenahan.

49th Ohio, Maj. Luther M. Strong.

Capt. Daniel Hartsough.

IN ALABAMA AND TENNESSEE.

Saturday, December 31, 1864, found us still in camp at the village of Lexington, Alabama, with orders to move to Huntsville. We marched 18 miles that day, in an easterly direction, over very rough country, and camped within 4 miles of Elk River. Thus closed the year '64; and when the new year came in, we moved on to Elk River, where we celebrated the holiday by building a pontoon bridge, on which to cross that stream. We were then 10 miles northwest of Athens, and were subsisting largely off of the fat of the land — which was pretty fat at that time. Our headquarters mess will never forget our New Year's dinner. Its chief component was the largest shoulder of pork any of us had ever seen, and looked like it had been taken from a young elephant. Another feature of the banquet was an immense camp-kettle of mush. The pork was sliced and fried in its fat. Placing a slice on each tin-plate, the cook piled on as much mush as would stay on, dabbed a hole in the top, and filled the cavity with gravy. The way we absorbed the natural products of that section, must have created in the minds of the natives grave apprehension of a famine. "Are you-uns-all gwine t' ruin we-uns-all?" they asked; and we assured them that we had come *to sure them!* Then we went on *suring* the fine sweet potatoes, dried fruit, pork, honey, etc., which these hypocritical people had been industriously cultivating and preserving to feed the rebel army with. We had little else to do, save to write letters and wash and mend our clothes; but were in constant fear of being disturbed in our enjoyment.

From this time till about the first of August, we were included in the 1st Brigade, 3d Division, 4th Army Corps, Department of the Cumberland.

Our respite was of short duration, and ended on the 3d without a moment's warning. All over camp, those who were not on regular detail, were reposing quietly, or were engaged in the usual games or household duties. Captain Scearce, Adjutant Harris and the writer were occupying a rail shebang, over which a fly was thrown ; and the first two worthies were down on a bed of corn-blades — their feet elevated on sacks of corn — telling old-time yarns, and having a roaring time. The sergeant-major was writing a letter home. Just then "Mother" Richeson, who was the captain's hostler, made his appearance with a deck of cards, followed by two other fellows. Instantly the officers and their visitors squared themselves for a game of euchre. At brigade headquarters a fine band was discoursing beautiful music. Before the letter was finished or the game ended, the call was sounded, to "fall in" and cross the river. The flapjacks and taffy and parched corn were dumped unceremoniously into haversacks, the curtailed letter was slipped into the office desk, the cards were hastily bunched and crammed into "Mother's" blouse, and a general rush was made to get into line. We passed through Athens the same night, and bivouacked three miles east of there ; our mail being delivered to us on our arrival at that point. Here we received the following announcement of the casualties in the two days' fight at Nashville, Dec. 15-16, '64 :

Losses.	Killed.		Wounded.		Aggregate.
	Off.	Enl'd.	Off.	Enl'd.	
89th Illinois.	1	3	2	14	20
51st Indiana.		15	3	85	103
8th Kansas		8	2	30	40
15th Ohio.	2	1	1	23	27
49th Ohio.		10	5	39	54
Total.	3	37	13	191	244

"CAMP GREEN"—SILVER LAKE.

Reaching Huntsville next day, we proceeded to Silver Lake, a beautiful body of water, a few miles south of there, that spread its bright bosom out among the grand forest trees, over which a premature spring was beginning to scatter its verdure. We found here several "dug-out" boats, in which the boys often sported on the shining water. Our camp was known as "Camp Green." We built comfortable shanties out of poles, over which our "dog-tents" were drawn for roofs. Some of these had single-pane windows, and many had doors with leather hinges. Chimneys were constructed by crossing the ends of sticks, and plastering the stack with mud. Tables and stools and bunks were made by driving forks into the ground. Our kitchen utensils comprised every variety, which the boys picked up on the way. By a system of borrowing, these were made to do a wonderful amount of service. Wash-bowls were hewed out of logs, like sugar-troughs. As soon as it was ascertained that we would probably remain there some time, a commodious log church was erected, in which we held some glorious services. The lake was full of geese and ducks when we went there, and for a time thousands of birds in the trees enlivened us with their music. But our pleasure was not characterized with much hilarity. While we were marching and fighting, the excitement of the campaign gave us little time for sentiment; but with rest came reflection, and with that a sense of our loss of many comrades. According to the regimental report, at Pulaski, before the retreat, we numbered 815; now we numbered 469. Where were they?

January 8, '65, General Wood wrote to General Whipple, chief of General Thomas' staff, recommending Colonel Streight's promotion to be brigadier-general, "for the skillful manner in which he managed his brigade in the battle of Nashville, for his personal gallantry in the battle, and for his uniform good and soldierly conduct." Like many another worthy plan, its operation was delayed too long, and the answer came too late.

"BATTLE OF GREEN LAKE."

It is strange, upon what slight provocation men may fall out with each other. Political parties split on tariff or protection or free silver; churches ostracise each other on account of some article of faith; medicine has its "code," and the veriest ninny who has been rushed through a "regular" institution, would see his patient expire in agony, ere he would disgrace his holy "code" by consultation with an "eclectic."

> " Mountains interposed,
> Make enemies of nations, who had else,
> Like kindred drops, been mingled into one."

Soldiers from the same State, but in different regiments, frequently agreed; but those from different States, while bound together by the common bond of patriotism and loyalty, often found cause for dispute. They stood on "rank," too; it was the standard by which almost everything was determined. The Fifty-First was regarded by part of the others as the pet of the commander; and naturally enough those soldiers were full of envy. This finally led to a rupture. Some of the boys of the 89th Illinois, that laid on our immediate left, got into an altercation with some Co. B boys one day, over a trifling matter; and kept it up till long after "taps." Finally, one of the old veterans swore that he always ranked "troopees," meaning raw recruits. This was an insult that no veteran could make any allowance for. Like an emetic, one thing brought up another; and in a few minutes a hundred brave soldiers of those two grand old regiments were out in line, shivering in their night-clothes, but with their guns in their hands, ready to settle the matter right there and then. They were quieted down, however, without bloodshed; and in time came to be the best of friends. But that chilly night of January 31,

'65, is remembered by most of our comrades, as the date of the "Battle of Silver Lake."

A FRUITLESS EXPEDITION.

Wednesday morning, February 1, at 8 o'clock, our regiment and the 41st Ohio—of Post's brigade, broke camp, and started ostensibly for Eastport, Miss., to guard a train consisting of two batteries and about 250 wagons and ambulances. There were also with us four companies of the 35th Indiana, having charge of a pontoon train, that was to accompany us as far as Elk River. The whole was commanded by Lt.-Col. Robert L. Kimberly, of the 41st Ohio. We marched 15 miles that day, and went into camp in the midst of a heavy fog. We reached Athens, 16 miles further on, the next evening, and on the 3d, made 15 miles; reaching Buck Island Ford, on Elk River, about 4 P. M. Finding the river shallow enough to ford, the pontoons were sent back; and early Saturday morning, the 4th, we crossed in wagons, and moved out 12 miles, to Blue Water Creek, a small stream, near the Tennessee State line. The road was very soft, and frequently the wagons sank to the hubs. Several mules mired, and had to be dragged out by hitching others to them. It also snowed while we were at this point. What was our surprise, on the morning of the 5th, to receive orders to retrace our steps. That evening we recrossed Elk River, and camped about a mile from the stream, at the residence of a very outspoken and offensive rebel named Strauss.

As foraging was at that time exceptionally good, strict orders were deemed necessary to prevent straggling. On the evening in question, after we had crossed in wagons, the writer was ordered to remain at the ford, and take the names of all stragglers. Seventeen of the Fifty-First and 8 or 10 of the 41st Ohio came to the river some time after the last wagon had crossed; and, of course, were compelled to wade. The water was about waist deep, almost freezing cold, and the bed of the stream quite rough and slippery. Two of them fell down in the deepest part. The writer had built a fire for his own comfort; and when he beheld the plight of his comrades, he heaped on more fuel, and made a royal bonfire, and received his guests warmly. Then he took the name of each transgressor, while they dressed. Of these, 2 sergeants and 4 privates of the Fifty-First stood guard that night; as many more the next night; and so on, till all had paid the penalty. The names were soon forgotten by the writer, so far as that transaction was concerned; but in 1883, in conversation with Sergeant Wm. Roberts, of Co. H, away down in Indiana, he recalled his hospitable reception on the bank of Elk River, where he thawed himself out, while his name was recorded for extra duty.

We proceeded next morning toward Athens, in snow, that turned to cold rain before night. Arriving at Athens about sundown, we occupied our former camp at that place. On Tuesday morning, 7th, we started early in 3 inches of snow, and marched 12 miles. As we halted, opposite the residence of a man named Cartright, preparatory to going into camp, the writer became so cold, that he obtained permission to go into the house, to keep from freezing. There he met a bevy of bright, interesting and neatly clad little girls, whose intelligence astonished him. One blue-eyed miss of 4 or 5 years, in a stainless check apron, began to entertain her guest by spelling great words, at her father's dictation. He had been afflicted for two years with heart disease and partial paralysis, and his wife had been dead a number of years. To an inquiry as to how he managed, he replied by casting his eyes toward a window, in the seat of which shrank a beautiful girl of 16 years. "There is our school teacher," he said. He had taught her; and she, in turn, was educating her sisters and brothers. In a brief conversation with her, she proved to possess a rare mind and sweet, winning disposition. The guest was rapidly losing himself under the irresistible influence of this noble

young creature, when in came Doc. King and a lot of other
headquarters savages, and dispelled the beautiful dream;
their spurs and traps clanging and clattering like a troop
of cavalry, which so confused and scared the little darling,
that she disappeared like a suddenly obscured sunbeam,
and was seen no more.

The rest of our journey was monotonous and unimportant. Next morning we started quite early, and marched
to Athens in the snow. We arrived there at sundown, in
a cold rain, and went into camp in our former quarters.
On Tuesday, 7th, we got an early start, and made 12 miles
in three inches of snow. On the 8th we had but 13 miles
further to go; but the bad roads made it hard on the teams,
and a fresh fall of snow made our progress quite difficult
and disagreeable. We entered our old camping ground at
Silver Lake about nightfall, and found our fine bunks all
gone, and our shanties in ruins. We had a hard time re-
constructing our domiciles; but our troubles were soon lost
and forgotten in the opening of an 8-days' mail.

February 13, '65, Colonel Streight was in Indianapolis.
Nothing of importance occurred; the usual camp duties occupying all our time. The diary of Will Wicker, of Co. F,
mentions, however, the startling fact that on that same day
he and Pete Camper caught a coon while on picket. The
weather moderated immediately after, and we had considerable rain during the rest of that month.

On the evening of February 20, we received news of
the capture of Charleston, S. C., by General Sherman; and
the boys made the night hideous with their vociferous yells
and bursting of blank cartridges. The brigade band came
out and played "Hail, Columbia!" We all got out on the
parade ground, and listened to an excellent speech by one
of the chaplains; which he closed by proposing three cheers
"for old Bill Sherman and his noble army!" which was
responded to by a miniature earthquake; and the entire
brigade went wild that night.

19

Wednesday, March 1, a very sad accident occurred in the 8th Kansas, which aroused our sympathy almost as if it had happened in our own regiment. Some one in felling a large tree, let it drop on the quarters, killing 1 and badly injuring 3 others.

On the same day, Wm. Armstrong, of Co. F, a recruit of '62, was discharged, by reason of expiration of service, and started for home.

Wednesday, March 8, we received the first copy of the Huntsville *Union*, whose name indicates the political sentiment of the paper. Up to this time, the newspapers in the South had been so thoroughly subsidized or terrorized, that nothing but the most virulent disloyalty and political malignity, sectional hatred, ostracism and abuse of loyal Union citizens, ever appeared in their columns; while their readers were kept in constant ignorance of the real status of their mushroom confederacy, until they were startled as by a thunderclap from a clear sky, to find their Utopia but the mirage of diseased minds, already being forever dissipated. It was therefore refreshing, to receive damp from the press the news from almost every part of the world, unburdened of the disgusting pretense of lordlings whose chief boast lay in the number and variety of their own half-brothers and half-sisters the law and usage of that section entitled them to. It was a bold venture in journalism; for, as soon as the Union army was gone, the *Union* paper would go into rapid dissolution, and its projector would find little peace or comfort in that locality.

The weather continued cloudy and cold, with an occasional clear day. On such days we had brigade or company drill. Several officers were absent; some on leave, and a few whose time had expired, were mustered out. On the 12th, word was received that Colonel Streight had resigned. Captain Hamilton, being the senior or ranking officer, was in command of the regiment. There were lively times at headquarters then. Adjutant Harris made the complement of a team that would be hard to beat. Hamilton once declared that Al. Harris was the most generous fellow he ever knew — he would give away anything in the world that he had. He said, "He gave me the itch at Huntsville, and I liked to have never got over it. I almost scratched my limbs off!"

Monday, 13th, we witnessed the spectacle of a soldier of the 41st Ohio being paraded before the brigade, with a placard on his back bearing the legend "Mutiny." The precise nature of his offence was not published; but he had concluded the war was about over, and undertook to loosen the bandage, that he fancied was a little tighter than necessary for his comfort. We had more of such trouble before the year was gone.

GOOD-BY TO ALABAMA.

We remained at Silver Lake until Wednesday, March 15, when we received marching orders. By this time that lovely pond had succumbed to the inevitable, and everything within sight or sound had become only distressing features of a howling wilderness. We longed for fresh pastures; so we welcomed the order to "get ready to march." Rations were issued that afternoon, and we marched to the railroad depot in Huntsville, where we got aboard a train about sunset. The next morning we awoke at Stevenson, where we spent the summer of '62, and where we learned the difference between "pegged" and "sewed" pies. Here we debarked, washed up and made coffee. At Bridgeport we waved a long and lasting adieu to Alabama, as we sped across the river, and soon after entered the Tennessee border. We experienced a real scare in crossing the Falling Water, a small stream with very high banks, near Whiteside's, over which a very rickety bridge had been thrown. It consisted of long saplings spiked together; and as our train came upon it, it swayed from one side to the other, as though it would scarcely require the weight of another man

to break down the entire structure. One car jumped the
track, and bumped over several ties; but we were running
very slowly, and were easily stopped. Had the car gone
off, it must certainly have pulled the train with it, and we
would all have been dashed to pieces on the rocks 150 feet
below. Then we proceeded, without further incident, to
Chattanooga, where we arrived about noon, and laid until
2 P. M., when we resumed our journey toward the east. As
the boys were a little short of rations — or thought of going
up about Knoxville, where they would be — they managed
to absorb 25 or 30 boxes of hard-tack, which they found
lying loose in the depot-yard, during our stay there. From
Chattanooga we flitted rapidly by most of the villages, only
stopping for fuel and water for the engine. Many sweet
memories were revived as we passed Cleveland, Athens,
Charleston, Calhoun and Loudon. At a deserted station,
we found a number of very nice cedar buckets; and as we
had just exhausted our assortment of cedar buckets, this
was a good opportunity to replenish our stock. And they
came in very handy the next morning, 17th, when we got
to Lenoir, where we had to carry water for the engine. A
nice old fellow who lived just over the mountain, had also
left several barrels of cider for us at this place; and again
the cedar pails came in excellent play.

We passed through Knoxville during that night, and
arrived at New Market, East Tennessee, Saturday morning, March 18.

The railroad from Huntsville to New Market, which is
about 30 miles east of Knoxville, was at that time in an
execrable condition; but the soft clay roads were so much
worse, we were glad to put up with the cinders and bumped
heads and bruised bones incurred in the jolting journey.

AT NEW MARKET.

We found the people of New Market the most loyal of
any we had met in the South; and they seemed also pos-

sessed of a higher and purer civilization. They were plain
spoken, but not rude nor coarse; they were pious, and the
women were modest and polite; and their conversation,
songs and all their conduct indicated a refinement that was
natural, and rendered them attractive. And in this lovely
month of March all nature seemed in harmonious keeping.

We were camped about half a mile from town, which
made it convenient for us to attend church. On Sunday
morning, 19th, there was preaching at the church nearest
to our camp, by the chaplain of the 8th Kansas, in which
he took occasion to score the rebels mercilessly. There was
present a fair representation of ladies, who seemed highly
delighted. The evening service was conducted by Chaplain
Randall Ross, of the 15th Ohio. Then we had "social"
meeting every evening through the week, the church being
crowded on each occasion.

In a quiet, sunny spot in the little cemetery, we found
the grave of our former comrade, Miltiades Cash, a member of the band, who left us March 26, '62, and joined a
New Jersey cavalry regiment. Loving hands had kept the
humble mound in order, and a neat head-stone with an appropriate inscription, marked the place.

ESCAPE OF MAJOR DENNY AND CAPTAIN GUDE.

Wednesday, 22d, our regiment experienced a real sensation by the arrival at our picket line, near this place, of
Major Wm. N. Denny and Capt. Alfred Gude, of Co. H,
both of whom had escaped from rebel prison at Chester.
S. C., about five weeks before, and had traveled on foot all
the way, about 250 miles, over mountains and through a
most desolate country. They made their first appearance
at our line on Mossy Creek, and from their dress were supposed to be rebel deserters. As soon as it was discovered
where they belonged, and were informed of the proximity
of the Fifty-First, they were almost prostrated by the announcement. They were conducted to our boys, who were

overjoyed to see them. Instantly the travel-worn and tattered refugees were caught up and borne into camp on the shoulders of the delighted comrades, amid deafening shouts and wildest demonstrations of joy. They were completely disguised by the suits of dirty dingy grey, and the changes in their countenances produced by hardship. As soon as they were able to talk coherently, they gave a very graphic and affecting description of their sufferings; having met on their way with barbarous treatment by the most cruel and depraved class of people they had ever known. The women had proved their worst foes during their difficult journey, being generally debauched, drunken and filthy in both conduct and conversation, and committed every kind of indecency that tongue could describe or fancy picture. Fit inhabitants they of the leading State in the murderous attempt on the life of the Nation! The poor fellows were soon stripped of their rebel rags, and provided with comfortable suits of blue; and were made to feel as happy as was possible under the circumstances.

At the same time, Captain McQuidden, of the 5th Tennessee, who was captured with our command, and escaped from rebel prison, also came to the Union lines, and was escorted to our camp. He was an excellent man, of plain, practical sense, and a good soldier; and we treated him as one of our own.

After a day or two of rest and recuperation in camp, the refugees were given leaves of absence, and proceeded to their homes.

Colonel Streight's resignation was accepted March 16, and he was at Indianapolis on the 20th. The same day, Captain Anderson, having recovered from the wound he received at Overton Hill, left that city for the front.

Our camp at New Market was a very nice one. We built fine quarters, and decorated them with cedar, which grew plentifully thereabout. General Wood visited us on Sunday, 26th, and complimented our boys highly on the

handsome appearance of our camp. This was of short duration, however; for on the following Tuesday we received
orders to prepare for campaigning. We had since the last
winter's campaign been supplied with "wall" tents; these
we turned over, with our camp equipage, and got ready to
take the road again.

Wednesday morning, 29th, we struck tents at 6 o'clock,
and moved out for Bull's Gap, distant about 45 miles east;
crossing Mossy Creek, 4 miles out, and marching 13 miles
that day. Next day it poured down rain all the forenoon;
but we pushed right ahead, passing through Morristown, a
railroad station 5 miles further on, and Russellville, 7 miles
more, where we camped that night. Friday, 31st, brought
us to Bull's Gap, about noon. There we built board shanties, with "dog-tent" roofs, and made ourselves as nearly
comfortable as we could; thinking we would remain some
time. The country was a desolate barren, consisting of a
succession of bluff backbone ridges and narrow ravines,
covered with a sandy alluvium, in which the boys found a
great quantity of small quartz polygons, resembling diamonds; the first specimens of which produced a fever of
excitement in camp, when they were exhibited. The whole
command was soon out hunting diamonds; and every one
expected to go home soon a millionaire. We found also
many fine specimens of petrifaction, which Longstreet's
men had turned out with their picks and shovels while for-
tifying against Burnside.

We were always eager for our mail. Frequently it was
delayed, as there were innumerable causes for interruption
both ways; and the transportation of the mails was always
attended with danger of capture by guerrillas. Our chaplain was a cowardly kind of soldier, and never ventured to
the rear — or any other direction, out of sight of the regiment. After he resigned, our mail was delivered for a long
time by a brigade orderly, and was distributed to the companies by the sergeant-major. It was, therefore, a matter

of great satisfaction to every one, that at this place, Corpoporal Taswell Dodd, of Co. K, was appointed regimental postmaster. He continued in this position until he was mustered out of the service, October 4, '65, by reason of expiration of term of service; and the postoffice was established in the adjutant's tent.

It was during this month of March, '65, also, that the indignity was thrust upon Co. C, of a drunken "troopee" being promoted to a lieutenancy over many old war-worn veterans, and then hastily advanced to the captaincy of that company. He completed the disgraceful farce by deserting the following September. *Vale! Emazetta!*

AT GREENVILLE, TENN.

On Tuesday, April 4, we left Bull's Gap, and marched through Blue Springs, the next railroad point, to Greenville, 18 miles; reaching the latter place at night. After going into camp, and when our tents were partly up, we were again ordered into line, and moved to the east side of town, where the boys erected nice shanties and bunks. We went to sleep with the cheering news that Grant had captured 20,000 prisoners in front of Richmond. There was great joy all over camp.

Our camp was located on a beautiful green mound, selected with special regard to the health of the boys. We had a fine view from here, of the surrounding country. On one side rose the town, while on the other we looked away to the Blue Ridge Mountains, the nearest spur of which was distant 10 miles, but which the peculiarity of the atmosphere made to appear not more than 2 or 3. The State line of North Carolina was about 15 miles away, and was plainly discernible, running along upon the summit of the mountains.

Thursday following, a large detail was made from the Fifty-First, to cut railroad ties. The work of general repairs was being vigorously prosecuted along this line, and

our boys again exhibited the skill that had been developed
under the colonel's direction during the earlier days of the
war. The 80th Illinois was camped near us; and many
little tokens of fraternal feeling were exchanged with our
former fellow-prisoners of war.

NEWS OF LEE'S SURRENDER.

April 10, we received news of Lee's surrender. The
intelligence seemed almost too good to be true; yet we had
been daily expecting it, and were ready for the unbounded
and universal rejoicing that followed. The enthusiasm in
the 4th Corps manifested itself in a manner that must certainly have convinced the people of that section, of our
total disregard for expense when we undertook to celebrate.
It began in the 2d Division, and was the result of a mad
freak of one company. That company, just before "taps"
that night, marched out along the railroad, and discharged
their guns. Another company followed suit; and it was
not long until the whole division was engaged. It lasted
nearly three hours. Our boys were just retiring, when an
orderly came galloping down with the order to "fall in."
The order was instantly obeyed; and in a very few minutes
every man was in line. We remained in line about an
hour, when another orderly announced that the men might
return to their quarters. Gradually the noise subsided;
and by midnight the camps were as quiet as a cemetery.

"LIKE A HOG!"

We passed, in town, the Williams residence, where the
noted horsethief and murderer, John Morgan, of Lexington, Ky., was killed, while skulking from his captors. The
snaggle-toothed old hag who survived the family, and who
stood guard over the house, treated the very civil and cour-
teous inquiries of our boys quite contemptuously, and shut
the door violently in their faces. The guerrilla Morgan
was killed in that house, or just as he jumped from the low
gallery into the garden below, by Andrew G. Campbell, of

a Tennessee cavalry troop. Some time previous to that, Morgan had discovered Captain Keenan, a United States officer, at his home, near this place, very sick. He is said to have killed the officer, and placing him in an old wagon, ordered his men to "haul him off like a hog!" It is also said that when Campbell shot Morgan, he took the body up on his horse, carried it out of town a short distance, and threw it down in the road, saying, "There *you* are, like a hog!" Campbell was promoted to a lieutenancy for this service, as he deserved to be.

Further down the street was the home of Andy Johnson, in front of which still hung his old sign, that read:

A. JOHNSON, TAILOR.

A dilapidated sign, on a dilapidated house; fit token of the dilapidated record of a very dilapidated citizen; who would have served this Nation a million times better, if he had continued to make and mend breeches for the people of that obscure village, than he did in "making treason odious" by placing traitors on top, and by helping to neutralize a large part of what had been accomplished by the war; and thereby putting a stain upon our flag and Government, that has ever since brought the blush of shame to every patriot's cheek.

Martin Clinesmith, a German boy in Co. D, who was sadly afflicted with epilepsy, bit his tongue so severely in a fit, one day, that he died from the result, and was buried here. George McCormick, of Co. A, is also recorded as having died at this place.

On Tuesday, April 11, a heavy rain set in, that continued unceasingly until about noon of the 13th; and the entire surface of the earth in that section was reduced to an immense puddle of mud. The atmosphere was a misty soggy, aguish sort, that penetrated one's bones even; and all nature seemed ashamed of itself.

Friday, 14th, was observed as a day of thanksgiving. We had no turkeys, save the kind

> "which our commissary found,
> While we were marching through Georgia;"

and they were precious scarce just then. But the battery opened its chorus of patriotic voices, and 100 rounds went roaring away to the distant Blue Ridge, and bounding over the rocky bed of the French Broad River, whose head was found among the neighboring foothills. Our hearts were full of gratitude for the great deliverance of our land from anarchy and ruin and shame. War was over, and peace was declared; and official acknowledgment, made by the authorized leaders of the so-called "Confederate States of America," that they were whipped, was formally and universally published. The infamous rebellion of hot-headed slave-drivers of the South and white niggers of the North, was crushed out; and the tag-ends that occupied East Tennessee, West Virginia and North Carolina, were fleeing before the wrath of the loyal natives, and were glad to find refuge under the protecting folds of the stars and stripes they had so lately insulted and outraged.

PRESIDENT LINCOLN'S DEATH.

But our joy was turned to deepest gloom and sorrow on the following day, when the news of the assassination of President Lincoln came. It spread like a pall over every heart; and the whole day was a season of humiliation and awe toward the Almighty Father, who controlled the destinies of nations and individuals, and was bringing our land through the divided waters to the fruition of our long deferred hopes. In our grief, therefore, we rejoiced, though we were no longer jubilant. The Moses of our pilgrimage was only permitted to look over into the promised glory of our great Nation, but not to possess it; and the shadow of our martyred President floated over our sad hearts. The sacrifice was a worthy one, and fit to crown the pyramid of noble lives that had already been yielded up for the cause of human liberty. Our cause was triumphant, and the Nation was saved.

> "Who said that the stars in our banner were dim —
> That their glory had faded away?
> Look up and behold! how bright through each fold
> They are flashing and smiling to-day!"

Sunday, 16th, two 3d Ohio officers, who had escaped from some rebel prison, came into our lines here, dressed in rebel uniforms. They were soon supplied with decent clothing, and forwarded to their homes.

Next day stragglers from Lee's vanquished army began coming in. They were nearly starved, and devoured the provisions our boys gave them ravenously.

On the 20th, the work on the railroad was completed, and a train of cars arrived. They were the first that had run here since the Union troops had occupied this place.

BACK TO NASHVILLE AGAIN.

Saturday, April 22, we struck tents at sunrise, and bidding adieu to Greenville, retraced our steps to Bull's Gap, arriving there at 3 P. M. Scarcely were we settled in camp, before Lee's men, by thousands, began to swarm in, who having stacked their guns and piled up their traps on the field where they surrendered, had proceeded this far on their way back to their homes. We divided our rations with them; which, in their half-starved condition, were gladly, if not gratefully, received.

Next day our wagon train moved out early for Knoxville, with orders to turn over everything there to the department. Things looked very much like we were going home; but we had been deceived so many times, that we did not bank much on mere appearances. Our brigade remained at Bull's Gap till Thursday, 27th. During this time large detachments of paroled rebel soldiers from Lee's army continued to pass through; one entire brigade camping near us on the 26th. On the 27th, we embarked on a railroad train for Knoxville, where we arrived at 3 P. M., the same day, and remained till 11 o'clock that night. We proceeded thence, in comfortable box-cars, to Chattanooga, which we reached at noon; but we did not stay for dinner. Possibly our last experience there had some relation to our hasty passage through the town. We got to Stevenson at sunset, and laid there till 9 o'clock, when we proceeded on our way, reaching Murfreesboro about 9 o'clock Saturday morning, April 29, and Nashville about noon. Thence we moved out to a point 4 miles from that city, on the Chicken pike, which led into the Murfreesboro pike, and was close to a beautiful little stream called Mill Creek. This stream was about 75 feet wide, and 3 to 12 feet deep. Our camp was named in honor of our former brave young commander, Gen. Charles G. Harker. Here we were shortly joined by Major Denny, who was then the ranking officer of the regiment. He had enjoyed his furlough, and was greatly improved in appearance. Other officers and enlisted men, of whom it has been impossible to obtain either names or any particulars, also returned to the regiment in this camp.

May came in with smiling face; and the boys, inspired with the confident expectation of speedy discharge, spruced up a little in anticipation of the meeting that awaited them with "the girl they left behind them."

DISSOLUTION.

THE LAST REVIEW.

On the 5th, orders were received to prepare for a grand review. That day and the next we had regimental drill, and on Sunday, 7th, regimental inspection. The following day was occupied very actively by every one in burnishing guns and bayonets and swords, and trimming up wagons, ambulances, artillery, tents and camp equipage of all sorts, and otherwise perfecting each command for the review.

Tuesday, May 9, was a lovely day; and every one was in fine spirits; though each was impressed with a degree of seriousness that was always present. We were soon to be forever disbanded; and it was desired that when we doffed the soldier uniform, we would have one particular occasion by which we would remember our last association as an organization. The ground on which General Thomas was to review his splendid army for the last time, was well chosen, being the same on which we had accomplished our glorious victory over the rebel hosts under Hood, the winter before. The lines were formed at 10 o'clock, A. M., and a salute of 13 guns announced the presence of the commander, and was the signal for the commencement of the review. The general, accompanied by his staff, then taking position on the right, rode slowly down the line, proudly waving his hat at the boys, who responded enthusiastically by presenting arms, dipping of colors and glad shouts. There was hand-shaking and tears, as the meaning of this occasion

crept into the intelligence of the brave boys who formed
this historic assemblage of the greatest army that ever was
organized on earth ; and which was to be the last general
gathering this side of eternity. Four tedious years of tiresome marches, bloody battles, watching and enduring, had
we been together, commander and command ; through the
dark valley of the shadow of death, that brought destruction, but never real disaster ; and down the pleasant slopes
of final triumph and victory! Well might the tattered
flags, that told the whole story, droop low to our hero and
our pride, as he passed! The boys remembered it all. In
those lines were the bronzed veterans who had been with
him at Mill Springs, while the Fifty-First was constructing
corduroy road at Hall's Gap, in order to furnish his command with supplies ; at Stone River, where Harker's brave
brigade withstood Breckenridge's vaunted division ; at the
slaughter of Chicamauga ; at Missionary Ridge, Atlanta,
Franklin, Nashville, and a hundred other fields, brought
to full view by our decimated ranks. The thought that the
old Cumberland Army, one of the proudest and most uniformly successful armies that ever was organized, was to be
disbanded forever, produced in advance a sense of loneli-
ness that few could resist. None of us were fond of war ;
but there had grown up between the boys an attachment
for each other, they never had, nor ever will have, for any
other body of men. This fraternity is still preserved ; and
they will treasure forever and aye, the affection cemented
on field of battle and on weary march, in sickness, hunger
and cold ; and that bound equally, as with cords of steel,
commanders and commanded.

In the Cumberland Army there was no "feather-bed"
business — no toadyism. Those soldiers — with rare exceptions ; and we didn't call *them* soldiers — won their honors ;
and deservedly they now enjoy them wherever loyalty and
patriotism hold over copperheadism and bossism. Those
boys who had lain on the cold, damp ground ; marched in

the sweltering, scorching heat of southern summer suns, in
clouds of dust and drifts of sand; through storms of rain
and sleet and hail; and endured all manner of hardship
and trial and suffering that mortality is capable of, through
four long years; and all for the noble cause we had all so
freely espoused, will not forget each other while life lasts;
but there will ever linger a fond recollection of the multitude of incidents of mutual interest, that shall tend to
unite them even more firmly, as their lives approach the
end; and that will be calculated to make ours a better Nation. We had learned many things. Our experience in
state affairs had been considerably extended, our wits were
brightened, and our judgment strengthened. We had not
scented out nice hams and shoulders in underground bins,
salt in fodder-shocks, potatoes and other good things in obscure corners, to no purpose. We all realized this, and we
believed along with it that, conversely with the prediction
of demagogue copperheads, "that the dissolution of the
army would scatter broadcast, as an epidemic in the land,
a horde of thieves and cutthroats such as no nation ever
was afflicted with,"—we were better men, save physically,
than we were when we went in.

The review closed about 3 P. M.; being witnessed by
thousands of citizens. Accompanying the review, the following general order was issued:

"GENERAL ORDERS   HDQRS. DEPT. OF THE CUMBERLAND, }
        No. 30.   NASHVILLE, TENN. May 10, 1865. }

The general commanding the department takes pride in conveying
to the Fourth Army Corps the expression of his admiration, excited by
their brilliant and martial display at the review of yesterday.

As the battalions of your magnificent corps swept successively before
the eye, the coldest heart must have warmed with interest in contempla-
tion of those men who had passed through the varied and shifting scenes
of this great modern tragedy, who had stemmed with unyielding breasts
the rebel tide threatening to engulf the landmarks of freedom, and who,
bearing on their bronzed and furrowed brows the ennobling marks of the
years of hardship, suffering and privation, undergone in defense of freedom and the integrity of the Union, could still preserve the light step,
and wear the cheerful expression of youth.

Though your gay and broidered banners, wrought by dear hands far away, were all shred and war-worn, were they not blazoned on every stripe with words of glory—Shiloh, Spring Hill, Stone River, Chickamauga, Atlanta, Franklin, Nashville, and many other glorious names, too numerous to mention in an order like this? By your prowess and fortitude you have ably done your part in restoring the golden boon of peace and order to your once distracted but now grateful country, and your commander is at length enabled to give you a season of well-earned rest.

But, soldiers, while we exult at our victories, let us not be forgetful of those brave, devoted hearts, which, pressing in advance, throbbed their last amid the smoke and din of battle, nor withhold our sympathy for the afflicted wife, child and mother, consigned, far off at home, to lasting, cruel grief.

BY COMMAND OF MAJOR-GENERAL THOMAS.

WM. D. WHIPPLE,
Assistant Adjutant-General.

IN CAMP HARKER, NASHVILLE.

During our stay in Camp Harker, we had many visitors, both from the city and from home. Among the latter, was the wife of Capt. J. A. Delano, who was an excellent lady, and was greatly admired and respected by all who knew her. She visited our camp on Saturday, May 13, in company with the captain; on which occasion the boys of Co. F gave her a reception.

On the 16th a number of the comrades visited the battle-field on Overton's Hill, where on December 16, '64, our command covered itself with glory by its successful assault on the enemy's stronghold, and by sweeping from existence Lee's entire corps of rebels. Many relics were picked up, which were subsequently sent home as souvenirs of that historic ground and its remarkable associations.

Friday, May 19, we had brigade drill, under the direction of our new commander, Gen. Chas. C. Doolittle, who also inspected the regiment on the following Tuesday. We continued each Sunday to have regimental inspection.

A very distressing accident occurred on the 22d. Two soldiers, Wm. S. Woodsworth, of Co. H, and another comrade, whose name could not be learned, were drowned in

20

Mill Creek, while bathing. Their bodies were recovered, and properly cared for.

Saturday, June 3, orders were received for all '62 men to be mustered out of the service. This created quite a sensation throughout the entire army; the veterans intuitively foreseeing a continuation of their service, in some capacity. The solution was not long delayed; and a deep murmur of disappointment involuntarily issued from the boys who, having borne the heat and burthen of the war, had indulged a fond dream that its end was very near; yet no one uttered a word of complaint, when it was officially announced that the 4th Corps was ordered to Texas. There was great activity among the '62 boys, from that time on, completing muster-out rolls, taking inventory of arms, accouterments and camp equipage. On the 6th, they signed the pay-rolls, and on the 9th, they turned over their guns, etc., and on the 14th, were formally mustered out.

A circular was issued about this time from corps headquarters, directing regimental and battery commanders, the terms of service of whose regiments or batteries would not expire till after the 31st of October, to prepare their rolls immediately for payment to April 30, 1865. Our rolls were soon completed, and forwarded; they were for eight months. There was little said about this among the veterans, but there was a settled conviction that something was behind it. This was, however, largely removed on receipt of the Cincinnati *Commercial* of May 27, containing the following. Governor Morton was doing all he could, now that the war was over, to have his boys relieved and sent home. He had telegraphed to Washington for information regarding the muster-out of Indiana soldiers, and this was the reply:

" WASHINGTON, May 26, 1865.

GOVERNOR MORTON:

I have just returned from General Grant. He says all muster out rolls will be made here, but no discharge papers will be given to the men, who will be taken in a body to Indianapolis, and paid there.

All veterans will remain in service, unless Kirby Smith has surrendered; in which case they also will be mustered out at once. Western troops are to be sent home first, immediately after the first of June."

"Unless Kirby Smith has surrendered!" Aye, there was the rub! The boys were filled with delight by a report that Kirby Smith had surrendered. But he had not; and Secretary Stanton had gotten it into his head that he had no thought of surrendering, but would keep up the war in Texas. Besides this, Maximilian with an army of French soldiers had invaded Mexico; and it could not be told what sort of combination might not be made to thwart the purpose of the Government, and prolong hostilities. So it was determined to send the 4th Corps to Texas.

About the 10th of June, word was received at regimental headquarters that we would certainly go at once to New Orleans. This intelligence was general, and soon became the all absorbing topic of conversation. It was reported that one brigade openly declared they would not go; and we anticipated a little trouble on their account and those who might be influenced to mutiny. Wiser counsel prevailed, however, and these fears were all dispelled before the time came to move.

NEWSPAPER CORRESPONDENTS.

One class of persons that annoyed us, was that sort of newspaper correspondents who, having secured a very soft assignment, without adequate qualification for such position, were ready to grasp at anything that came their way. They furnished a fine mark for our wags, and were made the mediums of a good deal of sport among the comrades. They were about as brave as the average of quartermasters' clerks, and about as intelligent. One of these news-suckers would fasten onto an old soldier with

"Aw, beg pawdon! I learn you are going to Texas. Saw several transports at Nashv'l, which the soldiers said were to take you down the river."

And whipping out his little scratch-pad and pencil, as

he adjusted his eye-glasses, he got ready for a stunning report. And he got it.

"Yes," replied the veteran, "we knew that several
days ago. Our general commanding has orders to take his
command to Corpus Christopher, and fit 'em up for a two
years' campaign in Western Texas and Mexico."

"Possible? Aw, by Jove! that's a long time."

"Yes; we've had all our guns packed in boxes, so they
won't be in our way. Each man is to be promoted as captain, and our present officers are to be put into nigger regiments and sent to the Sandwich Islands, to promote order
in that colony."

"Wonderful scheme, that! And—"

"Well, we are to be presented with a thousand acres
apiece of the best land in the South, with incomes of five
to ten thousand a year."

So he would run on, with one big yarn after another;
appealing to some other comrade for corroboration, whenever the astonished pencil-driver's credulity seemed to take
a check or to waver; occasionally weaving in something a
little plausible, to make the rest appear at least possible.
Then the delighted correspondent would seek a quiet spot,
and fix up a great story for some one of the enterprising
dailies. Nine out of ten of these smart reporters, or those
who were not old soldiers, could not be relied on for a true
report; their dialect "gave them away" instantly, and prevented their gaining information to which the shibboleth of
the old soldier would have obtained for him ready and welcome access. We were clannish, and besides we despised
the pedantry and quackery that characterized the majority
of war correspondents.

Surgeon Collins, being the ranking surgeon of our division, was placed in charge of the general field hospital.
He at once detailed Ast. Surgeon King and Steward Fitch
for duty at his headquarters. Dr. King was intrusted with
the care of several wards of the hospital, where he distin-

guished himself by his efficiency and industry. The dispensary and medical supplies were supervised by Steward Fitch, assisted by 3 prescription clerks and 7 nurses. This detail was materially increased afterward. The necessity for this detail will be seen, when it is known that sometimes there were 300 patients in the various wards at one time. Most of these, however, were sent to the hospital after we had been in Texas some time, and were afflicted with malaria peculiar to that country, known as "breakbone" fever, a sort of combination of every ache and pain and disagreeable feeling or condition known to humanity, and that is more fully described further on.

THE REASON OF IT ALL.

As the dissolution of the Cumberland Army began at this time ; our removal from Nashville being the first scene in the great final act ; the following, from Van Horne's History of the Army of the Cumberland, vol. 2, page 369, will probably fit in here better than elsewhere ; and it will certainly be of genuine interest to every one of the Fifty-First veterans :

The surrender of the remaining Confederate armies and forces east and west of the Mississippi river soon followed the capitulation of General Johnson and the capture of Mr. Davis. Preparations were then promptly made to disband the national armies, with the retention of such forces only as were necessary to prevent political and social chaos in the Southern States.

The formal unity of the Army of the Cumberland was restored before its dissolution by the return of the Fourteenth and Twentieth Corps within the territorial limits of the Department of the Cumberland. This reunion of the grand units under their revered commander was eminently appropriate as well as historically imperative. Their dismemberment at Goldsboro, North Carolina, occurring after their last battle had been fought, did not really impair the historical unity of this great army. Still, there would have been a painful lack of complete roundness in its mere organic unity, had two corps been disbanded outside the territorial limits of the department.

During the summer of 1865, the 4th Corps was also temporarily detached, and sent upon a mission to Texas under General Sheridan. But it, too, was soon remanded to the Department of the Cumberland, to be disbanded, as were the Fourteenth and Twentieth, by General Thomas.

From the 1st of June, 1865, to February 1, 1866, there were mustered out of the service of the United States, from the Army of the Cumberland, five thousand and eighty-three commissioned officers and one hundred and thirty-seven thousand five hundred and thirty-three enlisted men, exclusive of sixteen regiments of cavalry, whose strength was not definitely reported. About twenty thousand volunteer troops were retained within the Military Division of the Tennessee, under the command of Major-General George H. Thomas, until a later period. From the data given, the strength of the Army of the Cumberland, at the close of the war, may be placed, with approximate correctness, at one hundred and seventy-five thousand men. And when these heroic citizen soldiers were remanded to the duties of civil life, the Army of the Cumberland passed from organic existence to live in history as an army unsurpassed, if equaled, by any of the great armies which participated in our gigantic civil war—as one of the grandest that ever battled for country or freedom.

This army fought, unaided, the battles of "Mill Springs," "Perryville," "Stone River," "Chickamauga," "Wauhatchee" and "Bentonville;" gave essential aid to the Army of the Tennessee, at "Fort Donelson" and "Pittsburg Landing;" in combination with that army, but in twofold strength, gained the decisive victories on Lookout Mountain and Missionary Ridge; furnished more than half the forces for the Atlanta campaign, placing upon its banners the historic fields of "Buzzard's Roost," "Resaca," "Rome," "New Hope Church," "Kenesaw Mountain," "Peach Tree Creek," "Atlanta," and "Jonesboro;" at Jonesboro, represented by the Fourteenth Corps, made the only successful assault, in force, during the Atlanta campaign, carrying intrenchments held by Hardee's corps; formed the left wing of the army which marched from Atlanta to Savannah, and then swept through the Carolinas to Richmond and Washington; divided the glory of "Franklin" with the Army of the Ohio, and that of "Nashville" with the Armies of the Tennessee and Ohio; and, represented by the troopers of Generals Wilson and Stoneman, rushed through Alabama, Georgia, Tennessee and North Carolina, in swift and brilliant sequence to the great central battles of the war. This army, in its unity, never gave but one field to the enemy. But when it yielded the bloody ground of Chickamauga, it had revealed, under conditions of battle greatly unequal, its invincibility within fair terms of conflict. But even here it gained the fruits of victory, under the semblance of defeat, as it held Chattanooga, the objective of the campaign.

A QUERY RAISED.

Would the veracious chronicler state when, and the exact locality, within the territory of the Department of the Cumberland, when the act of remanding occurred, to which the 4th Corps was taken? According to the official order of Gen. D. S. Stanley, afterward commanding the

District of Texas, the principal part of it was mustered out in Texas, and were then "remanded" to the States whence they volunteered or were drafted from, for final discharge. The Fifty-First came directly by way of steamship to New Orleans; thence, without delay, to Cairo, on steamboats; and by the shortest railroad line thence to Indianapolis; as will be detailed further on. Now, it is possible, that, in order to preserve this "complete roundness in its organic unity," some of the troops were switched off en route, and posed in interesting and impressive tableaux to be photographed for future newspaper enterprises. But the Fifty-First was denied this additional pleasure.

What a happy thought, though, there was in "completing the roundness of our organic unity!" What sublimity and transcendent "appropriateness" in the "reunion of the grand units," that caused the loss of hundreds of noble lives that went out on the plains of Texas, and on the way there and return! What a blessed reflection upon the intelligence and judgment and justice and mercy of the authorities, who had but to command the loyal 4th Corps, to insure prompt and thorough obedience! Some would have denounced it all as sheer assumption and nonsensical display; but only because they were incapable of fathoming and appreciating the beautiful and eternal *thingness of the what!* The war of the rebellion had ended, and our hearts had fondly contemplated the glad reunion with the dear ones at home. But in this was repeated, for the millionth time, the old couplet,—

> "O, ever thus, from childhood's hour,
>   I've known my fondest hopes decay!

and we made up our minds for another tedious campaign. The boys could find no other cause for the movement, save that certain ends of personal aggrandizement were not yet consummated; and it was determined to test the gauge a little further. They were philosophical, though, and loyal to the core; and resolved to stand it.

Think of the boys who "went at their country's call," enduring every species of hardship incident to war in the South; and in addition to this, think of them breathing fever, penetrating mesquite jungles, making their beds in the presence of slavering wolves and with the ubiquitous greybacks; fighting clouds of gallinippers; guarding themselves with empty guns against the hyenas, alligators and murderous Texans; constantly in peril of death in some form — all to gratify the whim of an excited and pertinacious official, or for the purpose of making somebody military governor, or of securing a fat railroad contract — for such was the conviction of many other than ignorant privates; and there is great wonder that human integrity and fidelity should be able to endure this last test. Thousands of those who went the circuit of that campaign, are still no nearer its solution than they were when they entered the Lone Star State.

OFF FOR NEW ORLEANS.

Friday morning, June 16, 1865, the 4th Corps "fell in and counted off," and at the command took up its sorrowful tramp to Nashville, where cars were waiting to convey us to Johnsonville, on the Tennessee River, distant eighty miles almost due west from Nashville. The boys did not relish this trip much; but as we were whirled across that battle-scarred State for the last time, each tried to solace his partner by predictions of a surprise, and of speedy return to their homes. We arrived at Johnsonville the same evening in time to stow our baggage safely in the steamers that lay at the most convenient landings at and near that town. The Fifty-First was consigned to the boat "W. F. Curtis," Captain Hunt, master, and Thomas Benton Middleswart, the gentlemanly and big-hearted clerk. On this snug craft we loaded our traps, and got to bed as soon as practicable, the enlisted men distributed about the decks, and the commissioned officers occupying the state-rooms.

All the boys had plenty of money, having retained their recent 8-month's allowance, with the thought of taking it home, and would have been glad to pay for the luxury of a state-room; but all were tired, and such distinction faded out soon, as sweet Morpheus wafted them to their far-away homes, which were gradually growing more dimly distant. and the chances of going there more beautifully less. As we proceeded down the Tennessee, they found some compensation in the lovely landscape on either shore of the river, as our fleet, consisting of 11 boats, sped along; the murky trails of smoke streaming away from the lofty spectral stacks, down upon the bosom of the water. Here, on the right, is a clump of trees, whose branches overhang the margin, beneath whose grateful shadows has sported many a disciple of Isak Walton. A poetic comrade remarked that the scene reminded him of the "Lady of the Lake," and he looked to see her "leave the shore." Beyond rose the majestic spurs of the Cumberland Mountains, and they seemed to hover over us, as they reached away to the sky; and we were filled with adoration of the great Architect. who "measured the waters in the hollow of his hand," who "weighed the mountains in scales," and to whom "the nations are as a drop in the bucket." Cool springs trickled from the rocks, and sparkled in the sunshine, as they went to join the river in its course to the sea.

The first day out the boys began early to take observations about the steamer; and it was not long before they were on speaking terms with most of the crew, and had even penetrated the sacred precinct of the clerk's office, where a few, who were bolder than the rest, as dinner approached, had secured tickets for the first table. Soon others who felt keenly the necessity for "completing the roundness of their organic unity," strode bravely up to the desk and applied for dinner tickets. They were met by a volume of sulphurous vapor that rolled out from that office and down over the decks, while behind it was the clerk, in "fine frenzy rolling," and calling on all the gods of heathen mythology to deliver him from a lot of military orders he had received, as a sort of bills of lading, along with his human cargo, and which he was required to weave into his "log," which, being interpreted, signifies the journal of transactions and events of each trip.

SUBSTANTIAL GRATITUDE.

It is a strange fact, that humanity lives and prospers off of each other's distresses; and one man's extremity is another's opportunity. To one sympathizing inquirer, who was among the applicants at the window, the clerk replied by asking the soldier what his position was.

"I am sergeant-major."

The clerk had been a soldier himself, long enough to know something about the experience common to the office of sergeant-major. He exclaimed, joyously,

"You're an angel from heaven! You're the very fellow I want. Can't you help me?"

"Why, I guess so. What is it?"

"Well, for heaven's sake, come in here and straighten this out; and I'll make it interesting for you the rest of this trip!"

He said he had no trouble about the boat, nor with his regular business; but those blamed military orders took all the wind out of him.

It required about half an hour to "straighten out" his log; but before it was through, he had satisfied the hungry crowd at the window; and drawing his new assistant from the desk, the delighted clerk, with a grin that reached half way around his head, led him to the private table of the boat's officers. Seating him at a convenient corner, he beckoned the steward to him, and gave him special instruction to look after the new boarder; adding, "You take this place every meal!" After dinner, the steward escorted the soldier through the cabin, selected a state-room, and hand-ing the soldier the key, ordered the porter to put his baggage in that room. At the same time the steward inquired if his guest had a partner; and on being introduced to Comrade Dodd, he was invited to occupy the upper berth. So they lived like princes till we landed at New Orleans. The new assistant-clerk made himself useful at the desk, a few minutes each day, and kept the "log" clear of military snags; and the old master of the boat tried hard to induce him to get a discharge from the army, and continue on the boat, at a fine salary. But we were all in for "during the war," and it was a matter of conscience to see it through.

Quite early in the morning of the 17th, we passed Fort Henry, the scene of the early conquest of General Grant, and also of the harrowing events in the organization of the "Provisional Brigade;" and we quietly drifted as close as possible to the old stronghold, which had tumbled to ruins, and was overgrown with grass and weeds. While creeping leisurely along here, some of the boys on the different vessels of the fleet, realizing that their usefulness as soldiers was at an end, and desiring to transform their swords into pruning-hooks, noiselessly launched themselves into the river; but waved their hands wildly, when they saw the steamers' crews about to send out boats, thinking they had fallen overboard. They went home, enjoyed a brief visit, and joined us shortly after we reached Texas. They were, of course, reported "absent without leave," but a little "extra duty" squared the account, and removed whatever disability may have existed.

AT PADUCAH, KY.

Arriving at Paducah, Ky., at the mouth of the Tennessee River, and 500 miles below Cincinnati, on the Ohio, we were permitted to go ashore. This town before the war was the principal shipping point of that part of Kentucky, and vast quantities of pork, tobacco, mules, horses, etc., were sent up or down the Ohio River, to say nothing of an

extensive slave traffic that had been established with New
Orleans and other Lower Mississippi towns. Its glory had

"Gone, alas! like the many
    That bloomed —"

and luxuriated in that sacred soil of neutrality. As soon as
the boats landed, a swarm of men broke loose through the
town. Being Sunday, the business houses were all closed,
of course, as the law directs ; but, like a great many of our
alleged attorneys, "necessity knows no law ;" and the procession rallied on several stores, compelled the proprietors
to sell them whatever they required, and slipped back to
the boats, where General Willich, who was then commanding our brigade, was fluttering around like an old hen with
a litter of ducks in a pond. He made a fine little speech,
laying the whole mischief onto the Fifty-First, and swearing he would "hang every blanked rascal" he could find,
as an example to the rest. And that was the end of it. A
little more restriction was placed upon the whole command
that day ; but it only lasted till we got to Cairo.

We re-embarked soon after, and as soon as pilots were
secured for all of the boats, we proceeded down the Ohio.
The scenery along the Ohio River below Paducah is not
nearly so beautiful as it is above. We see only the worst
features from this point to its confluence with the Mississippi. The hills 200 to 500 feet high, and covered with the
verdure of an almost unbroken forest, approaching the
stream, and confining it on either side, which characterize
this lovely river from Pittsburg to Paducah, imperceptibly
fade away, and before we reach the Mississippi entirely dis-
appear.

The notes taken along the route, were made very hurriedly ; and many thanks are due Mr. Watson, the pilot,
for a great deal of information. He was a very intelligent
and interesting gentleman, and imparted a great deal of
useful knowledge to the boys, whom he welcomed kindly to
the wheel-house. He was at that time 69 years of age, and

had been on the river 35 or 40 years. His home was at Cape Girardeau, Missouri. He knew every town, point, plantation, bend, bar, eddy, snag, or other object of interest along or in the Ohio or Mississippi from their sources to the Gulf, with a vast amount of history connected with them. And notwithstanding his wandering sort of life, he had a great fondness for home, and spoke very tenderly of a sweet little granddaughter, who sometimes accompanied him on his trips.

Ten miles below Paducah, we passed Metropolis, Illinois. This was the first sight of "God's country" that had greeted our eyes for many a weary month; and as we sped past it, in that soft June evening, there came the painful thought that perhaps that was the last time that some of us would see the setting of our Northern sun. How true that prediction, let the black clods of Texas testify. Clearing a gunboat fleet lying at Mound City, 32 miles farther on, the ponderous hulks drifting like so many monster turtles, we swept by in the gathering gloam, with scarcely a sign of recognition.

CAIRO.

Eight miles more brought us to Cairo, at the junction of the two great streams. This place was always subject to inundation, which retarded the growth of the town. The levee built there to protect the town from these gushings, cost a million of dollars.

At Cairo the boys fitted up for the expedition. Linen coats and pants, straw hats, thin shoes and short hair were the order from this point on. And we learned, as we came nearer to the Tropic of Cancer, how sensible was this forethought.

DOWN THE MISSISSIPPI.

Out upon the broad swell of muddy water we drove, as a ready arrow from the hunter's bow. We were on the Mississippi, dashing along with no concern, save to gaze at

the shifting sights that like a grand moving panorama,
continually greeted the eye, only to pass out of view, filling
us at once with grateful pleasure at each succession, and
regret at their departure. The scenery on this river is no
less varied below the mouth of the Ohio than above. True,
there is more of the terrible seen in the cascades and lofty
rocks of the upper river; but below there is a happy blend-
ing of nature and art, an interesting struggle of essence
and circumstance for supremacy, not observed above. We
can appreciate the old raftsman's song,

"Down on the Mississippi river floating,
    Long time I traveled on my way,"

when we learn that the current is only 33 miles per day.
One peculiarity of the Mississippi, is its extremely winding
course. Sometimes a bend of 30 miles would occur, where
the distance across the neck did not exceed a mile. This
circumstance tended, no doubt, to check the current and
greatly facilitate navigation. It is a remarkable fact that
the water from many of the tributaries of this stream do
not reach the Delta for more than a month after inundation
above has been abating. The floods below vary in different
seasons. Usually these occur between the first of March
and the first of June, when they again subside. These ac-
cretions had ended before our journey began; and by the
time we reached the Mississippi, the river was in splendid
condition for navigation. The levees had broken through
in many places, causing great destruction of property and
loss of life. In some places great pools had been left, that
made excellent homes for the numerous alligators that in-
fest those Southern waters.

Columbus, Ky., is 20 miles below Cairo; Hickman, or
Mills' Point, 20 miles more. Then comes Island No. 10,
New Madrid, Ft. Pillow, Randolph and Memphis; all of
which are associated with some of the most thrilling events
of the war, with a dozen intervening points, of less interest. About 10 miles above the last named place, only two

months previous, had occurred the horrible explosion of the magnificent steamer Sultana, with 2,200 Union prisoners, who had just been released from the various hells all over the South, in which they had been confined for different periods, and who were hurled into the river at night, without a second's warning; many to find a watery grave, and many being scalded to death or otherwise injured so that they died soon after. Hundreds of those noble boys perished in that awful night, because somebody at Vicksburg got a percentage for every man that was crowded on board that boat.

The old wooden towns of Helena and Napoleon come a little farther on. They were made up entirely of frame buildings, because of the demoralizing effect of inundation and earthquakes on brick or stone structures. The latter is at the mouth of the Arkansas River, and just below the mouth of white River, which debouched by one channel into the Arkansas, and by another into the Mississippi. The Mississippi had cut through two years before, and we ran one mile in the old bed of the Arkansas.

We struck Vicksburg at a favorable hour; and many of the boys were permitted to stroll through that part of the city overlooking the river, that side being exceedingly precipitous. On the hill fronting the landing, were fine fortifications. Indeed, the whole place seemed a grand original series or combination of earthworks. There, on one hand, was the parapet from which "Whistling Dick" used to pitch "dinner-pots" over among the boys, during the memorable siege.

We then passed Warrington, Palmyra, Carthage and Bonjurant's. At the latter place, while we tied up a short time for wood, the boys had a great deal of sport with a little darkey, who resembled very much in size, shape and complexion, a ten-gallon demijohn. He was a marvel in the terpsichorean art, unequaled in song and dance, and a prince of bulesquity. Accompanying him was a juvenile of lighter tint, who varied the exercises by "patting juba," while the black one introduced feats, such as turning somersaults, forward and backward, hand-springs and jigs; all in perfect time with the music.

Natchez, 734 miles below Cairo, is the prettiest city on the Mississippi. Situated on a bluff 200 feet above the river, it affords an extensive view up and down the stream, and away off to the cypress swamps of Louisiana. It has wide, rectangular streets, beautiful flower gardens and luxuriant orange groves. Here we saw corn in the middle of June, with beautiful white tops waving in the soft wind, sugar cane, fig trees, rice fields, in an advanced condition, and feasted our senses of sight and scent on the extensive gardens filled with beautiful trees and rarest foliage and most delicate bloom.

THE CURSE OF THE SOUTH.

At all the plantations on either shore, little darkies seemed ubiquitous; decorating every projecting tree-stump like so many turtles, sunning themselves, and disappearing as nimbly, to reappear as suddenly as young toads dropped from the clouds. They were not all black by any means; many of them being as fair-skinned as our own brothers or sisters. We talked with some of these, who, with their mother, were huddled in a group near the landing. Their father had been reared in New Orleans. He was a white man, who had often comforted his innocent victim with the promise that she and her children should after while be sent North to freedom. But when the war broke out, he entered the rebel army, and forgot her; leaving her to the direction and control of a brutal planter, who without the fear of God or regard for man, stained his own soul with the same crime of her former owner, and perjured himself with the same lying promises of freedom. She was subsequently sent to work in the cotton-field, while her children were used as waiters. They had been told that the rebels.

had surrendered, and that they were free ; and the mother, still a handsome mulatto, bade her children hope for the promised deliverance.

Passing the mouth of Red River, 161 miles above New Orleans, we made no halt till we came to Baton Rouge, the capital of Louisiana. It was a pretty little city, filled with trees, and composed principally of small houses. This city derived its name from a majestic cypress that stood there in the early days of its settlement, and grew to an immense hight, perfectly straight, and branchless save at the very top. One of the visitors, a French gentleman, playfully referring to it, said *"le baton rouge!"* (which is French for "the red cane,") and this name was at once applied to the locality.

Below Baton Rouge the broad deep river swept through a plain occupied by luxuriant plantations of sugar cane, and adorned by splendid villas and gardens and groves of tropical fruit trees. As night approached, the sky became wonderfully clear, and in the distance rose gauzy cloudlets. Upon this soft background trees and foliage lay penciled in marvelous clearness. The brown water of the grand old river was broken into multitudes of little restless waves, begemmed with gleams of moonlight ; and as we sat out there in the silent night, there was not a sound

"To break the calm of nature;
Nor motion, I might almost say,
Of life or living creature,"

save occasionally the dismal hoot of an owl nestling among the shaggy locks of some old Spanish-moss-covered cottonwood. The rest of the trip was uneventful, save that the mosquitoes increased in numbers, noise and mordacity.

AT NEW ORLEANS.

At last we hailed the Crescent City, lined with a forest of masts, from oyster sloops to mammoth merchant ships and men-of-war. We landed at New Orleans, June 25, '65, and bidding our friends and comfortable quarters on the

21

steamboat good-by, fell into line on the broad wharf, and moved out south of the city, to the same ground on which General Andrew Jackson whipped the haughty Britisher, Packenham, on Sunday, January 8, 1815. As quickly as possible, a strong guard was thrown around the camp, and every one was set to work putting up quarters. An additional detail was also made for patrol service, whose duties were to prevent the soldiers from going into the city, and to arrest all of them found there without a pass; yet hundreds found their way there, possibly a few of them being members of the Fifty-First, who never ceased to regret the experiences of drunkenness and debauchery in the dens of that Sodom, into which they were enticed.

Some of us visited the famous markets; and as we meandered through the incongruous collection of French, Spanish, Sicilian and other foreign merchants, our ears were assailed by such a gabbling and chewing and grinding of languages as has probably not occurred since the fall of 2247 B. C. One comrade said he had never before heard so many different tunes on the jawbone at once.

Among other things we saw, and one that seemed very strangely out of place, was the statue of Henry Clay, on the pedestal of which were the burning words of that great statesman, in which he deemed the honor of the abolition of slavery the proudest earth could bestow. The exact language is not distinctly remembered. What would he have been, had he lived in the dark hour from which we were just emerging? He might have shared with Abraham Lincoln the proud honor of being the deliverer of four millions of people from the most brutal bondage that ever afflicted mankind.

New Orleans had several fine canals and bayous, on which many small boats, for pleasure or traffic, were constantly plying. These were delightful places for bathing, and thousands of the soldiers were accorded such privilege. Many visited the cemeteries, which were unique and beautiful. They were usually clothed with magnolias, cypresses and willows and a great variety of tropical flowers and foliage plants. Owing to the wet nature of the soil, bodies were not lowered into graves, but were placed in cell tombs built above ground, large enough to admit a coffin; rising often one above another to a hight of 8 or 10 feet. These were sealed with great care; some being very costly, but most of them plain and modest. Formerly they observed All Saints' and All Souls' days, at which times the graves were elaborately decorated with flowers and garlands; but in later years that custom yielded to the even more heathenish observance of Mardi Gras.

FOURTH OF JULY.

We celebrated the 4th of July in a very quiet manner. Regimental headquarters purchased a new tub, of the regulation washday size, and a huge chunk of manufactured ice — the first artificial ice we had ever seen — a quantity of lemons and a few other things to improve the flavor; and treated the entire regiment to lemonade. Several of us went into the city in the afternoon; and after partaking of a French dinner, we entered the train for Lake Pontchartrain. This road was about 9 miles long, the coaches being a little larger than ordinary street-cars. The route was one continuous stretch of swamp, said to be filled with hideous alligators. We soon accomplished the 9 miles, got some ice-cream at a little refectory, built out over the margin of the lake, and took an observation of the surrounding scenery, which for waterscape was magnificent; then we found an agreeable place for bathing. Entering the little booths, we were not long in divesting ourselves of our toggery; and soon we were immersed beneath the delicious briny liquid. To float upon this lake, and to revel in its delightful depths, had been one of the happiest dreams of boyhood. How we hugged that blessed lake — or tried to, and wanted to take it along, that we might lave in its refreshing depths every day. Plunging about, we buffeted the little soft waves that, like wine, seemed to impart new life and energy; diving and floating and frolicking to the complete fullness of our capacity. Then we sped back to the city, feeling a sense of relief—at least from lots of dirt.

New Orleans was scrupulously clean at that time, and the citizens treated us with marked civility; both being the results of General Butler's administration there. They had been humiliated. Formerly they had enjoyed unbounded prosperity; their population had increased phenomenally; and all went well, till, bent on secession, they went to work against every interest. They had "sowed to the wind, and reaped the whirlwind." These traitors sneered at our boys who read the Scriptures, and affected contempt for those "puling psalm-singers and canting Puritans who had wandered from Plymouth Rock down to the sunny fields of the South;" but they were now eating bread bountifully provided for them by the fathers and brothers of those they helped to starve in Andersonville and Salisbury and Libby. Yes, the religion which supported the mass of the Union army, was all that saved those sneering fire-eaters of the South from the merited halter and universal extinction. Thousands of men stood ready, whenever the word should be given, to desolate the entire territory south of Mason and Dixon's line. But love, the essence of the supreme authority to which they yielded obedience, was over all; and its gentle influences, though spent in vain upon many, have held sway over the hearts of the men and women who saved the Nation, and guided their words and actions in the great work of reconstruction.

About the time of our arrival at New Orleans, General Phil. Sheridan was appointed military commander of the Division of the Gulf, embracing the departments of Florida, Mississippi, Louisiana and Texas. Kirby Smith's rebel army was still in Texas, although he had agreed to surrender; and defying the United States Government, was committing depredations of every kind, and creating a panic wherever any considerable part of it appeared. When the rebel commander learned that Sheridan with a large force was certainly ordered to Texas, to bring him to terms, and finding also that his army was rapidly deserting him, he sent three of his prominent generals to surrender his entire force to General Canby, at New Orleans; and subsequently he ratified the surrender with his own signature at Galveston. He proved a very treacherous scoundrel, however, in the very last wriggle of his official authority; showing bad faith in disbanding his army, and permitting an indiscriminate plunder of public property. He and Magruder made their escape to Mexico. As his disbanded rebel horde still continued to devastate the country east of the Rio Grande, the 4th Corps was hastened to that part of Texas; and it was soon on its way thither, with Gen. D. S. Stanley in command. General Wood was again in command of his old division, and General August Willich commanded our brigade.

BOUND FOR TEXAS.

. Wednesday, July 5, '65, quite early in the morning, we struck tents and marched to the landing, where we loaded our stuff on the steamship "Cumbria," and embarked for Texas. Soon we were all aboard; and then the national colors were run up to the topmast amid the cheers of the crowd and the rattle of small arms. The engines groaned, and the steampipes wheezed, the ponderous screw that propelled the ship, creaked; and like a meteor we dissolved from the view of the Crescent citizens. Down the Delta we glided, past oyster-boats and vessels of all descriptions, out onto the "waste of waters." Yes, literally a waste; for nobody cared to save any of it; though there were numerous red-hot propositions to dam it. The prow of our ship sent the feathery spray dancing over the crests of the great waves, as they rolled away, and were mingled with the horizon. In many respects the ocean is very beautiful. We had read about how the spray like restless spirits floated across the briny peaks, as they dashed high against the dark ledges along the shore, and climbed in innocent fury above the rocky headland; awhile the surf chafed around the reef, and the howling gale slit into infinitessimal strips the proud sails whose corpulent bulge once lent majesty to the noble craft—how the hearts of the beholders leapt into their mouths, and their hands and voices went up in ecstasy over the glorious "life on the ocean wave;" and our hearts were all thrilled with expectation, only to be disappointed.

"One 'loves'—how he loves!—'the glittering foam,'
And 'the mad wave's angry strife;'
Just take that young genius who wrote the 'pome,'
Where the 'billows dash, and the sea-birds roam;'
And he'd give all he had to be safely at home,
He'd stay there the rest of his life."

It was the hardest trip we had made during the entire war. Four awful days we bobbed about on the "salt sea foam," with little beside a wide expanse of water to look at; and nothing to drink but nasty lukewarm water, if we may except a few pailfuls of slop, called coffee, made from the hot water pipe of the engine. The officers were, however, supplied, at a high price, with a few gallons of "ice water," made also of the same stagnant liquid.

OUT ON THE GULF.

Thousands of gulls flew around our vessel, or followed constantly in her track. The second day we encountered a school of porpoises, that bobbed and tumbled through the water like so many empty barrels. Sometimes they would jump several feet in the air, and drop into the water with a splash that could be heard a mile away.

Some of our boys were injudicious enough to take with them a lot of cakes, pies and fruit, to eat on the gulf; and others had liquor to protect them from sea-sickness. They were rewarded with a lovely combination of results.

As we passed Galveston — about four miles off, on the

second night, we encountered a gale. The sailors anticipated it; and everything was clewed down tight, and all
hands were set to work to clear the decks. All the soldiers
were sent below, and guards were placed at the hatchways
to keep them there. Then the word was given to the sailors, "Heave-yo-o!" and down went two ponderous anchors
to the bottom of the gulf, with a terrible rattling of chains;
and the vessel came to a halt, with a sudden jerk that mingled "red spirits and grey" in a babel of confusion. At
the same moment the storm struck her; and she groaned
and creaked and heaved and tossed under the awful trial.
Dishes and camp-kettles danced a Virginia reel all over the
decks; while the more delicate comrades yielded up the
contents of their stomachs with wonderful alacrity.

The master of the propeller paced the decks the whole
night long, his face blanched with a dread he dared not
communicate. He explained his restless manner next day,
by telling us that at that point the bottom of the gulf was
solid rock, and that we had been drifting all night toward
breakers, on which, had we reached them, the ship would
have been dashed to pieces in a little while, and we would
all have gone to the bottom. Ignorant of our great peril,
the writer, by an excuse, was permitted to go to the upper
deck; and crawling out the railing on the forecastle, to the
mast, he drew himself up by the great ropes, and stood
there in the starlight, and drank in the indescribable loveliness and grandeur of the scene. We were so near the
city of Galveston, that the street-lamps were plainly discerned. Tossing like a huge cork on the boiling waves,
whose crests glistened like ridges of diamonds in the mild
light of the stars; one moment the vessel pointed toward
the heavens,— the next as though she would plunge with
her precious cargo of humanity headlong to the bottom of
the gulf. But the crowded mass of soldiers shut up below,
in the dark, hot, noisome midship, tumbled about in agony
that was pitiable.

Arriving at the southwestern point of Matagorda Bay, at the Pass Cavallo, we came to land in the afternoon of July 9, '65. While awaiting orders outside the harbor, many of the boys took advantage of the occasion, to bathe in the gulf; and it was fine sport for them, as well as exciting entertainment for the spectators, to clamber out to the point of the bowsprit of the vessel, and plunge away down into the blue depths below. Then they would return to the deck by the ladders on the ship's side. The more timid ones contented themselves with swinging off on a rope's end. The water being entirely too shallow for our ship to enter the bay, we were transferred to "lighters" on which we steamed up to Indianola; where debarking, the boys at once prepared coffee, and had a feast.

We were now in the Central District of the Department of Texas, with headquarters at Galveston; and thus continued, with district headquarters afterward at San Antonio, until final muster-out at San Antonio; and were not again identified with the Department of the Cumberland.

TEXAS.

Robert Chevalier, Sieur de la Salle, led the first European immigrants to Texas, landing on February 18, 1685, near the same spot on which our patriotic little army first touched. He had discovered the mouth of the Mississippi, three years before, and returning from France to make a permanent settlement, erred in his calculations, and came to shore on the Texas coast. After two efforts to reach the Mississippi overland, in which his men suffered greatly, and which failed, La Salle, as Americans call him, started northward, to open communication with Canada. Trouble arising between some of his men, in the distribution of a quantity of grain; through the conspiring of one Duhaut, several of them were murdered. Then, fearing the anger of La Salle, they ambushed him, and shot him through the head; from which he expired in an hour.

Frequent storms occur along the gulf coast, in which the briny water sweeps over the adjacent low lands, filling cellars and wells, and ofttimes creating a water panic that is very distressful. In consequence of this, water has to be hauled a long distance, and is sold at a high price. Odd as it may seem, many of these people are delighted at such visitations. But this is easily understood; for when water is a dollar a gallon, and whisky is the same price, it does not pay to adulterate.

That part of Texas which the 4th Corps traversed, between Matagorda Bay and San Antonio, and on either side of a line drawn south from Austin, is almost entirely black prairie. The rivers that course through it are pretty regular in their flow, having their origin in large springs that are situated along the heavy slopes in the western part of the State, and extending from Austin southward. Those with which our six months' experience in Texas were principally connected, were the Guadaloupe and San Antonio. The latter is the western branch of the former, and empties into it 10 or 15 miles above the mouth of the Guadaloupe, which in turn empties into the Espiritu Santo Bay. Green Lake is situated at the mouth of the San Antonio River, on the line between the counties (or parishes) of Calhoun and Refugio, and is the chief watering-place for hundreds of thousands of cattle, that herd about its border.

THIRSTING TO DEATH.

Scarcely had the boys got their coffee drunk, before we were ordered into line ; and we moved out for Green Lake, distant 18 or 20 miles, but which, through the stupidity of a drunken guide, was extended to 32. To describe that march, would beggar the English language. About eight miles from the town of Indianola, we came to a cow pond, which was very muddy, on account of hundreds of cattle having waded through it just before we came to it. Most of the boys filled their canteens with this water, however ; for they had learned by the hardest kind of experience, to take anything, till they could get something better. That was the first opportunity to get water, after leaving Indianola ; and indications were good that it might be the last. Three miles further on, we came to another hole, or series of holes ; for they seemed more like big cow-tracks, filled from a summer shower. The water here was filthier, if possible, than the first ; yet those who had failed getting water before, did not slight it, but filled their canteens and little coffee-buckets with the vile stuff. From there on, we had not another drop of water of any kind until we reached the lake. Besides this, our progress was greatly impeded by the fact that we had our "sea-legs" on yet, and the ground seemed to roll just as the ship had; the strange deception causing many to fall; also making the distance seem twice as great as it really was.

It was hot enough "to roast a nigger" when we started on this march, and coats were a serious incumbrance; but we began soon after nightfall to realize the sudden change of temperature peculiar to that beautiful clime. The mercury in the thermometer slipped suddenly down to zero, and remained there till near midnight. The stupor produced by the sudden chill, added to the fatigue so greatly aggravated by the bobbing motion acquired on the vessel, rendered locomotion almost impossible. The soldiers could not be urged forward, and they dropped out by dozens and scores; until on the approach of day, it was discovered that not more than half of our brigade had pulled through. A number of them were afterward found as far back as 15 miles from camp. By 7 o'clock in the morning, nearly all who had kept anywhere near up, had reached the lake, and after a cup of strong coffee, were snoozing soundly beneath the broad shade of the shaggy live oaks that fringed the lagoon. But the poor fellows who, like the five foolish virgins, had "slumbered and slept," awoke to find that, like those same virgins, their vessels were empty.

Between the hours of 7 and 9 in the morning, there is a cessation of motion in the air; which on that morning was intensified by the intolerable heat of the sun, that was pouring down a flood of incandescent fury. One unaccustomed to this, cannot endure away from the shade scarcely an hour. A great many soldiers of other commands, as well as many from our own, were sunstruck at this season, during the war. A few of the unfortunate boys, after long search, managed to find, some distance off of the road, a pool of thick, stagnant water, that tasted like nectar to the parched throats; but most of them had none, and none could be gotten within 8 or 10 miles either way. When they were found by the details sent back after them, scores lay with their tongues out and terribly swollen ; others were trying to lick the dew off of the grass. Many had wandered away from the road in search of water, and it was with difficulty that they were found ; as they were too far gone to give any signal of distress that might lead to their discovery. Men, loaded with canteens filled at the lake, were dispatched on horseback in every direction ; yet, it is possible that some may not have been found, and died in horrible agony. Who can describe the feelings of those who were relieved, as the brave fellows saw life — most welcome, blessed life, coming to them — showers, canteens of life ! Finally, all who could be found, were brought in.

GREEN LAKE.

In a few days we had recovered in a manner our usual strength and spirits ; and having nothing else to do, we made a special requisition for ammunition, and amused ourselves shooting alligators ; varying this pastime with gathering grapes and pecans, which were quite abundant and of enormous size, and the usual routine of camp life. The war being over, we paid little attention to guns or any other part of our hostile apparatus, save as already indicated, and to despatch a "slow deer," when our supply of meat ran short. They were called "slow," probably, because of their dilatoriness in getting out of our way, and keeping up with the rest of the cattle.

Our reports of "able for duty" men were so meager, that there were hardly enough to make a respectable detail for anything. Most of the boys grumbled so, that the orderlies were almost afraid to detail them for duty at all. It came so frequently, that they each declared not more than half of the other boys had been on since they were. Then the orderly got a blessing ; and he laid it onto the sergeant-major. As there was nobody else to pass it on to, the latter had to bear the burden that might be shirked by every orderly in the regiment. But his heart was large, and his shoulders very broad.

The days continued scorching hot, and everything in nature was wrinkled or blistered or reduced to dust by the piercing rays of the vertical sun. But the oppressiveness of the day enhanced the delightfulness of the night. And, while at sunset the sky seemed like a huge oven, in which the earth was a mammoth roast, flanked by its majestic forests and towering mountains, and all humanity felt like the dried anatomy of what it started out in the morning; we were renewed and revigorated by the pleasant breeze and the peculiar soothiness of the night air. True, this succession of changes of temperature was severe on those who were subjected to extremes of both ; but those who sat in the live-oak shade all day, could philosophize, in spite of the common misfortune. Listen to one of them :

> " Day is done brown, and set away to cool ;
> And evening, like a salad fresh and moist,
> And peppered with her master's stars, comes on :
> The moon, like a large cheese cut just in half,
> Hangs o'er the landscape most invitingly ;
> The milky way reveals her silver stream
> ' Mid the blanc-mange-like clouds that fleck the sky ;
> The cattle dun, sleeping in pastures brown,
> Show like huge dough-nuts 'mid the deep'ning gloom.
> How like a silver salver shines the lake !
> While mimic clouds upon its surface move,
> Like floating islands in a crystal bowl ;
> The dews come down to wash the curled-up leaves,
> And night-winds follow them, to wipe them dry.
>
> On such an eve as this 'tis sweet to sit
> And thus commune with Nature, as she brings
> Familiar symbols to the thoughtful breast
> And spreads her feast of meditative cheer.
> Day with its broils and fiery feuds is o'er ;
> Its jars discordant and its seething strifes ;
> And all its boiling passions hushed to peace ;
> Old Earth, hung on her hook before the sun,
> Turns her huge sides alternate to his rays,
> Basted by rains and dews, and cooks away,
> And so will cook, till she is done — and burnt"

Green Lake was girdled by a beautiful green border of live-oak trees, whose branches hung quite low, and spread out to a distance of 30 or 40 feet on each side; furnishing a most umbrageous shelter from the broiling sun. These trees were covered with vines, which produced grapes of marvelous size and abundance, and of delicious flavor. Of these grapes we made a fine wine, splendid pies and cobblers, and a variety of other very palatable dishes.

Some of the trees hung thickly with Spanish moss, which we made to serve in lieu of straw for our beds. This moss is a parasite plant, found growing in vast profusion, clinging to many of the trees in Southern forests. When exposed to the process of "curing," as variously practiced, the outer bark or covering is decomposed, and an almost indestructible black fiber is disclosed, which closely resembles the article of commerce known as "curled hair;" and for all purposes to which the latter is applied, is equal to it, with the advantage of being vastly cheaper.

Eagles' nests were frequently found among the tops of these trees; but they were never disturbed.

The atmosphere of Southern Texas is very thin and elastic, and so transparent, that every star and planet in the heavens appears boldly defined; the beholder seems to see around and behind them. And there are constellations quite unknown to Northern skies; while the "milky way," instead of making a nebulous, almost unperceived light, absolutely flames through eternal space. Yet people are very foolish to seek there the famed "fountain of youth." Among the saddest chapters of suffering, are those of confirmed invalids going from the North, seeking health in "the balmy air of tropical cities." It is a delusion; and, if they survive it, they won't do it the second time.

Pleasure-seekers should not be deceived by illuminated pictures of this lovely Southwestern Texas; for, although more than a quarter of a century has passed, with its wonderful changes, no change is found there. The same tales of bloodthirsty transactions, the same lawless disregard for human life or any of the rights guaranteed by civilization, come to our ears from that God-forsaken region ; the same vile language, the same filthy habits, the same moral and intellectual obscuration are perpetuated. Accustomed to the careful housekeeping and domestic arrangments of the Northern home, the tourist finds himself or herself suddenly deprived of even a comfortable retiring room, and without the necessary convenience of even a bed to lie on. Every dish, unless imperatively ordered otherwise, reeks with red pepper, onions or garlic ; the language and habits of the people are strange and repulsive, and the climate enervating and exhausting to the most vigorous constitution.

The natives in that part of the State did not stable their horses nor pen their cattle. Every spring, (or once a year,) they would brand the new crop, and let them run ; then, when they wanted an animal, they would send or go out and get one bearing their brand. Little boys of 8 or 10 years would lasso a horse or a cow, as easily as our boys would jerk a pebble across the street. It's born in them.

VICTORIA.

Leaving Green Lake, about Monday, August 28, we proceeded to Victoria, the seat of Victoria county. Upon the beaten dirt road were teamsters with their merchandise packed in long white-covered ox-wagons, hauling freight to and from the gulf; half-breeds on Mexican ponies, bobbing along under their broad brown sombreros, nodding to us as we passed, with a half-articulate "How, senor?" looking more like murdering us, than having a Christian regard for our welfare.

There was very little of vegetable product there, save the bur-grass, on which the cattle feed. The bur on the grass was about the size of beet seed, and in shape reminded one of a jimson bur, with prickles so tough and sharp, that they would penetrate our thickest ponchos. This fact was discovered by most of the boys, by personal experience; as they learned nearly everything else. On spreading their ponchos, after a hard hour's march, and sitting down suddenly, they could scarcely suppress the involuntary oath that struggled up, as the ugly barbs pierced the nether cuticle, compelling instant removal to another spot.

"The wicked flea, which no man pursues," though not quoted with precise accuracy, was as plentiful there as the locusts in Egypt. Tarantulas and centipedes, also, were quite numerous, and dangerous; and the deadly scorpion was liable to turn up at any point. The writer, while employed upon the regimental books, one day, put his hand upon a dead scorpion, curled up between the leaves of one of the large volumes. Several cases of poisoning by these creatures were reported. The usual antidote for the bite, or sting, was whisky; though with some the cure was worse than the complaint. One man recovered from the bite of a tarantula, by the copious use of whisky, and the wound healed in two days; but the man died of delirium tremens.

The town of Victoria presented a very forbidding appearance, with its dirty streets, rough, unpainted, isolated buildings, broken-down doors and dingy rooms; and there was most harmonious correspondence between these and its greasy, disgusting inhabitants. The houses here, as well as nearly all along the line of our march, consisted of poles for walls, roof and chimney of sticks, plastered over, inside and out, with a sort of white pasty clay, that is found near the surface of the ground. The gables of some had boards that were hauled over 100 miles. In these close, filthy quarters, and covered with vermin, those people appeared to spend their lives cheerfully. The streets were filled with blinding dust, and were entirely innocent of shade trees. Reeking odors filled the air, and reminded one of the poet's description of the famed village in France:

"In Colin, a town of monks and bones,
And pavements fanged with murderous stones,

> And rags, and hags, and hideous wenches,
> I counted five and seventy stenches."

If cleanliness be akin to godliness, those people would not come in as "forty-second cousins" to divinity. There was little in the town to interest any one. Fronting upon a small sluggish stream, it recedes from the ragged shore, and occupies the acclivity and crest of a broad mound, that attains an elevation of perhaps 15 or 20 feet. To the east, west and north the adjacent country stretches away level to the horizon. To the southeast the eye rests on the low, blue outlines of the bluffs or ridges rising to the north of Galveston, about 50 miles away.

There was a railroad striking off from this place in some direction; and our boys were detailed to repair it. It must have been in a terrible condition, according to the report they made. The bridges had been propped up temporarily with rotten and decayed timbers; and, instead of replacing the old ties with new ones, only one new tie was placed at the ends of the iron rails, and one in the middle. Trains were known to run several miles without jumping off the track. A friend, who admitted having gone over it, says the improvements made on it since, are of the finest character in the world. But we got no benefit from it.

The writer visited the Catholic chapel, in which many relics had been preserved. Almost everything of any value had been carried away by Father Benoni, the priest, to a place of safety. All had deserted the place save the house-keeper, a young German woman, with more of Martin Luther's ideas of religion than of Romanism. She was very tired of the stupid existence she was forced to submit to; and sighed for freedom, that only the grave promised her. She despised the insincerity and meaningless mummery of the chapel service, and regarded with horror the ignorance and heathenism of the poor degraded masses, who,

> "In their blindness,
> Bow down to wood and stone."

It had been her habit to undeceive the poor creatures who

22

came from time to time for absolution and consolation, and to encourage them to rely upon God, instead of a besotted priest. As a token of her loyalty to our country's cause, she presented her visitor with a small brass crucifix, which had a history that would electrify the superstitious Romanist, and appall him with horror. The crucifix is still preserved, with its marvelous secret, among the choicest and most sacred of his war relics.

In the cramped little den occupied by the office of the Victoria *Gazette*, we met an old typo, who had at one time labored in the "art preservative" in the more appreciative North. In Texas his worth was not realized. The *Gazette* was a dingy little paper, printed on a sheet too small for a full form by a half-column; the last column being "half-measure." This man had been for several years a sort of journalistic shuttlecock in the upper districts of Michigan; had reported the proceedings of the original secession convention, and had traveled over most of the rebel "confederacy" as a topographical engineer. His experiences had been varied, and many of them quite interesting, as he narrated them. He had not been true to the land that had made him what he had been, and that would have continued to advance him, in the profession which moulds and directs public opinion; and, like the prodigal son, he was now feeding on the husks of intellectual existence in consequence, with very little either in his stomach or store to compensate.

A very exciting incident occurred in town, one day, the particulars of which interested a member of the Fifty-First, but whose name must be suppressed. He was a German; and in his search for something to eat, had dropped into a restaurant, where he soon got into a dispute with a French gentleman who ground hash for the establishment, and who attempted to convert our comrade into wurst, but got badly worsted himself. The gentleman from the west side of the Rhine stabbed the Teuton with a billet of wood,

and retired to the back yard, to cool off, satisfied with his
accomplishment. Not so he of the jaw-breaking dialect,
who rushed out frantically with a cheese-knife half as long
as a saber, and claimed to be master of the field. Africa
was also present, but being about equally divided on the
question, proposed to remain neutral. France made a fine
sorte, but Bavaria caught him on the flank, and enfiladed
him; leaving him scattered all over the field, slicing his
cotton uniform into convenient strips for a kite-tail. Then,
leaving word with the proprietor, to get a basket and sweep
the Frenchman up, he took the shortest cut for camp.

HOT WEATHER.

Those were such days as that in which Sidney Smith
wanted to take off his flesh, and sit down in his bones; or,
as Artemas Ward said of the final reward of the wicked, it
was a time and place in which "a man would sigh for his
summer clothes." At such a time we could sing with the
poet:

> "O, for a lodge in a garden of cucumbers!
>   O, for an iceberg or two at control!
> O, for a vale which at midday the dew cumbers!
>   O, for a pleasure trip up to the pole!
>
> O, for a little one-story thermometer!
>   With nothing but zeros all ranged in a row;
> O, for a big double-barreled hydrometer,
>   To measure this moisture that rolls from my brow!
>
> O, for a soda-fount, spouting up boldly
>   From every hot lamp-post against the hot sky!
> O, for a proud lady to look on me coldly!
>   Freezing my soul with a glance of her eye!
>
> Then, O, for a draught from a cup of cold pizen!
>   And, O, for a resting-place in the cold grave!
> With a bath in the Styx, where the thick shadow lies on
>   And deepens the chill of its dark running wave!

Think of it! The sun beating down, at a temperature
not a degree less than 100° in the shade; the sand in the
road glistening with heat; the leaves motionless; the little
birds panting for breath; the hot sweat standing in great

beads on the tent-poles; our ideas melted; our mental and physical capabilities thoroughly exhausted; when a cry salutes our ears, more terrifying than that of the horse-leech or the office seeker; more importunate than the claims of a creditor; and more irresistible than the smiles of a pretty widow :—

"Strike tents! Turn out, here, and roll 'em up right quick! Fall in! Forward, m-a-r-ch!"

And away we go for San Antonio. On our march we met more native teamsters; such long-bearded, murderous-looking fellows, with faces brown as autumn, and innocent of water for weeks at a time, their unkempt hair straggling in matted clusters or bunches; trudging along 15 or 18 miles a day, perfectly oblivious to the world of intelligence and refinement about them. They never settle anywhere; and their stay depends on their slyness in hiding and disposing of what they appropriate from others.

One day, about noon, and just as we had halted for dinner, we observed a dusty-looking cloud in the northwest. Not being familiar with all the peculiarities of that climate, we continued our season of refreshment a few minutes too long. Down they came, those bloodthirsty clouds, rattling a million fragments of dismembered vegetation into our milk — that had just been drawn on special requisition — and filling our eyes, ears, nostrils and mouths with vile dust. We gathered our stuff together, and prepared for a cyclone. Then followed the most tremendous tempest of wind and rain we had ever experienced. It seemed like the vault of heaven had uncorked itself, and we were about to have another Noahic visitation. It was worse, in its terrible portent and in our undefined apprehension, than Waterloo. It was a water-spout!

> Then there was hurrying to and fro,
> And gathering hard-tack, and yells of deep distress;
> And milk all spilt, which but an hour ago
> Produced the fervent envy of the mess;
> And swiftly forming in the ranks of war,

> Without the fife's shrill voice, or clattering drum,
> The shivering soldiers chattered, near and far,
> Or murmured with white lips, " I'm froze!" "I'm numb!"

In less time than it has taken to describe it, the rain
had passed entirely beyond the rear of our division, and
we began to collect ourselves; when, as if guided by the
evil one, the cloud about-faced, and passing back directly
over us, poured out upon us a deluge more violent and watery than before; drenching and soaking us as completely
as if we had been dipped in the river. The water stood in
the road and over the surrounding land, as far as we could
see, at least four inches deep; and as there were no fences,
nor sight of anything save the water, it seemed like the
gulf had broken its bonds and suddenly enveloped the entire State. We were compelled to wade thus for several
hours, till our arrival at Helena, a hungry-looking collection of half-a-dozen kennels, standing on a slight eminence
in the county of Karnes — so slight, however, that the elevation would hardly have been discerned, but that all the
water had run off, leaving the grass perfectly dry when we
got there, and safe to lie down upon. We learned there the
true philosophy of getting wet; which is to get soaked.
Moist clothing brings a hesitating discomfort; but in feeling that every thread is drenched, there is a desperate sort
of satisfaction.* At Helena we were given time to dry our
clothes, and restore our frozen limbs.

NATURE AND ART.

This county, as well as De Witt, which we had just
left, was almost destitute of trees; and for long stretches
without a trace of civilization. Over these wandered multitudes of cattle, browsing on the bur-grass, and watering
at the rivers and lagoons. At one place we saw a collection
of herds, going to water; which were said to number over
700,000; and further up the Guadaloupe River were fully
300,000 more — all within a radius of 10 miles. Here we
enjoyed one real luxury — pure milk and cream, unadul-

terated by chalk or water. As we advanced toward San
Antonio, things improved a little. Occasionally eggs were
obtainable, but at very exorbitant prices. Greenbacks were
becoming scarce, too, and it behooved the boys to devise a
proper variety of expedients by which they might obtain
their daily requirement of native product. Some fell back
on their more frugal comrades, to whom they gave an order
on the paymaster, for the amount of the loan, with liberal
interest; to be settled on next pay-day. Others, with more
elastic consciences, had provided a sort of currency that
was only resorted to in such a period of great stringency.
It consisted of an advertisement of an insurance and real
estate office at "Yohn's Block, No. 5, Indianapolis," done
in cheap lithography, and the figure 5 placed so as to give
it the appearance of a bank note, and printed with green
ink. It was a real invention in the interest of economy.

ANECDOTE ABOUT WILLICH.

One day, when the sun was broiling everything that
was exposed, the sergeant-major was sweating over an entry
in one of the regimental books. Having occasion to ask
Colonel Denny for information, he found that officer, with
General Willich and several others, seated under a tree,
in animated conversation. Obtaining the information he
sought, the subaltern turned to go, when he was accosted
quite sharply by the old general, who said:

"Hey, sawgent-majah; I ton't vant any more sich tam
reports vat you zent in! My atchitant dells me you zent
in de vorst reports vot come in de prigade!"

"How is that, sergeant?" said the colonel; "I thought
your reports were always pretty good."

"Vell, dey ain't! Dey're plotted und dutty, like dey
fallt in a hoss-pond!"

"I beg pardon;" said the sergeant-major, replying to
the colonel, "I trust there is a mistake somewhere."

"Don't dell me I'm mishtaken, ober I blay hell mit

you!" roared Willich, in a fierce rage, as he shook his fist.

The usual humiliation followed; and the brow-beaten youth sought his den, feeling like he would like to jump onto that old Dutchman, and pound him good.

Next morning, as usual, the daily report was made out and carried over to brigade headquarters by the sergeant-major. Laying the report on the adjutant-general's desk, he was quietly slipping away, when a voice came from the next tent:

"Sawgent-majah!—hey, you little fellow! come pack here! I vant to dell you vot a tam jeckess I mate mit my-zelf, yesterday. My atchitant dells me you make de best reborts vot come to dis hetquarters. It's dat tam 89t' Illi-nois feller. I play hell mit him!"

CAMP SALADO, NEAR SAN ANTONIO.

Finally, after traversing the county of Wilson, we came to San Antonio, the county-seat of Bexar, about the 30th of August '65; having marched over 200 miles from Indi-anola; and went into camp about 4 miles southwest of the city, on Salado [Sa-lah'-do] Creek.

As we did nothing there, and as there were scarcely enough able for duty in camp long enough to do anything, there is very little to say about it. Besides, the writer, in common with several hundred others in our division, had contracted that most horrible of all diseases, "breakbone" fever, and was incapable of chronicling anything that may have occurred. There was no doctor in our camp, and no one who had authority to issue medicine, but Easterling. The boys had no faith in him, as he had only a short expe-rience in a small drug-store, and knew nothing about dis-ease; so, all who could, got transferred to the division hos-pital, where Drs. Collins and King and the splendid nurses they had there, soon had the boys in good spirits, and on the way to speedy recovery.

San Antonio was a tough town. The principal part

of the male portion were inveterate gamblers, from the boy of 6 years, pitching "two-bits" (quarters,) to the grizzled veteran, venturing his remaining cow. Some of the soldiers entered into the spirit, with a zeal worthy of a better cause; and "fought the tiger" as hard as ever they fought rebels. A swarm of beer-blooded Mexicans occupied the plaza, in the center of the town, peddling watermelons and little hard apples. The pure whites had a sort of average intelligence, for they were principally from the North; but the nasty-looking, sallow, skinny natives were densely ignorant. The men seemed to be constantly "tight,"; but this could not be said of the women. Yet they all seemed happy in their squalor and depravity.

The stomach of the native Texan is something wonderful. One day, by way of variety, some of us dined at a popular hotel. Some of these comrades were of the first families of Indiana. Before one of them was a dish of fine large peppers, placed there as a "relish," and which are relished by the natives, as much as young radishes or little pickles are by the average Hoosier. The comrade's mouth watered, as he observed a native near him gulp down half-a-dozen of them in as many minutes. He gazed at the beautiful red pods; and then, as the waiter was a little slow with his order, he stuck his fork into one of them, and put it into his mouth. As his teeth closed on it, tears sprang to his eyes and strangled imprecations to his lips. With a gasp of despair, and a look of tenderest don't-give-me-away pleading, he tore the blazing cone from its resting-place, and clapped it on the table; and with an exclamation that would not be permitted to pass through a telephone, said, "Just lie there and cool!"

THE ALAMO.

This place was the scene of the hardest battles during the old Mexican troubles; and where Santa Anna's troops murdered the garrison under Col. David Crocket and Col.

Wm. B. Travis. The Alamo, from which the town had its origin, was a chapel, built by a Romish mission, said to have been planted in 1673; though it bore the date 1757. Its name in Spanish means "poplar," and was derived, no doubt in a manner similar to that of Baton Rouge. During the early conflicts, it was converted into a fort; and is known in history as Fort Alamo. The entire area included more than two acres, and was surrounded by a wall 9 to 12 feet high, and 3 feet thick. In 1835, the Mexican general surrendered San Antonio to the Texans; but early in 1836, Santa Anna, the Mexican dictator, came with an army of 3,000, and surrounded the town and fort, defended by 177 men. The Mexicans planted 2 batteries, and kept up an active cannonade on the fort. There were also frequent skirmishes by day and alarms by night. Finally, Santa Anna called a council of war; and it was decided to make a general assault at daybreak on the 6th of March. Three divisions advanced, while Santa Anna, taking his station with bands of music 500 yards south of the fort, sounded "No quarters!" The first division to attack, was repulsed handsomely; the second was checked for some time; but the third scaled the wall. Most of both officers and men were killed at their posts. Travis received a shot as he stood on the wall, cheering his men on. As he fell, a Mexican officer rushed forward to dispatch him; Travis met his assailant with a thrust of his sword; and they expired together. The garrison kept up a deadly fire from the doors and windows. Some were posted in the old chapel, which had long been unroofed; and there the last fighting took place. One was killed while attempting to fire the magazine. A few who escaped from the enclosure, were shot by the cavalry. One officer with his child was shot while leaping from a chapel window. The whole action occupied less than an hour; and Santa Anna, entering toward the close, grossly insulted the bodies of his victims, and ordered them burned. Some were afterward found under mattresses, and served like the rest. This spot has been called, from that battle, "the Thermopylæ of Texas."

The brutal Mexican leader supposed this would intimidate the natives; but it only aroused them to vengeance. Eight weeks later, at San Jacinto, Gen. Sam. Houston, at the head of 783 natives, came up with Santa Anna's army, charged them, shouting fiercely, "Remember the Alamo!" and routed the greasers; capturing their leader.

The town has grown to be a populous city; the census of 1890 giving it 38,681.

"BREAKBONE" FEVER.

This disease, which has already been mentioned, and which did not slight very many of us, is sometimes epidemic in that region. It occurs in this form at intervals of four or five years, and is known as "dengue." In many respects, it is identical with "yellow-jack;" but with the important difference that "breakbone" rarely kills. It is also no respecter of persons; and snaps its finger at acclimation. The natives, however, get away with it easily. They quackle down their orange-leaf tea, pack their heads in cold, wet cloths; and are soon over it. But it wasn't so with our comrades. One case describes the experience of nearly all.

Morning broke on the tired-out veteran, after a long and fearful night in pitched battle with a brigade or two of gallinippers; and he blessed the day, as the signal for retreat of the sanguinary foe. He answered with cheerful alacrity, the call to "grub-pile;" and contemplated the big cupful of black coffee and the hard-tack with pleasurable anticipation. But it was for only a moment; for a cold, disagreeable sensation began creeping up his spinal column. He put on his overcoat, but the sensation increased; and in an instant he had lost his appetite. He first sought relief in wine, made from the native grapes; but that was a failure. There was a sensation of nausea in the epigas-

tric region, attended with shooting pains in the back of his
head. Outside, the noisy soldiers, quarreling over a game
of "horse-shoe" quoits, or euchre, and anathematizing the
man who brought them to Texas, made racket enough to
distract a healthy brain; to the victim, groaning and tossing, with a raging headache, an aggravated toothache in
every muscle, currents of molten lead coursing through
every bone and bowel.—an earnest of sheol it seemed. To
be broken on the wheel, or stretched on the rack, would be
a sweet relief. Partial delirium attended the working of
the disease; and he became identified with everything in
the camp. Then it seemed like he were floating in space;
vainly trying to get away from the body in which all the
pain was centered, and with which he seemed to maintain
only a nominal connection; by no means pleasant, yet
necessary to the complete appreciation of his new acquisi-
tion. The alleged assistant-surgeon was applied to, and a
score or two of symptoms described; also the victim's sus-
picions were ventured. The wonderful man of science felt
the comrade's pulse, looked at his tongue, gave him three
or four lively shakes, informed him it was only a slight bil-
ious attack; and left him a dozen nasty-looking powders,
with the injunction to take one just before eating. He was
perfectly safe in the latter, so far as any good or evil result
was concerned; as the patient might have died forty times,
from lack of virtual benefit contained in those little packages, before he would have the slightest sign of an inclina-
tion to eat. Still the battle raged. The headache assumed
a spiral tone, like a huge auger, or the screw of a propeller,
boring into his brain. His "mess" did all they could to
relieve him; but there is no consolation for a man with the
"dengue." Every part of his physical composition, from
head to foot, seemed broken into inch bits of cartilage and
bone, and all grinding on each other. As the "breakbone"
finally gave signs of leaving, it was succeeded by an exaggerated attack of "fever 'n' ager," that threatened to finish

the subject. One shake of genuine Texas ague is equal to a dozen earthquakes, and almost as conclusive as an ordinary thunderbolt. Yet hundreds of comrades survived the terrible disease; and are now, that the vigor of youth has yielded to the natural disablements of advanced age, prematurely decrepit, gazing into open graves, in consequence of the awful experience of that summer and fall in Texas.

GENERAL WOOD'S FAREWELL ORDER.

About the middle of August, General T. J. Wood, by an order emanating from the War Department, relieving many general officers from their former commands, and assigning them to new ones, was transferred to the command of the Department of Arkansas. The first intimation we had of his removal, was received by the soldiers of his old division in the following order, which was read on the next dress parade. The reproduction below is almost a perfect fac-simile of the original copy sent to the Fifty-First, which is still preserved by the writer:

HEAD QUARTERS 3rd DIVISION, 4th ARMY CORPS,
GREEN LAKE, TEXAS, August 24th, 1865.

SOLDIERS:

An order assigning me to duty in another department, dissolves our official relations. It is therefore necessary I should take leave of you. Had it been consistent with the views and orders of the Government, I should have greatly preferred conducting you to a rendezvous near to your homes, there to have seen you mustered-out of the service, and bidden you a final adieu. It is ordered otherwise, and, as good soldiers, we must submit cheerfully, and perform with alacrity, whatever duty is imposed on us.

Your military career has been glorious. You can retrospect the history of your participation in the war for the suppression of the atrocious rebellion with the proudest satisfaction; unalloyed by any feeling of regret or sorrow, save that which you feel for the brave comrades who fell on the battle field, or who have been disabled and maimed for life. To the bereaved and afflicted I am sure you will ever extend the cordial sympathy of gallant soldiers.

As a right fairly won, you can blazon on your banners a long roll of the proudest historic names—names which symbolize some of the hardest fought fields and grandest victories of the war. Your fair fame as soldiers will be the richest legacy you can bequeath to your posterity. It will be a priceless inheritance.

Soldiers! Remember that as you have been the preservers of our nationality in the great and terrible domestic war, you must consider yourselves the custodians of our national honor and dignity and rights, and be ready to do battle for these great interests whenever they may be imperilled, whether by a domestic or foreign foe. Having asserted the principle of free government in the suppression of the rebellion, you must maintain it against all enemies.

It is highly probable that I may chance in the future to meet many of you in civil life and I now request if such should be the case, none of you will hesitate to make yourselves known to me. I make this request for the reason that the change produced in your appearance by doffing the uniform of the soldier and donning the attire of the citizen will prevent me from recognizing many of you. It will ever afford me pleasure to greet any soldier who has served under my command. Participation in common dangers, privations and hardships, and the sharing of common triumphs, have warmly attached me to all of you, and cause me to feel a deep interest in your future prosperity. I can wish you no better fortune than that in the peaceful vocations of civil life your career may be as prosperous, successful and happy as your military career has been brilliant, honorable and useful. To each one of you I bid a friendly good bye, with the assurance that from my inmost heart goes forth a sincere invocation for God's blessing on you. Soldiers, farewell!

TH. J. WOOD,
Maj. General Vols.

General Wood was indeed a friend to the common soldier; and had endeared himself to them by his many acts of genuine kindness. They will ever hold dear to memory the name of "Old Tommy Wood," as he was familiarly called, when spoken of, just as the idol of the Cumberland Army was called "Old Pap Thomas," and will always be proud of having belonged to the old division he had the honor to command through so many glorious campaigns, so many hard-fought battles and so many trying hardships. He was, on November 3, '65, by General Order No. 159, War Department, assigned to the command of the Army of the Tennessee.

General Wood's removal was the feather that broke the camel's back. He never knew it, though; and had he been present, he could have prevented the unhappy transaction which occurred. Some of the boys, like a certain impulsive element in every community, felt that they could stand no more; and now their indignation asserted itself. They did not know the cause of his removal; and did not stop to ask. They had a theory that it was in some way associated with their demand for muster-out; and that was quite enough. Hundreds of soldiers, who had preserved their integrity till that moment,—and preserved it to the end, were sorely tempted to throw off the yoke, and openly denounce those who were responsible for this disaffection. The more considerate, though, sought to calm the impatient ones, who were threatening all kinds of things, and to prevent any disgraceful act that might mar their thus far brilliant record. They succeeded in part. But some of the boys determined to demonstrate in some way; and these decided on a parade in mock honor of the individual who was holding them in Texas. They found a burro, which is a diminutive donkey, a native of that region, about the size of a calf two weeks old, whose head constitutes one-half of the beast, is as hard as an oak post, and is surmounted by most enormous ears. They then constructed an effigy, as nearly resembling the person intended to represent, as the able artists could get up under the circumstances — in full uniform; and strapping it onto the burro, paraded it thus through the whole camp, demanding, with terrible epithets and imprecations, the immediate muster-out of themselves and their comrades; while showers of pebbles and volleys of clods and sticks were hurled against the devoted paddy. The brass ornaments shone resplendent in the evening sun, and dazzled all beholders. The bosom of the uniform stuck out like that of a Thanksgiving turkey; the coat-tails floating gracefully behind, like a fashionable belle with a "Grecian bend." A ponderous saber clanked at his side, to which his spurs rattled a merry accompaniment. There was no response from headquarters; and everything soon quieted down.

About the first of September a large force was distributed along the Rio Grande, in consequence of the disturbed condition of affairs reported there, and the escape of many rebel soldiers and officers into Mexico, carrying with them arms and other property rightfully belonging to the United States. Along with this, a rumor prevailed, that General Sheridan had an ambition to fight Maximillian, and that he would try to take the 4th Corps across the Mexican border, on some pretext or other. The popular feeling among the rank and file was that a certain person was ambitious to be provisional governor, while another aspirant for honors was to be known as the great American invader of the land of the Montezumas. Several officers who called at headquarters, to make inquiry about the cause of our detention in Texas; there having been no development, since our entering the State, of any public interest necessitating the presence of a large and expensive body of veteran soldiers; reported that they were snubbed, and returned as wise as they went. Many believed all this; and it again threatened to demoralize the entire army in that section. Various methods were resorted to, to prevent insubordination, and to relieve the dreadful pressure that seemed about to find vent in some sort of folly.

Saturday, September 3, we were still in our old camp on Salado Creek. General Willich, who had been sick and absent from the command for a long time, had gone home, in accordance with the order from the War Deparment, referred to; and Brev.-Brig.-Gen. H. K. McConnell was commanding our brigade. Major-General Wright, who was at that time commanding the Department of Texas, reviewed our brigade, at which time he was presented with a petition signed by all the regimental commanders, and by the brigade commander also, for the immediate muster-out of our brigade; which he readily approved, and promised to leave orders with General Stanley, for carrying into effect, as soon as he arrived at Victoria.

October 4, Taswell Dodd, who was a recruit of '62, was mustered-out, by reason of expiration of service; and we were without a postmaster from that on.

Then began a disintegration, that continued during our stay there. At Camp Weidner, October 22, although Sunday, 100 one-year men started for home; their term of service having expired. We were cheered with the information that an order was at division headquarters for the muster-out of the Fifty-First; but grew gloomy when told we would be retained till after the State election. What did we care for the State election? All around us were the wasted forms of gallant boys, who in health marched up to the cannon's mouth, and charged serried hosts of rebels, to save the Nation, and to preserve the honor of the old flag. They wanted to go home, while they were able to get there. And they were hopefully waiting.

> "Waiting for health and strength;
> Counting each flickering pulse, each passing hour,
> And sighing, when the weary frame at length
> Sank like a drooping flower.
>
> Waiting for absent eyes,
> Brighter than sunrise to the lonesome sea;
> Lovely as life to youth's expectant gaze,
> And dear almost as heaven."

BREAKING UP.

Our brigade, that had included seven regiments, now began to be broken up. The 89th Illinois went to New Braunfels; the 15th Ohio to Stanley's headquarters, at Victoria; 8th Kansas to San Antonio; 49th Ohio to Gonzales; leaving with us the 71st Ohio, (General McConnell's old regiment,) and the 32d Indiana, (Willich's old regiment,) to preserve the "roundness of our organic unity." It was expected we would be sent to Galveston. Camp duty was almost entirely suspended; roll-calls were very irregular; and the boys who were able and inclined, found amusement in fishing, gathering pecans and smoking "jerked" beef for prospective consumption while crossing the gulf, and on the way home. Most of the boys were convalescing from "breakbone" fever and Texas ague; and simply sat around and waited.

MUSTERED OUT.

At length it came. About November 20, the following order was promulgated, and we got ready at once to march:

HDQRS. CENTRAL DISTRICT OF TEXAS, ꜱ
AST. ADJ. GEN.'S OFFICE,
San Antonio, Tex., Nov. 16, 1865.

SPECIAL ORDERS
No. 234. [Extract.]

In accordance with Special Orders No. 62, Par. 5, Head Quarters Department of Texas, dated Galveston, Texas, Oct. 23d, 1865, the following Regiments will be mustered out of service:

77th Pennsylvania V. V. I.,		15th Missouri V. V. I.	
31st Indiana,	"	28th Kentucky.	"
23d Kentucky,	"	13th Ohio,	"
21st Kentucky,	"	15th Ohio,	"
21st Illinois,	"	71st Ohio,	"
40th Indiana,	"	49th Ohio,	"
57th Indiana,	"	59th Illinois,	"
42d Illinois,	"	8th Kansas,	"
64th Ohio,	"	51st Indiana,	"
65th Ohio,	"	32d Indiana.	"
13th Wisconsin,	"		

By command of Maj. Gen. D. S. STANLEY,

W. H. SINCLAIR, A. A. Gen.

Certified to by W. NICHOLAS, Capt. & C. M., C. D. of Texas.

In this order the commanding officers were directed to forward reports, designating the rendezvous each regiment should be sent to, for final payment and discharge. The muster-out rolls of the Fifty-First were at once made out, to date December 13, 1865; our rendezvous for final discharge was Indianapolis; and as each comrade attached his signature to the roll, he was then silently and informally mustered-out. Some desired their final discharge in Texas, for various reasons; and were mustered-out accordingly. Some were too ill to undertake the trip across the gulf, and their partners did not want to leave them. A few wanted to invest their pay in cattle, and take them home for speculation. The rest of us retraced our steps by the nearest

23

route to Indianola, where we were to take the next ship to New Orleans.

"Though long of waves and winds the sport,
Condemned in wretchedness to roam;
Thou soon shalt reach a sheltering port,—
A quiet home!"

Merry Christmas came to us as we lay on the sandy beach of Matagorda Bay; the fifth anniversary of that day we had spent in the South; but we had no pleasant meditations specially suited to that holiday. We can all recall now the joys of childhood, the row of fat stockings hanging at the fire-place, and our quarrels over our treasures — as every one else might. But we didn't meditate in that way there, on that bleak, dreary beach. A variety of thoughts struggled for utterance; but we were weak, and tired and sleepy; and so we let them struggle on.

BACK TO GOD'S COUNTRY.

Next day we went aboard a ship, and sailed to New Orleans; arriving there in time to celebrate New Year's Day with a feast of delicious oranges, fresh from the trees. We marched to the steamboat landing in a drenching rain, which held on till we went aboard the steamer "Clara Dolson," that was to take us to Cairo, Illinois.

Just as we reached the landing, the commissary wagon came up and issued several barrels of mess pork; which, as the boys had supplied themselves before we left Texas, with an abundance of nicely smoked "jerked" beef, was a rather unwelcome ration. While they were pondering over its disposition, the steward of the steamer approached the sergeant-major, and proposed that if the boys would bring their pork around to the cook-house, he would buy every pound of it. This was immediately communicated to each company; and in a few minutes a line of soldiers formed half way round the boat, making their way to the steward's quarters; where they soon exchanged their fat meat for a good price in cash.

At Cairo we were delayed part of a day, on account of lack of transportation. Then we proceeded as rapidly as safety would permit, to Indianapolis; where we found delightful quarters awaiting us in the "Soldiers' Home" on West street, near Georgia street, a comfortable building, somewhat similar to the one described elsewhere; this one being capable of lodging 1,800 men, and having dining accommodations for 8,000. The building was fitted up by the State, and the rations were furnished by the Government; and it was one of the most complete institutions of the kind in the country. Regiments, as well as individuals, were furnished with warm meals and lodging, almost at a moment's notice. Here thousands of soldiers, continually arriving and departing, some en route to join their regiment in the field, others returning discharged, or on sick-leave or furlough, were provided for. At this place our final pay-rolls were signed, and we received our final pay and discharge.

During the brief interval between our arrival and discharge, the boys were permitted to visit the clothing stores; and it was very amusing to observe the wonderful variety of selections made by the boys, as they exchanged their soldier suits for such other styles as pleased their fancy.

The arrival of the paymaster, then, closed the last act in the great drama of our army life; and as each comrade departed with his vellum certificate and his money, the Fifty-First Indiana Regiment, Veteran Volunteer Infantry, as a legal and physical organization, faded like the mist before the morning sun.

RECAPITULATION AND ROSTER.

Adj.-Gen. Terrell's Report is very far from being exactly accurate; not nearly so much from his errors, as the result of carelessness and incapacity of many whose duty it was to furnish the data from which that report was made up. Incorrect as it is, yet it is the only comprehensive record attainable suited for this work; and it is therefore used just as it is, with such corrections as the compiler was enabled to make.

ENGAGEMENTS.

The following list of engagements in which the Fifty-First took part, is compiled from the Adjutant-General's Report; to which must be added the fight at Charleston, Tenn., December 27, '63, and at Duck River, Columbia, Tenn., December 23, '64; besides a great many heavy skirmishes and sorties, that were not officially reported:

1862. April 7, Shiloh, (Pittsburg Landing,) Tenn.
       April 11 to May 30, Siege of Corinth.
       August 9, McMinnville, Tenn.
       August 21, Gallatin, Tenn.
       "   27,   "   " (Second)·
       October 8, Perryville, (Chaplin Hills,) Ky.
       December 31 to January 2, '63, Stone River, (Murfreesboro,) Tenn.
1863. April 30, Day's Gap, Alabama.
       "   " Crooked Creek, Alabama.
       May 2, Blount's Farm, Alabama.
       November 25, Mission Ridge, (Chattanooga,) Tenn.

1864. January 10, Strawberry Plains, East Tennessee.
  " 12, Mossy Creek,   "   "
  " 17, Dandridge,   "
  August 15, Dalton, Georgia.
  November 26, Columbia, Tenn.
    " 30, Franklin, "
  December 15–16, Nashville, Tenn.

CAMPAIGNS.

Tennessee and Kentucky,	-	-	-		1862
Siege of Corinth,	-	-	-	-	1862
Pursuit of Bragg,	-	-	-	-	1862
Rosecrans in Tennessee,	-	-	-		1863
Streight's Raid	-	-	-	-	1863
Tennessee and Georgia,	-	-	-	-	1864
Hood — Pulaski to Nashville, (and return,)	-				1864
Texas,	-	-	-	-	-	1865

FLAGS IN THE STATE LIBRARY.

National Flag; silk; worn, torn and faded; inscribed, "51st Regt. Ind. Vols."; staff good.

Regimental Flag; blue silk; split and torn; inscribed, "51st Indiana Regiment Infantry," "Shiloh," "Corinth," "Chaplin Hills," "Stone River," "Day's Gap," "Crooked Creek," "Cedar Bluff," "Blount's Farm," "Shoal Creek," "Charleston," "Dandridge," "Battles of Nashville," "Columbia;" "Duck River," staff good.

Regimental Flag; blue silk; worn, torn and faded; inscribed, "51st Regt. Indiana Vols.;" "Stone River, Tenn.;" staff good.

————

The Adjutant-General's Report, vol. 3, p. 18, says:

"The Fifty-First Regiment was mustered out at San Antonio, Texas, on the 13th of December, 1865, and arrived at Indianapolis on the 10th of January, 1866, with 23 officers and 286 men, under command of Lieut. Col. Wm. W. Scearce. On the following day it had a public reception, after which its officers and men were finally discharged from service."

According to that authority, also, the Fifty-First had, from first to last, 43 original commissioned officers, 16 original non-commissioned officers, 880 original enlisted men, 654 recruits, 295 re-enlisted veterans, 69 unassigned recruits, 7 commissioned officers died, 259 enlisted men died, 130 deserted, 51 are unaccounted for; a total of 1644. The roster reduces this number to 1614, as follows:

COMPANIES.	A	B	C	D	E	F	G	H	I	K	TOTAL.
Killed............	7	5	7	1	0	5	0	3	1	3	32
Diseased	13	12	16	12	4	1	4	6	21	20	109
Unknown......	8	4	3	9	15	17	11	20	6	4	97
Wounded	5	2	1	0	5	0	0	5	4	1	23
Poisoned........	0	0	1	0	0	0	0	0	0	0	1
Drowned........	0	0	1	0	0	0	0	0	0	0	1
Drafted	7	0	15	32	13	21	9	14	27	26	164
Substitutes.....	13	1	8	13	13	6	19	12	11	7	103
Deserted	22	22	8	14	9	15	17	2	7	21	137
Veterans........	21	29	33	15	31	25	30	36	27	23	270
Non-Veterans	143	115	117	141	129	132	116	119	123	135	1270
AGGREGATE.	164	144	150	156	160	157	146	155	150	158	1540

FIELD AND STAFF..	29
UNASSIGNED..	45
GRAND TOTAL...	1614

RETROSPECTION.

DEAR COMRADES:

Stop and listen to what I have to say:
I want to scan your faces, and shake your hands to-day.
The years have rushed by swiftly, yet it seems an age to me,
Since "Old Pap" Thomas had his last review in Tennessee.

There was color in your faces then, and fire in your eyes,
And courage in your loyal hearts that nothing could disguise:
We marched and fought together in sunshine rain and snow,
On Southern plains and mountain-sides, many years ago.

A vision floats before me, a phantom troop goes by,
With bayonets glistening brightly, and banners waving high:
Down to the fields of strife they go, with proud and gallant tread;
Down to the feast of carnage — to the harvest of the dead.

Burdens of hardships on their backs, burdens of hunger and thirst:
Burdens of pictures on their hearts,—almost ready to burst;
Pictures of mother and sister, of sweetheart and of wife;
Pictures of boyhood's sunny home, dearer to them than life!

I hear again the sad good-bye, and the mother's piteous wail;
I hear the love-lorn maiden's sigh, as her lovely cheek turns pale;
I hear old Jim and Curt, as they fifed and drummed that day.
I hear the tramp in the morning damp, as my comrades march away,
And they stride with steady pace — with their faces all aglow
With youth and love and loyalty, as they did so long ago.

* * *

Now a bronze is on their faces, as I look along the line;
And rent and rip have sadly marred the uniform so fine;
A beard is growing on the lip so late by mother pressed;
The slender boy is stouter now than sweetheart once caressed;
And battle-scars show here and there, and some show signs of pain;
And some are sighing for the home they ne'er shall see again:
Some are dying —far from home, alone — and some are dead:
Killed by dread contagion, or by rebel lead;

Yet their spirits march before me, and their faces all I know,
As we comrades knew each other, in the long ago.

They've gone! — as all the years have gone, since we put off the blue ;
Some to watch above the graves where lie the brave and true ;
In "soldiers' home" and poor-house some find a bivouac brief,
While many drag along life's march in sorrow and in grief.

I cannot tell how you have fared, my comrades, — all so dear !
How, as the seasons came and went, you've wrought from year to year ;
Whether you've had to "forage" much to keep your "mess" supplied,
Or if the "fat" exceeds the "lean" in every "bacon-side ; "
Or if the "hard-tack" you have drawn is full of "worms" and "mould ; "
Or if you've lined your pockets with loads of shining gold ;
But there's a tie no others know — all will agree, I ween, —
That binds the boys of Sixty-one, who drank from the same canteen.

No matter what that vessel held, sweet milk or apple-jack,
Or water from some stagnant pool, or coffee strong and black,
Gurgled from its rusty neck, or emptied in a cup ;
As long as e'er it lasted, we divided, sup by sup.

We marched and bunked together on the mountain-side and plain ;
On barks of trees we made our beds at Shiloh, in the rain ;
You nursed me in my sickness, and brought me back to life ;
Your cheers inspired my courage, in the din and heat of strife :
When my haversack was empty, you opened wide your own ;
When sutler's checks were out, you knew just where to get a loan.

And so, my grizzled comrades, as we near life's ragged edge,
I warm to you, and here renew our old fraternal pledge.
Our tramping days are nearly done ; our sun is in the west ;
We're nearing camp ; — I see the light ! we soon will take our rest ;
But while we're on the tramp, let's go together down the slope ;
And be together in that land of life and love and hope.

So, here's a health to you and yours, my comrades true and brave, —
To the dear old flag we love so much, — forever may it wave !
Here's to the mothers, wives and girls, whose hearts were all aglow, —
Whose spirits marched and suffered with us in the long ago !

ROSTER OF FIFTY-FIRST INDIANA.

The uniform date of muster-in, which appears in each company, is by no means correct; as many soldiers enlisted and were mustered in as early as August; and should have been so recorded. The only explanation of this error is, that in making out the original company pay-rolls, it was easier for the scribes to make ditto marks, than to fill out the dates. The Adjutant-General's Report was doubtless made up from these pay-rolls. The excessive "red-tape" that prevailed then, may also have had something to do with it. The compiler has taken no liberty with the Report, save in a few instances, where he was requested to do so by the individuals interested.

EXPLANATION.—A date immediately after a name, indicates the *muster-in* of each individual; *except original muster-in*, which is given at the head of each Company. An italic *e* signifies "*veteran*." Other dates and abbreviations explain themselves.

FIELD AND STAFF.

Colonel.

Abel D. Streight, Dec. 12, '61; com'd Sept. 4, '61; resig Mar. 16, '65.

Lieutenant-Colonel.

Benj. J. Spooner, Dec. 4, '61; com'd same date; res June 16, '62; re-entered service as Colonel 83d Regiment.

Major.

Wm. H. Colescott, Dec. 7, '61; com'd Oct. 9, '61; pro Lt.-Col. June 7, '62; res Feb. 26, '63.

Adjutant.

Jno. W. Ramsey, Dec. 7, '61, com Dec. 4, '61, res Nov. 28, '62.

Quartermaster.

John G. Doughty, Sept. 30, '61; com'd Sept 27. '61; hon dis Sept. 30, '64.

Chaplain.

Elias Gaskins, Dec. 14, '61; com'd Oct. 22, '61; res Mar. 26, '63.

Surgeon.

Erasmus B. Collins, Dec. 6, '61 ; com'd Nov. 19, '61 ; res.
Mar. 22, '63 ; re-com'd Apr. 6, '64 ; must-out Dec. 13, '65.

Assistant Surgeons.

David Adams, Dec. 9, '61 ; res. Nov. 8, '62.
Wm. Moorehead, pro tem ; com'd Apr. 25, '62.
Wm. P. Parr,   "   "   "
John W. Pearce, com'd Sept. 27, '62 ; res. Apr. 15, '65.

Sergeant-Major.

Wm. M. Cochran, Dec. 14, '61 ; dis. June 19, '62, disability.

Hospital Steward.

Henry R. King, Dec. 14, '61 ; pro. Ast. Surg. Dec. 6, '62 ;
must-out Dec. 13, '65.

Quartermaster's Sergeant.

Henry C. Long, Dec. 14, '61 ; pro. Q. M. 124th Regt.

Principal Musicians.

James H. Todd, Dec. 14, '61 ; must-out (about) Mar. 20, '62.
Alonzo D. Coe,   "   "   "   "

Musicians.

[Mustered-in December 14, 1861 ; mustered-out (about) March 20, 1862.]

Alvin B. Charpie,   Geo. W. Coil,
James Douglas,   John H. Murphy,
Newton H. Morgan,   Otho Olinger,
Wm. R. Beckwith,   Samuel Lavey,
Jesse D. Zern,   Ira Mason,
Elias Olinger,   Charles West.
Bartley Marrer,

COMPANY A.

[Original muster-in, December 13, 1861.]

Captain.

Jacob H. Fleece, com'd Oct. 11, '61 ; res. Aug. 9, '62.

First Lieutenant.

Milton Russell, com'd Oct. 11, '61 ; pro. Captain Aug. 10,
'62 ; hon. dis. Dec. 30, '64.

Second Lieutenant.

Harvey Slavens, com'd Oct. 11, '61 ; died Mar. 27, '62.

First Sergeant.

Wm. A. Adair, pro 2d Lt. Apr. 24, '62; 1st Lt. Aug. 10, '62; honorably discharged Mar. 12, '65.

Sergeants.

John Harlan, discharged May 2, '62, disability.
Geo. A. Proctor, died May 30, '63.
Amos C. Weaver, dis Mar. 11, '65, wounds at Dalton, Ga.
Wm. N. McLevad, dis Oct. 25, '63, disabiliy.

Corporals.

Jeremiah Givens, pro Captain May 1, '65; mustered-out Dec. 13, '65.
Silas Gardner, deserted May 1, '62.
Wm. T. Linn, mustered-out Dec. 14, '64.
John Emmons, pro 1st Lt. May 1, '65; mustered-out Dec. 13, '65.
Mahlon A. Dyer, r, pro 2d Lt. May 1, '65, must-out Mar. 6, '66, to date Dec. 13, '65.
Willis Slavens, discharged June 29, '62, disability.
George W. Shackelford, r, mustered-out Dec. 13, '65.
Wm. B. Gibson, mustered-out Dec. 14, '64.

Privates.

Geo. W. Adams, killed May 28, '63.
David Alley, r, mustered-out Dec. 13, '65.
John Allen, deserted Aug. 1, '62.
Patterson J. Brown, deserted June 9, '64.
Abner A. Bryan, died May, '62, at Evansville.
Francis M. Barber, r, pro corporal; must-out Dec. 13, '65.
David Budd, killed at Murf'boro, Jan. 2, '63.
Oscar F. Brown, discharged July 5, '63, disability.
Joseph Buchanan, died Feb. 10, '64.
Robert A. Condiff, killed at Columbia Jan. 19, '65.
Samuel G. Cook, r, pro sergeant; must-out Dec. 13, '65.
John R. Cook, r, pro corporal;   "   "
Warner L. Cole,   "   Feb. 14, '65.
Geo. W. Crayner, r, pro corporal;   "   Dec. 13, '65.
Wm. Duckworth, killed at Murfreesboro Jan. 2, '63.
Wm. Davis, discharged Oct. 27, '62, disability.
Francis M. Davis, mustered-out Dec. 14, '64.
Martin Debard, deserted Aug. 15, '62
John J. Ellington, discharged June 23, '62, disability.
Joseph B. Fleece, killed at Nashville, Dec. 16, '64.

Geo. J. Frenyear, died Aug. 1, '63.
Richard Frazier, deserted Nov. 1, '62.
John R. Givens, discharged June 29, '63, disability.
Thomas Gardner, deserted June 17, '65.
Samuel Gwinn, discharged July 5, '62, disability.
Anthony Gardner, died Dec. 7, '63.
Wm. Houston, r, mustered-out Dec. 13, '65.
Wade H. Harrison,   "   Dec. 14, '64, exp. service.
John W. Hunt, discharged Mar. 1, '63, disability.
Wm. P. House,   "   July 10, '62, disability.
Wm. H. Harvey, pro 2d Lt. Sep. '62; must-out Dec. 14, '64.
Jesse Jones, discharged July 4, '62, disability.
Wm. T. Jordan, r, pro corp; mustered-out Dec. 13, '65.
Samuel A. Johnson,   "   "
Francis Kelly, r, pro corporal;   "   "
Henry T. Kirk, r.   "   "
James S. Linn, r, pro sergeant;   "   "
John Lookabaugh, r, deserted June 17, '65.
Wm. Lovell, mustered-out June 4, '65.
George W. Moore, discharged June 25, '62, disability.
Henry C. Moore, r, discharged Dec. 13, '65.
Eli Marshall,   "   Dec. 2, '61.
Mason Morris, r, deserted June 17, '65.
John Morris, discharged May 1, '62, disability.
G. W. McCormick, died Apr. 5, '65.
Berriman McCormick, deserted June 17, '65.
Richard S. Marun, died Sept. 16, '62.
John Osborn, discharged June 18, '62, disability.
Josephus Osborn, "   June 11, '62, disability.
Wm. D. Osborn, died Mar. 3, '62.
James B. Proctor, r, pro sergeant; discharged Dec. 13, '65.
Williamson Page, discharged Feb. 1, '63, disability.
Logan Russell,   "   Sept. 18, '62, disability.
Thomas Rose,   "   Sept. 10, '62, disability.
James I. Rose, died Sept. 18, '62.
John Roberts, r, pro corporal; discharged Dec. 13, '65.
Thomas B. Riggins, died Dec. 10, '61.
Joseph Sears, killed at Stone River, Jan. 2, '63.
Milton Slavens, discharged June 25, '62.
James Southerland, died July 1, '62.
Edward Shepherd, died at Camp Chase, June 1, '63.
James Sheckles, discharged Aug. 1, '62, disability.

Ira F. Shurley, discharged June 18, '62, disability.
Ed. L. Shurley, *r*. transferred to 1st U. S. Eng. July 16, '64.
David Steers, discharged Dec. 14, '64.
John P. Smith, pro Hospital Steward, dis Dec. 14, '64.
Caleb Smith, discharged Apr. 17, '65.
Daniel Schrayer, discharged Dec. 14, '64.
Franklin F. Soots, died Nov. 1, '62.
John C. Trotter, discharged Aug. 10, '62.
William Tout, *r*, mustered-out Dec. 13, '65.
Jas. M. Warren, died Jan. 30, '62.
John E. Walker, transferred to the marine Sept. 20, '62.
Montreville Waddel, discharged May 29, '65, wounds.
Amos Warrick, *r*, discharged Dec. 13, '65.
John M. White, *r*, pro corporal; discharged Dec. 13, '65.

Recruits.

David S. Adams, Sept. 11, '62; died Jan. 25, '63.
John A. Anderson, June 29, '63; deserted July 10, '65.
John J. Armstrong, Oct. 13, '64; drafted, des June 14, '65.
Marcellus Brown, accid killed, Athens, Tenn., Apr 20, '64.
John W. Brooks, Aug. 10, '63; deserted June 17, '65.
James A. Booher, Oct. 6, '64; sub, dis May 20, '65, wounds.
Alpheus Booher.   "   "   "   Oct. 19, '65.
James Beaver, Oct. 14, '64;   "   "   July 18, '65.
Nicholas Berget, Sept. 28, '64, drafted, dis July 18, '65.
Frederick Berget, Oct. 9, '64, discharged Oct. 19, '65.
Francis Buler, Sept. 16, '64, drafted, never reported.
Frederick Barker, Oct. 17, '64, substitute, never reported.
Lewis A. Concliff, Aug. 4, '63, died Oct. 29, '64.
John H. Crabb, Oct. 5, '63, transf'd to V. R. C. Apr. 6, '66.
John H. Crabb.   "   died Feb. 15, '65, wounds.
John Christy, Oct. 18, '64, died Feb. 17, '65, at Nashville.
Noah Cloe, Oct 7, '64, substitute, discharged Oct. 19, '65.
Carey Cooper, Oct 14, '64, "   "   "
Allen Danner, June 15, '63, discharged Dec. 13, '65.
William S. Dayton, Sept. 24, '63, "   "
John Douglas, Mar. 28, '64.   "   "
George W. Davis, Oct. 14, '64,   "   Oct. 19, '65, subst.
George W. Durand, ———, deserted Apr. 20, '65.
William A. Ellis, July 29, '63, discharged Dec. 13, '65.
John T. Ellis, Mar. 28, '64.   "   "
Marion Fitch, Oct. 22, '62, pro Hosp. St'd, dis Oct. 22, '65.
Peter Fuhrer, Oct. 15, '64, substitute, dis July 17, '65.

Francis M. Green, Oct. 8, '63, discharged June 9, '64.
George S. Givens, Nov. 11, '64,   "   Dec. 13, '65.
William Hockman, Oct. 13, '64, drafted, dis Aug. 14, '65.
Alpheus P. Job, Mar. 11, '65, discharged Dec. 13, '65.
Jacob Kurz, Oct. 7, '64, substitute, deserted June 17, '65.
George W. Manley, July 6, '63, discharged Dec. 13, '65.
John W. McCormick, July 22, '63, died Mar. 13, '65.
William S. McCormick, Aug. 21, '63, transf V. R. C. Apr.
    1, '65.
Aq. S. McCormick, Apr. 7, '64, discharged Dec. 13, '65.
Stephen L. McCormick, Mar. 29, '64, deserted June 17, '65.
William Matthew, Aug. 29, '63,   "   "
Frederick Mosier, Sept. 28, '64, drafted, dis June 14, '65.
Jacob Mosiman,   "   "   "   "
William P. Moore, Aug. 12, '63, deserted June 15, '65.
Levi Olmstead, Oct. 22, '64, discharged Dec. 13, '65.
James F. Ohaver, ——, deserted, arrested, time made up.
Wm. T. Parkhurst, Sep. 8, '62, transf V. R. C. Dec. 12, '63.
Dudley H. Parker, June 24, '63, discharged Dec. 13, '65.
Wm. A. Phillips, Oct. 15, '63, pro corp, "   "
James Price, Oct. 6, '64, sub, died of wounds."
Wm. A. Pratt, Oct. 4, '64, substitute, deserted Nov. 18, '65.
James D. Pickard, Oct. 15, '64, " discharged Oct. 11, '65.
Warren Rice, Nov. 23, '63, deserted June 15, '65.
John P. Round, Nov. 11, '64, discharged Nov. 15, '65.
Peter Reitz, Oct. 15, '64, substitute, discharged Oct. 19, '65.
Elwood E. Richards, Oct. 14, '64, died Aug. 23, '65.
John Smith, Apr. 18, '62, died July 4, '62.
Thomas J. Smith, Apr. 18, '62, dis Dec. 1, '62, disability.
George E. Shiner, June 29, '63, deserted July 10, '65.
Thomas J. Spurgeon, Oct. 13, '64, drafted, dis Dec. 13, '65.
Frederick Scott, Oct. 14, '64, died of wounds Dec. 17, '65.
William T. Tout, June 6, '63, died Apr. 10, '63.
Ephraim Tull, Sep. 30, '64, substitute, killed Dec. 16, '64.
William T. White, Sep. 11, '62, died Dec. 28, '62.
John A Ward, July 29, '63, died of wounds Jan. 15, '65.
Henry N. Ward, July 29, '63, discharged Dec. 13, '65.
John M. Watts, Sep. 24, '63,   "   "
William H. Watkins, Oct. 6, '64, discharged Oct. 19, '65.
William P. Ward, Oct. 14, '64,   "   "
Roland F. Wiltshire, Oct. 12, '64,   "   "
Jonathan Woter, Oct. 22, '63,   "   "

Henry Wivel, ——. deserted Apr. 20, '65.
William W. Watts, Apr. 3, '65, discharged Dec. 13, '65.
Richard L. Watts, Feb. 24, '65, "   "

COMPANY B.

[Original muster-in, December 14, 1861.]

Captain.

David A. McHolland, com'd Oct. 11, '61, pro Major Apr.
25, '63, pro Lt.-Col. June 30, '63, pro Col. Mar. 17, '65,
mustered-out as Major Apr. 17, '65.

First Lieutenant.

Albert Light, com'd Oct. 11, '61, died Feb. 24, '62.

Second Lieutenant.

Adolphus H. Wonder, com'd Oct. 14, '61, pro 1st Lt Mar.
15, '62, pro Capt June 30, '63, died in prison Charleston, S. C., Sept. —, '64.

First Sergeant.

Jeremiah Sailor, pro 2d Lt Mar. 15, '62, died —.

Sergeants.

Wm. R. Lewis, pro 2d Lt June 30, '63, pro Capt Nov. 23,
'64, resigned June 11, '65.
J. Skinner, discharged Apr. 7, '63, by order.
Jeremiah Fogerty, deserted Oct. 16, '62.
Edwin R. Arnold, pro 1st Lt June 30, '63, mustered-out
Jan. 25, '65.

Corporals.

J. F. Shafer, discharged Jan. 13, '63.
Aaron Kenoyer, r, pro sergeant, discharged Dec. 13, '65.
John D. Morgan, pro 1st Lt Feb. 6, '65, pro Capt June 12,
'65, mustered-out Dec. 13, '65.
G. E. Tiffany, r, killed Nov. 26, '64, at Columbia, Tenn.
J. S. Hurst, r,   "   "   "   "
William Deweese, discharged Dec. 2, '63, disability.
A. Arnold, discharged Dec. 14, '64.
D. Doty, unaccounted for.

Musicians.

Samuel Yoman, deserted July 1, '62.
J. Bramble, discharged Mar. 26, '63, by order.

Wagoner.

K. Ferguson, discharged Oct. 12, '63, by order.

Privates.

Robert Barr, *r*, discharged Dec. 13, '65.
John Burk,   "   Dec. 14, '64.
John Bridgman,   '   "
John Branson, *r*, pro sergeant, discharged Dec. 13, '65.
Robert Barkhurst, died at Nashville, Nov. 30, '62.
Isaac N. Bush, deserted June 2, '62.
Samuel Bechtel, died Feb. 7, '62.
William Board,   "   "
John Bigger, *r*, discharged Dec. 13, '65.
Abraham Cornelius, discharged May 21, '62.
Samuel Clark, killed at Day's Gap, Apr. 30, '63.
William Collins, *r*, unaccounted for.
John Coshow, killed at Day's Gap, Apr. 30, '63.
Thomas Crawn, discharged Mar. 13, '65.
Reece A. Denny, *r*, discharged Dec. 13, '65.
Smiley Dawson, discharged Nov. 20, '62.
Daniel C. Darroh, deserted Sept. 15, '63.
Bartholomew Davis, *r*, discharged Dec. 13, '65.
James Ennis, deserted June 16, '63.
Thomas Evans, died at Bowling Green, Mar. 16, '62.
Alexander Ekey, discharged Nov. 12, '62.
John Feely,   "   May 15, '62.
Patrick Griffin, transf to V R C Jan. 14, '64.
John Greer, discharged Feb. 28, '63, disability.
George W. Haney, discharged Dec. 14, '64.
Walter Hawkins,   "   "
Jacob Hosier,   "   "
John T. Harris,   "   "
William Haney, *r*,   "   Dec. 13, '65.
George W. Hershman, died Apr. 22, '62.
James H. Harrington, discharged July 3, '62, disability.
Ezra G. Handley, *r*, discharged Dec. 13, '65.
Henry Howery, died Dec. 24, '61.
James Helms, *r*, pro sergeant, discharged Dec. 13, '65.
James Hatfield, *r*,   "   "
Ephraim T. Ham, died Apr. 23, '63.
Lemuel J. Johnson, discharged July 16, '62, disability.
Isaac P. Johnson, *r*, discharged Dec. 13, '65.
Eli Jackson, died at Louisville, Feb. 16, '62.

James Kenoyer, r, pro sergeant, discharged Dec. 13, '65.
Leroy H. W. Kelly, discharged Nov. 11,'62, by order.
James Keenan, deserted Dec. 20,'61.
John Karnes, died Mar. 15,'62, Nashville, disease.
Samuel Lyon, discharged Dec. 14. '64.
Abel Lyon, deserted May 2, '62.
John B. Lyon. dis June 13,'62, disability. re-enl'd Feb. 16. .
    '64, pro Hospital Steward, discharged Dec. 13,'65.
Cyrus Lowthain, discharged Dec. 13. '65.
John Lowe, discharged Dec. 27,'62, disability.
Robert Love, died Jan. 2,'62, wounds at Stone River.
John F. McKee, discharged Dec. 14,'64.
William G. McIntosh, died Jan. 20,'62.
Perry C. McIntosh, r, discharged Dec. 13, '65.
Dennis P. Morris. r, mustered-out Dec. 13,'65.
Henry W. Meredith r. pro sergeant, pro 2d Lt Oct. 1, '65,
    discharged Dec. 13,'65.
Alexander A. Myers, r, mustered-out Dec. 13,'65.
Charles Mallet, r, pro 1st Lt June 12,'65, dis Dec. 13,'65.
Martin V. Manly, discharged Dec. 14.'64.
James Nottingham, died Feb. 4,'62.
Stark Olmsted, r, discharged May 29,'65.
Jonathan Pruett, r, discharged Dec. 13,'65.
William Perigo, deserted Dec. 1.'62.
William H. Reeves, r, pro corp, mustered-out Dec. 13,'65.
Alfred Smythman, discharged Jan. 28, '63, disability.
George W. Smith, mustered-out Dec. 14,'64.
David G. Smith, died May 7.'62.
Benjamin Y. Smith, discharged Dec. 14.'64.
Jonathan Staton, r, deserted June 21,'65.
Thomas Scott. r. pro corp. mustered-out Dec. 13,'65.
Edward Sherman. r. "   "   "
Harry Troup, r, killed at Overton Hill., Dec. 16,'64.
Harvey J. Thomas, deserted Mar. 3,'62.
William J. Wilcox, r, deserted June 21,'65.
Barden B. West, r. mustered-out Dec. 13,'65.
Ira Yoman, discharged July 3,'62, disability.

Recruits.

Sylvester Bennett. Sept. 19,'63, discharged Dec. 13,'65.
Henry Bishop, Nov. 4,'64, discharged Nov. 11,'65.
Lewis I. Bailey, Oct. 15,'64. discharged June 13,'65.
John S. Black, Oct. 22,'64. deserted July 10,'65.

24

Thomas J. Bennett, ——, discharged Dec. 13,'65.
John Beckdol, Feb. 24,'64, discharged Dec. 13,'64.
James Corn, Aug. 29,'63,   "   "
John S. Christopher, Sept. 29,'63, deserted Jan. 29,'64.
Charles W. Clifton, Oct. 3,'63, pro Q M Sergt., discharged
    Dec. 13,'65.
George Cutsinger, Oct. 29,'64, discharged Dec. 13,'65.
Isaac C. Denny, Apr. 13,'64, discharged May 17,'65.
Jesse Dodson, Mar. 24,'64, discharged Dec. 13,'65.
Charles B. Davis, Nov. 3,'64, discharged Nov. 19,'65.
Moses Edgings, Oct. 8,'64, discharged Oct. 29,'65.
Amos Easterling, Sept. 23,'64, to date Dec. 19,'63. pro Ast
    Surg June 7,'65. discharged Dec. 13,'65.
John A. Gwinn, Aug. 29,'63, dis July 4,'65, disability.
John J. Horn,   "   deserted June 21,'65.
Ephraim Haney,   "   discharged Dec. 13,'65.
Robert F. Humphrey, Aug. 15,'63, discharged June 5,'65.
George W. Hotenstein. Sept. 19,'63, discharged May 23,'65
Levi Haney. Sept. 29,'63, died May 23,'65.
George W. Hayton. Apr. 8,'64, discharged Dec. 13,'65.
James Hamilton. Oct. 22,'64, discharged Oct. 29,'65.
Robert Johnston, ——, deserted June 21,'65.
Francis P. Jones, Dec. 9,'63, discharged Dec. 13,'65.
Samuel D. Kilgore, Oct. 20,'64. deserted July 10,'65.
Thomas F. Landrum, Sept. 12,'63, deserted Dec. 25,'63.
Charles W. Lynch, Oct. 12,'63, discharged Dec. 13,'65.
Elijah Long, Oct. 21,'63. discharged Dec. 13,'65.
David A. Lunday, May 20,'64, discharged Dec. 13,'65.
Joshua Matthews, Aug. 10,'63, discharged Dec. 13,'65.
John G. Messersmith, Aug. 17,'63, discharged Dec. 13,'65.
John Musson, Mar. 24,'64. died Dec. 18,'64, wounds.
John N. Maxwell. Oct. 24,'64, discharged Aug. 24,'65.
Edmund A. McClintock, Oct. 28,'64, discharged Oct. 29,'65
Hiram H. McClain, Nov. 3,'64, discharged Nov. 14,'65.
Warren Marsh, Nov. 15,'64, dischárged Nov. 14,'65.
Albert Myers. Dec. 8,'63, discharged Dec. 13,'65.
James M. Owens. Aug. 10,'63, discharged June 5,'65.
John Quarterman, Sept. 2,'63, deserted June 21,'65.
Michael Ryan, July 7,'63, discharged Dec. 13,'65.
John Robinson, Sept. 19,'63, discharged June 5,'65.
Naman C. Roney, Mar. 24,'64, discharged Dec. 13,'65.
George W. Reed, Nov. 3,'64, deserted June 21,'65.

Henry Stafford, ——, dis S O War Dep Aug. 3,'65.
Tyler Stafford, ——, deserted Feb. 25,'65.
Joseph P. Tyler, July 7,'63, deserted Sept. 15,'65.
Wm. W. Thoroughman, Sept. 29,'63, dis July 22,'65.
James Tegart, Feb. 2,'64, discharged Dec. 13,'65.
Benjamin F. Wheeler, Oct. 24,'64, sub, dis Oct. 29,'65.

COMPANY C.

[Original muster-in, December 14, 1861.]

Captain.

James W. Sheets, com'd Oct. 11,'61, pro Lt-Col Apr. 25,'63,
died as Capt, wounds at Day's Gap, June 21,'63.

First Lieutenant.

Samuel Lingerman, com'd Oct. 11,'61, pro Capt June 30,
'63, died May 1,'64.

Second Lieutenant.

Aaron T. Dooley, com'd Oct. 11,'61, pro 1st Lt June 30,'63
discharged May 12,'65.

First Sergeant.

Charles E. Stephens, pro 2d Lt June 30,'63, dis Mar. 1,'65.

Sergeants.

William F. Hadden, discharged Oct. 20,'62, disability.

John T. Dinwiddie, r, discharged Dec. 13,'65.
David C. Lane, discharged Dec. 14,'64.
William Kelly,   "   "

Corporals.

James M. Munday, discharged Dec. 14,'64.
Joseph A. Munday, killed at Stone River, Dec. 31,'62.
Joseph Wagner, deserted Sept. 20,'62.
Calvin Dickerson, discharged Dec. 14,'64.
Floyd Dickerson,   "   "
John C. Call, r, discharged Dec. 13,'65.
John V. Parker,   "   Dec. 14,'64.
William V. Brown,   "   "

Musicians.

William C. Welshans, discharged Dec. 14,'64.

Wagoner.

William M. Crawford, discharged Dec. 14,'64.

Privates.

Gabriel H. Adams, r, pro 2d Lt May 1,'65, 1st Lt June 1, '65, discharged Dec. 13,'65.

Joshua G. Adams, r, pro corporal, discharged Dec. 13,'65.

Francis M. Arbuckle, discharged Jan. 9,'65.

Lewis T. Armstrong, discharged July 15,'62, disability.

John F. Bates, discharged Dec. 14,'64.

Francis M. Brittain, discharged Aug. 15,'63, disability.

James Bryant, discharged Dec. 14,'64.

Joseph Brown, transf Invalid Corps June 23,'63.

William C. Clements, r, pro corporal, dis Dec. 13,'65.

Huey Curtis, discharged Aug. 30,'62, disability.

Charles P. Cox, r, discharged Dec. 13,'65.

John M. Champion, discharged Dec. 14,'64.

James L. Davidson, discharged July 12,'62.

James A. Dickinson, died June 29,'62.

Arthur Dooley, discharged Dec. 14,'64.

Norman L. Dixon,   "   "

Reuben Eaton, r. discharged Dec. 13,'65.

Richard H. Ellis, died at Mooresville, Ala., July 4,'62.

Thomas Elburn, died Mar. 4,'63.

Mason Flinn, deserted Nov. 16,'62.

John Gasper, r, discharged June 19,'65, disability.

James S. Griggs, r, pro 1st Sergt, pro 1st Lt Oct. 1,'65, discharged Dec. 13,'65.

William Greenlee, discharged Dec. 14,'64.

James A. Godfrey, r, discharged Dec. 13,'65.

William Hancock, transf to Corps d'Afrique June 20,'64.

Stephen Hilton, died at Mooresville, Ala., July 2,'62.

William T. Hensley, died Mar. 29,'62.

Robert C. Hall, r, discharged Dec. 13,'65.

John W. Hensley, r, discharged Dec. 13,'65.

Isaac Hensley, died Feb. 6,'62.

Enoch Hill, died Jan. 15,'62.

Jeremiah B. Hodson. r, discharged Dec. 13,'65.

William D. Holder, died June 8,'65.

William R. Hartpence, r, pro Sergt-Major Nov. 12,'64, discharged Dec. 13,'65.

Jacob O. Iddings, died Apr. 12,'62.

Alexander W. Jones, deserted May 14,'62.

William H. Jelf, r, pro sergeant, discharged Dec. 13,'65.

Cornelius S. Kurtz, r, pro corporal, discharged Dec. 13,'65.

James M. Landon, r, discharged Dec. 13,'65.
William D. Lewis, r, pro sergeant Oct. 1,'63, 2d Lt Oct. 1, '65, discharged Dec. 13,'65.
Tilman A. McDaniels, killed while prisoner. May 12,'63.
John F. McKinley, r. discharged Dec. 13,'65.
Chares A. McWilliams, killed at Blountsville, May 2,'63.
Archibald Nesbit, r, discharged Dec. 13,'65.
Charles Newnam, discharged Nov. 9,'64, disability.
Silas Osborn, killed at Day's Gap, Apr. 30,'63.
William B. Osborn, r, pro sergeant, discharged Dec. 13,'65
Oliver H. Pike, discharged Dec. 14,'61.
Eli Phillips, killed at Stone River, Jan. 1,'63.
Henry C. Rumney, r, discharged Dec. 13,65.
Thomas N. Runnels, discharged June 24,'62, disability.
Thomas A. Reynolds, died Nov. 7,'62.
Henry S. Rounds, died Feb. 19,'62.
Thomas J. Shirley, discharged May 18,'63, disability.
William Shockley, r, pro sergeant, discharged Dec. 13,'65.
Silas Sturman, deserted Sept. 10,'62.
William C. Summers, discharged Dec. 14,'64.
William A. Summers, r, pro sergeant dis Dec. 13,'65.
John B. Scherer, discharged Nov. 14,'62, disability.
William Sharpe, discharged Dec. 14,'64.
James M. South.   "   "
Reuben T. Templin, r, discharged Dec. 13,'65.
James W. Tout, r, pro corporal, discharged Dec. 13,'65.
David Thompson, discharged May 15,'63, disability.
Elkin Toney, discharged Dec. 14,'64.
Milton B. Vannice, discharged June 28,'62, disability.
John F. Williams, died Nov. 13,'62.
Henry M. Welshans, r, discharged Dec. 13,'65.
Samuel W. Watts, r, pro corporal, discharged Dec. 13,'65.
John W. Wells, r, killed at Overton Hill, Dec. 16,'64.
Elijah C. Whitaker, r, pro chief musician, dis Dec. 13,'65.
John T. Whitaker, r. discharged Dec. 13,'65.

Recruits.

John Arnold, Oct. 15,'64, substitute, died Dec. 27,'64.
Stephen Alexander, Oct. 15,'64, substitute, dis Oct. 19,'65.
George Bilheymer, Mar. 28,'62, discharged Mar. 28,'65.
John T. Bell, Oct. 13,'63, discharged Dec. 13,'65.
Abraham Barkley, Sept. 23,'64, drafted, dis June 14,'65.
Andrew Barkley, Sept. 22,'64, drafted, dis Dec. 13,'65.

Elias Barkley, Sept. 22,'64, drafted, dis June 14,'65.
Isaac Barton, Oct. 3,'64, drafted, dis Dec. 13,'65.
Joshua Bennett, Sept. 28,'64, drafted, discharged June 14,
    '65, reported also died at Nashville.
William Bolton, Oct. 19,'64, discharged Dec. 13,'65.
Edward Bartleman, Sept. 28,'64, drafted, dis June 14,'65.
William H. Burgett, Oct. 20,'64, deserted Mar. 28,'65.
Henry J. Craig, Sept. 25,'63, discharged Dec. 13,'65.
Robert L. Carter, Nov. 6,'63, discharged May 18,'65.
Richard Carman, Oct. 14,'64, substitute, dis Oct. 3,'65.
Henry Cobbin, Sept. 28,'64, drafted, dis June 14,'65.
John S. Davis, Nov. 6,'62, died Dec. 15,'62.
Almond Ducher, Oct. 3,'64, drafted, dis Dec. 13,'65.
William W. Davis, Oct. 19,'64, discharged Dec. 13,'65.
James H. Davis, ——, discharged Oct. 19,'65.
Andrew J. Foster, Oct. 21,'64, discharged July 21,'65.
George Gregg, r, Jan. 2,'62, pro 2d Lt Mar. —,'65, pro 1st
    Lt May 1,'65, pro Capt June 1,'65, deserted Sept. 5,'65
    dropped from rolls as deserter May, '65.—[vol 3, p 18.
James G. Grasshopper, Sept. 22,'64, draft, died Mar. 28,'65
William H. Gray, Oct. 6,'64, deserted Mar. 28,'65.
Frederick Galliger, Oct. 3,'64, deserted Mar. 28,'65.
William T. Gilbert, Jan. 21,'62, r, discharged Dec. 13,'65.
Alexander W. Hollett, July 14,'63.   "   "
Eli B. Hodson, Oct. 5,'63,   "   "
William Hardwick, Oct. 6,'63.   "   "
James M. Harrison, Oct. 24,'64, discharged Oct. 19,'65.
John Hyton, Oct. 13,'64, substitute,   "   "
David W. Hamilton, Oct. 6,'64, prom Capt Oct. 29, '64 re-
    signed May 23,'65.
Noah N. Irwin, Oct. 20,'64, discharged July 19,'65.
John S. Leonard, Sept. 28,'64, discharged June 14,'65.
Martin Lord, Oct. 15,'64, substitute, discharged Oct. 19,'65.
Scott W. Lewis, Nov. 2,'62, died Mar. 3,'63.
Caleb B. Mendenhall, Jan. 2,'62, died, not reported.
Henry Morrison, Mar. 10,'64, drowned in a well at Chatta-
    nooga, May 10,'64.
George W. Mumma, Oct. 20,'64, substitute, dis July 10,'65
Amos Mast, Sept. 20,'64, drafted, discharged June 14,'65.
John L. McCammack, Oct. 22,'64, discharged Dec. 13,'65.
Emery Morrison, Sept. 30,'64, substitute, dis June 13,'65.
Seth Myers, Sept. 28,'64, drafted, discharged June 14,'65.

Samuel Norman, Sept. 20,'64, drafted, dis June 10,'65.
James Nenius, Sept. 28'64, drafted, dis June 14,'65.
Harrison Owens, Oct. 2,'62, dis Apr. 20,'64, wounds.
Samuel Patterson, Oct. 14,'64, killed Ov'n Hill Dec. 16,'64.
Josephus Rumney, Oct. 6,'64, discharged Oct. 19,'65.
Michael Robbins, July 24,'63, discharged Dec. 13,'65.
Patrick Ryan, Oct. 21,'64, deserted Mar. 28,'65. (shot)
Richard F. Raney, Oct. 7,'63, dis May 18,'65, wounds.
Harney Risley, Sept. 28,'64, drafted, dis June 14,'65.
Daniel R. Rice, Oct. 26,'64, substitute, dis Oct. 19,'65.
John T. Sielhymer, Aug. 3,'63, discharged Dec. 13,'65.
Silas Strange, Oct. 24,'64, discharged Sept. 13,'65.
Jacob Sawyer, Sept. 28,'64, draft. "   "
Levi H. Sipes, Oct. 22,'64, discharged Aug. 3,'65.
Alfred Snow, Oct. 21,'64, discharged Oct. 19'65.
Richard F. Watts, Feb. 24,'65, deserted Mar. 28,'65.
John Walker, Oct. 21,'64,   "   "

COMPANY D.

[Original muster-in, December 14, 1861.]

Captain.

Sylvester R. Brown, com'd Oct. 11,'61, resigned Sep. 5,'62

First Lieutenant.

Wilber F. Williams, com'd Oct. 11,'61, res Apr. 15,'62.

Second Lieutenant.

Leonidas Fox, com'd Oct. 14,'61, resigned Apr. 15,'62.

First Sergeant.

Marion T. Anderson, pro 2d Lt Apr. 30,'62, Capt Dec. 11, '62, resigned June 16,'65.

Sergeants.

Evan E. Sharp, pro 1st Lt Apr. 30,'62, dis Mar. 24,'65.

Seth Marsh, r, pro 2d Lt May 1,'65, Capt June 17,'65, discharged Dec. 13,'65.

Thomas R. Wetherald, r, pro 1st Lt June 17,'65, disch'ged Dec. 13,'65.

John Curry, discharged June 19,'62, by order.

Corporals.

William Curry, discharged June 30,'63, by order.

Porter A. Crawford, deserted Oct. 1,'62.
James D. Rodman, discharged Dec. 14, '64.
Henry C. Duncan, died at Greenfield, June 8,'62.
Richard Kinkle, discharged June 25,'62, by order.
Charles Nelson, discharged Dec. 14,'64.
John Hook, died at Jeffersonville, Mar. 28,'62.
George W. McKeihan, discharged Oct. 27,'62, by order.

Musicians.

Sebron S. Jones, died at Bardstown, Ky., Jan. 5,'62.
Asa H. Hewin, deserted June 3,'62.

Wagoner.

Wilson Rittenhouse, died at Murfreesboro, Mar. 26,'63.

Privates.

Christopher Alt, died at Nashville, Mar. 20,'62.
Howard V. Adams, died at Savannah, Tenn., Apr. 14,'62.
Hiram C. Adams, r, pro sergeant, 2d Lt June 17,'65, discharged Dec. 13,'65.
William C. Adams, pro sergeant, dis Dec. 13,'64.
James Bayles r, discharged Dec. 13,'65.
Moses Burris, died at Nashville, Nov. 28,'62.
Taylor M. Burris, discharged June 25,'62, by order.
Thomas Brown, r, deserted June 19,'65.
Rufus Basset,r, discharged Dec. 13,'65.
John Commer, discharged Dec. 14,'64.
Ebenezer Cross, died at Nashville, Mar. 20,'62.
Cyrus W. Creviston, discharged Apr. 17,'63, disability.
Samuel D. Case, died at Nashville, Nov. 1,'62.
Thomas Comar, r, discharged Dec. 13,'65.
John W. Dickson, discharged Dec. 14,'64.
Absolom Davis, discharged July 3,'62.
James Dorman, discharged Dec. 14,'64.
Isaac East, unaccounted for.
William Evans, discharged Jan. 25,'62, disability.
John Ell, deserted Oct. 3,'62.
James Eads, r, pro 1st Sergeant, discharged Dec. 13,'65.
Jerry Ferrin, r, discharged Dec. 13,'65.
James Grannis, deserted Nov. 19,'61.
Benjamin Hudson, discharged Aug. 14,'62, disability.
John Hood, discharged Dec. 14,'64.
John Hamilton, died at Cicero, Ind., never reported.
David S. Herbst, r, pro sergeant, discharged Dec. 13,'65.

James Hensley, discharged Jan. 1,'63.
William C. Hewey, discharged June 25,'62. disability.
Luke Hariban, discharged May 24,'62.
Oliver P. Hodges, deserted Mar 7,'62.
John W. Johnson, deserted Mar. 2,'62.
Charles W. Lewis, discharged Apr. 29,'63.
Francis M. Mingee, discharged, date unknown.
Charles Pool, died at Bowling Green, Ky., Dec. 10,'62.
William Peters, r, deserted July 9,'65.
James Polson, discharged May 29,'63, enl'd marines.
Wesley Polson, died at Murfreesboro, Jan. 31,'63.
Henry Powell, deserted Oct. 31,'62.
John Rittenhouse, sr., muster-out unknown.
John Rittenhouse, jr., r, discharged Dec. 13,'65.
Nathaniel Rittenhouse, discharged June 28,'62.
Daniel Rittenhouse, discharged July 24,'62.
George Robinson, r, discharged Dec. 13,'65.
Jerry Randolph, discharged Jan. 8,'63, disability.
Jesse Stump, r, discharged Dec. 13,'65.
George Slifer, discharged June 25,'62.
James F. Snow, died at Nashville, Nov. 1,'62.
John Terry, deserted Oct. 1,'62.
Samuel C. Thompson, discharged June 25,'62.
Ralph L. Thompson,   "   "
John H. Vanvalkenberg.   "   "
Elisha Whorton, died at Nashville, Mar. 5,'64.
Marcus D. L. Weaver, died at Nashville, Apr. 14,'62.
Joseph M. Westfall, discharged Nov. 7,'62.
Henry Westfall, died at Munfordsville, Mar. 9,'62.
Henry Winter, r, discharged Dec. 13,'65.
George Windsor, died at Indianapolis, Aug. 20,'63.
John Yates, discharged June 24,'64, disability.

Recruits.

Frederick Armstrong, Sept. 26,'64, draft, dis June 13,'65.
James M. Archibald, Oct. 3,'64, discharged July 21,'65.
Haman Allen, Oct. 13,'64, substitute, dis Oct. 19,'65.
James K. Banks, Feb. 16,'64, discharged Sept. 9,'65.
Eli Banks, Apr. 10,'62, discharged Apr. 14,'65.
Austin C. Beaman, Jan. 18,'64, discharged Dec. 13,'65.
Simon Black, Oct. 15,'64, substitute, dis Oct. 19,'65.
Francis Bibler, Sept. 26,'64, discharged June 8,'65.
Ernest Boach, Oct. 3,'64, drafted, discharged June 6,'65.

Reuben D. Barber, Oct. 14,'64, substitute, dis Oct. 19,'65.
William R. Bone, Oct. 15,'64,   "   "
Lewis A. Brickley, Oct. 12,'64, dis May 22,'65, wounds.
Alfred Burkley,   "   deserted July 11,'65.
Martin V. Buckley, Sept. 26,'64, drafted, dis June 14,'65.
William Bly, Oct. 3,'64, drafted, discharged Aug. 21,'65.
John Balzo,   "   "   "   Dec. 13,'65.
William Chandler, Oct. 15,'64, substitute, dis Oct. 19,'65.
William W. Christy,Sept. 21,'64, drafted, dis June 14,'65.
Martin Clinesmith, Oct. 14,'64, substitute, died Apr. 9,'65.
William W. Cline, Sept. 26,'64, discharged June 6,'65.
John Chapman,   "   drafted, dis June 14,'65.
Solomon Dill,   "   discharged May 19,'65.
John H. Duff, Oct. 12,'64, discharged May 29,'65.
Daniel Davis, Apr. 10,'62, deserted Oct. 20,'62.
Christian W. Fells, Sept. 22,'64, drafted, dis June 16,'65.
Francis D. Foster, Oct. 20,'64, substitute, dis Sept. 22,'65.
Solomon Funderburg, Sept. 26,'64, discharged July 20,'65.
James L. Gilpatrick, Apr. 7,'64, discharged May 26,'65.
John Goodmiller, Sept. 26,'64, drafted, dis June 14,'65.
Jacob Goodmiller,   "   "   "
Frank Galmeyer. ——, discharged Dec. 13,'65.
Henry Gresh, Oct. 3,'64, drafted, discharged Oct. 19,'65.
John Gordon, Oct. 12,'64, drafted, discharged Dec. 13,'65.
Michael Holland,   "   discharged July 22,'65.
Joseph Harrell, Nov. 21,'64, drafted, dis Aug. 21,'65.
Davis Higgin, Sept. 26,'64, drafted, dis June 14,'65.
John Hardin,   "   died at Mt. Etna, Apr. 10,'65.
Samuel W. Hamrick, "   killed at Columbia, Dec. 22,'64.
John S. Kerbox, Aug. 25,'62, discharged Feb. 12,'66.
Valentine Kirsh, Oct. 3,'62, drafted, dis July 22,'65.
Royal Kingsley, Dec. 4,'63, discharged Dec. 13,'65.
George B. Lowrey, Dec. 16,'63, deserted June 17,'65.
John W. Lyell, Jan. 18,'64, discharged Dec. 13,'65.
John Lahr, Oct. 22,'64, substitute, discharged Oct. 19,'65.
Andrew J. McKinley, July 23,'63, discharged Dec. 13,'65.
Simon Miller, July 12,'63, drafted, discharged July 21,'65.
William Maddocks,   "   drafted, died at Nashv, July 3,'65.
William Norvolt, July 3,'63, drafted, dis Aug. 25,'65.
George Ormsby, July 19,'63, substitute, dis Oct. 19,'65.
Peter Pressey, Apr. 17,'63, discharged Sept. 8,'65.
John Parks, Sept. 26,'64, drafted, discharged June 14,'65.

William S. Pedigo, Oct. 13,'64, substitute, dis Oct. 19,'65.
Alva C. Roach, Aug. 5,'62, pro 2d Lt Dec. 11,'62, pro 1st Lt May 1,'65, resigned June 14,'65.
Jacob Roller, Mar. 31,'64, discharged Dec. 13,'65.
William H. Redding, Oct. 12,'64, died May 14,'65.
Jones Redding, " drafted, dis Aug. 21,'65.
Ransom Redding, Oct. 12,'64, drafted, dis Sept. 15,'65.
Milton Rodenbaugh, " " " Oct. 19,'65.
George W. Schlenker, Mar. 8,'65, discharged Dec. 13,'65.
John F. Schultz, Sept. 26,'64, drafted, dis June 16,'65.
Jacob Sheffield, Oct. 10,'64, substitute, dis Oct. 17,'65.
Frederick Stetzell, Sept. 26,'64, drafted, dis June 16,'65.
John W. Shambaugh, " , " "
Samuel Straw, Oct. 12,'64, drafted, deserted July 7,'65.
Henry J. Smith, Oct. 3,'64, drafted, discharged Oct. 19,'65
Daniel Stoner, Sept. 26,'64, drafted, dis June 16,'65.
Hiram Schoonover, Sept. 12,'64, deserted, bounty-jumper.
Jacob Smith, Oct. 13,'64, " "
Wellington Thomas, Sept. 11,'63, discharged Dec. 13,'65.
Andrew Thorp, Oct. 17,'64, substitute, " "
Warren B. Thorn, Sept. 26,'64, drafted, dis June 14,'65.
John W. Walker, Apr. 10,'62, discharged Apr. 14,'64.
Conrad Woebbeking, Oct. 31,'64, drafted, dis Oct. 19,'65.
William G. Welch, Oct. 15,'64, substitute, dis Oct. 19,'65.
Jesse D. Wilson, Sept. 22,'64, sub, pro corp, dis Oct. 19,'65
Andrew Wolf, Sept. 21,'64, drafted, discharged June 14,'65
Elijah Walters, Sept. 22,'64, " " "
Jacob Yeager, Oct. 3,'64, drafted, discharged Aug. 25,'65.

COMPANY E.

[Original muster-in, December 14, 1861.]

Captain.

William Denny, com'd Oct. 11,'61, resigned Feb. 5,'62.
William N. Denny, Feb. 23,'62; entered service as 2d Lt Co. G, 14th Ind., pro 1st Lt Apr. 24,'61, pro Captain Feb. 6,'62, and transf'd to Co. E, 51st Ind.; pro Major June 30,'63, Lt-Col. Mar. 17,'65, Col. June 1,'65, discharged Dec. 13,'65.

First Lieutenant.

Daniel Trent, resigned Jan 22,'62.

David L. Wright, Feb. 1,'62, pro Capt. June 30,'63, discharged Mar. 14,'65.

Second Lieutenant.

John A. Welton, com'd Oct. 11,'61, resigned June 20,'64.

First Sergeant.

William S. Marshall, pro Adjt Nov. 29,'62. dis Mar. 22,'65.

Sergeants.

Samuel W. Dunn, discharged Dec. 14,'64.

Henry Gilham, transf'd to 120th Ind. Dec. 25,'63.

Weston Howard, r, discharged Dec. 13,'65.

David A. Denny, pro 1st Lt June 30,'63, res Aug. 21,'64.

Corporals.

James S. Little, discharged Dec. 14,'64.

Martin S. Miller, transf'd to V R C Apr. 10,'64.

William Hogue, discharged Apr. 27,'63.

Emanuel Reel, discharged Dec. 14,'64.

William W. Johnson, discharged May 2,'62, by order.

James Threlkeld, transf'd to V R C, no date.

Arthur Hatfield, deserted Feb. 6,'62.

William Purcell, discharged Dec. 14,'64.

Musicians.

John H. McClure, discharged Dec. 14,'64.

Martin Phillippe, discharged Dec. 14,'64.

Privates.

Robert H. Alexander, died at Stevenson, Aug. 2,'62.

James Ashby, r, pro corporal, discharged Dec. 13,'65.

Matthias Berry, r,   "   "   "

William Byers, died at Nashville, Dec. 25,'62.

Daniel B. Boyles, r, pro corporal, discharged Dec. 13,'65.

William T. Bruce, discharged Feb. 14,'65.

Henry C. Byers, r, pro 1st Lt May 1,'65, dis Dec. 13,'65.

Moses J. Betcher, discharged Dec. 14,'64.

Herman Buchthal, r, pro 1st Sergt, dis Dec. 13,'65.

John Byers, r, died Jan. 14,'65, wounds at Nashville.

Charles H. Colgrove, r. discharged Dec. 13,'65.

David Cook, transf'd to V R C Apr. 30,'64.

George Casey, r, discharged Dec. 13,'65.

John L. Chambers, discharged May 9,'64, disability.

William Chambers, died at Murfreesboro, Mar. 6,'63.

James H. Crooks, discharged Jan. 3,'62.

Jasper Cooper, r, died Dec. 18,'64, wounds at Nashville.

George W. Donaldson, r, deserted July 3,'65.

David Donaldson, r, discharged Dec. 13,'65.

Francis M. Ellis, discharged Aug. 26,'62.

William D. Eeves, discharged Aug. 15,'62.

Ephraim Foster, r, pro sergeant, discharged Dec. 13,'65.

Amos Farmer, deserted Oct. 10,'62.

Andrew Frederick, discharged Oct. 18,'62.

Mansfield Gee, discharged May 21,'62.

Christopher Godfrey, discharged Feb. 20,'63.

Augustus Hoag, discharged Nov. 15,'62.

William W. Harper, transferred to V R C.

Jacob Harvey, r, discharged Dec. 13,'65.

Lawson A. Huett, died at hospital, Feb. 27,'63.

Jackson Huett, discharged Dec. 14,'64.

Ellis House, pro 1st Lt Aug. 22,'64. Capt. Mar. 15,'65. discharged Dec. 13,'65.

William Justice, discharged Dec. 14,'64.

Wilson Little, died at Indianapolis, Dec. 21,'61.

Alfred Little, discharged Dec. 14,'64.

William Lamb,   "   "

William Lankford,   "   "

Noah P. McClure,   "   "

Abram McGankry, discharged Sept. 18,'62.

Levi Moore, died July 4,'62.

William H. Martin, died at Lebanon, Ky., Feb. 10,'62.

James H. Norton, r, discharged Dec. 13,'65.

John Pressey, discharged May 23,'62.

Joab Peak, r, discharged Dec. 13,'65.

Benjamin Peck, discharged May —,'62.

William K. Palmer, discharged Feb. 6,'63.

James M. Peck, r, discharged Dec. 13,'65.

Peter Phillippe, discharged May 25,'62.

Marion M. Puett, r, discharged Dec. 13,'65.

Columbus Parker, r.   "   "

James H. Parker, died at Mooresville, Ala., July 1,'62.

James M. Peck, r, discharged Dec. 13,'65.

Jasper Rader, r,   "   "

William Reel, r, discharged June 17,'65.

Alfred B. Racey, discharged June 19,'65.

William Robbins, discharged Dec. 14,'64.

Herod Risley, discharged Nov. 6,'63.

William Rowe, discharged Dec. 14,'64.

Solomon Stuckey. *r*, discharged Dec. 13,'65.
Samuel H. Stuckey. *r*. pro corp, discharged Dec. 13,'65.
Levin Sullivan, deserted Oct. 30,'62.
Elias Shoemaker. transferred to V R C Apr. 10,'64.
Thomas F. Smith, discharged Mar. 27,'63.
Samuel Snapp. died at Bardstown, Jan. 28,'62.
James Stipes, died at Murfreesboro. Feb. 6,'63.
William Shelton, discharged Dec. 13,'65.
Samuel H. Seltzer. discharged Dec. 14,'64.
Alva A. Sowers, died Jan. 1,'65, wounds at Nashville.
Columbus Sutt, *r*, discharged Dec. 13,'65.
Noah P. Scott, *r*, pro 2d Lt May 1,'65, dis Dec. 13,'65.
William H. H. Smith, *r*, died of wounds at Nashville.
Rankin Steele, discharged July 18,'62.
Daniel Smith, died at Nashville Mar. 25,'62.
William Tapp, died at Munfordsville, Mar. 10,'62.
Ira G. Thorn, *r*, died of wounds received at Nashville.
Solomon Thorn, discharged May 21,'62.
James H. Welton, *v*, pro sergeant, discharged Dec. 13,'65.
Samuel A. Warner, discharged June 19,'62.
William H. H. Wilson, *r*, discharged Dec. 13,'65.
Tilghman Whalen, died at Sullivan, Ind., May 22,'62.
Jacob R. Wanzer, died at Lebanon, Ky., Mar. 24,'62.
Joseph Zerr, *r*, died at Nashville, May 11,'65.

Recruits.

Jacob Ahr, drafted, Sept. 22,'64, discharged June 14,'65.
William M. Buck, Aug. 21,'62, deserted, date unknown.
Abraham Brunemer, Oct. 16,'64, died Dec. 29,'64.
Jefferson Baughman. Dec. 21,'64, discharged June 14,'65.
John V. Bishop, Oct. 15,'64, substitute, dis Oct. 19,'65.
Joseph H. Christy, Oct. 18,'64,   "   "
Alvin H. Clifford, Oct. 19,'64,   "   "
George Crouse, Oct. 17,'63, discharged Dec. 13,'65.
Charles Casey, Oct. 21,'63,   "   "
Andrew J. Cooper, Apr. 9,'64.   "   "
Joseph Crabb, Nov. 30,'64,   "   "
Washington Crabb.   "   "   "
John Davenport, Sept. 21,'64, substitute, dis June 14,'65.
Harvey N. Denny, Sept. 21,'64, drafted,   "
Daniel Diel, Sept. 21,'64, drafted, died Dec. 18,'64.
John Diel,   "   "   discharged June 14,'65.
William M. Diel,   "   "   "

Daniel Diel, Sept. 21,'64, drafted, discharged June 14,'65.
Jacob Diel, " " "
Christy Dolen, Oct. 28,'64, deserted, bounty-jumper.
James Eagan, Apr. 9,'64, discharged Dec. 13,'65.
Edward Frazier, June 20,'63, unaccounted for.
Washington Fairhurst, Oct. 17,'63, discharged Dec. 13,'65.
Patrick Glanzy, Oct. 28,'64, deserted, bounty-jumper.
John W. Harvey, Oct. 17,'63, pro corporal, dis Dec. 13,'65.
George Halleck, June 20,'63, dishon. dismissed Dec. 13,'65
James E. Hunnyent, Oct. 17,'63, discharged Dec. 13,'65.
Willis Hodge, Jan. 1,'64, deserted July 3,'65.
Martin V. Helton, Nov. 21,'64, drafted, dis June 14,'65.
Charles W. Ingersoll, Mar. 3,'64, discharged Dec. 13,'65.
Josiah Kierlin, Oct. 10,'64, substitute, died Dec. 16,'64.
Alfred C. Kidwell, Oct. 23,'63, discharged Apr. —,'65.
William Lincoln, Oct. 15,'64 substitute, dis Oct. 19,'65.
Joseph Myers, Sept. 21,'64, drafted, dis June 14,'65.
Ezra Poling, Oct. 15,'64, subst, transf'd V R C May 2,'65.
Andrew Poling, " " discharged Oct. 19,'65.
John A. Polum, Sept. 21,'64, drafted, dis June 14,'65.
Peter Phillippi, Aug. 27,'62, discharged May 25,'65.
Job Riddle, Sept. 21,'64, drafted, discharged June 14,'65.
Samuel F. Rork, Nov. 30,'64, discharged Dec. 13,'65.
Patrick Riley, Oct. 24,'64, deserted, bounty-jumper.
Martin V. Small, Oct. 17,'64, discharged Dec. 13,'65.
George Swisher, Oct. 8,'64, substitute, dis Dec. 13,'65.
George Sickling, Sept. 21,'64, substitute, dis June 14,'65.
William Saladay, " " "
John H. Taylor, Oct. 17,'63, pro Prin Mus, dis Dec. 13,'65.
Samuel F. Terrell, Sept. 22,'64, dis May 31,'65, wounds.
William B. Vestal, " drafted, dis June 14,'65.
William H. Watts, Oct. 24,'64, discharged Oct. 19,'65.
James H. Wallace, Feb. 12,'64, discharged Jan. 13,'66.
James L. Whitson, Oct. 14,'64, substitute, dis Dec. 13,'65.
Timothy Whitmore, Oct. 15,'64, died Jan. 1,'65, wounds.
Michael Welch, Oct. 24,'64, deserted, bounty-jumper.
James Waugh, Mar. 24,'64, discharged Dec. 15,'65.
Van S. Waugh, " "
Clinton Wallace, "
Green Wallace, " "
Henry York, Oct. 18,'64, substitute, dis Oct. 19,'65.

COMPANY F.

[Original muster-in, December 14, 1861.]

Captain.

James E. McGuire, com'd Oct. 11,'61, resigned Oct. 24,'62.

First Lieutenant.

John M. Flinn, com'd Oct. 11,'61, pro Capt Oct. 25,'62, discharged Dec. 14,'64.

Second Lieutenant.

Joel A. Delano, com'd Oct. 11,'61, pro 1st Lt Oct. 25, '62, Capt Dec. 15,'64, Major Oct. 1',65, dis Dec. 13,'65.

First Sergeant.

Gideon T. Hand, pro 2d Lt Oct. 25,'62, dis Mar. 15,'65.

Sergeants.

Robert Montgomery, r. discharged Dec. 13,'65.

Thomas J. Morgan, discharged Dec. 14,'64.

John A. McLaughlin, r. discharged May 8,'65, wounds.

Leonidas Smith, pro 2d Lt Apr. 7,'65, 1st Lt Apr. 10,'65, Capt Oct. 1,'65, discharged Dec. 13,'65.

Corporals.

Andrew J. Pyle, discharged Sep. 23,'63, wounds Dry's Gap.

Benjamin F. Payne, discharged Dec. 14,'64.

John M. Gatewood, died at Nashville Mar. 29,'62.

James Hendricks, deserted Oct. 7,'62.

James McCarty, deserted June 2,'62.

Ethan A. Kendall, killed at Day's Gap, Apr. 30,'63.

Thomas C. Walton, r. pro sergeant, dis Dec. 13,'65.

Joel Gatewood, r, pro sergeant, 2d Lt Oct. 1,'65, discharged Dec. 13,'65.

Musicians.

Job A. Howland, discharged Oct. 14,'62, disability.

Elijah Henby, died at Nashville, May 2,'62.

Wagoner.

Jackson McGrew, discharged Nov. 17,'62, disability.

Privates.

Joseph H. Allen, deserted Dec. 15,'61.

Edward Ayers, r. discharged Dec. 13,'65.

Henry J. Bowers, r.   "

James K. Bowers, discharged Dec. 14,'64.

John Cassida,   "

Henry W. Camper, r. discharged Dec. 13,'65. .

George W. Collins, *r*, pro corporal, discharged Dec. 13,'65.
Joshua S. Crosby, discharged Feb. 10,'65.
John C. Darmer, *r*, deserted June 9,'65.
Joseph Dennis, discharged June 16,'62, by order.
John W. Dicks, *r*, transf'd to 1st U. S. Eng. July 30,'64.
Martin Dwyre, transferred to V R C May 1,'64.
Richard Fosset, *r*, deserted June 19,'65.
William A. Gilchrist, discharged May 2,'62, disability.
William Garland, *r*, pro sergeant, discharged Dec. 13,'65.
Robert Gatewood, died at Nashville Jan. 28,'63.
Ellison Gatewood, discharged Mar. 18,'65.
John Goodrich, discharged June 8,'62, disability.
John Harry, *r*, pro corporal, discharged Dec. 13,'65.
Silas Henderson, deserted June 2,'62.
Benjamin Heistand, *r*, discharged Dec. 13,'65.
Hiram Henderson, discharged May 5,'62, disability.
Nelson Hemphill, discharged Dec. 14,'64.
George Howrie,
Willis Hord, died at Pittsburg Landing, Apr. 16,'62.
John R. Henby, discharged Apr. 25,'65, wounds.
Oscar James, deserted Dec. 15,'64.
Robert D. Kendall, *r*, pro sergeant, discharged Dec. 13,'65.
James B. Kendall, discharged Feb. 28,'62, by order.
Wesler Kenderling, discharged Mar. 4,'65.
Lewis Linville, discharged Dec. 4,'65.
William A. Linville, *r*, pro sergeant, dis Dec. 13,'65.
Levi Lock, died at Woodsonville, Ky., Mar. 21,'62.
Smith Martin, deserted Mar. 13,'62.
Fielding J. Miller, died at Bardstown, Jan. 4,'62.
Thomas A. Morrison, *r*, pro 2d Lt Apr. 10,'65, 1st Lt Oct.
    1,'65, discharged Dec. 13,'65.
James Moroney, discharged Dec. 14,'64.
Robert A. McGuire, deserted Dec. 15,'64.
John E. McConnell, died at Nicholasville, Ky., Mar. 27,'62
Samuel A. McKenzie, discharged Feb. 12,'62, by order.
Edward Newman, discharged July 23,'62.
William A. Overman, died at Louisville, Ky., Dec. 21,'61.
John M. Overman, deserted Dec. 15,'64.
Gideon Palmer, discharged June 16,'62.
James Palmer, died at Bardstown, Jan. 5,'62.
Washington Parker, died at Day's Gap, May 3,'63.
Rufus Perry, transferred to V R C May 31,'64.

25

Andrew J. Plank, r, discharged Dec. 13,'65.
Anderson Rhoads, r, deserted June 19,'65.
Lewis Rhoads, transferred to V R C Jan. 14,'64.
Robert Rains, died at Camp Morton, Ky., Jan. 11,'62.
Adam Shryock, discharged May 22,'62, by order.
John Shryock, died at Indianapolis, Dec. 29,'61.
William T. Smith, discharged Dec. 14,'64.
George J. Smith, r, pro corporal, discharged Dec. 13,'65.
William E. Stafford, unaccounted for. (?)
John Stevens, discharged Dec. 14,'64.
George Steele, deserted Dec. 15,'61.
John Simpson,   "   "
James Todd, discharged Dec. 14,'64.
Washington Turner, r, discharged Dec. 13,'65.
George F. Walker, discharged May 15,'62, by order.
James Whitcomb, r, deserted June 19,'65.
Isaac Winton, r, pro corporal, discharged Dec. 13,'65.
John Yager, r, pro corporal, discharged Dec. 13,'65.

Recruits.

William Armstrong, Mar. 1,'62, discharged Mar. 1,'65.
Alexander B. Blythe, Dec. 12,'63, discharged Dec. 13,'65.
Horace G. Bates, Dec. 18,'63,   "
John Baugh, Aug. 27,'62,   "
Samuel C. Birdwell, Oct. 1,'64, substitute, dis Oct. 19,'65.
John C. Campett, Aug. 28,'63, discharged Dec. 13,'65.
Matthew A. Cherry, Sept. 10,'62, discharged June 4,'65.
James K. Campett,   ·   "   "
James M. Conaway, Sept. 24,'64, drafted, dis Aug. 14,'65.
Peter E. Clinger, Sept. 18,'63, discharged June 25,'65.
William H. Copp, Oct. 23,'62, died Shelbyville Apr. 14,'64
Benjamin A. Dennis, Sept. 4,'63, discharged Dec. 13,'65.
Morgan Gaylor, Oct. 21,'64 discharged Oct. 19,'65.
James T. Gatewood Aug. 1,'63 discharged Dec. 13,'65.
James Hendrickson Sept. 24,'63   "   "
James F. Harrison, Apr. 12,'64,   "   "
George W. Holbrook, Dec. 23,'61, killed Murf'b, Dec. 29,'62
Thomas B. Hendrickson, Sept. 10,'62, substitute, pro cor-
     poral, discharged June 14,'65.
William Hutchinson, Dec. 24,'64, drafted, dis Aug. 14,'65.
Samuel Hawley, Oct. 21,'64, drafted, dis July 11,'65.
John W. Hutchinson,   "   "   discharged July 6,'65.
Elijah B. Hester, Oct. 23,'62, died at Murf'boro Feb. 4,'63.

Silas Hill, Oct. 15,'64, drafted, deserted June 15,'65.

Hiram F. Justice, Sept. 5,'63, pro corporal, dis Dec. 13,'65.

William C. Johnson, Dec. 14,'63, discharged Dec. 13,'65.

Benjamin F. Jones, Sept. 24,'64, drafted, dis Aug. 11,'65.

Daniel C. Jameson, Oct. 21,'64, drafted, transferred to V
   R C May 24,'65.

Elijah S. Knight, Aug. 18,'63, discharged Dec. 13,'65.

William Kines, Sept. 10,'63, discharged May 29,'65.

Samuel Knoble, Oct. 21,'64, drafted, dis May 26,'65.

Amos Kimball, Sept. 24,'64, substitute, dis Aug. 4,'65.

James M. Linville, Sept. 10,'62, discharged June 14,'65.

Valentine Langhnet, Sept. 24,'64, drafted, dis Aug. 14,'65.

William Langhnet, Oct. 21,'64, drafted, dis Oct. 19,'65.

David Linville, Oct. 23,'62, transf'd to V R C Apr. 10,'64.

Matthew B. Leonard, Sept. 7,'63, discharged Dec. 13,'65.

Sylvester L. Monronea, Aug. 24,'63,   "

Neal McClain, Aug. 27,'62,   "

David C. McCowan, Oct. 20,'64, substitute, dis Oct. 19,'65.

James Noland, Sept. 24,'64, drafted, dis Aug. 11,'65.

Samuel Phipps, Sept. 24,'63, discharged Dec. 13,'65.

Joseph V. Post, Sept. 10,'63, pro corporal, dis Oct. 13,'65.

James L. Phares, Sept. 10,'62, discharged June 14,'65.

Robert T. Phares,   "   "

James Pyle   "   "

Enoch Rhoads, Oct. 23,'62, killed Crooked Cr., Apr. 30,'63.

John L. Rhoads, Oct. 6,'62, discharged Oct. 3,'65.

John L. Rodky, Oct. 7,'64, substitute, dis May 26,'65.

George Rader, Oct. 21,'64, drafted, discharged June 26,'65.

Thomas Ruse, Sept. 24,'64, drafted, discharged Aug. 14,'65.

Matthew B. Ross, Jan. 28,'62, deserted Aug. 9,'62.

Henry E. Ross, Mar. 8,'64, deserted Aug. 10,'64.

George W. Stafford, Dec. 10,'63, discharged Dec. 13,'65.

Charles Shoemaker, Dec. 9,'63,   "

Loona L. Sally, Sept. 4,'63,   "

Isaac H. Storms, Sept. 24,'64, drafted, dis Aug. 11,'65.

Abraham Skidmore,   "   "

Francis B. Sims,   "   "

Zachariah Scott,   "   "

James Stanley, Oct. 15,'64, substitute, dis Oct. 19,'65.

Charles C. Sellers, Oct. 21,'64, drafted.   "

William Storms,   "   "   died at Jeffersonville
   Dec. 17,'64.

Levi Todd, Sep. 4,'63, killed at Dalton, Aug. 17.'64.
Andrew J. Treon, Dec. 9.'63, discharged Dec. 13,'65.
Anderson Talbert, Sept. 4.'63.   "
Isaac O. Taylor, Sept. 24,'64. drafted, dis Aug. 14,'65.
William L. Taylor   "   "   "
Joseph A. Talbert, Sep. 4,'63, died San Antonio. Sep. 30,'65
George Walker, Oct. 23,'64, killed at Nashville Dec. 16,'64.
William T. Wicker, Sept. 10,'63, discharged June 14,'65.
James N. Winton, Sep. 18,'63, died at Nashv. Apr. 20,'64.
Greenup Weekly, Nov. 4,'62, deserted June 15,'65.
James W. Zike, Sept. 10,'62, died at Nashville Dec. 19,'62.

COMPANY G.

[Original muster-in, December 4, 1861.]

Captain.

Francis M. Constant, com'd Oct. 11,'61, res Mar. 25,'65.

First Lieutenant.

Joseph Y. Ballou, com'd Oct. 11,'61, resigned Feb. 19,'63.

Second Lieutenant.

William Wallick, com'd Oct. 11,'61, pro Capt June 30,'63,
    discharged Dec. 14,'64.

First Sergeant.

Abraham G. Murray, pro 1st Lt June 30,'63, discharged
    Jan. 25,'65.

Sergeants.

Elisha Buck, transferred to Engineers July 24,'64.
Charles B. Mason, died at Bowling Green Mar. 15,'62.
Jasper N. Brown, pro 2d Lt June 30,'63, res Nov. 11,'64.
William Crooks, died at Nashville Sept. 18,'62.

Corporals.

Thomas B. Crooks, r, pro 1st Sergt, discharged Dec. 13,'65
William O. Piper, discharged Dec. 14,'64.
Francis M. Brown, r, pro sergeant, discharged Dec. 13,'65.
Caleb Boggs, discharged Sept. 20.'62.
Louis P. Holman, r, pro 2d Lt May 1',65. dis Dec. 13,'65.
Josiah Metsker, discharged July 28.'65.
Aaron M. Hurtt, r, discharged Dec. 13,'65.

Musicians.

Allen S. Hurtt, r. transferred to 1st U S Eng Aug. 8.'64.
John Burgess. deserted Feb. 1,'63.

Wagoner.

Samuel Jackson, deserted Dec. 21,'63.

Privates.

Robert Baker, died at Stanford, Ky., Feb. 19,'62.
Luman B. Black, discharged Dec. 14,'64.
Thomas Booher, deserted Mar. 27,'62.
William Bolles, r, pro corporal, discharged Dec. 13,'65.
William S. Bolles, r, pro sergeant, discharged Dec. 13,'65.
Thomas R. Bolles, r, pro corporal, discharged Dec. 13,'65.
William H. Bolinbaugh, discharged Dec. 14,'64.
Philander Boner, discharged Feb. 19,'63, disability.
Michael Bowas, discharged July 18,'63.
Joseph Brown, r, missing in action Nashville, Dec. 16,'64.
William C. Bryant, r, pro Q M Feb. 20,'65, dis Dec. 13,'65.
Alden W. Bryant, r, pro corporal, discharged Dec. 13,'65.
Lawrence P. Campbell, discharged Feb. 6,'63, disability.
Avery B. Charpie, r, pro 2d Lt Nov. 23,'64, Capt Dec. 15,
    '64, discharged Dec. 13,'65.
John Charles, discharged Dec. 14,'64.
John Chitester, discharged Feb. 29,'64, disability.
Ira S. Chitester, r, pro corporal, discharged Dec. 13,'65.
John W. Coan, died at Munfordsville Mar. 10,'62.
Moses Clingensmith, discharged June 22,'62, disability.
Hamilton Crouthers, r, discharged Dec. 13,'65.
Andrew J. Curtis, discharged Mar. 21,'63, wounds.
Wilson Deniston, deserted Apr. 25,'62.
Daniel Diebert, r, transferred to 1st U S Eng July 24,'64.
Francis M. Doles, r, discharged Dec. 13,'65.
Alexander Duncan, discharged Aug. 7,'62, disability.
William M. Dunnuck, discharged June 28,'62, disability.
Charles Dyer, died at Lebanon, Ky., Feb. 19,'62.
Thomas Ewing, died at Nashville Mar. 30,'62.
Thomas Faley, r, died at Bowling Green Sept. 17,'62.
Jonas Foss, discharged June 22,'62, disability.
Sebastian Ferguson, r, deserted June 19,'65.
John Gale, transferred to V R C Apr. 30,'64.
Jacob Glaze, discharged Dec. 13,'65.
James Hamlin, r, discharged Dec. 13,'65.
Charles W. Harper, discharged Feb. 27,'63, disability.
William S. Harris, discharged June 21,'62, disability.
Nelson Harvey, deserted June 2,'62.
David Holmes, deserted Nov. 1,'61. (?)

John Holt, discharged Jan. 9,'63, disability.
Charles L. Hoover, discharged Jan. 22.'62, disability.
Edward Hinds, deserted Aug. 1,'63.
Joshua Jackson, died at Munfordsville, no date.
Martin V. B. James. died at Peru, Aug. 15,'63.
Francis Kannay. r. discharged Dec. 13,'65.
John J. Kennedy. discharged Jan. 2,'62, disability.
John Kiles, r, transferred to U S Eng July 24,'65.
Theodore Kuhns, discharged June 27,'63, disability.
John II. Larue. discharged Dec. 10.'63, disability.
Thomas S. Lay, died at Nashville, Oct. 7,'62.
William II. Lavett, discharged Dec. 14.'64.
Oscar F. Loomis, deserted Oct. 1,'62.
Cornelius Lucey, died Sept. 22.'62.
John Malone, r. discharged Dec. 13,'65.
Conrad Metsker, discharged Dec. 14,'64.
John II. Miller, r, discharged Dec. 13,'65.
Francis M. Moody, r.   "
Michael Oliver, discharged Apr. 1,'62. disability.
Francis M. Piper, discharged Dec. 14,'64.
Benjamin F. Petticrew,   "
George Pomeroy, r, discharged Dec. 13,'65.
Jeremiah Richeson. r.   "
Henry C. Richeson. discharged Dec. 14,'64.
Thomas Roberts.   "
Frederick Rupley,   "
Eli Shortridge, discharged Aug. 9,'62, disability.
Nathan W. Scott, discharged Dec. 14,'64.
Walter M. Still, deserted Feb. 10.'62.
Perry Slagle, r, discharged Dec. 13,'65.
Andrew J. Trimble, deserted Feb. 10,'62.
James N. M. Tuttle, deserted Mar. 10,'62.
William F. Tudor, discharged Dec. 14.'64.
Joseph Walker, discharged Aug. 5,'62. disability.
Alexander Ward, r, discharged Dec. 13,'65.
George W. Whiteside. r, pro sergeant, dis Dec. 13,'65.
Daniel Wortemberger, died at Bardstown. no date.
John C. Young. r. pro 2d Lt Feb. 6,'65, dis Dec. 13,'65.

Recruits.

Charles W. Ashley, Feb. 24.'64, discharged Oct. 31,'65.
James M. Blystone, Oct. 13,'64, drafted, dis Dec. 13,'65.
Josephus Blystone, Aug. 21,'64, drafted, dis Aug. 14,'65.

George W. Burroway, Sept. 30,'64, discharged June 14,'65
Daniel F. Beckdal, Feb. 24,'64, discharged Dec. 13,'65.
John Combs, Aug. 1,'63, deserted Dec. 21,'63.
Alva Copper, Oct. 6,'63, pro corporal, dis Dec. 13,'65.
David B. Carter, Feb. 12,'64, discharged Dec. 13,'65.
Nathaniel R. Carter   "   "
Joseph A. Cowdry, Mar. 9,'64,   "
William H. Downs, Oct. 7,'64, sub, trans V R C May 1,'65.
Henry J. Dunkelberger, Oct. 8,'64, subst, dis Oct. 19,'65.
Alfred Edwards, Feb. 12,'64, discharged Dec. 15,'65.
John C. Fremont, Oct. 14,'64, substitute dis Oct. 19,'65.
Thomas Gorham, Sept. 20,'64, substitute, dis June 17,'65.
George Gardner, Aug. 25,'63, discharged Dec. 13,'65.
Thomas J. Griffith, Dec. 30,'63, discharged Oct. 19,'65.
John S. Hitchcock, Sept. 21,'64, drafted, dis Aug. 15,'65.
Elmore J. Harry, Oct. 18,'64, substitute, dis Dec. 13,'65.
Jesse D. G. Hasler, Oct. 8,'64, substitute, dis Oct. 19,'65.
George W. Heisler, Apr. 15,'64, discharged Dec. 13,'65.
Noah N. Isam, Oct. 20,'64, substitute, dis June 6,'65.
Jacob L. Kirkendall, Sept. 21,'64, drafted, dis Aug. 14,'65.
Logan Kell, Oct. 18,'64, substitute, discharged Oct.. 19,'65.
Isaac Kelly, Oct. 26,'64,   "   "
Henry H. Leavell, Sept. 7,'63, discharged Dec. 13,'65.
Stephen C. Leavell, Oct. 1,'63,   "
William Lang, Oct. 16,'63, pro corporal, dis Dec. 1,'65.
Andrew Murphy, Sept. 21,'64, drafted, dis Aug. 16,'65.
Smith F. McKey, Sept. 13,'64, drafted, dis June 25,'65.
John F. Michael, Sept. 21,'64, drafted, dis Aug. 14,'65.
Nelson Michael, Oct. 13,'64, drafted, died May 25,'65.
John W. Miller, Oct. 21,'64, substitute, dis Oct. 19,'65.
Robert F. McClain, Sept. 29,'64, substitute, dis June 17,'65
Cornelius H. Martin, Mar. 9,'64, transf to Co. A, 86th Ind.,
     transferred to V R C, discharged Nov. 11,'65.
Charles Purdy, Sept. 20,'64, substitute, dis June 17,'65.
Richard Roberts, Oct. 14,'64, substitute, dis June 10,'65.
Jacob Simmons, Apr. 25,'63, discharged Dec. 13,'65.
George Sullivan, Sept. 3,'63, died at Peru July 19,'64.
Alonzo B. Shaw, Oct. 20,'64, substitute, dis Oct. 19,'65.
Marion Smarl, Oct. 14,'64.   "   "
George W. Songer,   "   "   dis Aug. 4,'65.
John W. Skidmore, Aug. 6,'63, deserted June 19,'65.
Peter F. Thatcher, Sept. 21,'64, discharged Aug. 14,'65.

John T. Taylor, Oct. 15,'64, discharged June 5,'65.
Squire Taylor, Oct. 6,'64, substitute, dis Dec. 13,'65.
Seabury Thorpe, Oct. 14,'64, substitute, dis Oct. 19,'65.
Winfield S. Tipton, Jan. 1.'63, discharged Dec. 13,'65.
William Westetter, Oct. 6,'63, pro corporal, dis Dec. 13,'65.
George W. Woodruff, Sept. 21,'64, drafted, dis Aug. 14,'65.
Francis H. Walls, Oct 17,'64. dis Feb. 28,'65, disability.
John Walker. Oct. 12,'64, substitute. dis Sept. 7,'65.

COMPANY II.

[Original muster-in, December 14, 1861.]

Captain.

Clark Willis, com'd Oct. 11,'61, pro Major June 17,'62, resigned Mar. 17,'63.

First Lieutenant.

Thomas F. Chambers, com'd Oct. 11,'61, pro Capt June 17,
'62, resigned Mar. 16,'63.

Second Lieutenant.

James W. Haley, com'd Oct. 11,'61, pro 1st Lt June 17,'62,
pro Capt Co. I. Dec. 31,'62, discharged Dec. 14,'64.

First Sergeant.

Alfred Gude, pro 2d Lt June 17,'62. 1st Lt Jan. 1,'63, Capt
May 18,'63, discharged Mar. 31,'65.

Sergeants.

Hiram Mallory, pro 2d Lt May 18,'63, dis Jan. 25,'65.
Samuel J. Baird, unaccounted for.
William Willis, pro 2d Lt Jan. 1,'63, 1st Lt May 18,'63,
discharged Feb. 5,'65, Circ. 75.
James Dunn, discharged July 3,'62.

Corporals.

Emory H. Stuckey, *r*, discharged Dec. 13,'65.
William Roberts, *r*, pro 1st Sergt, discharged Dec. 13,'65.
John E. Pickett, discharged May 23,'62, by order.
Joseph A. Bruce, discharged Nov. 10,'62, by order.
William H. Dunn, *r*, pro 1st Lt May 1,'65, dis Dec. 13,'65.
John W. Manning, *r*, pro 2d Lt　　　"　　　　　"
James M. Falls, died of wounds Dec. 16,'64.
Samuel H. Dunn, discharged Dec. 14,'64, by order.

Musicians.

Frederick A. Stuckey, *r*, discharged Dec. 13,'65.

John T. Simpson, r, pro Com Sergt, dis Dec. 13,'65.

Wagoner.

Samuel P. Ruble, discharged Dec. 14,'64.

Privates.

James R. Alexander, discharged Oct. 2,'62, disability.
William F. Atkins, r, discharged Dec. 13,'65.
William W. Bruce, killed at Nashville, Dec. 16,'64.
Elliott Bruce, discharged July 14,'63, by order.
George W. Bruce, r, discharged Dec. 13,'65.
Alexander C. Bowen, r, pro corporal, dis Dec. 13,'65.
George W. Burris, r, transferred to U S Eng.
Leander Bond, discharged Dec. 14,'64.
Thomas Chambers, deserted Oct. 1,'62.
John S. Cox, r, discharged June 7,'65.
Peter Collop, transferred to V R C.
Austin P. Cox, discharged Mar. 18,'63, by order.
Andrew Cook, r, pro corporal, discharged Dec. 13,'65.
Charles Chambers, discharged Dec. 14,'64.
Harvey J. Cox, "
William I. Dunning, "
George W. Debord, discharged May 16,'63, by order.
Spear S. Dunning, r, discharged June 14,'65.
John Donaldson, died at Paducah, June 1,'63.
Joseph Dillinger, died at Stanford, Ky., Feb. 20,'62.
John R. Edmonds, discharged Dec. 14,'64.
George W. Frederick, died at Lebanon, Ky., Mar. 14,'62.
William Frederick, died at Bowling Green, Mar. 11,'62.
Samuel Foreman, died at Bardstown, Jan. 11,'62.
James W. Farris, r, pro corporal, discharged Dec. 13,'65.
George Frederick, transf. to V R C, died at Lebanon, Ky.
William S. Getty, died at Evansville.
John Getty, discharged, no date.
Thomas J. Hollingsworth, discharged June 1,'62, by order.
Perry Hollingsworth, killed at Nashville, Dec. 25,'62.
Thompson Hollingsworth, r, discharged Dec. 13,'65.
Albert Hollingsworth, discharged Dec. 31,'64.
Milton Hollingsworth, r, discharged Dec. 13,'65.
William C. Harbin, died at Bardstown, Dec. 29,'61.
John B. Houck, r, pro sergeant, discharged Dec. 13,'65.
Franklin Jerrel, died at Nashville, Jan. 21,'63.
William G. Keith, r, discharged May 21,'65.
John L. Keith, r, pro corporal, died Dec. 30,'64, wounds.

Thomas N. Keith, died at Nashville Jan. 24,'63.
Frederick Kixmiller, died at Murfreesboro Apr. 6,'63.
Stephen J, Leas, discharged Dec. 14,'64.
Christopher B. Long, unaccounted for.
Henry M. Luking, r, pro corporal, discharged Dec. 13,'65.
Edward Limen, discharged Dec. 14,'64.
John H. Malcolm, discharged July 13,'62, by order.
Daniel McKea, died at Nashville, Jan. 27,'63.
Eli Myers, discharged Dec. 14,'64.
William P. McClure, r, pro 1st Lt Feb. 10,'65, Capt May
　　1,'65, discharged Dec. 13,'65.
Charles W. McClure, r, pro sergeant, dis Dec. 13,'65.
William H. H. McCormick, died at home.
George W. McKinley, r, pro sergeant, dis Dec. 13,'65.
Thomas H. Paddock, r, discharged June 14,'65.
Alexander Palmer, died at Bowling Green, Ky.
Henry F. Piper, r, pro sergeant, discharged Dec. 13,'65.
Michael A. C. Robertson, r, discharged May 22,'65.
Thomas B. Robertson, died at Murfreesboro Apr. 17,'63.
Martin I. Ruble, discharged Dec. 14,'64.
William E. Steffey,　　　　　　"
George W. Scrogin, r, died, Nashville Dec. 21,'64, wounds.
Joseph H. Scrogin, discharged Dec. 10,'62.
James A. Sanders, died at Corinth, Miss.
John W. Setzer, unaccounted for.
James H. Shouse, r, discharged May 22,'65, wounds.
William Simpson, discharged July 13,'62, by order.
Frederick A. Smith, r, pro corporal, discharged Dec. 13,'65
James H. Stephenson, r　　"　　　　　　"
Harrison Scrogin, died at Nashville.
Henry M. Thompson, died at Murfreesboro, Feb. 25,'63.
Benjamin E. Thorn, died Dec. 21,'62.
Frederick Tellsman, r, discharged Dec. 13,'65.
Elijah G. Teague, r,　　　　　　"
John B. Vincent, r,　　　　　　"
James Vankirk, died at Louisville Nov. 11,'62.
William O. Ward, discharged May 20,'62, disability.
William S. Woodsworth, r, drowned, Nashville May 22,'65.
Miranda Westfall, died in Knox Co.
Clark I. Willis, r, discharged Jan. 20,'65, disability.
John W. Wilson, discharged Feb. 24,'65.
William H. Williams, discharged Nov. 10,'64.

Recruits.

Thomas Alexander, Jan. 23,'63, died, Chatt'ga, May 5,'64.
Levi H. Booker, Aug. 15,'62, discharged June 14,'65.
Hamilton G. Bond, Aug. 5,'63,   "
David M. Bruce, Mar. 12,'63, discharged Dec. 13,'65.
John D. Beaver, Oct. 18,'64, substitute. dis Nov. 19,'65.
Robert S. Brown Mar. 9,'64, discharged Dec. 13,'65.
Jacob Bugh, Oct. 10,'64, drafted, discharged May —,'65.
Garver M. Brown, Jan. 4,'64, discharged Dec. 13,'65.
Richard Burgess, Oct. 20,'64, substitute, dis Oct. 19,'65.
Alexander Bolds, Sept. 22,'64, drafted, dis May 13,'65.
Giles Borden, Apr. 19,'64, discharged Dec. 13,'65.
Levi Bowman, Oct. 10,'64, drafted. discharged Oct. 19,'65.
Landis Boyer, Mar. 24,'64, discharged Dec. 13,'65.
James W. Cable, Aug. 21,'62, discharged Sept. 1,'63.
David R. Chambers, Apr. 9,'64, discharged Dec. 13,'65.
George W. Craigmill, Oct. 30,'64, substitute, dis Dec. 13,'65
Joseph Creek, Oct. 10,'64, drafted, discharged Nov. 19,'65.
Oliver P. Dunn, June 23,'63, discharged Dec. 13,'65.
Theodore Deafenbaugh, Sept. 22,'64, died Louisv. Jan. 1,'65
John B. Farris, Apr. 9,'64, discharged Dec. 13,'65.
John F. Grizzle, Aug. 15,'62, discharged June 14,'65.
Bernard Hollingsworth, Jan. 5,'62, r, killed Dec. 16,'64.
William H. Hageman, Apr. 8,'64, discharged Dec. 13,'65.
John Haget, Aug 15,'62, died at Camp Chase May 26,'63.
William Hall, Oct. 16,'64, substitute. dis Oct. 19,'65.
Daniel Heller, Sept. 22,'64, dis May 24,'65, wounds.
William H. Harris, Oct. 19,'64, substitute, dis Oct. 13,'65.
Madison Heaton, Oct. 10,'64, drafted, dis Oct. 19,'65.
James Hancock, Oct. 24,'64, substitute,   "
Jonas Ikes, Oct. 10,'64, drafted. discharged Oct. 19,'65.
John G. King, Sept. 20,'64, drafted, dis June 14,'65.
Daniel E. Maddocks. Oct. 17,'64, substitute, dis Oct. 19,'65
Handsbury Murphy, Apr. 9,'64, discharged Dec. 13,'65.
Daniel T. Myers, Oct. 18,'64, subst. died Nashv. Jan. 19,'65
John A. G. Miller, Oct. 10,'64, drafted, dis June 3,'65.
Madison McBroom, Oct. 14,'64, substitute, dis Oct. 19,'65.
Christopher C. McRea, Aug. 21,'62, discharged Feb. 24,'63
William Miller, Aug. 21,'62, died at Murf'boro Feb. 1,'63.
Elliott H. Pearce, Aug. 15,'62, discharged Apr. 26,'63.
Horace S. Polk,   "   , discharged June 14,'65.
Daniel Pontius, Oct. 7,'64, drafted, discharged Oct. 19,'65.

William T. Richardson, Apr. 9,'64, pro corp, dis Dec. 13,'65
Samuel A. Risley, Aug. 21,'62, died Murf'boro, Mar. 5,'65.
Thomas P. Ruble, Apr. 9,'64, discharged Dec. 13,'65.
James Rodgers, Oct. 19,'64. substitute, dis Oct. 19,'65.
John C. Roberts, Oct. 10,'64, drafted, dis May 27,'65.
Joshua H. Stuckey, Sept. 16,'63, discharged Dec. 13,'65.
James A. Shrock, Oct. 10,'64, drafted, dis June 2,'65.
John B. Sandall,   "   "   dis Oct. 19,'65.
Allen Sacra, Oct. 14,'64, discharged June 20,'65, disability.
Joseph Shoemaker, Oct. 18,'64, substitute, dis Oct. 19,'65.
Alva Townsend, Oct. 10,'64, drafted, deserted Aug. 17,'65.
Aaron Wolverton, Aug. 7,'62, discharged June 14,'65.
James Watson, Oct. 16,'63, discharged Dec. 13,'65.
William Walton. Oct. 18,'64, substitute, dis Oct. 19,'65.
James Whitehead, Nov. 1,'64, discharged Dec. 13,'65.
Matthias Yoos, Sept. 22,'64, drafted, dis June 14,'65.

COMPANY I.

[Original muster-in, December 8, 1861.]

Captain.

Marquis L. Johnson, com'd Oct. 11,'61, resigned Aug. 13,'62

First Lieutenant.

James S. Reeves, com'd Oct. 11,'61, resigned Dec. 8,'62.

Second Lieutenant.

John Bowman, com'd Oct. 11,'61, resigned Feb. 13,'63.

First Sergeant.

James W. Barlow, pro 2d Lt Feb. 14,'63, Capt May 1,'65,
    discharged prisoner of war.

Sergeants.

Frederick J. Brownell, pro 1st Lt Dec. 31,'62, discharged
    Mar. 31,'65.
Arthur W. Sargent, discharged, no date.
Ephraim Donavan, discharged June 30,'62.
George W. McCauley, r, pro 1st Lt May 1,'65, Capt July 1,
    '65, discharged Dec. 13,'65.

Corporals.

Henry B. McCauley, dis Apr. 29,'63, wounds at Day's Gap.
Marquis D. Losey, unaccounted for.

William R. Barlow, discharged Oct. 25,'62.
Joseph S. King, discharged Oct. 21,'62.
Joseph E. Campbell, r, pro sergeant, dis Dec. 13,'65.
George Snyder, discharged Dec. 14,'64.
Martin V. Williams, r, pro sergeant, dis Dec. 13,'65.
Lewis R. Burr, died at Louisville, Jan. 7,'62.

Musician.

Francis O. Williams, died at Lebanon, Ky., Feb. 6,'62.

Wagoner.

William D. Parker, r, discharged Dec. 13,'65.

Privates.

Leander Z. Burr, discharged Dec. 14,'64.
William T. Barlow, r, pro sergeant, dis Dec. 13,'65.
Samuel Barrow, r, discharged Dec. 13,'65.
George W. Boring, died Mar. 12,'62.
James Berry, deserted Oct. 4,'62, ret, dis June 14,'63.
Aaron Creviston, died at Nashville, Mar. 26,'62.
James Chambers, r, died at New Orleans, July 14,'65.
Thomas Coffee, r, pro corporal, discharged Dec. 13,'65.
John Cartmill, discharged ——, disability.
George W. Copple, discharged Dec. 29,'64, disability.
Richard Carpenter, r, discharged Dec. 13,'65.
Jonathan P. Curtis, deserted Jan. 2,'62.
Henry H. Doolittle, r, discharged Dec. 13,'65.
Charles Davice, discharged Feb. 10,'65.
Samuel Doyle, r, discharged Dec. 13,'65.
Albert Ellington, died at Bardstown, Dec. 28,'61.
Edward Fogarty, r, discharged Dec. 13,'65.
William H. Fair, discharged Dec. 10,'62, by order.
George W. Farris, discharged Dec. 14,'64.
William F. Fry, r, pro sergeant, discharged Dec. 15,'65.
Harrison Graves, r, pro corporal, discharged Dec. 13,'65.
Joseph A. German, discharged July 8,'62.
Charles E. German, died at Bardstown, Dec. 29,'61.
John H. Griffis, discharged Dec. 14,'64.
Dennis Garrity, r, discharged Dec. 13,'65.
Charles Gott, r,
Charles Holden, died at Stanford, Ky., Feb. 1,'62.
Thomas Harrison, discharged Jan. 1,'63, disability.
S. Hyner, died July 27,'62, disease.
Rine Houzlot, deserted Sept. 15,'63.

Enoch Hines, died at Nashville, July 27,'62.
Albert S. Hartley, r, pro 1st Sergt, discharged Dec. 13,'65.
John W. Hamilton, died, Greenwood, '62. unaccounted for.
Benjamin Johnson, discharged Dec. 14,'64.
Jeremiah Johnson. deserted.
John J. Jeter, transferred to V R C
John Jarvis, died at Huntsville, July 2,'62.
Joseph Jarrett, died at Nashville, Dec. 7,'62.
Benjamin Jones, discharged Feb. 28,'63, disability.
Jacob B. Kitchen, r, pro corporal, discharged Dec. 13,'65.
John Kitchen, r,   "   "
Joseph Lowe, discharged Jan. 3,'62. disability.
Henry B. Lipscomb, discharged Dec. 14,'64.
Eli L. Marsrush, unaccounted for.
James M. Manners, r. discharged Dec. 13,'65.
George Martin, r, pro corporal, discharged Dec. 13,'65.
Benjamin Martin, discharged June 9,'63.
James Martin. discharged June 27,'62.
Ezekiel McCurdy. died at Indianapolis. Dec. 18,'61.
George W. Moore. r, deserted June 29,'65.
Charles F. Mount, discharged Mar. —,'63.
James McCoarte, dis Sept. 9,'63, wounds at Day's Gap.
Thomas J. Prescott, deserted '62.
John W. Phillips. discharged Dec. 14,'64.
Martin Philpot, died Jan. 18,'62.
Nathan Riley, transf'd to Inv Corps, wounds Nov. 1,'63.
John W. Rumrill, deserted Apr. 1,'63.
Andrew Roach, died Feb. 22.'63, wounds at Stone River.
Ira Roach, r, deserted Apr. 3,'64.
Samuel Smith. died at Bardstown, Feb. 4,'62.
Isaac Simpson, discharged July 18.'62, disability.
Abraham Simpson. discharged July 11,'62.
Ransom Smith, r, discharged Dec. 13,'65.
Henry Simpson, died June 19,'62.
Benjamin Simpson, r, discharged Dec. 13,'65.
John R. Trimble, r. pro sergeant, discharged Dec. 13,'65.
John Tibbit. r, unaccounted for.
Lewis P. Taylor. died at Bardstown, June 15,'62.
Leroy Wagner, discharged Dec. 14,'64.
Henry Willis, deserted Oct. 16,'63, dis by order War Dep.
Allen Warren, died at Stanford, Ky., Feb. 21,'62.
James Wallace, discharged Feb. 8,'63, disability.

George Youngman. died at Bardstown, June 4,'62.

Recruits.

James Aldridge, Sep. 6,'62. killed at Stone Riv, Dec. 31,'62.
William H. Arnold, Sept. 1,'63. discharged Dec. 13,'65.
Mahlon E. Blackford, Sept. 17,'63. discharged May 30,'65.
Isaac Boring, Apr. 9,'64, discharged Dec. 13,'65.
Haman Backtell, Sept. 26,'64, drafted. dis June 27,'65.
Christian Bender, Oct. 2,'64. drafted, dis Aug. 11,'65.
Francis M. Campbell, June 30,'63, discharged Dec. 13,'65.
Silas Cook, Oct. 17,'64, substitute, discharged Sept. 12,'65.
James Dowden, Oct. 15,'64, substitute, dis Oct. 19,'65.
John T. Disinger, Oct. 19,'64, drafted. dis Oct. 19,'65.
Henry H. Englerth, Oct. 24,'64, substitute, dis Oct. 19,'65.
Thomas Fisher, Oct. 3,'64, drafted, discharged May 23,'65.
Samuel Flinn, Oct. 15,'64, sub, died at Pulaski, Jan. 10,'65.
George Fellers, Oct. 19,'64, drafted, discharged Dec. 13,'65
John W. Foutz, Oct. 19,'64, drafted. discharged Aug. 26,'65
Henry Fuhrman, Oct. 3,'64, drafted, dis Sept. 15,'65.
George M. Green, Aug. 25,'63, discharged Dec. 13,'65.
Joseph Grey, Oct. 6,'64, substitute, discharged Oct. 19,'65.
Jasper N. Hushaw, Sep. 1,'63, transf'd to V R C Apr. -,'64.
Engelbert Hittenbrock, Sept. 1,'63. discharged Dec. 13,'65.
James A. Hill, Sept. 22,'63, pro corporal, dis Dec. 13,'65.
Isaac B. Harman, Oct. 18,'64, drafted, dis Dec. 13,'65.
Henry Heler. Oct. 15,'64, substitute. died Jan. 22,'65.
Joseph A. Hendricks, Oct. 14,'64, substitute, dis Oct. 19,'65
Joseph Johnson, Sept. 22,'62, discharged June 14,'65.
John A. King, Dec. 16,'63, discharged Dec. 13,'65.
William N. Kitchen, Mar. 31,'64, discharged Dec. 13,'65.
William A. King, Dec. 18,'64, drafted, dis Aug. 14,'65.
William Kline, Sept. 22,'64, drafted, dis June 14,'65.
Joseph Link, Oct. 15,'64, substitute, discharged Oct. 19,'65
Enoch Martin, Sept. 15,'63, discharged June 14,'65.
George Mugler, Oct. 6,'63, died Dec. 23,'64. disease.
William J. Miller, Oct. 13,'64, drafted, dis Aug. 11,'65.
Obadiah Miller, Oct. 13,'64, drafted, dis Aug. 14,'65.
Jesse Miller.   "   "   "
James W. Miller, Oct. 18,'64, drafted, dis Oct. 2,'65.
William S. Ogle, Aug. 10,'63, unaccounted for.
George W. Owens, Mar. 31,'64, discharged Dec. 13,'65.
John Phillips, Oct. 18,'64, drafted. discharged July 13,'65
Henry F. Pierce, Sept. 30,'64, substitute, died June 8,'65.

John Quinn, Oct. 19,'64, drafted, discharged Oct. 19,'65.
Cornelius W. Roan, Aug. 25,'63, discharged Dec. 13,'65.
Emanuel H. Rotroff, Oct. 19,'64, drafted, died Jan. 1,'65.
David Reuchler, Oct. 3,'64, drafted, dis Oct. 19,'65.
Lewis Reapert, Oct. 3,'64, drafted, died Apr. 1,'65.
Richard Shaw, Apr. 9,'64, died at Chatt'ga, July 14,'64.
Cyrus D. Smith, Oct. 13,'64, drafted, died Mar. 24,'65.
George Soopler, Sept. 22,'64, drafted, died Feb. 7,'65.
William H. Stewart, Oct. 15,'64, substitute, dis Oct. 19,'65.
Joseph N. Snell, Oct. 19,'64, drafted, dis Nov. 14,'65.
Sylvester Spangler, Oct. 3,'64, drafted, dis Oct. 19,'65.
Wesley E. Thomas, ——, died Dec. 14,'64, wounds.
Thomas Tull, Sept. 7,'63, discharged Dec. 13,'65.
Charles H. Tully, Mar. 29,'64,
Adam Trout, Oct. 13,'64, drafted, discharged Aug. 14,'65.
David Welty, Oct. 19,'64, drafted, died Dec. 28,'64, wounds.
Aaron Woodruff, Sept. 30,'64, substitute, dis June 14,'65.
Solomon Zurfes, Oct. 15,'64, drafted, died of wounds, at
    Nashville, Jan. 1,'65.
William E. Zartman, Oct. 19,'64, drafted, dis Oct. 19,'65.

COMPANY K.

Captain.

William W. Scearce, com'd Dec. 8,'61, pro Major May 1,
    '65, Lt-Col June 1,'65, discharged Dec. 13,'65.

First Lieutenant.

Jonathan Dunbar, ——, resigned Mar. 20,'63.

Second Lieutenant.

Samuel C. Owen, ——, died, no date.

First Sergeant.

Roman Salter, Feb. 23,'62, pro 1st Lt Mar. 21,'63, dis Feb.
    23,'65.

Sergeants.

Allen R. Harris, Feb. 18,'62, pro Adjut Apr. 13,'65, dis-
    charged Dec. 13,'65.
James A. Lawson, Dec. 10,'61, discharged Dec. 14,'64.
George W. Scearce, Dec. 16,'61, pro 2d Lt Mar. 21,'63, dis-
    charged Jan. 25,'65.
Thomas B. Hawkins, Feb. 22,'62, r, discharged Dec. 13,'65

Corporals.

Alfred Goffen, Feb. 22,'62, died at Terre Haute May 26,'62.
Solomon Stanfield, Feb. 23,'62, r, deserted.
John H. Moore, Feb. 22,'62, pro 1st Lt Feb. 28,'65, Capt
May 1,'65, discharged Dec. 13,'65.
Joseph Simpson, Feb. 22,'62, dis Feb. 18,'63, disability.
Jonathan Grantham, Dec. 11,'61, discharged Dec. 14,'64.
George W. Kelshaw,   "   "
Alando Hemphill, r,   "   pro sergt, dis Dec. 13,'65.
Marcus Sperry, ——, discharged Aug. 8,'62, disability.

Musicians.

Jeremiah M. Mayes, Dec. 11,'61, dis Apr. 27,'63, disability.
Ebenezer C. Mayes,   "   dis Feb. 22,'63, disability.

Wagoner.

John Bockley, Dec. 11,'61, died, Green Co, June 1,'62.

Privates.

James V. Arthur, Dec. 11,'61, died at Lebanon, Ky., Feb.
13,'62.
Benjamin F. Adams, Feb. 23,'62, dis Feb. 18,'63, disability.
Squire M. Adair, Feb. 22,'62, r, pro sergt, dis Dec. 13,'65.
William Anderson,   "   r,   "
David E. Barnes, Dec. 11,'61, r, pro corp,   "
Henry C. Black, Feb. 23,'62, r,   "   "
Abraham Bensinger, Feb. 22,'62, deserted Apr. 2,'62.
Miltiades Cash, Dec. 16,'61, discharged March 26,'62.
Peter H. Carnahan, Feb. 22,'62, died at Nashv. May 16,'63
Ephraim Carpenter, Feb. 2,'62, r, pro 1st Sergt, discharged
Dec. 13,'65.
William Chappell,   "   r, pro sergt, dis Dec. 13,'65.
John W. Chappell, Feb. 22,'62, r, discharged Dec. 13,'65.
John L. Duncan, Dec. 11,'61, died at Bardstown, Jan. 13,'62
Jerome W. Dyers,   "   died Feb. 6,'63, wounds Stone
River.
Charles D. Eves, Feb. 23,'62, r, pro corp, dis Dec. 13,'65.
George W. Fuller, Dec. 11,'61, discharged, no date.
Henry Fisher, Feb. 23,'62, dis Nov. 17,'62, disability.
Hiram Grider,   "   discharged Feb. 28,'65.
William B. Goodman, Feb. 23,'62, deserted Oct. 30,'62.
Levi Harna, Dec. 15,'61, discharged Dec. 14,'64.
William Holcom, Feb. 23,'62, dis July 1,'63, disability.
26

Benjamin F. Hensley, Jan. 29,'62, deserted Oct. 18,'62, ret, deserted July 9,'65.

John F. Hensley, " " "

James A. Harvey, Feb. 23,'62, dis Nov. 11,'62, disability.

Ephraim P. Herold, " died, Evansville May 12,'62.

Matthias Herold, " transf'd Inv Corps Dec. 8,'63.

David A. Harvey, Feb. 22,'62, r, died Nashv. Dec. 22,'64.

Reason Hawkins, " transf'd Inv Corps Dec. 8,'63.

James M. Kelly, Dec. 11,'61. dis June 28,'62, disability.

James M. Lester, sr., " dis Oct. 4,'62, disability.

Francis M. Leach, Dec. 15,'61, died at Lebanon, Ky., Feb. 4,'62.

James M. Lester, jr, Dec. 11,'61, died Evansv. May 12,'62.

Michael Long, Feb. 22,'62, r, pro corporal, dis Dec. 13,'65.

John Long, " discharged Feb. 23,'65.

William McKinley, Feb. 23,'62, r, pro 2d Lt May 2,'65, discharged Dec. 13,'65.

John J. Mitchell, Dec. 11,'61, dis June 30,'62, disability.

William Mitchell. " dis Oct. 1,'62. disability.

Benjamin F. Moore, " r. pro sergt, dis Dec. 13,'65.

Willis F. Moore, Feb. 22,'62, r, pro 2d Lt May 1,'65, 1st Lt May 2,'65, discharged Dec. 13,'65.

George W. Powell, Dec. 11,'61. died Nashville, Jan. 19,'64.

James Parker, " dis Dec. 10,'62. disability.

Samuel R, Perkins, Dec. 16,'61, deserted Mar. 26,'62.

Jacob Pitzer. Dec. 11,'61, discharged Dec. 14,'64.

Charles Price, Feb. 22,'62, transf'd to U S Eng July 25,'64.

Franklin Price, " " "

Jeremiah L. Rice, Feb. 23,'62, r, discharged Dec. 13,'65.

George W. Richards, " died, Louisville, Nov. 4,'62.

Samuel Racy, " r, pro corp, dis Dec. 13,'65.

John T. Rose, Dec. 11,'61, disch'd Jan. 13,'63, disability.

Joseph Rees, " died at Nashville Mar. 26,'62.

Solomon T. Stafford, Feb. 23,'62, r, trans U S E, July 25,'64

David S. Strain, Dec. 11,'61, r. killed at Overton's Hill, Dec. 16,'64.

Thomas E. Stanley, Feb. 23,'62, died, Nashv. Feb. 1,'64.

William H. Smith, " discharged June 14,'65.

Squire Stepleton, " died at Nashv. Apr. 27,'62.

Ditter C. Stringer, " deserted Jan. 18,'63.

Eli A. Stringer, Feb. 23,'63, r. dis Mar. 22,'65, disability.

Joseph Shuts, Feb. 23,'62. missing in action, Stone River.

David Snow. Feb. 23,'62, *r*. discharged Dec. 13,'65.
William Sutherlan, Feb. 22,'62, discharged Mar. 13,'63.
John Walford, Dec. 11,'61, discharged Aug. 19,'63.
John W. Wolford,   "   deserted Mar. 26,'62.
William Y. Weir, Dec. 15,'61. died Dec. 29,'62.
James B. Whitlock, Dec. 11,'61, died, Nashv. Mar. 30,'62.
John Wisner,   "   discharged Dec. 14,'64.
Noah Wisner,   "   died. Nashv. Aug. 14,'62.
Joseph West,   "   dis June 28,'62, disability.
William W. Yeates, Feb. 22,'62, *r*, pro corp, dis Dec. 13,'65.

Recruits.

Samuel C. Astley, Apr. 26,'64. discharged Dec. 13,'65.
Alexander Bridges, Oct. 27,'63,   "
Francis M. Butcher, Oct. 10,'64, substitute, dis Dec. 13,'65.
John Burns, Oct. 21,'64. drafted, deserted May 13,'65.
Thomas Brown, Oct. 25,'64, drafted.   "   "
Daniel Burden, Oct. 21,'64,   "   "
James Butcher, Oct. 19,'64,   "   "
George Coonce, Apr. 12,'64. discharged Dec. 13,'65.
Joseph Crown, Oct. 21,'64, subst. killed Nashv. Dec. 16,'64
Christopher Clapper, Oct. 10,'64. drafted, died Jan. 22,'65.
Charles F. Drummond, Sep. 27,'62. dis Apr. 6,'63, disability
Taswell Dodd, Oct. 2,'62, pro sergeant, dis Oct. 4,'65.
Roger Doyle, Oct. 21,'64. deserted May 13,'65.
Dennis Davis, Oct. 22,'64,   "
William Elder, Jan. 6,'64, discharged Dec. 13,'65.
Henry Feith, Oct. 25,'64. deserted May 13,'65.
John Flinn, Oct. 22,'64,   "
Robert P. Grey, Oct. 15,'64. substitute. dis Dec. 13,'65.
Samuel L. Gadbury, Oct. 10,'64. drafted, dis Oct. 19,'65.
Manoah W. Grim. Oct. 3,'64. substitute,   "
William Grey, ——, discharged Oct. 19,'65.
George Green, Oct. 22,'64. drafted, deserted May 13,'65.
Emanuel C. Garber, Oct. 20,'64. drafted. deserted   "
Abram Hanna, June 17,'63. died, Victoria. Tex.. Aug. 10,'65
Abram J. Heavelin, Sept. 20,'64. drafted. dis Mar. —,'65.
John Higgins, Oct. 20,'64. drafted. deserted May 13,'65.
John Howard, Oct. 25,'64,   "   "
John Hays, Oct. 22,'64,   "   "
Albert Hodges,   "   "   "
Amos M. Hanes, Oct. 25,'64. substitute. dis Dec. 13,'65.
Marshall Jennings, Oct. 20,'64. drafted, dis June 14,'65.

Elias B. Keller, Nov. 12,'64, dis May 26,'65, disability.
Samuel Kemper, Sept. 4,'62, discharged Dec. 13,'65.
Henry Kiefaber, Sept. 20,'64, drafted dis, Aug. 24,'65.
Richard H. Lewis, June 22,'63, discharged Dec. 13,'65.
Thomas A. Lawson, ——, died Dec. 18,'64.
Henry Long, Oct. 22,'64, deserted May 13,'65.
Ormal L. Musgrave, Aug. 22,'63, discharged Dec. 13,'65.
Jacob McMertrie, Oct. 27,'63, discharged Dec. 13,'65.
William B. Mahan, Apr. 12,'64,   ''
Justice Minnick, Mar. 9,'64,   ''
Thomas J. Newton, Oct. 27,'63, pro corp, dis Dec. 13,'65.
Henry Newport, Sept. 20,'64, drafted, dis June 14,'65.
Michael O'Conner, Sept. 13,'62, dis May 29,'65, disability.
Andrew J. Perkins, June 17,'63, died at home Aug. 16,'63.
Allen C. Parker, Sept. 13,'62, discharged June 14,'65.
William D. Parker, Apr. 7,'64, discharged May 29,'65.
William Polsom, Sept. 21,'64, drafted, dis June 14,'65.
Levi S. Ransopher, Feb. 16,'64, discharged Dec. 13,'65.
Samuel Richardson, Oct. 4,'64, substitute, dis Oct. 4,'65.
Sanford Reynolds, Sept. 20,'64, drafted, dis June 14,'65.
Charles W. Salter, Aug. 29,'62, discharged June 14,'65.
James P. Sillery, June 24,'63, discharged Dec. 13,'65.
Jacob Stepler, Sept. 21,'64, drafted, discharged Aug. 24,'65
John Sutton, Apr. 8,'64, died at Nashville May 17,'64.
Solomon Standley, Sept. 20,'64, drafted, dis June 14,'65.
John Schraer, Sept. 22,'64, drafted, discharged Oct. 2,'65.
Daniel Schearer, Sept. 21,'64, drafted, dis June 14,'65.
Alvin B. Tibbits, Apr. 7,'64, died at Chatt'ga. Aug. 22,'64.
Thomas Tinsley, ——, discharged Oct. 19,'65.
Joseph Trump, Sept. 20,'64, drafted, dis May 22,'65.
Christian Trump, ——, drafted, discharged June 14,'65.
Levi Whitehead, Sept. 13,'62, discharged Dec. 13,'65.
Joel Whitehead, Oct. 27,'63,   ''   ''
Samuel T. White, Apr. 26,'64,   ''   ''
Wesley C. Wyant, Feb. 24,'65, discharged Dec. 13,'65.
Adam Wolf, Sept. 21,'64, killed at Nashville, Dec. 16,'64.
Nathan Wheeler, Oct. 15,'64, substitute, dis Aug. 2,'65.
Henry Worling, ——, drafted, discharged Oct. 4,'65.
Andrew Worling, Oct. 3,'64, drafted, dis Oct. 4,'65.
Thomas J. Yeates, June 3,'63, discharged Dec. 13,'65.

UNASSIGNED RECRUITS.

ACCOUNTED FOR.

William Brown, Oct. 3,'64, drafted, transf'd Co. G, 21st Ind.
Levi P. Bivans, Sept. 22,'64, " "
Joseph Blanchard, " " "
Jacob Harsh, Oct. 19,'64, " "
James Davidson, Oct. 2,'63, discharged Jan. 10,'65.
George W. Fitzpatrick, Sept. 7,'64, subst, dis June 14,'65.
John Simpson, Sept. 10,'62, discharged June 14,'65.

UNACCOUNTED FOR.

Hiram F. Baxter, Sept. 5,'63.
Wm. Bennett, Oct. 21,'64.
John A. Dunbar, Oct. 27,'64.
Wm. Ehlarding, Oct. 3,'64.
Wm. Linter, Oct. 18,'64.
Charles La Pettitt, Oct. 18,'64.
James Martin, Sept. 22,'63.
John Russell, Oct. 22,'64.
James McMunigal, "
Patrick Rengold, Oct. 25,'64.
Geo. H. Smeltzer, June 30,'62.
Henry P. Stallsmith, Oct. 6,'62.
Alvin M. Smith, Apr. 14,'62.

Wm. D. Barbor, May 20,'64.
Daniel Bioden, Oct. 22,'64.
Henry Davis, "
Joseph Forunty, Oct. 26,'64.
John McMahan, Oct. 19,'64.
Wm. H. Levillager. "
Thomas Myers, Oct. 20,'64.
Nathan McCarthy, "
John Murrell, Oct. 18,'64.
John Ragan, Oct. 22,'64.
John Riley, "
Charles Willard, "
John Wilson, "

James L. Conklin, Oct. 12,'64, drafted.
Henry G. Colburn, Sept. 28,'64, drafted.
James Glendering, Sept. 22,'64, drafted.
Marshall Hale, Oct. 13,'64, drafted.
Darres Hagall, Sept. 26,'64, drafted.
Frederick Kannaman, Oct. 19,'64, substitute.
Nelson Moore, Oc. 18,'64, drafted.
John Mason, Sept. 22,'64, drafted.
Ewenry Moorse, Sept. 30,'64, substitute.
James M. McCullough, Sept. 21,'64, drafted.
William Snyder, Sept. 22,'64, drafted.
Marshall Vance, " "